Armenian Constantinople

The UCLA conference series, "Historic Armenian Cities and Provinces," has been organized to convey the historical, political, cultural, religious, and economic legacy of a people rooted on the Armenian Plateau for more than three millennia.

Other Publications by Richard G. Hovannisian

Armenia on the Road to Independence, 1918
The Republic of Armenia (4 volumes)
The Armenian People from Ancient to Modern Times (2 volumes)
The Armenian Genocide in Perspective
The Armenian Genocide: History, Politics, Ethics
Remembrance and Denial: The Case of the Armenian Genocide
The Armenian Image in History and Literature
Enlightenment and Diaspora: The Armenian and Jewish Cases
Islam's Understanding of Itself
Ethics in Islam
Poetry and Mysticism in Islam: The Heritage of Rumi
"The Thousand and One Nights" in Arabic Literature and Society
The Persian Presence in Islam
Religion and Culture in Medieval Islam
Looking Backward, Moving Forward: Confronting the Armenian Genocide
The Armenian Genocide: Cultural and Ethical Legacies
Armenian Van/Vaspurakan
Armenian Baghesh/Bitlis and Taron/Mush
Armenian Tsopk/Kharpert
Armenian Karin/Erzerum
Armenian Sebastia/Sivas and Lesser Armenia
Armenian Tigranakert/Diarbekir and Edessa/Urfa
Armenian Cilicia (with Simon Payaslian)
Armenian Pontus: The Trebizond-Black Sea Communities.

Other Publications by Simon Payaslian

US Foreign Economic and Military Aid: *The Reagan and Bush Administrations*
International Political Economy: Conflict and Cooperation in the Global System (with Frederic S. Pearson)
The Armenian Genocide, 1915-1923: A Handbook for Students and Teachers
United States Policy toward the Armenian Question and the Armenian Genocide
The History of Armenia: From the Origins to the Present
Armenian Cilicia (with Richard G. Hovannisian)

UCLA ARMENIAN HISTORY AND CULTURE SERIES
Historic Armenian Cities and Provinces, 9

Armenian Constantinople

Edited by

Richard G. Hovannisian
and
Simon Payaslian

MAZDA PUBLISHERS Costa Mesa, California
2010

Mazda Publishers, Inc.
Academic publishers since 1980
P.O. Box 2603
Costa Mesa, California 92628 U.S.A.
www.mazdapub.com
A. K. Jabbari, Publisher

Library of Congress Cataloging-in-Publication Data

Armenian Constantinople / edited by Richard G. Hovannisian
and Simon Payaslian.
p. cm. — (Historic Armenian cities and provinces ; no. 9)
Includes bibliographical references and index.

ISBN 978-1-56859-156-8 (alk. paper)

1. Armenians—Turkey—Istanbul—History. 2. Armenians—Turkey—
Istanbul—Social life and customs. 3. Armenians—Turkey—Istanbul—
Intellectual life. 4. Istanbul (Turkey)—Ethnic relations. 5. Istanbul
(Turkey)—Social life and customs. 6. Istanbul (Turkey)—Intellectual
life. I. Hovannisian, Richard G. II. Payaslian, Simon.
DR727.A75A76 2010
949.61'800491992—dc22
2010031563

CONTENTS

LIST OF MAPS AND ILLUSTRATIONS

Maps

Illustrations

CONTRIBUTORS

SARKIS BALMANOUKIAN is the architect of the Armenian Genocide memorial complex in Deir-el-Zor and two other genocide memorials. A native of Aleppo, Syria, he earned an advanced degree in architecture from the Polytechnic Institute in Erevan. He has designed several churches and monuments, including the Holy Cross Armenian Catholic Church and community center and the renovated altars in the historic chapel within Karasun Manuk (Forty Martyrs) Armenian Apostolic Cathedral in Aleppo and was involved in the renovation and restoration of the ancient square of Aleppo as well as in the design of several municipal buildings. Since his immigration to the United States in 1987, he has taught the history of Armenian art and architecture and lectured extensively on the subject, while also designing many homes. His most recent project has been the interior design of Saint Gregory the Illuminator Church in Pasadena.

MARLENE R. BREU is Professor Emerita from the Textile and Apparel Studies Program at Western Michigan University. She has published articles on the sacred historical textiles and other artifacts in the Armenian Apostolic (Orthodox) Churches of Istanbul in collaboration with Ronald T. Marchese. They collaborated on two books on this subject, *Splendor and Pageantry: Textile Treasures from the Armenian Orthodox Churches of Istanbul*, and *Sacred Relics and Artifacts from the Armenian Orthodox Churches of Istanbul*, both forthcoming. In addition to her work on the sacred artifacts in the Armenian Church collections of Istanbul, she has published scholarly articles and chapters on traditional Turkish material culture. She is a former Senior Lecturer at Izmir Economic University under the auspices of the Fulbright-Hays foreign exchange of scholars program.

DAVID STEPHEN CALONNE is the author of *William Saroyan: My Real Work Is Being*, and *The Colossus of Armenia: G.I. Gurdjieff and Henry Miller*. He has edited prepared introductions to a work on California poet and novelist Charles Bukowski, *Sunlight Here I Am: Interviews and Encounters, 1963-1993*, and two volumes of Bukowski's previously uncollected stories and essays, *Portions from a Wine-Stained Notebook* and *Absence of the Hero*. He has lectured on Armenian American literature and especially Saroyan at noted universities in the United States and at the Saroyan Centennial in Erevan in 2008. He has taught a seminar on Saroyan at the University of Chicago and currently teaches at Eastern Michigan University.

S. PETER COWE is Narekatsi Professor of Armenian Studies at the University of California, Los Angeles, and previously held positions at the Hebrew University of Jerusalem and Columbia University. His research interests include medieval Armenian intellectual history and modern Armenian nationalism. The author of five books in the field and editor of seven, he is completing an investigation of the post-Soviet publishing industry in the Republic of Armenia. A regular contributor to scholarly journals, he is the past co-editor of the *Journal of the Society for Armenian Studies*. The recipient of the Garbis Papazaian award for Armenology, he is currently collaborating on a study on the earliest Armenian encyclopedia, for which he has received a National Endowment for the Humanities fellowship, and researching royal ideology in the Cilician Armenian state, for which he has received a NEH summer grant.

SUREN DANIELYAN is the Director of the "Spyurk" Scientific Educational Center in Yerevan and a specialist on Western Armenian literature and has published extensively on the subject, including *Hetanosakan grakan sharzhman patmutiunits* (From the History of the Pagan Literary Movement); *Amerikahay vipagirner: Hamastegh, Hakob Asaturyan, Andranik Andreasyan* (American Armenian Novelists: Hamasdegh, Hagop Asadurian, and Antranig Antreassian), and has co-authored with Zareh Khrakhuni *Azatergutiunner* (Songs of Freedom). He has organized summer Armenian language enhancement courses for Armenian teachers in the Diaspora, and appears frequently on television and in the print media on issues relating to Armenian culture.

HERVE GEORGELIN is the author of *La fin de Smyrne: Du cosmopolitisme aux nationalismes* (2005), also in Greek (2007) and in Turkish (2008). He has also translated Aram Andonian's *Ayn sev orerun* as *En ces sombres jours* (2007) and published several research articles and review essays relating to Armenian, Greek, and Turkish history and society. With a Ph.D. from the Ecole des Hautes Etudes en Sciences Sociales, he focuses primarily on the Christian communities of the Ottoman Empire and their successor communities in the Diaspora. He has held teaching positions at the universities of Paris, Montpellier, and Bern.

TIM GREENWOOD is Lecturer in Eastern Christianity in the Department of Mediaeval History at the University of Saint Andrews. He has written widely on Armenian political, social, and cultural history between the fifth and thirteenth centuries, utilizing and analyzing and literary, epigraphic and architectural sources. He is the co-author of *Hakob's Gospels: The Life and Work of an Armenian Artist of the Sixteenth Century*, a study of Hakob Jughayetsi. Recent publications include a study of the late seventh-century *Anonymous Chronicle* and aspects of Sasanian Iran reflected in a range of Armenian texts. He is presently completing the translation and commentary of an Armenian eleventh-century composition, the *Tiezerakan Patmutiun* or *Universal History* by Stepannos Taronetsi.

ROBERT H. HEWSEN is Professor Emeritus of History at Rowan University and has taught Armenian history as a visiting professor at several universities in the United States and Europe and most recently at the Hebrew University of Jerusalem. He is the co-founder of the Society for the Study of Caucasia and a contributor to the *Journal of the Society for Armenian Studies*, *Revue des études arménnienes*, and other publications. A specialist in the historical geography of Armenia, he has prepared *Armenia: A Historical Atlas*, contributed several maps for the *Tübingen Atlas of the Middle East*, and translated with critical commentary the *Ashkharhatsoyts*, an early geography that he attributes to Anania of Shirak.

RICHARD G. HOVANNISIAN is Holder of the Armenian Educational Foundation Chair in Modern Armenian History at the University of California, Los Angeles, and serves as the editor of this series on historic Armenian cities and provinces. His numerous publications include *Armenia on the Road to In-*

dependence, the four-volume *The Republic of Armenia*, five volumes on the Armenian Genocide, the most recent being *Remembrance and Denial: The Case of the Armenian Genocide*; *Looking Backward, Moving Forward*; and *The Armenian Genocide: Cultural and Ethical Legacies*, and fifteen other volumes and sixty research articles relating to Armenian, Caucasian, Middle Eastern, and Islamic studies. A Guggenheim Fellow, he has received many honors, including encyclicals from the supreme patriarchs of the Armenian Church, two honorary doctoral degrees, and election to membership in the National Academy of Sciences of Armenia. He is the initiator and six-time president of the Society for Armenian Studies (SAS).

LUCINA AGBABIAN HUBBARD is Adjunct Instructor in Thornton School of Music at the University of Southern California, where for twenty years she has taught "Introduction to Armenian Music" and "Armenian Musical Culture." She has also been a lecturer in the Department of Ethnomusicology at UCLA and in the Teachers' Training Program of La Verne University, as well as a presenter of Armenian music in diverse venues. A graduate of UCLA's Department of World Arts Cultures, she has focused her studies on Armenian music and identity, with work at the Erevan Komitas Conservatory of Music and research under the direction of professors Robert Atayan, Margaret Proudyan, and Nigoghos Tahmizian,

DIKRAN M. KALIGIAN is managing editor of the *Armenian Review*. He has served as a visiting professor of the Kaloosdian/ Mugar Chair in Modern Armenian History at Clark University and of history at Westfield State College and at Regis College. He is the author of *Armenian Organization and Ideology under Ottoman Rule, 1908-1914*; "A Prelude to Genocide: CUP Population Policies and Provincial Insecurity," in *Late Ottoman Genocides*, ed. Dominik J. Schaller and Jurgen Zimmerer; and "The Use and Abuse of Armeno-Turkish Dialogue," *Armenian Review* (Fall-Winter 2008).

OHANNES KILIÇDAĞI is a Ph.D. candidate in History at Boğaziçi University, Istanbul. He is also a teaching and research assistant at Bilgi University. His Master of Arts thesis is titled "The Bourgeois Transformation and Ottomanism among Anatolian Armenians after the 1908 Revolution." He has translated a number of stories by William Saroyan into Turkish as part of a two-volume work published by Aras Press. His research centers on Ottomanism in the late Ottoman period, non-Muslims in the Ottoman Empire, and the social history of cities in Asia Minor before the establishment of the Turkish republic, particularly missionary activities and bourgeois society and ideology.

ROBERT OWEN KRIKORIAN is a Professorial Lecturer at George Washington University and an Associate of its Institute for European, Russian and Eurasian Studies. He earned a Ph.D. in History and Eurasian Studies at Harvard University and has worked with a variety of organizations, including Medecins sans Frontieres and the USAID Office of Foreign Disaster Assistance. He also serves as an Armenian-language interpreter for the State Department's Office of Language Services. He is the co-author of *Armenia: At the Crossroads* and has published articles and reviews in periodicals such as the *International Journal of Middle East Studies, Middle East Journal, Journal of Cold War Studies, Annual of the Society for the Study of Caucasia*, and *Armenian Review*.

INA BAGHDIANTZ McCABE is Holder of the Darakjian and Jafarian Chair in Armenian History at Tufts University. She has taught at Columbia University, University of Michigan, Bennington College, and University of Chicago. Her books include *The Shah's Silk for Europe's Silver: The Eurasian Trade of the Julfa Armenians in Safavid Iran and India (1530-1750); Du bon usage du thé et des épices en Asie: Réponses à Monsieur Cabart de Villarmont;* and *Orientalism in Early Modern France: Eurasian Trade, Exoticism, and the Ancien Régime.* She is also co-author of *Slaves of the Shah: New Elites of Isfahan* and co-editor of *Diaspora Entrepreneurial Networks: Four Centuries of History.* She has published articles on New Julfa, the Armenian silk trade, the spice trade, slavery, travel accounts, Orientalism, and the Armenian Diaspora.

RONALD T. MARCHESE is Professor of Ancient History and Archaeology at the University of Minnesota at Duluth. He has conducted archaeological, historical, and ethnographic research in Greece and the Middle East for thirty years. A two-time recipient of a Fulbright-Hays Senior Research award, he is the author or editor of a number of books and articles. He has been actively involved in the study of nomadic life in the Middle East and has participated in various ethnographic projects, including international, national, and regional exhibitions and conference presentations. For more than a decade, he has been involved in the study of Armenian material culture, especially religious culture, at the Armenian Patriarchate of Istanbul and All Turkey. This work has given substance to the "Constantinople style" in Armenian religious art. He has been a participant in the national lecture series of the Archaeological Institute of America and is currently conducting geophysical research at the ancient town of Plataiai in Greece.

VARTAN MATIOSSIAN is affiliated with the School of Oriental Studies, University del Salvador, Buenos Aires, and currently resides in New Jersey. He has written extensively about Armenian history and literature, both ancient and modern, in Armenian, Spanish, and English. Among his five books in Armenian are *Gostan Zariani shurj* (Concerning Kostan Zarian) *Haravayin koghmn ashkharhi: Hayere Latin Amerikayi mej skizben minchev 1950* (The Southern Side of the World: Armenians in Latin America from the Beginnings to 1950), and *Grakanbanasirakan usumnasirutiunner* (Literary-Philological Studies). He has also translated twelve books and a number of articles from Armenian into Spanish.

BARBARA J. MERGUERIAN is the Director of the Women's Information Center of the Armenian International Women's Association in Boston. She has been a visiting professor at Tufts University, Erevan State University, and California State University, Fresno. She is the former editor of the *Journal of Armenian Studies* and the *Armenian Mirror-Spectator* newspaper and is the co-editor of three books: *Exploring Gender Issues in the Caucasus*; *Voices of Armenian Women*; and *Armenian Women in a Changing World*. Her major research interest has been the role of the American missionaries in their work among the Armenians of the Ottoman Empire in the nineteenth and early twentieth centuries, about which she has published several articles.

MIKAËL NICHANIAN is curator of Armenian manuscripts at the Bibliothèque Nationale de France. His Ph.D. thesis from Paris University is titled "Byzantine Aristocracy and Imperial Power (7th-9th Centuries)." He has taught medieval history at the universities of Lyon and Paris and is a member of the Centre de recherche d'histoire et civilisation de Byzance (CNRS-Collège de France). He is the author *of Le monde byzantin, économie et société: du 8ᵉ siècle à 1204* (2006) as well as articles on Byzantine society and state, iconoclasm, and the Armenian nobility.

SIMON PAYASLIAN is Holder of the Charles and Elisabeth Kenosian Chair in Modern Armenian History and Literature at Boston University. He is the author of *The History of Armenia: From the Origins to the Present*; *United States Policy toward the Armenian Question and the Armenian Genocide*; *The Armenian Genocide, 1915-1923: A Handbook for Students and Teachers*; *U.S. Foreign Economic and Military Aid: The Reagan and Bush Administrations*; and *International Political Economy: Conflict and Cooperation in the Global System* (co-author with Frederic S. Pearson); as well as articles on the United Nations, international law and human rights, peace studies, the Kurdish question, U.S. foreign policy, and Armenian literature.

VICTORIA ROWE is the author of *A History of Armenian Women's Writing, 1880-1922* and co-editor of a bilingual volume of the poetry of Shushanik Kurghinian. She is the translator of Inga Nalbandian's 1917 classic *Your Brother's Blood Cries Out* and Aleksandr Shirvanzade's play *Did She Have the Right*. She has taught at universities in Canada, Japan, and the United Kingdom. Her current research focuses on international humanitarian organizations, including the work of the League of Nations with survivors of the Armenian Genocide. Among her articles on this subject is "Armenian Women Refugees at the End of Empire: Strategies of Survival," in *Refugees and End of Empire,* ed. Panikos Panayi and Pippa Virdee (forthcoming). She is the author of *A History of Armenian Women's Writing: 1880-1922*, has translated Inga Nalbandian's 1917 account of the Armenian Genocide as *Your Brother's Blood Cries Out,* and is co-editor of a bilingual volume of Shushanik Kiurghinian's poetry. She is the author of articles on Armenian literary and gender history, including "Armenian Writers and Women's Rights Discourse in

Turn-of-the-Twentieth-Century Constantinople," published in *Aspasia*, and "Modernity and Masculinity in Aleksandr Shirvan-zade's *Did She Have the Right*," published in *Ararat*.

MANEA ERNA SHIRINIAN is Professor of History in Erevan State University's Faculty of Theology and the head of the Department of Research and Editing of Ancient Armenian Texts in the Mashtots Matenadaran. She has been a visiting professor at universities in Germany, France, Israel, the Netherlands, and Switzerland. Her specializations are Armenian and Greek manu-scripts; Early Byzantine and Armenian historiography; Late Antique, Byzantine, and Armenian philosophy; and Eastern Christian Studies. She has published books and articles on Ar-menian translations of the Hellenizing School, textual criticism, Byzantine-Armenian cultural and historical connections, and the *Book of Causes* as a witness of the Armenian reception of the Greek philosophical and patristic theological heritage in Late Antiquity. She is chief editor of *Armeniaca* (English summaries of Armenological publications in Armenia) and the Armenian Studies periodical *Ashtanak,* the vice-president of the National Commitee of Byzantine Studies, and the coordinator of the *Orthodox Encyclopaedia* in Armenia.

VERJINE SVAZLIAN is Professor and Leading Researcher in the Institute of Archaeology and Ethnography, National Acade-my of Sciences of the Republic of Armenia. For the past half century, she has collected and studied the oral traditions of the Western Armenians and survivors of the Armenian Genocide. In addition to more than 500 articles, she has published twenty-three books, including *The Folklore of Musa Dagh*; *Cilicia: The Oral Traditions of Western Armenians*; *The Oral Tradition of the Armenians of Constantinople*; *The Armenian Genocide: Testi-monies of the Eyewitness Survivors* (all in Armenian), as well as *"The Armenian Genocide and the People's Historical Memory* (in several languages) and the entry "Armenia" in *The Green-wood Encyclopedia of World Folklore and Folklife*.

ROBERT W. THOMSON is Calouste Gulbenkian Professor of Armenian Studies Emeritus at Oxford University. A co-founder of the Society for Armenian Studies, he was the first Mashtots

Professor of Armenian Studies at Harvard University, 1969-1992, and served as Director of Dumbarton Oaks in Washington, DC, from 1984 to 1989. His research centers on classical and medieval Armenian literature within the context of Eastern Christian Studies. He has edited texts in Armenian, Syriac, and Greek and has translated many Armenian histories and commentaries. A comparative study of the versions of the *History* of Agathangelos with translations of the Armenian, Greek, Syriac, and Arabic texts is at press. He is currently working on medieval Armenian ideas about the natural world and the influence of Greek science. In 1995, he was elected a Fellow of the British Academy.

PREFACE

Armenian Constantinople is based on the papers delivered in the series of semi-annual international conferences on *Historic Armenian Cities and Provinces* held at UCLA since 1997. Publication of the edited proceedings began with *Armenian Van/Vaspurakan* (2000), followed by *Baghesh/Bitlis and Taron/Mush* (2001), *Tsopk/ Kharpert* (2002), *Karin/Erzerum* (2003), *Sebastia/Sivas and Lesser Armenia* (2004), *Tigranakert/Diarbekir and Edessa/Urfa* (2006), *Armenian Cilicia* (2008), and *Armenian Pontus* (2009). Future publications in this series include Kars and Ani; and the Armenian communities of Smyrna/Izmir; Caesarea/Kesaria and Asia Minor; Musa Dagh, Kessab, and Dort Yol; Jerusalem; New Julfa and Iran; and the Indian Ocean.

The challenge of bringing consistency in style and format to a variety of essays in different disciplines is formidable, requiring of the editors substantial rewriting and careful attention to detail both in form and in content. The views expressed by the individual contributors, however, are their own. In this series, a simplified system of transliteration is used to make the words and titles recognizable for persons who are proficient in Armenian but who would find it difficult to comprehend scholarly transliteration systems with non-phonetic diacritical marks—for example, *c'* representing "ց" (ts) as in the English word "lots." The drawback of this adaptation is that it does not allow for a precise conversion from the Latin alphabet back to the original Armenian script, as, for example, the transliterated character "e" in this volume may stand for any one of four Armenian letters (է, ե, ը, ի). In the citation of works that use diacritical marks, however, the form as it appears on the given title page has been retained. The transliteration of identical Armenian words may vary slightly depending on the orthography used in the original. Hence, the word "history" or "story" may appear as *patmutiun* (պատմութիւն) when taken from works published in traditional Armenian orthography or as *patmutyun* (պատմություն) when transliterated from the reformed orthography that was adopted in Soviet Armenia.

In this modified transliteration system, Eastern Armenian phonetic values are used in the citations, but, if it is the author's preference, exceptions have been made in the text in chapters using the more familiar Western Armenian forms of place names and personal names, as Bolis rather than Polis, Balian rather than Palian, and Gomidas rather than Komitas. This has led to seeming inconsistencies, but the variance has been intentional. Thus, one may see Gomidas or Baronian in the text but Komitas or Paronian in the corresponding citation in the footnote. Turkish names are rendered in the style commonly used before the Turkish alphabet reform of 1928—thus, for example, Javid rather than Cavit, and Beshiktash rather than Beşiktaş. Terms in foreign languages, such as *millet*, are italicized only the first time they appear in each chapter. In certain instances, the editors have not required absolute consistency when there are discrepancies in the information given or data cited by different authors.

The editors gratefully acknowledge the use of illustrations from the works of Pars Tuğlacı, Raymond H. Kévorkian, Ronald T. Marchese and Marlene R. Breu, and the *Nor Hayastan Daily*. The map on the front cover of the Armenian churches and neighborhoods and the insert on the back cover of an old Armenian neighborhood in Constantinople are from Marchese and Breu. Timothy Singer and Arpi Payaslian assisted in the editing of the preliminary drafts of several chapters. A. Kamron Jabbari, the publisher of this series, has been helpful throughout. As has been the case since the first volume in this series, Dr. Vartiter Kotcholosian Hovannisian has collaborated closely with the editors at each stage leading to the publication of *Armenian Constantinople*.

❉ 1 ❉

ARMENIAN CONSTANTINOPLE

Richard G. Hovannisian and Simon Payaslian

The Armenian presence in Constantinople contributed to the cultural and material wealth of the imperial city—*Kostandnupolis*, the City of Constantine, often referred to simply as "Polis" or "Bolis." Armenians had contacts with the Roman rulers in the eastern reaches of the imperial frontier for centuries when in the fourth century Emperor Constantine I, the Great, designated the city of Byzantium on the Bosphorus as Constantinople, his new or second Rome, the capital of the Eastern Empire.

Armenian cultural and military ties with Constantinople assumed particular significance after the Arshakuni/Arsacid king Trdat/Tiridates the Great adopted Christianity as the official state religion at the beginning of the fourth century. Because of the Persian Sasanian threat to the Arshakuni domains and the Byzantine-Persian partition of Armenia in 387, an increasing number of Armenians emigrated to Byzantine lands and eventually to Constantinople. In the fifth century, Mesrop Mashtots, the creator of the Armenian alphabet, and his disciples journeyed to the Byzantine capital in efforts to render a perfect translation of the Bible into Armenian. In 450, Armenian political and religious leaders opposed to the Sasanian aggressive policy in Armenia dispatched a delegation, headed by the famed commander-in-chief *Sparapet* Vardan Mamikonian, to Constantinople in an urgent but futile call for military support against the Persian invaders. In a similar vein, in 572, another Vardan Mamikonian, who had led a rebellion against the Persians, sought refuge in Byzantine lands.

Beginning in the middle of the seventh century, the Arab occupation of Armenia under the Umayyad Caliphate and subsequently the Abbasid Caliphate and the resultant political upheavals caused by rebellions of the noble *nakharar* families led to the migration of thousands of Armenians to the Byzantine Empire. Their growing presence in Constantinople escalated the Armenian role in the affairs of the empire. As demonstrated by Peter Charanis, Sirarpie Der Nersessian, and Alexander Kazhdan, among others, some Armenian nobles in Byzantium even rose to the rank of emperor, while others attained prominence within the military establishment and the Orthodox Church. They were kings and princes, bishops and patriarchs, rebels and usurpers, intellectuals and diplomats, all operating within the Byzantine context.

The Seljuk invasions and the disintegration of the Armenian Bagratuni/Bagratid kingdom in the eleventh century caused new waves of migration to the Byzantine Empire. The disastrous Byzantine defeat by the Seljuks at Manzikert in 1071 signaled the decline of the imperial army. Although Constantinople survived for nearly four centuries thereafter despite external and internal threats, the sustained Ottoman offensives proved too debilitating. The Byzantine military finally collapsed in 1453 when the Ottoman army under Sultan Mehmed II, the Conqueror, captured the coveted city. By the end of the fifteenth century, approximately 1,000 Armenian households existed in Constantinople, and that number increased rapidly as political turmoil spread across the region.

As the Ottoman Empire consolidated power and stabilized, many Armenians in the capital and its environs registered impressive cultural and economic development despite their legal status as second-class citizens. Armenians were placed under the religious-civil jurisdiction of the Armenian Patriarch of Constantinople, as the *Ermeni millet* or religious community, a convenient and practical system of control for the Ottoman rulers. The Patriarchate, the origins of which, according to the traditional view, date back to the fifteenth century, or, according to later scholarship, to the sixteenth century, played a central role in the reforms initiated for the Armenian millet in the nineteenth century. These included ratification in 1847 by the sultan's government (Sublime Porte) of the establishment of the Armenian Spiritual Council and the Supreme Council, and the imperial *iradé* (decree) in 1863 confirming the regulations that became known as the Armenian National Constitution (Hayots Azgayin Sahmanadrutiun). The Patriarchate, a conservative institution, had the unenviable task of representing an increasingly polarized community. The *amira* class, consisting of the wealthy and influential Armenian elite, rejected structural reconfigurations of power and authority within the community and viewed the *esnafs* or trade guilds and the radicalization of Armenian national sentiment with a deep sense of apprehension. Belonging to the amira class, the Balian, Bezjian, Dadian, and Duzian families, for example, had cultivated close ties with the sultanate and opposed any intellectual currents that could potentially undermine their position and patronage. Such relations, they maintained, were necessary for the benefit of the Armenian community and enabled them to contribute generously to the construction of schools, churches, and hospitals. Demands for fundamental reforms for the redistribution of power and privilege both within the Armenian community and Ottoman society in general threatened the amira class. The internal difficulties notwithstanding, the fact that there had emerged Armenian amiras, esnafs, and nationalists, and that Armenians created their own councils and constitution demonstrated the dynamic nature of the community of Constantinople.

By the middle of the nineteenth century, the internal and international tensions were exacerbated by the military and economic decline of the empire. In 1876, the government itself, under Sultan Abdul Hamid II (1876-1908/09), promulgated a liberal Ottoman Constitution, which instituted a seemingly democratic political system with guarantees for civil and political freedoms. In less than two years, however, the sultan found excuses to suspend the constitution. The reforms promised for the political liberalization of the Ottoman state never materialized nor did the reforms for the Armenian communities. The Treaty of San Stefano (1878) concluding the Russo-Turkish war of 1877-78 provided for the effective implementation of reforms under direct Russian supervision, but the Treaty of Berlin, signed only months later, revised the related article and placed the question of reforms under collective European responsibility. The Ottoman government, however, showed little tolerance toward demands for civil and administrative change. Reforms in the name of modernization and liberalization threatened the status quo, a particularly troubling potentiality for the political elite and Muslims in general, as the Armenians and other Christians were deemed the principal beneficiaries. Disillusionment with the European powers and the failure of the Armenian Patriarchate to effectuate changes within the Armenian communities further radicalized Armenian nationalist movements and led to the emergence of a number secret societies in the provinces and the creation of the three major political parties: the Armenakan Party in Van (1885), the Hnchakian Social Democratic Party in Geneva (1887), and the Armenian Revolutionary Federation or Dashnaktsutiun in Tiflis (1890). Significantly, the fact that none of these political parties was founded in Constantinople was indicative of the degree to which security concerns restricted open political activities in the Ottoman Empire.

While promising reform, the sultan was determined to quell any public manifestations of political grievances, as in the case of the Kumkapu demonstrations in July 1890, when a small group of Armenian activists instigated turmoil inside the patriarchal church during mass, which, continuing outside, led to clashes with the police. A more serious crisis occurred in October 1895, when a demonstration organized by the Hnchakian Party to petition the Sublime Porte led to the death of more than 200 Armenians in another clash with the police. Government repression reached unprecedented levels in the eastern provinces (*vilayets*) between 1894 and 1896 when between 100,000 and 200,000 Armenians were massacred and thousands more were forced to convert to Islam. Armenians in the capital could not remain indifferent to the escalating hostilities and the bloodshed in the provinces. In August 1896, a number of activists of the Dashnaktsutiun reacted by seizing the Ottoman Imperial Bank in hopes of soliciting an immediate response to the crisis from the European powers. The revolutionaries clearly failed. Moreover, the government in turn responded by unleashing an armed mob to deliver murder and mayhem upon the Armenian neighborhoods. In a community of about 150,000 Armenians, more than 5,000 were killed within a couple of days, and many thousands more left the city in the following weeks and months.

Constantinople was unquestionably the most important Armenian center of the Ottoman Empire, just as Tiflis was the largest and most active Armenian center of the Russian Empire. Both cities were beyond the historic bounds of Armenia, yet the Armenians did not regard themselves as living in Diaspora. Here, in the cosmopolitan environment of Constantinople, new generations of Armenian intellectuals, working as editors and journalists, artists and musicians, poets and teachers, gave shape to their nation's cultural renaissance and enlightenment, in spite of the increasingly repressive political environment. Among the notables (whose names are given here in Western Armenian transliteration) were Krikor Odian (1834-1887) and Nahabed Rusinian (1819-1876), who formulated the Armenian National Constitution; Odian also worked with Midhat Pasha in drafting the Ottoman Constitution of 1876. Mgrdich Khrimian "Hayrig" (Patriarch of Constantinople from 1869 to 1873; Catholicos of All-Armenians from 1892 to 1907) published *Artsvi Vaspurakan* (Eagle of Vaspurakan) beginning in 1855 in order to bring the life and culture of the eastern provinces to the attention of the Constantinopolitan community. Hagop Baronian, the famed satirist, published the journals *Tadron* (Theater) and *Khikar*, in addition to his own works casting a critical eye on Constantinopolitan habits and customs. Among the leading writers were Mgrdich Beshigtashlian (1828-1866), Bedros Turian (1851-1872), Srpuhi Diusap (1841-1901), Arpiar Arpiarian (1852-1908), Misag Medzarents (1886-1908), Rupen Sevag (1885-1915), Taniel/Daniel Varoujan (1884-1915), Siamanto (Adom Yarjanian, 1878-1915), and Zabel Yesayan (1878-1943). In 1914, Hagop Oshagan (1883-1948), Kegham Parseghian (1883-1915), and Gosdan/Kostan Zarian (1885-1969) published the journal *Mehyan* (Pagan Temple). These romanticist, realist, and radical intellectuals debated issues related to modernization and enlightenment, religion and secularization, political reforms and democratization, national liberation and social and cultural liberalization.

Their hopes and emotions, aspirations and disappointments, failed reform programs and nascent resistance movements of the nineteenth century gave way to new hopes and emotions evoked by the Young Turk revolution in 1908 and Sultan Abdul Hamid's final abdication of the throne in 1909. Yet ironically it was the Young Turks who were to spell the end of the Ottoman Armenians. The unwillingness of the major powers to intervene to stop the massacres of 1894-96 and to rectify the situation in the provinces indicated to the Armenians that they could not rely on outside support for protection. More ominously, however, the indifference shown by the powers to the plight of the Armenians for decades convinced the future virulently nationalist political leaders of the empire, the triumvirate of Mehmed Talaat, Ismail Enver, and Ahmed Jemal within the Committee of Union and Progress (CUP; Ittihad ve Terakki Jemiyeti), that atrocities committed against the Armenians could be carried out with impunity. They seized power through a military coup in January 1913, and the following year mobilized the empire for World War I. Military campaigns were in full swing when on February 12, 1915, the authorities ordered the removal of all Armenian officials from their government posts in Constantinople. Then on the night of April 24-25, more than 200 Armenian intellectuals and community leaders were arrested in the city and exiled to Ayash, Changhiri (Changri), and Chorum. This was followed by the arrest of nearly 3,000 other Armenians.

While the genocidal policies of massacre and deportation by the Ittihadists continued to unfold across the empire, the authorities in January 1916 notified Patriarch Zaven Der Yeghiayan (Ter-Eghiayan) and Catholicos Sahag II Khabayan (Sahak Khapayan) of the Great House of Cilicia at Sis of their intent to terminate both institutions and to nullify the Armenian National Constitution. On August 10 (July 28, old style), 1916, the Ittihadists abolished the Patriarchate of Constantinople and exiled Patriarch Zaven to Baghdad and thence to Mosul, where he remained until the conclusion of the war. The government also ordered Catholicos Sahag to transfer to Jerusalem with the title of Catholicos-Patriarch.

The Allied victory and occupation of Constantinople forced the defeated Turkish government on November 20, 1918 to reinstitute the legal status of the Armenian Patriarchate and the Catholicosate of Cilicia. Patriarch Zaven returned to Constantinople on the British destroyer *Acacia* on February 19, 1919. The Patriarchate commenced the task of reorganizing the community and, in co-operation with a number of compatriotic associations, introduced various social services to care for the orphans. The Orphan Collection Agency, the Orphan Care Agency, along with others, oversaw the operation of orphanages and relocation posts, as in the Beylerbey orphanage and the Beshiktash orphanage for girls. By the end of 1922, approximately 3,000 Armenian orphans had been rescued in Constantinople. In the meantime, military tribunals in Constantinople tried a number of the perpetrators of the massacres as war criminals. Soon, however, the Nationalist forces under Mustafa Kemal (Ataturk) consolidated power against the postwar government in Constantinople and pressed forward in a campaign that culminated in the expulsion of the remaining Christian population in Asia Minor, Cilicia, and the Pontus and the establishment of the Republic of Turkey.

Constantinople was formally renamed Istanbul in 1930. Since

then, the Armenian community, totaling about 50,000, has remained relatively isolated, in sharp contrast with its cultural vi-
brancy in the nineteenth century. The murder of Hrant Dink, the
editor of *Agos* newspaper in Istanbul, on January 19, 2007, evoked
profound fear and anger. The community was calmed by the
heartening display of thousands of Turks and Armenians marching
together at his funeral procession and carrying placards reading
Hepimiz Ermeniyiz (We Are All Armenians), *Hepimiz Hrant
Dink'iz* (We Are All Hrant Dink). The Armenian community of
Istanbul has survived despite the decades of difficult circumstances, trying to maintain an identity and a continuing presence.

The Contributions

This volume offers an overview of the history of the Armenian
community in Constantinople from its earliest times to the twentieth century. The book cannot claim to present a comprehensive
history, for an effort to capture the community's rich heritage
would require separate volumes devoted to Armenian literature,
theater and drama, art and architecture, music, education, and the
church. Nevertheless, it is hoped that collectively the twenty
chapters that follow will open an enticing window into the history
and culture of the largest and strongest Armenian community of
the Ottoman Empire.

Robert W. Thomson reviews the link between Constantinople
and the development of Armenian literature as found in the works
of the classical writers Agatangeghos, Movses Khorenatsi, and
Ghazar Parpetsi. From the earliest period, Constantinople served
as a center for secular and theological learning. Armenian monarchs placed a premium on their political ties with Constantinople
in hopes of securing military support against repeated Persian in-
cursions. Mesrop Mashtots visited Constantinople and is said to
have secured the emperor's approval to establish schools in
western Armenia to train the next generation in the use of Armenian script for church services. Mashtots subsequently dispatched
his disciples Ghevond, Eznik, and Koriun to Constantinople, who
returned with copies of the Bible for translation.

Mikaël Nichanian examines the engagement of the nascent
Armenian elite in Byzantine politics, drawing attention to the role
of a group of Armenian military officers in a coup to overthrow

Emperor Justinian II (705-11). Because of the emphasis on the Macedonian dynasty founded by Emperor Basil I (867-86) as the principal Armenian aristocratic family in Constantinople, the literature has tended to neglect the earlier Armenian presence among the Byzantine elite. A case in point is that of the Emperor Philippikos-Vardanes (Philippicus Bardanes, 711-13), whose Armenian family is believed to have settled in Byzantium in the sixth century. During his short reign, Philippikos-Vardanes reverted to a compromise religious doctrine known as Monotheletism and pursued diplomatic ties with various leaders in the Caucasus for the unity of the Christian Church, while also pressing his own Armenian subjects to accept the Byzantine (Orthodox) Church. Philippikos-Vardanes himself was overthrown by an army rebellion.

Erna M. Shirinian analyzes the relationship between Emperor Basil I and Patriarch Photius I (858-67, 877-86). She notes that by the ninth century, the Armenian presence in Constantinople had increased and several elite families had gained prestige and power in Byzantium. Upon assuming the throne, Basil removed Photius as patriarch because of the strained relations with the Roman Church. Yet, Basil and Photius eventually developed close ties. While in exile, Photius, perhaps a descendant of the Armenian Kamsarakan noble family, hoped to demonstrate that Basil had descended from the illustrious Arshakuni dynasty. It may be relevant that Basil even requested a crown from Prince Ashot, the future King Ashot Bagratuni, of Armenia.

Tim Greenwood considers the relations between Constantinople and Armenia from 860 to 976. He outlines the changes taking place along the eastern frontier. The Armenian princely Bagratuni and Artsruni houses were both within the sphere of influence of the caliphate and its deputies when, from the reign of Emperor Romanos I Lecapenus (920-44) to the death of John I Tzimisces (969-76), Constantinople widened its interests in Armenia, acquired rights to territories, and thereby challenged the position of the Arabs and the Sadjid emirate. Among the ruling Armenian dynasties, the Bagratunis remained more cautious than the Mamikonians and the other noble houses in their Western orientation, while the Artsrunis favored closer ties with the empire and appeared more willing to make concessions in matters of land and loyalty. The Byzantine emperors, for their part, considering the Armenian nobility generally untrustworthy as allies, demanded territorial concessions as the only acceptable proof of their loyalty.

Ronald T. Marchese and Marlene R. Breu present a detailed analysis of the closely intertwined nature of Armenian material culture and social identity, artisanship and religion, as manifested in the sacred objects of the Armenian Apostolic Church and the revival of Armenian religious art in Constantinople. The amira class, through patronage, strengthened the authority of the Patriarchate and enhanced the prestige of the Armenian Church. The authors note that donations of objects of faith served a number of purposes. They represented an expression of the glorification of God and direct participation in communal religious life. Furthermore, contributions functioned as cultural markers delineating the boundaries between the Armenians' Christian identity and the Muslim world surrounding them.

Ina Baghdiantz McCabe stresses the relationship between commerce and culture by linking a Bible produced in 1623 with Armenian merchants in Constantinople and their counterparts in Iran. The Armenian community in the Ottoman capital experienced a renaissance of manuscript illumination in the seventeenth century, which the Armenians of New Julfa sought to imitate. Bibles were commissioned and imported from the scriptoria in Constantinople under the patronage of wealthy amiras, and the city became one of the principal distribution centers for manuscripts to other parts of the Diaspora.

Barbara Merguerian focuses on the American missionary teacher Cyrus Hamlin, who under the auspices of the American Board of Commissioners for Foreign Missions (ABCFM) established Robert College (now Boğaziçi University) in Constantinople in 1863. As president of the college, Hamlin, who directed the college until 1875, witnessed a rapid growth in enrollment but encountered numerous difficulties with college trustees and some of the American faculty who found him too tolerant of local diversities. By the early twentieth century, Robert College had emerged as one of the most prominent institutions of higher learning in the Middle East.

Ohannes Kılıçdağı describes some of the key characteristics of the Constantinopolitan Armenian community in the second half of the nineteenth century and the early years of the twentieth century. The Armenian *tagh* or neighborhood played a significant role as an organizational unit within the administrative system as established under the Armenian National Constitution of 1863. The governance of the neighborhoods and the various societies was a contentious affair, as their leaders vied for power while seeking to maintain order and preserve traditional moral norms. Competing values and priorities generated tensions between the traditional and the modern, between loyalty to the Ottoman state and opposition to its repressive rule. The social and political difficulties notwithstanding, the Armenian neighborhoods were dynamic, vibrant quarters.

Victoria Rowe emphasizes the significance of Constantinople as the center of modern Western Armenian intellectual life. By the second half of the nineteenth century, expanding opportunities for education for Armenian men and women also widened the cultural circles for the cultivation of talents for a growing range of artists. Armenian women created networks of communication through the salons and journals, participated in public debates on modernity, society, politics, and culture, and were active through educational institutions, philomathic and charitable societies, and literary groups. Among the most gifted women were Srpuhi Dussap, Sibyl, and Zabel Yesayan. Their works captured the cultural changes and challenges brought about by modernization in general and education in particular. Armenian women in Constantinople gained greater visibility in the public sphere than had been possible for earlier generations.

Sarkis Balmanoukian gives an overview of the architectural works by four generations of the distinguished Balian family. Working under six sultans from the late eighteenth century to the early twentieth century, the Balians constructed palaces, military barracks, mosques, churches, and other buildings in Constantinople and contributed to the development of European architectural styles in the city. Garabed Balian, the leading architect among the family members, built four palaces, including the popular Dolmabahche Palace, two military barracks, and a number of schools and factories. Yet, as the author notes, despite its contributions to Ottoman and Turkish culture, the Balian dynasty of architects is often excluded from public memory and discourse.

Lucina Agbabian Hubbard, in her essay on Armenian music in Constantinople, contends that after centuries of Ottoman rule, Armenian cultural memory appeared to have lost the nation's musical traditions. That legacy consisted of secular and sacred songs and poetry but was gradually replaced by Turkified Armenian music whereby the Armenian liturgy in churches and schools was sung with Turkish musical intonations. This Turkified style was criticized by prominent Armenian musicologists such as Hampardzum Limonjian in the nineteenth century and Gomidas Vartabed (Komitas Vardapet) in the early twentieth century. Armenian musicians trained in Western conservatories nevertheless were able to further a cultural reawakening through their performances, publications, and education of the next generation and in so doing enriched the Armenian musical world.

Souren Danielyan analyzes the poetry and philosophy of Daniel Varoujan. Born in the village of Brgnik in Sebastia (Sivas), Varoujan composed most of his poetry in Constantinople. He maintained that Armenian cultural reawakening required a return to pre-Christian Armenian values and traditions and accordingly emphasized a revival of heathenism. Nature and beauty, blood and soil were the essential ingredients that permeated his works. Yet, despite Varoujan's fame as one of the leading Western Armenian poets, Eastern Armenian intellectuals, especially Vahan Terian, severely criticized him and the heathenist movement. Prior to World War I, Daniel Varoujan, in cooperation with Kostan Zarian and others, worked to create the journal *Mehyan* for the purpose of propagating pre-Christian values. He was among the intellectuals who were arrested and murdered in 1915 in the early stages of the Armenian Genocide.

Vartan Matiossian assesses Kostan Zarian's contributions to Armenian cultural life in the Ottoman capital in the early twentieth century. Zarian, who while in Europe had refused to write in the Armenian language, reacted to the horrendous news regarding the Adana massacres in 1909 by re-embracing his Armenian identity and culture. In 1910, he spent nine months in Constantinople, where he contributed a number of articles to the local Armenian newspaper, *Azatamart*. He also became active in Armenian literary circles and specifically the literary Mehyan movement along with Daniel Varoujan and Hagop Oshagan. The advent of World War I and the Armenian Genocide abruptly ended the movement. Despite the genocide, a number of leading intellectuals returned to Constantinople to revive Armenian culture in the community. Zarian took part in the formation of the House of Armenian Arts (Hay Arvesti Tun) in 1921 and the literary journal *Bardzravank* the following year. Soon, however, the spread of Kemalism and the burning of Smyrna in September 1922 were to compel many Armenian intellectuals, including Zarian, to flee the capital never to return.

Robert Krikorian contemplates the role of Armenian intellectuals in Constantinople between 1908 and 1915. Comprised of individuals of various ideological predilections, they performed various functions in the community and within the broader Ottoman society. They represented their people and in doing so served as a bridge between the community and the outside world. Educated in foreign universities, some Armenian intellectuals propagated Western cultural values as they sought to construct a modern Armenian national identity. Yet, from the perspective of the Ottoman state and Muslims in general, the motivations and activities of the Armenian intellectuals were ambiguous at best, as they were considered instruments of foreign interference in domestic affairs.

Dikran Kaligian reviews the relationship between the Armenian Revolutionary Federation (ARF) and the Committee of Union and Progress. Both parties collaborated against Sultan Abdul Hamid II, who in 1908 was forced to restore the Constitution of 1876 and finally to abdicate the throne in 1909. The ARF supported Ottoman territorial integrity but also advocated a federal structure to allow for local autonomy and guarantees for civil liberties and political rights. It appeared that the two parties would pursue mutually supportive aims after the reinstitution of the constitution. However, the 1909 massacres in Adana and throughout Cilicia, which claimed more than 20,000 Armenian lives, raised a host of questions concerning the feasibility of cooperation, particularly as Turkish nationalism gained wide support among the Young Turk leadership. The outbreak of the world war ended all efforts for further cooperation, with disastrous results for the Armenian population.

Hervé Georgelin introduces *La Renaissance*, a daily newspaper published under the auspices of the Armenian Patriarchate of Constantinople for two years following World War I. Under the editorship of Tigrane Tchaïan, the paper sought to convince the Allied Powers of the urgency of action to assist the Armenian orphans and refugees. Further, it advocated just punishment for the crimes committed against the Armenian people during the war and demanded reparations for the material losses suffered. In the end, however, *La Renaissance* and the community leadership failed to influence Allied opinion. The rapidly changing political situation created by the Kemalist forces and Allied geopolitical considerations did not permit a just resolution favorable to the Armenian community.

Peter Cowe evaluates the works of twentieth-century popular poets Zahrad (Zahrat; Zareh Yaldizian) and Zareh Khrakhuni (Artin Jiumbiushian), both born in Istanbul. They have sought to make literature more accessible to the general reader, as they delve into matters pertaining to cultural identity, tensions, and conformity, while, especially in the case of Khrakhuni, also stressing the particular experiences of Armenians in their social milieux in Istanbul. The discussion highlights the similarities and differences between the works of the two writers. Zahrad aspires to capture the individual and the universal dimensions of daily life in his native city, the monotony of the routine, and the universality of alienation, while Khrakhuni deals more explicitly with Armenian themes and symbols but without losing sight of the universality of the human condition.

Robert H. Hewsen looks at the life and work of Vahram Papazian (1888-1968), an Armenian celebrity in the theatrical profession. Born in Constantinople, Papazian studied acting in Milan and performed in many cities, including Tiflis, Baku, and Moscow. As an actor, he gained fame and popularity, particularly with women. He taught at the Sundukyan State Theater in Erevan and staged numerous productions. In recognition of his talent and contribution to Soviet theater, Papazian was awarded the titles of People's Artist of Armenia, Georgia, and Azerbaijan and the People's Artist of the USSR. His fame is immortalized by the national theater in Stepanakert named in his honor.

Verjiné Svazlian offers samples of morality stories and fables from the Armenian oral tradition collected in Istanbul. Consisting of proverbs, didactic aphorisms, and riddles, the oral tradition in prose and verse is said to capture in embellished narrative and adorned imagery actual events and characters endured in the nation's collective memory. They emphasize ethics and morality, customs and religion. The survival of this rich oral tradition demonstrates the ability of the Armenian community in Istanbul to maintain and transmit its cultural traditions from generation to generation.

David Stephen Calonne writes about the novelist Peter Sourian, whose works touch on various themes, ranging from father-son relations and triangular love affairs to wealth and class relations in the United States and Armenian identity. At first rejecting his Armenian heritage, Sourian eventually accepted his identity. Above all, however, it was French culture and literature that had the greatest influence on his work. Through his fictional characters, Sourian struggles with his diasporan identity and his Armenian past rooted in Constantinople. The tensions generated by such emotional conflicts are further exacerbated by the dichotomous, paradoxical self-perceptions of belonging on the one hand to seemingly culturally superior privileged circles of intellectuals, and on the other hand to an ancient people with an extensive historical record of victimhood.

The Armenian community in Constantinople had emerged far from the historic Armenian homeland, but by the nineteenth century it had evolved into the foremost cultural center. The community in Istanbul today and Armenians across the Diaspora and the current Republic of Armenia remain the beneficiaries of the rich cultural legacy inherited from the generations of Srpuhi Diusap and Zabel Yesayan, Hagop Baronian and Daniel Varoujan. The editors trust that this volume will provide useful glimpses into the history and culture of Armenian Constantinople and an appreciation of the continuing Armenian presence in this great crossroads metropolis—Bolis.

Armenian Patriarchate, Kumkapu

Samatia and Galata

Rumeli Hisar and Bebek

18

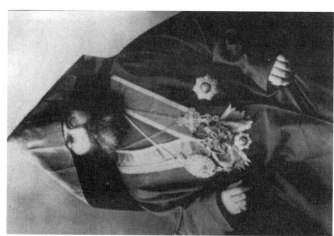

Patriarchs Malachia Ormanian and Zaven Der Yeghiayan

❋ 2 ❋

CONSTANTINOPLE
AND EARLY ARMENIAN LITERATURE

Robert W. Thomson

Constantine I the Great (306-37) established Constantinople in 330 as his new capital at Byzantium and named it after himself. Over the centuries an Armenian community gradually developed there, the process greatly accelerating after the fall of the city to the Ottoman Sultan Mehmed Fatih in 1453. This essay is concerned only with the earliest period, concentrating on the importance of the Armenian link with Constantinople in the development of early Armenian literature.

The historian Ghazar Parpetsi describes in some detail the building of the new capital on the site of the earlier city.[1] He explains, quite correctly, the advantages of the peninsula, encircled on all sides by the sea except for a short stretch of dry land on the western side. From then on, says Ghazar, streams of wisdom have been flowing from the royal capital, where the greatest scholars from all regions of Greece are anxious to shine. Movses Khorenatsi gives a more detailed picture of Constantinople, naming several of the buildings on the older site of Byzantium.[2] Unlike Ghazar, he states that Constantine I named the city "New Rome," but "the world" popularly called it Constantinople. The foundation of such an important capital was also known to Armenians from other sources that deal with the reign of the emperor Constantine—for

---

[1] Ghazar Parpetsi, *Patmutiun Hayots ev tught ar Vahan Mamikonian*, ed. Galust Ter-Mkrtchian and Stepan Malkhasian (Tiflis: Aragatip Mnatsakan Martirosiants, 1904; reprinted Delmar, NY: Caravan Books, 1985); trans. Robert W. Thomson, *The History of Łazar P'arpec'i* (Atlanta: Scholars Press, 1991), pp. 3-5.

[2] Movses Khorenatsi, *Patmutiun Hayots*, ed. Manuk Abeghian and Set Harutiunian (Tiflis: Aragatip Mnatsakan Martirosiants, 1913; repr. Delmar, NY: Caravan Books, 1981); trans. Robert W. Thomson, *Moses Khorenats'i: History of the Armenians* (Cambridge, MA: Harvard University Press, 1978), Bk II, ch. 88.

example, the translation of the *Ecclesiastical History* of Socrates Scholasticus.[3]

Early Armenian Visitors to Constantinople

Ghazar mentions that he had studied in Roman territory, that is, in the Eastern Roman Empire, the area now known as Byzantium,[4] while Movses explicitly states that he visited Constantinople himself.[5] These historians were of course writing well after the invention of the Armenian script and the development of an original literature in the Armenian language. But contacts had been established between Constantinople and Armenia prior to the invention of the Armenian script by Mesrop Mashtots and the beginning of writing in the Armenian language.

In the well known story of the conversion of King Trdat to Christianity, Agatangeghos provides an account of a journey that the king and Saint Gregory the Illuminator undertook in order to visit the emperor Constantine and to congratulate him on his own conversion to Christianity. He claims that Trdat and Gregory went to the old Rome in Italy, and there concluded a pact of mutual aid and support.[6] Although the visit to Rome of an earlier Trdat in the reign of the emperor Nero attracted much attention and was described in great detail by Dio Cassius and Suetonius,[7] this later visit of Trdat is not mentioned in Greek or Latin sources. None-

[3] Socrates Scholasticus, *Sokratay Skolastikosi ekeghetsakan patmutiun ev patmutiun varuts srboyn Silbestrosi episkoposin Hrovmay*, ed. M. Ter-Movsesian (Echmiadzin: Catholicosate of Echmiadzin, 1897), Bk I, ch. 16; English translation of the second, shorter, Armenian version, Robert W. Thomson, *The Armenian Adaptation of the Ecclesiastical History of Socrates Scholasticus* (Leuven: Peeters, 2001). For the founding of Constantinople, see Averil Cameron and Stuart G. Hall, *Eusebius: Life of Constantine* (Oxford: Clarendon Press, 1999), Bk III, chs. 47-49; C. Sanspeur, "La version arménienne de la Visio Constantini, BHG 396," *Handes Amsorya* 88 (1974): 307-20.

[4] Ghazar Parpetsi, *Patmutiun Hayots*, p. 185.

[5] Khorenatsi, *Patmutiun Hayots*, Bk III, ch. 62.

[6] Agatangeghos, *Patmutiun Hayots*, ed. Galust Ter-Mkrtchian and Stepan Kanayiants (Tiflis: Mnatsakan Martirosiants, 1909; repr. Delmar, NY: Caravan Books, 1980); trans. Robert W. Thomson, *Agathangelos: History of the Armenians* (Albany, NY: State University of New York Press, 1976).

[7] For the visit of this Trdat to Rome in the first century, see Dio Cassius, *Epitome of Book LXIII*; Suetonius, *Life of Nero*, XIII, and XXX, 6 for Trdat as a "magus," Latin and Greek texts with English translation in the Loeb Classical Series.

theless, Constantine did receive innumerable delegations of foreign dignitaries in his new capital, the New Rome, as described by the historian Eusebius of Caesarea in his *Life of Constantine*:

> There were constant diplomatic visitors who brought valuable gifts from their homelands. . . . We saw before the outer palace gates waiting in a line remarkable figures of barbarians, with their exotic dress, their distinctive appearance, the quite singular cut of hair and beard. . . . The faces of some were red, of others whiter than snow, of others blacker than ebony or pitch . . . [Eusebius elaborates on their various gifts and treasures]. . . . The emperor responded with equal gifts. . . . He honoured the most distinguished of them with Roman titles, so that very many now longed to remain here, forgetting any thought of returning to their homes.[8]

As for the visit to Rome of the newly converted Trdat with Saint Gregory in the fourth century, early Armenian writers refer frequently to the mutual pact between their king and the emperor Constantine.[9] The first reference to this pact occurs in the *Buzandaran* in the reign of King Tiran (338-50?).[10] In response to a request from the Armenians, who recalled the treaty of alliance, the Greeks sent an army to help repulse an invasion of the Persian shah. The description of the Persian defeat is somewhat rhetorical: supposedly the emperor went himself as a spy to reconnoitre the Persian camp disguised as a cabbage-seller! At a later date, the Armenian patriarch Nerses was sent to the imperial palace,[11] "because of the existence of an alliance between the realm of Armenia and the emperor of the Greeks."[12] Although there are problems

---

[8] Eusebius, *Life of Constantine*, Bk IV, ch. 7; quotation from the translation in Cameron and Hall.

[9] Later the tradition takes on a life of its own with fabulous elaborations. See details in Robert W. Thomson, "Constantine and Trdat in Armenian Tradition," *Acta Orientalia Academiae Scientiarum Hungaricae* 50 (1997): 277-89.

[10] The Armenian text of the *Buzandaran* was attributed to Pavstos Buzand, *Pavstosi Buzandatsvoy Patmutiun Hayots*, ed. Kerope Patkanian (St. Petersburg: Imperial Academy of Sciences, 1883; repr. Delmar, NY: Caravan Books, 1984); trans. Nina G. Garsoïan, *The Epic Histories Attributed to P'awstos Buzand (Buzandaran Patmut'iwnk')* (Cambridge, MA: Harvard University Press, 1989), Bk III, ch. 21.

[11] On both occasions, the *Buzandaran* only refers to the *palat*, not to Constantinople by name.

[12] *Buzandaran*, Bk IV, ch. 5.

with the dating of these visits, the important point is that the author of the *Buzandaran* emphasized the long-standing treaty of friendship.

This appears again in the famous work of Eghishe, *Vasn Vardanay ev Hayots paterazmin* (The History of Vardan and the Armenian War). In 450, the Armenian delegation seeking help after the Persian invasion took with them a letter. This document recalls Roman assistance in restoring King Trdat to his throne, and states that he received the faith in Christ from the archbishop of Rome. This is somewhat at variance with the tradition known to Agatangeghos.[13] More relevant here is the statement in Eghishe that when the Armenian request and the records of their ancestors were presented to Theodosius II (408-50), confirmation of the same covenant was found in Greek books. The later historian Sebeos also emphasizes the pact that had been agreed upon between Constantine and Trdat. In 572, a different Vardan Mamikonian had rebelled against the Persians and killed their governor in Dvin; but he was forced to take refuge in Constantinople. The emperor Justin II (565-78), confirming the old pact, sent an imperial army to support the Armenians. Subsequently, the Persians suffered a defeat at the hands of a Greek army.[14]

The visit of the second Vardan to Constantinople was of some consequence, for the Armenians were pressured to accept Greek Orthodoxy in an attempt to enforce reunion of the churches. On this occasion Vardan at first refused, stating that his church authorities would not permit it; however, he summoned Armenian clerics to discuss the question. The gathering, which ended with Armenian submission, was convoked at the Cathedral of Saint

---

[13] Eghishe, *Vasn Vardanay ev Hayots paterazmin*, ed. Ervand Ter-Minasyan (Erevan: Armenian Academy of Sciences, Institute of Literature, 1957; repr. Delmar, NY: Caravan Books, 1993), p. 72; trans. Robert W. Thomson, *Elishe: History of Vardan and the Armenian War* (Cambridge, MA: Harvard University Press, 1982). Here the emphasis on Rome as a source of faith suggests the influence of the legend of Silvester. The *Life of Silvester* was translated into Armenian in 677. A revised and shortened version was then added to the "shorter" Socrates in 695/96. For details, see Manea S. Shirinyan, "Ricerche sulla *Storia ecclesiastica* di Socrate Scolastico e sulle sue versioni armene," *Annali di Ca'Foscari* 33 (1994): 151-67.

[14] Sebeos, *Patmutiun*, ed. Georg V. Abgaryan (Erevan: Armenian Academy of Sciences, 1979); trans. Robert W. Thomson and James Howard-Johnston, *The Armenian History Attributed to Sebeos* (Liverpool: Liverpool University Press, 1999 [pub. 2000]), pp. 67-68.

Sophia, and from that time on a tradition arose that the eastern door was called "the door of the Armenians." Later sources referring to this tradition confuse the date and associate the Armenian-Greek meeting with the much larger fifth ecumenical council held in 553.[15]

There is a long tradition in Armenian sources about this "Armenian door" of Saint Sophia. It was later adapted to the interests of the Bagratuni family after their rise to power in the ninth century, despite its earlier association with the Mamikonians, to which noble family this Vardan, and his more famous predecessor, belonged. This "Armenian door" has been misinterpreted as referring to an Armenian quarter of the city of Constantinople.[16] There is no evidence for such an Armenian quarter in the vicinity of Saint Sophia in the sixth century, nor does the Armenian term *dur* or *durn* (door) signify a quarter. Nevertheless, it was the establishment of ecclesiastical contacts and similar ties of this nature, beginning with Mashtots and his pupils, which influenced the development of Armenian literature.

Koriun, the biographer of Mashtots, states that in his devising of an individual script for Armenian Mashtots was assisted by Rufinus, a scribe of Greek literature in Samosata. The invention was thus effected in a city of Syria which had a significant Greek population. This emphasizes the twofold background which from the very beginning had characterized the Armenian Church and also profoundly affected the development of Armenian literature—the influence of the Syrian and the Greek traditions.

Samosata and Edessa, with their mixed populations of Greek and Syriac speakers, were important early centers of Christianity close to Armenia. But the missionary and educational activity of Mashtots and his pupils was carried out in eastern Armenia—the much larger part of the country under Iranian suzerainty since the partition of 387.[17] It was only after he had secured the success of his enterprise there that Mashtots crossed the border to seek im-

---

[15] See the detailed discussion of these events in Gérard Garitte, *Narratio de Rebus Armeniae* (Louvain: Imprimerie Orientaliste, 1952), pp. 175-254.

[16] See the Armenian texts quoted in Haïg Berbérian, "Les Arméniens ont-ils acheté une des portes de Sainte-Sophie?" *Byzantion* 20 (1950): 5-12.

[17] See map in Robert H. Hewsen, "The Geography of Armenia," in *The Armenian People from Ancient to Modern Times*, vol. 1: *The Dynastic Periods*, ed. Richard G. Hovannisian (New York: St. Martin's Press, 1997), p. 97.

perial permission to teach the new script to Armenians in Roman territory. Koriun gives few dates for events, but it was before the year 425 that Mashtots arrived in Constantinople.[18] He traveled by public transport since his visit had the approval of the emperor Theodosius II. This is a rare reference in Armenian to the Roman transport system, the *cursus publicus*, or in Greek, *dromos*.

Along the roads of the empire that linked major centers, carts or wagons would haul baggage, and donkeys or mules would pull carriages. These were not all grand conveyances, the more humble having wooden wheels which made (and make still) the most horrendous creaking. There were inns of varying comfort at appropriate intervals where changes of animals could be procured.[19]

The actual route taken by Armenian visitors to Constantinople is never described. According to the *Itinerary* attached to the seventh century Armenian *Geography*, the *mghonachapk* or "measurement of miles," the road from Dvin to Karin (Erzerum) was 200 Roman miles (roughly 10 percent shorter than our modern miles), and a further 100 miles to the frontier ditch. The road then proceeded to Coloneia (90 miles) and Niksar (Neocaesarea, 100 miles). Next appeared Amasia (80 miles), Gangra (another 105 miles), and Angora (Ankara, 80 miles). From there, it was a final 120 miles to Constantinople (which is wrong, the variant of 320 miles being more accurate).[20] This is a northerly route. Since Koriun says that Mashtots stopped at Melitene on the way, he must have gone directly west from there to Caesarea, then up to Angora and along the main road to Constantinople. A century earlier, Gregory the Illuminator had traveled to Caesarea for consecration as the first bishop for Armenia. According to Agatangeghos, he was accompanied by an impressive escort of nobles. Gregory was put in the royal carriage, which was drawn by mules. But his route is not described. On his return Gregory passed through Sebaste,

---

[18] Gabriele Winkler, *Koriwns Biographie des Mesrop Maštoc'* (Rome: Pontificio Istituto Orientale, 1994), pp. 329-30.

[19] See Lionel Casson, *Travel in the Ancient World* (Baltimore: Johns Hopkins University, 1994), ch. 11.

[20] Armenian text in *Anania Shirakatsu matenagrutyune* [Anania Shirakatsi's Bibliography], ed. Ashot Abrahamyan (Erevan: Matenadaran, 1944), pp. 355-56; trans. Robert H. Hewsen, *The Geography of Ananias of Širak (Ašxarhac'oyc')* (Wiesbaden: Ludwig Reichert Verlag, 1992), pp. 320-21. Note that the 320 miles from Angora to Constantinople does appear in a variant reading, whereas the text has 120 miles.

northeast of Caesarea, and from there, passing many stages, he reached Armenia.[21]

The term in Armenian for stage, *awtevank*, means both a day's distance and the inn where one lodged for the night. The *Buzandaran* mentions such inns in Armenia being established by Catholicos Nerses I (353-73).[22] When Koriun describes the journey of Mashtots to Constantinople he uses similar expressions. On leaving Melitene, he mounted a public *andrvar*;[23] while on the return he traveled along the imperial road in a carriage provided by the emperor (*i despaks ev i kars arkunaturs*). Not every Armenian visitor to Constantinople traveled in such luxury!

The historian Sebeos refers to official travel warrants in his description of the return to Armenia of Atat, prince of the Khorkhorunik, in the early seventh century.[24] Summoned to Constantinople to provide military support for the imperial army in Thrace, Atat had traveled there with seventy retainers. But after his reception in the capital, while on his way northwest to Thrace he resolved to rebel, to return to Armenia, and to throw in his lot with the Persian shah: "Turning aside from the road, he made his way to the coast [that is, the west coast of the Black Sea], and encountering a ship he said to the sailors: 'Take me across to the other side, because I have been sent on an important task by the emperor.' He duped the sailors who took him across." All travelers who had an imperial warrant traveled free on the Roman system. Presumably Atat pretended that he had such a document, which obliged the sailors to accommodate him and his escort. Koriun states clearly that Mashtots had an imperial warrant for his travels and that when he reached Greek territory he was received by the imperial governor, Anatolius, who sent word to the capital and received an official reply. Anatolius is well known. At this time he was the *magister militiae orientis* and later a high official in

---

[21] Agatangeghos, *Patmutiun Hayots*, §§791-808.

[22] *Buzandaran*, Bk V, ch. 31, where the expression used is *awtaratunk*, literally, "rest houses for strangers."

[23] Koriun, *Vark Mashtotsi*, ed. Manuk Abeghyan (Erevan: Haypethrat, 1941; repr. Delmar, NY: Caravan Books, 1985), with English translation by Bedros Norehad, ch. 16, pp. 66, 68. For a German translation of both recensions of Koriun with extensive commentary, see Winkler, *Koriwns Biographie*.

[24] Sebeos, *Patmutiun*, p. 104.

the capital.[25] Eghishe mentions him as being unfriendly to the
Armenian delegation in 450, and as an appeaser of the Persians.[26]

Mashtots and Translations from Greek

In Constantinople, Mashtots would have had no difficulty in com-
municating with imperial officials, for in his youth he had received
a good Greek education.[27] On this visit he was accompanied by
Gint, bishop of Derjan on the upper Euphrates west of Karin on the
Greek side of the border. Gint, too, would have been a fluent
speaker of Greek. They were lodged at the monastery of the
Akoimetoi, the "sleepless" monks, which was famous for its library.[28] Mashtots and Gint obtained from the emperor official
authorization to establish schools in western Armenia for youths
to learn the new script and to be trained to use it for the conduct
of services in church.[29] According to Koriun, before Mashtots returned to Armenia proper, "he acquired many inspired books of the
Fathers of the church" to deepen his knowledge further.[30] Koriun
implies that Mashtots brought these books from Constantinople,
which in turn reinforces the description of his continuous zeal,
from the time of the invention of the script until his death, in
making available in Armenian the treasures of Greek (and Syriac)
religious literature.

   Some years after his visit, Mashtots sent further disciples to
Constantinople: Ghevond, Eznik, and his biographer to be, Koriun.[31]
Koriun informs that they brought back to Armenia copies of the
Bible, the canons of the councils of Nicaea and Ephesus, and the

---

[25] See *Prosopography of the Later Roman Empire*, ed. J.R. Martindale (Cambridge: Cambridge University Press, 1980), vol. 2, pp. 84-86, s.v. "Anatolius."

[26] Eghishe, *Vasn Vardanay*, pp. 61, 124.

[27] Koriun, *Vark Mashtotsi*, p. 36.

[28] Ibid., p. 64. For the library of the monastery of the Akoimetoi, see Paul Peeters,
Le tréfonds oriental de l'hagiographie byzantine (Brussels: Société des Bollandistes,
1950), pp. 150-51.

[29] Cf. the later account in Khorenatsi, *Patmutiun Hayots*, Bk III, chs. 57-58 and
the commentary on Koriun by Winkler, *Koriwns Biographie*. No Greek source confirms
the account of Koriun. Would the dissemination of Armenian written works have enjoyed imperial patronage? Perhaps this would not have been a problem until the policy
of Justinian I in the sixth century to integrate the Armenian provinces into the empire.

[30] Koriun, *Vark Mashtotsi*, p. 68.

[31] Ibid., pp. 74-76.

testaments (*ktakaran*) of the Holy Church.[32] Koriun adds that Catholicos Sahak relied on these new copies of the Bible to revise earlier translations and that Sahak translated many commentaries. These books, at least, must have been in their original Greek versions, although whether Koriun and his colleagues translated the other works in Constantinople and brought back copies in Armenian is not clear. In fact, many works were translated from Greek (and Syriac), but the actual locations of these translations are rarely known. Nor is information available as to whether the originals were brought to Armenia or the new translations. During his patriarchate, Sahak coordinated this activity in Vagharshapat. But after his death, and that of Mashtots, there are no references to organized translating or to the circulation of Greek books in Armenia.[33]

The kinds of books that were brought from Constantinople had broader implications. In the first place, Koriun stresses the Bible and indicates that Catholicos Sahak directed a revision of the earlier translation based on these copies from the Byzantine capital, considered the authoritative source of the most reliable text. Twice he emphasizes that these Greek copies were more authoritative (*hastatun*) than the previous rendering into Armenian based on Syriac texts.[34] Sahak also translated many commentaries on the Bible.

Further, Koriun refers to the works of the Church fathers but fails to mention the authors which were translated. Space does not permit here to name all the texts which could be ascribed to the fifth century.[35] What is significant in this regard is that the Ar-

---

[32] The "testaments" cannot refer to the Old and New Testaments since the Bible was just mentioned; they are presumably works of patristic theology.

[33] The question of coordinated activity is relevant for the development of the later style of translation called "Philhellene," discussed below. There is no direct evidence whether the similarity of style in these translations was deliberately controlled or was more or less spontaneous on the part of the translators.

[34] Koriun, *Vark Mashtotsi*, p. 76. There is a large bibliography of modern studies on the text of the Armenian biblical translation. Since the Bible was not translated at one go, the versions of the different books show different models in Syriac and Greek. There were also revisions over time. For a brief bibliography see Robert W. Thomson, *A Bibliography of Classical Armenian Literature to 1500 AD* (Turnhout: Brepols, 1995), pp. 235-49: "Apocrypha" and "Bible." Note also the very extensive bibliography in Hakob S. Anasyan, *Haykakan matenagrutyun* (Erevan: Armenian Academy of Sciences, Institute of History, 1976), vol. 2, cols. 305-670.

[35] For the foreign authors, see Thomson, *Bibliography*, pp. 29-88: "Translations

menians rapidly absorbed much of the Greek theological traditions of the fourth and early fifth century. Great figures such as Athanasius, Gregory Nazianzenus, Basil of Caesarea, and John Chrysostom, who had expounded the meaning of the Christian faith in terms of current Greek philosophy and set the foundations of orthodoxy, were accepted as authorities for the Armenian exposition of faith.[36] Their works were also cited in defense of the Armenian positions after the age of Sahak and Mashtots, when doctrinal conflicts developed between the churches of the eastern Christian world. In the realm of historical writing, the historians Eusebius and Socrates Scholasticus were held up as models.[37] Remarkably soon the Armenians formed their own canon of orthodox writings. Although they continued for centuries to translate new texts from Greek, these were rarely the works of contemporary Byzantine theologians or historians, but were mostly patristic texts written prior to the Council of Chalcedon which had not yet been made available in Armenian.[38]

---

into Armenian." Note also Levon Ter-Petrosyan, *Hay hin targmanakan grakanutyun* (Erevan: Matenadaran, 1984), which has been translated into several languages; English version by Krikor Maksoudian, in Levon Ter Petrosian, *Ancient Armenian Translations* (New York: Saint Vartan Press, 1992). See also Constantine Zuckerman, *A Repertory of Published Armenian Translations of Classical Texts* (Jerusalem: Hebrew University of Jerusalem, 1995). For exegetical texts, see Jean-Pierre Mahé, "Traduction et exégèse: Réflexions sur l'exemple arménien," *Mélanges Antoine Guillaumont* (Geneva: Patrick Cramer, 1988), pp. 243-55. Nerses Akinian dated translations of the following authors to the fifth century on the basis of style alone: the Bible, John Chrysostom, Severian of Gabala, Eusebius of Emesa, Cyril of Alexandria, Basil of Caesarea, Eusebius of Caesarea, Evagrius of Pontus, Hippolytus of Bostra, Gregory Thaumaturgus, Aristides of Athens, Ephrem the Syrian, Afrahat, Zenob of Amida, Aithalla of Urha, Labubna, and letters by Proclus of Constantinople, and Acacius of Amida. See Nerses Akinian, "Hay matenagrutian oskedare" [The Golden Age of Armenian Literature], *Handes Amsorya* 46 (1932): 105-28.

[36] The Armenian versions of Athanasius and Gregory Nazianzenus reflect an early stage of the "Philhellene" style of translation and may be of the sixth rather than the fifth century. The only modern critical edition of these patristic authors is that of Gregory's works, currently directed by Bernard Coulie, of which three volumes have appeared to date. For an overview, see Guy Lafontaine and Bernard Coulie, *La version arménienne des discours de Grégoire de Nazianze* (Louvain: Peeters, 1983).

[37] Socrates carried the story of the church from the time of Constantine, where Eusebius left off, down to the time of Theodosius II. For the Armenian version and the later adaptation, see notes 3, 13 above.

[38] There is an Armenian version of the *Hexaemeron* by the seventh-century George of Pisidia, but no Armenian translation of any of the noted Byzantine historians, such as Procopius, Agathias, and Theophanes.

Finally, with respect to ecclesiastical authority enshrined in written texts, Koriun explicitly refers to the canons of the church councils of Nicaea and Ephesus. The Council of Nicaea (325) was summoned by the emperor Constantine for various reasons but primarily to deal with the conflict caused by Arius and his views about the Trinity, which were condemned as heretical. This is alluded to in the *Buzandaran*, where the holy status of Constantine is emphasized.[39] Agatangeghos, too, describes this first ecumenical council and the presence of Gregory's son Aristakes as the Armenian representative.[40] He notes that Aristakes brought back the canons of Nicaea, to which Gregory made additions appropriate to the situation in Armenia. But since Agatangeghos was writing after Koriun and borrows a great deal of descriptive material from his predecessor,[41] it is not clear how well known these canons were in Armenia before the time of Catholicos Sahak. When the *Buzandaran* describes the work of Catholicos Nerses, it refers only to the Apostolic canons which he imposed as normative. In any event, there could have been no written Armenian translation of any canons until the time of Mashtots.

The Council of Ephesus (431) took place in the time of Mashtots himself. It was summoned by Theodosius II to deal with the opinions of Nestorius about the nature of Christ. No representative from central Armenia attended this council,[42] but immediately following it there was extensive correspondence between the Armenian and Greek ecclesiastical leaders about the theological issues involved.[43] The Council of Ephesus was in fact the third of

---

[39] *Buzandaran*, Bk III, ch. 10.

[40] Agatangeghos, *Patmutiun Hayots*, §§884-85. For bishops from areas around central Armenia present at Nicaea, see Nina G. Garsoïan, "Some Preliminary Precisions on the Separation of the Armenian and Imperial Churches: I. The Presence of 'Armenian' Bishops at the First Five Ecumenical Councils," *Kathegetria: Essays Presented to Joan Hussey on Her Eightieth Birthday* (Camberley: Porphyrogenitus, 1988), pp. 258-63.

[41] For the relationship between the Armenian text of Agatangeghos in its present form and Koriun, see the Introduction to Thomson, *Agathangelos*.

[42] For bishops at Ephesus from the regions of Melitene and Amida, see Garsoïan, "Some Preliminary Precisions," pp. 263-65.

[43] These letters are collected in the *Girk tghtots* [Book of Letters]. There are two editions of the Armenian texts, Hovsep Izmiriants (Tiflis: Tparan Rotiniants, 1901) and Norayr Pogharian (Jerusalem: St. James Press, 1994). For French translations of the Armenian-Greek correspondence, see Nina G. Garsoïan, *L'Eglise arménienne et le grand schisme d'orient* (Leuven: Peeters, 1999), pp. 412-37, and ch. 2, "Les crises

the "ecumenical" councils. The second of these, which Koriun does not mention, was held at Constantinople in 381, at the end of the prolonged Arian controversy. Although no representative from central Armenia had participated at this council, later Armenian historians erroneously asserted that the patriarch Nerses attended, even though he had died eight years earlier. The presence of Nerses in the capital for other reasons is described at some length in the *Buzandaran*, leading to some confusion.[44]

The decisions of these three councils had a pivotal role in defining the orthodox faith and in condemning heresy. To these councils the Armenians always remained committed. In the correspondence of succeeding centuries, much of it preserved in the famous *Book of Letters*, Armenian theologians continued to base their position on this foundation, refusing to accept the "innovations" of Chalcedon, the fourth ecumenical council, held in 451. Their interpretation of Ephesus was much influenced by contacts with Constantinople in the time of Sahak and Mashtots, with permanent effects for the creation of Armenian orthodoxy.[45]

In their quest for learning and scholarship, Armenians did not frequent only Constantinople. Prior to Mashtots, young Armenians had studied at universities elsewhere in the eastern Mediterranean. The famed teacher Libanius at Antioch, for example, had a succession of Armenian pupils spanning two generations. Prohaeresius from eastern Armenia made a name for himself as a teacher in Athens; and Armenians are mentioned in Beirut.[46] Koriun notes that Mashtots sent students to Melitene and Syria.[47] Nonetheless, Constantinople remained the source of learning par excellence, and this included secular as well as theological studies.

---

et la transformation du Ve siècle," pp. 45-134.

[44] *Buzandaran*, Bk IV, chs. 5-11; cf. Khorenatsi, *Patmutiun Hayots*, Bk III, ch. 33. Nerses died in 373; see Garsoïan, *Epic Histories*, pp. 395-96.

[45] Here the influence of Constantinople is emphasized. But for a full understanding of early Armenian theology, the influence of Syrian traditions (not least in matters of practice and ritual) must also be taken into account. See Garsoïan, *L'Eglise arménienne*, ch. 2.

[46] See Robert W. Thomson, "The Formation of the Armenian Literary Tradition," in *East of Byzantium: Syria and Armenia in the Formative Period*, ed. Nina G. Garsoïan, Thomas F. Mathews, and Robert W. Thomson (Washington, DC: Dumbarton Oaks, 1982), pp. 135-50.

[47] Koriun, *Vark Mashtotsi*, p. 64.

Influence of Greek Texts on Armenian Literature

Eznik Koghpatsi, who was in Constantinople with Koriun, was the first to compose in Armenian an original treatise in which philosophical themes based on classical learning are addressed. The wide range of authors on whom Eznik drew includes a few pagan writers as well as many Christian ones. He was clearly familiar with most of these texts in the original and presumably had put his time of study in Constantinople to good use.[48] Ironically, despite being the first study of free will and the nature of evil in Armenian, it was not much quoted in later times, perhaps because the main topic—the conflict of Christian with non-Christian philosophies—soon became outdated. After the fifth century, Armenians were no longer concerned with refuting Zoroastrianism or pagan views, but rather with refuting Christian views inimical to their own positions. Be that as it may, it was not until Anania Shirakatsi (Ananias of Shirak) that more precise information was compiled about scientific studies. His brief *Autobiography* provides a good starting point, even though he lived in the seventh century, two hundred years after Mashtots.[49]

Anania Shirakatsi states that he had studied Armenian literature and wished to pursue philosophy, especially the science of numbers which he considered the mother of all knowledge. Finding no one to assist him in central Armenia, he went to Roman Armenia, only to discover that the teacher there had limited skills. After six months, he decided to further his studies in Constantinople; however, before his journey he met some acquaintances coming from the Byzantine capital, who were traveling to Trebizond to study with the Greek scholar Tychikos. Anania

---

[48] See Louis Mariès, "Le *De Deo* d'Eznik de Kolb connu sous le nom de 'Contre les sectes': Etudes de critique littéraire et textuelle," *Revue des études arméniennes* 4 (1924): 113-205; 5 (1925): 13-130; also reprinted separately (Paris: Imp. nationale, 1924). Cf. Levon Ter Petrosyan, "Eprem Asoru 'Hobi meknutyune' Eznik Koghbatsu aghbyurnerits [Ephrem the Syrian's 'Commentary on Job' as a Source for Eznik of Koghb]," *Banber Matenadarani* 16 (1994): 7-15; trans. Monica J. Blanchard and Robin Darling Young, *A Treatise on God Written in Armenian by Eznik of Kolb* (Leuven: Peeters, 1998).

[49] Armenian text in Ashot Abrahamyan, *Anania Shirakatsu matenagrutyune* (Erevan: Armenian Academy of Sciences, 1944), pp. 206-09; trans. Haïg Berbérian, "Autobiographie d'Anania Shirakats'i," *Revue des études arméniennes*, n.s. 1 (1964): 189-94.

joined them to study mathematics.[50]

When he met Tychikos in Trebizond, Anania was surprised that his Greek teacher was fluent in Armenian. In his brief biographical account of Tychikos, Anania notes that Tychikos had learned Armenian when on military service in Armenia. He was wounded in battle when the Persians attacked Antioch (around 606-07), and on recovering he decided to devote himself to scholarship. He spent three years in Egypt, one year in Rome, and then completed his training in Constantinople before returning home to Trebizond.[51]

Learning and scholarship in Armenia based on Greek models necessitated translation of the basic textbooks used in the universities of the late Roman Empire. By the time of Anania Shirakatsi, the standard curriculum consisted of courses on grammar, rhetoric, and philosophy (the trivium), followed by the four sciences of logic, physics, mathematics, and theology (the quadrivium).[52] The trivium was essential in preparing for a career in the law or the civil service, while higher learning was based on the quadrivium. The standard works on grammar, rhetoric, and philosophy were soon rendered into Armenian, and some of these texts were influential over a long period. The introductory book of philosophy by Davit Anhaght (David the Invincible), for example, was used in Armenian schools for more than a thousand years.[53]

These technical treatises were translated into Armenian in a more literal fashion than the biblical and patristic texts mentioned above. The translators, sacrificing good Armenian style for a word-to-word rendering, created new Armenian words to render the Greek technical expressions, a style commonly referred to as

---

[50] Anania describes these persons as *tsanawtk*, which in his French rendering Berbérian translates as "compatriotes." But Anania does not explicitly indicate whether they were Armenians, Greeks, or of other national origin. Nonetheless, since Anania had not visited Constantinople, "acquaintances" were most likely to have been fellow Armenians.

[51] This grand tour has echoes in Armenian texts, as discussed below.

[52] On this subject, see the important study of Jean-Pierre Mahé, "Quadrivium et cursus d'études au VIIe siècle en Arménie et dans le monde byzantin," *Travaux et mémoires* 10 (1987): 159-206.

[53] See Bridget Kendall and Robert W. Thomson, *Definitions and Divisions of Philosophy by David the Invincible Philosopher* (Chico, CA: Scholars Press, 1983), pp. xx-xxi.

"Philhellene." Opinions vary as to the exact purpose of such a method of translation; the writing appears quite artificial and often becomes incomprehensible. Clearly, every language changes and adapts itself to new times and problems. Over the centuries many innovations were absorbed into standard Armenian, while others were omitted and lost.

Concerning the connection of these books with Constantinople, unfortunately, despite years of efforts to analyze the numerous products of the Philhellene style, their grammar and syntax, and their linguistic innovations, practically nothing is known as to the identity of the translators, who translated what, where, or when. The main difficulty in this regard is that the information about Armenians engaged in such studies abroad are largely derived not from their contemporaries but from later authors who in many cases were influenced by legends concerning the disciples of Mashtots. In general, however, the main works of the Philhellene style may be dated to the sixth and seventh centuries, and a connection with Constantinople is more likely than with the other major centers such as Antioch, Beirut, or Alexandria.[54]

Although Anania Shirakatsi never reached Constantinople, his *Autobiography* mentions acquaintances who had been in that city. Also in the seventh century the historian Sebeos refers to Davit from Bagrevand, who had not only visited Constantinople but made a career there. In 649, Davit brought a letter from the emperor Constans II and the Greek patriarch to the Armenians, which prompted a gathering of Armenian bishops at Dvin; Sebeos records the long response they composed on that occasion.[55] Davit is said to have become versed in the art of philosophy at Constantinople. He was clearly a Chalcedonian Armenian, since he

---

[54] The use of the term "school" for this style of translation is rather misleading, as there is no evidence of any central direction in organizing such activity. For a general overview of the main characteristics of this style, see Charles Mercier, "L'école hellénistique dans la littérature arménienne," *Revue des études arméniennes* n.s. 13 (1978/79): 59-75. Abraham Terian places its activity in Constantinople. See his "The Hellenizing School: Its Time, Place and Scope of Activities Reconsidered," in Garsoïan, Mathews, Thomson, *East of Byzantium*, pp. 175-86. Further bibliography appears in Thomson, *Bibliography*, pp. 22-27.

[55] Sebeos, *Patmutiun*, pp. 148-61. On this response and the question of the authenticity of the text in Sebeos, see Robert W. Thomson, "The Defence of Armenian Orthodoxy in Sebeos," in *AETOS: Studies in Honour of Cyril Mango*, ed. Ihor Sevcenko and Imgard Hutter (Stuttgart: B.G. Teubner, 1998), pp. 329-41.

was entrusted with an official mission, but no further details about his origins or career are given.

One of the most important Armenian scholars to visit Constantinople and return to his homeland was Stepannos, later bishop of Siunik. He is attested in Constantinople between the years 712 and 718 both by later Armenian historians and by colophons to the translations he made there. Siunik, east and south of Lake Sevan, was a large area whose relationship to central Armenia, Ayrarat, remained ambiguous for many centuries. Its metropolitan bishops cherished a certain independence, which the catholicoses in Echmiadzin were not always happy to concede. In his patriotic *History of Siunik*, Stepannos Orbelian, bishop of Siunik from 1287 to about 1309—that is, nearly six hundred years after the above-mentioned Stepannos—devoted a lengthy chapter to his predecessor.[56] According to the historian, the young Stepannos was teaching theology at the seminary at Dvin when he became engaged in a theological dispute with the duophysite *aspet* or military commander of Armenia, Smbat Bagratuni. Lacking sufficient knowledge of the philosophical arts, Stepannos lost the argument and therefore decided to go to Constantinople for further studies.

Whatever the veracity of this explanation, the colophons of his translations leave no doubt that Stepannos completed Armenian versions of three important works of philosophical theology in Constantinople. The first is the corpus of texts attributed to Dionysius the Areopagite, who at that time was universally considered to be the Dionysius who became a Christian after hearing Saint Paul preach in Athens. In fact, the texts are of the late fifth century and are much indebted to neoplatonic ideas.[57] The other two texts translated by Stepannos were Gregory of Nyssa's *Treatise on the Formation of Man* and the similar work by Bishop

---

[56] Stepannos Orbelian, *Patmutiun nahangin Sisakan* [History of the Province of Siunik] (Tiflis: N. Aghaniants, 1910), ch. 31; trans. Marie Brosset, *Histoire de la Siounie par Stépannos Orbélian* (St. Petersburg: Imperial Academy of Sciences, 1864).

[57] For the Armenian version, see Robert W. Thomson, *The Armenian Version of the Works Attributed to Dionysius the Areopagite* [Corpus Scriptorum Christianorum Orientalium, 488 and 489, Scriptores Armeniaci, 17 (text) and 18 (translation) (Leuven: Peeters, 1987). The Introduction to the volume of text presents the colophons and other evidence for the work of Stepannos.

Nemesius of Emesa, *On the Nature of Man*. These writings had a significant impact on medieval Armenian thought, as some of the major activities of monasteries like Tatev and Gladzor involved the study of such philosophical texts and the writing of commentaries on them. Much of this activity still remains to be properly studied, and the medieval commentaries remain mostly unpublished.

Stepannos did not work alone in Constantinople. He was assisted by a certain David, "consul and kinarios of the royal table," who was not unknown to the Byzantine world. A seal dated to the first quarter of the eighth century gives his name and the title "royal kinarios" (that is, "butler").[58] Whether or not he was also an Armenian cannot be determined; as in the case of Tychikos, it was not unknown for a Greek to know the Armenian language. But the colophons definitely state that David and Stepannos worked together on the translations.

The travels of Stepannos are described in more elaborate detail by later historians. Curiously, the tradition of his going as far as Rome is first reported by Movses Daskhurantsi, the tenth century historian of the Aghvank, another region whose relationship with central Armenia was ambiguous. Like Stepannos Orbelian, Movses Daskhurantsi recorded many traditions and legends concerning the earlier history of the outlying regions, which often are at variance with the received tradition in Ayrarat. According to his account, after the debate between Stepannos and Smbat Bagratuni, Stepannos traveled to Constantinople to study.[59] Smbat sent word to the emperor that Stepannos was a heretic, and when he was arraigned before the emperor, Stepannos asked for the chests of books to be opened. There he found a book on the Faith (Movses does not mention the title). The emperor then sent him to Rome to fetch three further books of similar content. On his way back, however, Stepannos avoided Constantinople altogether and headed

---

[58] See W. Seibt, "Kinarios - ein 'neuer' Würdenträger an Hof des Byzantinischen Kaisers," *Handes Amsorya* 88 (1974): 369-80; *Oxford Dictionary of Byzantium*, s.v. "kinarios." The seal is no. 600 in G. Zacos and A. Veglery, *Byzantine Lead Seals*, vol. 1 (Basel: Augustin, 1972).

[59] Movses Daskhurantsi (also known as Kaghankatuatsi), *Patmutiun Aghvanits ashkharhi*, ed. Varag Arakelyan (Erevan: Armenian Academy of Sciences, 1983), Bk III, chs. 17-18; trans. Charles J.F. Dowsett, *The History of the Caucasian Albanians by Movsēs Dasxuranci* (London: Oxford University Press, 1961).

straight to Dvin, where he was consecrated bishop for Siunik. Daskhurantsi then appends an extremely garbled account of Homer's *Iliad* and of Virgil's *Aeneid*, tracing the succession of capitals from Troy to Rome to Constantinople.

This version of events is greatly elaborated in the *History of Siunik* by Stepannos Orbelian.[60] Not only does he have the earlier Stepannos also study in Athens (which by the eighth century was no longer a center of learning), but he also names the three books brought from Rome as writings by Cyril of Alexandria, Athanasius of Alexandria, and Ephrem the Syrian, all classic patristic texts. The point of the story is to demonstrate the orthodoxy of the Armenians and the willingness of the Greek emperor to accept that faith as defined by authoritative fathers of the church.

Legendary details about visits to Constantinople by Armenians from the entourage of Mashtots share a common purpose with the fabled travels of Stepannos—namely, to bolster the Armenian claim to orthodoxy against the Greek imperial church. Two figures play central roles, Movses Khorenatsi and Davit Anhaght (the Invincible). In his *History of the Armenians*, Movses Khorenatsi described his own travels as a student. He claims to have been sent by Sahak and Mashtots to study at the academy in Alexandria. He gives a rhetorical description of that city, contrasting the pagan deities of its past with the Christian worship of his own day. Returning by way of Greece, Movses Khorenatsi says his ship was blown off course to Rome, where he visited the tombs of Peter and Paul. Subsequently, he stayed at Athens for a while and then moved on to Constantinople. There he learned of the death of Sahak and Mashtots and returned disconsolate to Armenia.[61]

Movses Khorenatsi refers to the cities where in the fifth century important schools of philosophy existed, although Alexandria (unlike Athens or Constantinople) is not mentioned by other Armenian sources in this context. The sketchy account given by the historian, however, was insufficient for later historians, who record much more elaborate details of the travels of Movses Khorenatsi and his companions. By the eleventh century, the outline of these legendary additions had been fleshed out. According

---

[60] Stepannos Orbelian, *History of Siunik*, ch. 31.
[61] Movses Khorenatsi, *Patmutiun Hayots*, Bk III, ch. 62.

to the historian Asoghik (that is, Stepannos of Taron), Movses Khorenatsi had a brother Mambre, who is also mentioned earlier by Tovma Artsruni, and among his disciples was David.[62] The three had traveled abroad together. By the thirteenth century, the chronicler Vardan had associated their travels with the defense of Armenian orthodoxy, which they successfully accomplished in debates against the Greeks.[63] In a colophon of 1297, written in Cilicia,[64] it is even claimed that both Movses and David had taught philosophy in Athens. This represents the adaptation to Armenian hagiography of the presence as students of Basil the Great and Gregory Nazianzenus in Athens. Their works were well known in Armenia, and many centuries after their death the same pattern of travel for study was attributed to great figures of the Armenian past.

The important point here is that Armenians, too, studied in the notable universities of the ancient world. By the sixth century, Christian Constantinople had taken the place of pagan Athens. From the time of Mashtots, there was regular traffic between the Byzantine capital and Armenia, as Armenians visited that city to study. Some remained, like Davit from Bagrevand, while others returned with books that they had translated from Greek, like Stepannos of Siunik. More than any other center of learning, Constantinople provided the impetus for broadening Armenian interests into patristic and secular literature. Of course, this is not to neglect the Syriac legacy which strongly influenced the early Armenian Church and Armenian culture generally. Constanti-

---

[62] Stepannos Taronetsi, *Patmutiun tiezerakan*, ed. Stepan Malkhasian (St. Petersburg: Imperial Academy of Sciences, 1885), Bk II, ch. 2; trans. Edouard Dulaurier, *Etienne Asoghig de Daron: Histoire universelle* (Paris: Leroux, 1883), Bks I-II; Fréderic Macler, *Etienne Asolik de Taron: Histoire universelle* (Paris: Leroux, 1917), Bk III; Tovma Artsruni, *Patmutiun tann Artsruniats*, ed. Kerobe Patkanian (St. Petersburg: Imperial Academy of Sciences, 1887; repr. Delmar, NY: Caravan Books, 1991), p. 44; trans. Robert W. Thomson, *Thomas Artsruni: History of the House of the Artsrunik'* (Detroit: Wayne State University Press, 1985).

[63] Vardan Areveltsi, *Havakumn patmutian Hayots*, ed. Ghevond Alishan (Venice: Mekhitarist Press, 1862; repr. Delmar, NY: Caravan Books, 1991), pp. 54-55; trans. Robert W. Thomson, "The Historical Compilation of Vardan Arewelts'i," *Dumbarton Oaks Papers* 43 (1989): 125-226.

[64] Jerusalem Ms 1303. For fuller details of these legends, see Kendall and Thomson, *Definitions*, p. xvii; Robert W. Thomson, "A quoi Movses Xorenac'i doit-il sa réputation?" *Movses Xorenac'i et l'historiographie arménienne des origines*, ed. Dickran Kouymjian (Antelias: Catholicosate of Cilicia, 2000), pp. 55-70.

nople, however, exercised paramount influence on Armenian learning and scholarship. The Armenian evidence from the first two or three centuries after Mashtots is rather scanty, and later historians added much legendary material to what little their predecessors had recorded. Nonetheless, even the legends point to the significance of the Constantinopolitan connection and the enduring respect paid to that city as "the mother of the sciences."

❈ 3 ❈

BYZANTINE EMPEROR PHILIPPIKOS-VARDANES: MONOTHELITE POLICY AND CAUCASIAN DIPLOMACY

Mikaël Nichanian

The Armenian aristocracy in Byzantium is rarely credited with having a significant presence before the ninth century.[1] The Macedonian dynasty founded by Emperor Basil I (867-86) has overshadowed the earlier presence of other Armenian aristocratic families in Constantinople. During the eighth century, for example, a small group of Armenian military officers participated in a coup d'état against Justinian II (705-11), suggesting that some Armenians either belonged to or had close associations with the Byzantine court more than a century before Basil's reign. The ability to ascend to the throne of an empire signifies integration into the highest echelons of society, as it required established political networks among the ruling class. The case of Emperor Philippikos-Vardanes (Philippicus Bardanes) (711-13), whose family arrived in Byzantium probably in the sixth century, is just such an example.[2]

---

[1] See Nicolas Adontz (Nikoghayos Adonts), *Études arméno-byzantines* (Lisbon: Calouste Gulbenkian Foundation, 1965); Isabelle Brousselle, "L'intégration des Arméniens dans l'aristocratie byzantine au 9ᵉ siècle," in *L'Arménie et Byzance*, ed. Jean-Pierre Mahé (Paris: Centre de recherches d'histoire et de civilisation byzantines, 1996), pp. 43-54; Peter Charanis, "The Armenians in the Byzantine Empire," *Byzantinoslavica* 22 (1961): 196-240; Nina G. Garsoïan, "The Problem of Armenian Integration into the Byzantine Empire," in *Studies on the Internal Diaspora of the Byzantine Empire*, ed. Hélène Ahrweiler and Angeliki E. Laiou (Washington, DC: Dumbarton Oaks, 1998), pp. 53-124; Joseph-François Laurent, *L'Arménie entre Byzance et l'Islam, depuis la conquête arabe jusqu'en 886* (Paris: Fontemoing et cie [E. de Boccard], 1919; rev. ed., Marius Canard [Lisbon: Librairie Bertrand, Calouste Gulbenkian Foundation, 1980]); Cyril Toumanoff, *Studies in Christian Caucasian History* (Washington, DC: Georgetown University Press, 1963).

[2] Two seals published by Boris A. Panchenko may shed new light on Vardanes' career before his reign: the first one (no. 88) is that of *Bardanes hypatos* and the other

Prominent Armenian officials until the sixth century tended to be either eunuchs attached to the imperial house, such as the great Narses, or temporary auxiliaries serving in the imperial army. By the early seventh century, Armenian nobles had developed close relations with the Constantinopolitan aristocracy, their ties further strengthened in the aftermath of the Arab invasions of Asia Minor beginning in the middle of the seventh century when many Armenians joined the Byzantine army as soldiers and officers. By the eighth century, the Armenian aristocracy was fairly integrated into the ruling class.

The case of Philippikos-Vardanes shows the first successful coup led by an officer of Armenian descent.[3] He in turn was removed from power in June 713. The adoption of the name Philippikos at the time of his proclamation by the army indicated a preference for a familiar, albeit rare, name within the imperial circles.[4] By contrast, the name Vardanes was certainly considered unworthy of the throne, as it lacked an imperial background.[5] The modification of the status of an individual had precedence and justified the adoption of new names for emperors with Oriental or

---

(no. 156) is of *Bardanes patrikios* and *strategos*. See Boris A. Panchenko, "Kollektsii Russkago Arkheologicheskago Instituta v Konstantinopol, Katalog molivdovulov," *Bulletin de l'institut d'archéologie russe à Constantinople* 8 (1903): 199-246, and 9 (1904): 341-96. These seals, housed at the Hermitage Museum in St. Petersburg, require more precise dates. See also *Prosopographie der mittel-byzantinischen Zeit*, ed. Ralph-Johannes Lilie et al. (Berlin: W. de Gruyter, 2000), nos. 752-53.

[3] See *Oxford Dictionary of Byzantium*, ed. Alexander P. Kazhdan et al., 3 vols. (London: Oxford University Press, 1991), vol. 3, p. 1654, s.v. "Philippikos, emperor"; Andreas N. Stratos, *Byzantium in the Seventh Century*, trans. Marc Ogilvie-Grant, 5 vols. (Amsterdam: Adolf M. Hakkert, 1968-1980), vol. 5, pp. 155-77; *Prosopographie der mittel-byzantinischen Zeit*, no. 6150; *Prosopography of the Byzantine Empire*, ed. John R. Martindale (London: King's College, 1993), s.v. "Philippikos I"; Judith Herrin, "Philippikos 'the Gentle'," in *From Rome to Constantinople: Studies in Honour of Averil Cameron*, ed. Hagit Amirav and Bas ter Haar Romeny (Leuven: Peeters, 2007), pp. 251-62.

[4] *Nikephoros, Patriarch of Constantinople, Short History*, ed. and trans. Cyril Mango (Washington, DC: Dumbarton Oaks, 1990), §45, p. 110. The name is rare, as attested by the *Prosopographie der mittel-byzantinischen Zeit* and the *Prosopography of the Later Roman Empire*.

[5] Garsoïan, "Integration," p. 97 and note 166; idem, "Notes préliminaires sur l'anthroponymie arménienne du Moyen Âge," in *L'Anthroponymie, document de l'histoire sociale des mondes méditerranéens médiévaux*, ed. Monique Bourin, Jean-Marie Martin, and François Menant (Rome: Ecole française de Rome, Palais Farnèse, 1996), pp. 230-31.

humble backgrounds, as in the case of Vardanes, in addition to other emperors, such as Leo Leontios (695-98), Tiberios III Apsimar (698-705), Anastasios Artemios (713-15), and Leo III the Syrian (Isaurian) (717-41).

Further, as the only famous Philippikos at the time was the brother-in-law of Emperor Maurice Tiberios (582-602), Philippikos and Vardanes probably had familial ties. In 583, the elder Philippikos[6] had married Gordia, the sister of Maurice, and until 614, during the reigns of the emperors Maurice and Heraclius (610-41), had held some of the highest offices in the Byzantine army, including *Comes Excubitorum* and *Magister militum per Orientem*. In all likelihood, Vardanes' choice of the name Philippikos was derived from Maurice's brother-in-law and was adopted to confer a certain imperial legitimacy on Vardanes. The latter's name was affiliated with the Mamikonian family, which had been present in Byzantium since 575, when one of the leading members of the dynasty, Vardan, sought refuge in the empire after assassinating the Persian *marzpan* or governor of Armenia.[7] A member of the Mamikonian family must have gained enough leverage in the Byzantine state to be involved in an alliance with the family of Emperor Maurice.

Philippikos' father, Nikephoros (a common name in Byzanti-

---

[6] Theophylactus Simocatta, *Theophylacti Simocattae Historiae*, ed. Carolus de Boor and Peter Wirth (Stuttgart: B.G. Teubner, 1972); Theophylact Simocatta, *The History of Theophylact Simocatta*, trans. with intro. and notes, Michael and Mary Whitby (Oxford: Clarendon Press; New York: Oxford University Press, 1986), p. 13; Theophanes, the Confessor, *Chronographia*, ed. Carolus de Boor, 2 vols. (Leipzig: B.G. Teubner, 1883-1885), vol. 1, p. 253; George Zacos and Alexander Veglery, *Byzantine Lead Seals*, 2 vols. (Basel: J.J. Augustin, 1972-1985), vol. 1, no. 468, *Philippikos Patrikios*; *The Prosopography of the Later Roman Empire*, vol. 3: A.D. 527-641, ed. John R. Martindale (Cambridge: Cambridge University Press, 1992), vol. 3B, pp. 1022-26; *Pascal Chronicle*, ed. Ludwig A. Dindorf (Bonn: E. Weber, 1832), p. 695; Michael and Mary Whitby trans. (Liverpool: Liverpool University Press, 1989), p. 144; *Nikephoros, Patriarch of Constantinople*, §2, p. 40.

[7] *Prosopography of the Later Roman Empire*, vol. 3B, p. 1365, s.v. "Vardan Mamikonian"; *La Narratio de Rebus Armeniae*, ed. Gérard Garitte (Louvain: L. Durbecq, 1952), §77-78, pp. 37, 175-90; Jean-Pierre Mahé, "*La Narratio de rebus Armeniae*," *Revue des études arméniennes*, n.s., 25 (1994-95): 434. "Vardan, ayant tué Suren, le tyran perse, contre qui il s'était révolté, s'enfuit d'Arménie pour Constantinople, la quatrième année de Xosrov (= 594) et la trentième année de Justinien (= 557)." None of these dates is consistent with the chronology of Vardan's career who rose against Persian rule in 572.

um) had held the high rank of *patrikios* at court. The description provided by Agatho the Deacon regarding the background of Nikephoros as "Persarmenian" does not mean that he had recently arrived from Armenia, but, more probably, that the author saw a connection between the foreign origins of the emperor and his religious policy, which aimed to revert to Monothelitism.[8]

Heraclius the Elder (the father of the emperor Heraclius), Vardan Mamikonian, and the elder Philippikos were contemporaries of Emperor Maurice Tiberios. Their children belonged to the same generation as the emperor Heraclius. Nikephoros, the father of the emperor Philippikos, must have been a contemporary of Constans II (641-68). There was a Nikephoros who held the rank of patrikios and led an expedition to Africa in 665-66 during the reign of Constans II. Warren Treadgold identifies him as the father of the emperor Philippikos. Another Nikephoros headed an expedition against the rebellious Saborios strategos of the *Armeniac Theme* in 667-68. Andreas Stratos identifies this general as the father of the emperor Philippikos. The *Prosopographie der mittel-byzantinischen Zeit* and Wolfram Brandes abstain from any identification because of the alleged frequency of the name.[9]

The background to the coup by Philippikos-Vardanes in 711 is significant.[10] Vardanes was twice condemned to banishment:

---

[8] Agatho the Deacon, in *Acta Conciliorum Oecumenicorum*, ser. II, vol. 2:2, ed. Rudolf Riedinger (Berlin: W. de Gruyter, 1992), p. 899: Johannes Dominicus Mansi, ed., *Sacrorum conciliorum nova, et amplissima collectio*, 12 vols. (Florence: Expensis Antonii Zatta, 1759-1798; repr. Graz: Akademische Druck, 1960), vol. 12, col. 192. On this word, see Heinrich Gelzer, "Pergamon unter Byzantinern und Osmanen," *Abhandlungen des K. p. Akademie der Wissenschaften* (Berlin, 1903), pp. 25-30; cf. Wolfram Brandes, "Armenier in Pergamon?" *Byzantinische Zeitschrift* 86/87 (1993-94): 69-74, and *Prosopographie der mittel-byzantinischen Zeit*, no. 5258. The emendation of the text has not always been acknowledged; see Garsoïan, "Integration," p. 97. See also Agatho the Deacon, *Acta Conciliorum Oecumenicorum*, p. 900.

[9] Stratos, *Byzantium*, vol. 3, pp. 223-24, vol. 5, p. 165; Denys Pringle, *The Defence of Byzantine Africa from Justinian to the Arab Conquest* (Oxford: B.A.R., 1981), pp. 47-48; Warren Treadgold, *A History of the Byzantine State and Society* (Stanford: Stanford University Press, 1997), p. 320; *Prosopographie der mittel-byzantinischen Zeit*, nos. 5253-54; Theophanes, *Chronographia*, p. 350; Agapius, Bishop of Hierapolis, *Kitab al-'Unvan, Histoire universelle, écrite par Agapius (Mahboub) de Menbidj*, ed. and trans. Alexandre A. Vasiliev, 4 vols. (Paris: Firmin-Didot, 1910-1947); *Patrologia Orientalis* 8:3 (1912): 489.

[10] For a general analysis of the plot, see Walter E. Kaegi, *Byzantine Military Unrest (471-843): An Interpretation* (Amsterdam: Adolf M. Hakkert, 1981), pp. 189-

first, by the emperor Tiberios III Apsimar and again later during the second reign of Justinian II (first reign, 685-95; second reign, 705-11). He was exiled the first time to Cephallenia (Cephalonia) because of his seditious intentions.[11] There are two versions of this event. According to the first, Vardanes had a premonitory dream of an eagle above his head, which he was imprudent enough to discuss with those around him and which was subsequently communicated to the emperor.[12] A second story reports that a heretic monk foresaw the imperial destiny of Vardanes and was responsible for the heretical policy adopted by the emperor. The chronicler Theophanes alleges that these tales of prediction, though contradictory, caused Vardanes to be exiled to Cephallenia. With respect to the prediction concerning the heretical emperor, sources traditionally connect the prophecy of a monk, always presented as possessed by the devil, to the iniquitous reversion to Monothelitism.

Vardanes was recalled from Cephallenia during the second reign of Justinian II.[13] His chroniclers, however, do not explain the reasons for his presence in Cherson in the Crimea in 711. At first glance, it seems strange that Justinian II would recall Vardanes from Cephallenia only to send him back into exile. It is also possible that Vardanes was sent to Cherson as a member of a punitive expedition.[14] The references to his banishment in Cherson might simply be confused references to his earlier Cephallenian exile. But Vardanes is never mentioned as one of the leaders of the expedition ordered by Justinian II to Cherson; on the contrary, he is often referred to as "the outcast" by the two main chroniclers.[15] Vardanes may have been sent into exile a second time during the reign of Justinian II for reasons which remain unclear but which probably are related to the threat he still represented to the emperor in Constantinople. Since the military campaign against

---

91.

[11] Theophanes, *Chronographia*, pp. 372, 381.

[12] The brother-in-law of Maurice, Philippikos, was also suspected of imperial ambitions. See Theophanes, *Chronographia*, p. 285.

[13] *Nikephoros, Patriarch of Constantinople,* §45,12-13 p. 108; Theophanes, *Chronographia*, p. 378.

[14] See *Oxford Dictionary of Byzantium*, vol. 2, p. 1654.

[15] Theophanes, *Chronographia*, p. 379; *Nikephoros, Patriarch of Constantinople,* §45,52 p. 110.

Cherson in 711 failed, the imperial army decided to support Vardanes, who had already been proclaimed emperor by the people of Cherson. His fame as a political opponent, his imperial ambitions, and his status as an exile made him the ideal individual for the people of Cherson and the army to rally around. Certainly Vardanes was also courted for his military experience and the social distinction needed to occupy the throne. Besides his connection to the relatives of Emperor Maurice, his social distinction is confirmed by the close relationship Philippikos had with the most aristocratic families during his reign.[16] He invited the most distinguished members of the senatorial aristocracy to the Zeuxippos bath, where he built a statue of himself.

The Restoration of Monothelitism

Traditionally, historians have interpreted the Byzantine policy of Monothelitism as a means for the emperors to close the doctrinal chasm between the Monophysites and Duophysites, as the Chalcedonian and anti-Chalcedonian churches drifted apart. The Monothelete doctrine professed that Christ possesses two natures but a single will. It was a compromise solution in the intense Christological debate about the nature of Christ and was propagated by the official "Decree of Faith," the *Ekthesis* of Emperor Heraclius.[17] The reason behind this compromise doctrine was that the imperial administration considered, from the sixth century on, such religious divisions politically dangerous and insisted on union. As a result, the Monophysites (Syrians, Egyptians, and Armenians), whose churches and officials were at times per-

---

[16] Theophanes, *Chronographia*, p. 383. For an interpretation of this passage, see Judith Herrin, "Philippikos and the Greens," in *Novum Millennium: Studies on Byzantine History and Culture: Dedicated to Paul Speck*, ed. Claudia Sode and Sarolta Takács (Aldershot and Burlington: Ashgate, 2001), pp. 137-46.

[17] On Monotheletism, see Garegin Owsepian, *Die Entstehungsgeschichte des Monothelismus nach ihren Quellen geprüft und dargestellt* (Leipzig, 1897); Venance Grumel, "Recherches sur l'histoire du monothélisme," *Echos d'Orient* 27 (1928): 6-16, 257-77; 28 (1929): 19-34, 272-82; 29 (1930): 16-28; François-Xavier Murphy and Polycarp Sherwood, *Constantinople II et Constantinople III*, vol. 3: *Histoire des conciles œcuméniques*, ed. Gervais Dumeige (Paris: Editions de l'Orante, 1974), pp. 133-322; Friedhelm Winkelmann, "Die Quellen zur Erforschung des monoenergetisch-monotheletischen Streites," *Klio* 69 (1987): 515-59; Gilbert Dagron, "Le Christianisme byzantin," pp. 40-60.

secuted by Byzantine emperors, resented and resisted imposition of unity by the central authorities of Constantinople.

Religious divisions bore enormous geopolitical ramifications. After the loss of Syria to the Persians in the early seventh century and of Jerusalem in 614, Emperor Heraclius urged a religious compromise to reunite the churches. At first, he attempted to coerce the Monophysites into supporting the Byzantine Church. Having met with stubborn resistance, however, he then tried to strike an agreement through Monothelitism under the *Ekthesis* in 638. The hardliners on each side immediately rejected that compromise, but the imperial government continued to promote Monothelitism after the death of Heraclius until the reign of Constantine IV (668-85) and the Sixth Ecumenical Council (Constantinople III) in 680-81, which condemned Monothelitism as a heresy. The successors of Heraclius pursued this religious policy not only to regain the lost territories of Syria, Armenia, and Egypt, but also for religious reasons, as it sought to mollify the supposed "wrath of God," as manifested in the Arab victory at Yarmuk in 636, the capture of Jerusalem in 638, and the final loss of three quarters of the imperial territories between 636 and the end of the century.

During his short rule (November 24, 711-June 3, 713), Philippikos-Vardanes implemented two emergency policies.[18] First, he restored Monothelitism as a state doctrine and ordered the destruction of the acts of the Sixth Ecumenical Council and the

---

[18] On the chronology of Philippikos' reign, see Philip Grierson, *The Tombs and Obits of the Byzantine Emperors, 337-1042* (Washington, DC: Dumbarton Oaks, 1962), pp. 51-52; Graham V. Sumner, "Philippicus, Anastasius II and Theodosius III," *Greek, Roman, and Byzantine Studies* 17 (1976): 287-89. There are doubts concerning the day of his coronation, November 4 or 24, 711, and concerning that of his deposition, June 3, 713, or May 26, 714. According to the Chronicle of 1234, the reign of Philippikos lasted a little less than two years, from the beginning of the "indictional" year 711/12 to the end of 712/13 (The *Constantinopolitan indiction,* like the Greek year, commenced with the month of September. This tradition was followed in the Eastern chronicles). See "Dionysius Reconstituted," in *The Seventh Century in the West-Syrian Chronicles,* trans. and annotated Andrew Palmer (Liverpool: Liverpool University Press, 1993), p. 210. According to Theophanes, *Chronographia,* pp. 383, 386, who follows two different traditions at the same time, the reign lasted either less than two years or else two years and nine months. According to Nikephoros, *Patriarch of Constantinople,* §48, 15, p. 114, Philippikos was deposed in the second year of his reign. Most probably, the date was June 3, 713.

removal of the image of that council from the palace precincts.[19] Second, he forced the withdrawal of the Armenian population in the empire to parts of Armenia under Arab rule, which effectively caused them to cooperate with the Arab army in the frontier zone.[20] The chronicler Theophanes reports these two events without connecting them, but Michael the Syrian, writing from the perspective of the twelfth century, argues that the religious policy of Philippikos-Vardanes was directly related to the mass departure of Armenians from the empire.[21] In fact, the military context of the early eighth century provided a strong incentive for Philippikos-Vardanes to arrive at a compromise formula in the Christological debate with the Armenian Church and princes and more generally with the eastern churches in the Heraclian tradition.[22] This effort to unite the churches, to come closer to the Armenian princes *outside* the empire in Armenia, and to strengthen the coalition against the Arabs led to a forced union of the churches *inside* the empire, since the emperor thought he had established a common ground for Chalcedonian and anti-Chalcedonian churches with the Monothelite compromise. The forced conversion of the Armenians within the empire was clearly the reason for the population shift toward the frontier zone.[23] In this context, the edict of 712 ordering all Armenians within the empire to recognize the

---

[19] The events are related in a letter of Agatho the Deacon to Pope Constantine. See Agatho the Deacon, in Mansi, *Sacrorum conciliorum nova*, vol. 12, cols. 193-96, and in Riedinger, *Acta Conciliorum Oecumenicorum*, pp. 898-901; Gilbert Dagron, "Le Christianisme byzantin du 7ᵉ au milieu du 11ᵉ siècle," in *Apogée de la papauté et expansion de la Chrétienté, 1054-1274*, ed. André Vauchez (Paris: Desclée, 1993), p. 49; John F. Haldon, *Byzantium in the Seventh Century: The Transformation of a Culture* (Cambridge and New York: Cambridge University Press, 1990), pp. 320-22.

[20] *Chronicle of 1234*, p. 210; Agapios, p. 240; Theophanes, *Chronographia*, p. 382. See also Leone Caetani, ed., *Chronographia Islamica, ossia, Riassunto cronologico della storia di tutti i popoli musulmani dall'anno 1 all'anno 922 della higrah (622-1517 dell'èra volgare)*, 5 vols. (Paris: P. Geuthner, 1912), vol. 1, pp. 1120, 1135, A.H. 92 (710-11) and A.H. 93 (711-12).

[21] Michael the Syrian, *Chronique de Michel le Syrien, Patriarche jacobite d'Antioche, 1126-1199*, ed. and trans. J.-B. Chabot, 5 vols. (Paris: Ernest Leroux, 1899-1924), vol. 2, p. 482.

[22] Dagron, "Le Christianisme byzantin," pp. 41, 47; Jean-Pierre Mahé, "L'Eglise arménienne de 611 à 1066," in Vauchez, *Apogée*, pp. 468-70.

[23] According to *Oxford Dictionary of Byzantium*, vol. 3, p. 1654, s.v. "Philippikos," and vol. 2, p. 1336, s.v. "Melitene," the emperor intended to colonize Melitene and Armenia IV. These territories, however, were clearly outside the empire's sphere of influence, as attested by Michael the Syrian, *Chronique*, vol. 2, p. 482.

authority of the Patriarch of Constantinople must be attributed to Philippikos-Vardanes rather than, as John Haldon has argued, to Justinian II.[24]

The reversion to Monothelitism by Philippikos-Vardanes is often ascribed to his Armenian background, as he allegedly favored the Monophysite doctrine. Considering the pressure he exerted on the Armenian Church and the forced conversion of the Armenian population, however, this interpretation falls short. Agatho the Deacon, who recopied the acts of the Sixth Ecumenical Council which had been destroyed on Philippikos-Vardanes' orders, was largely responsible for this view, as he eagerly sought to attach the revival of the heresy to the foreign origins of the emperor and to the doctrine of the Armenian Church. Thus, he simultaneously condemned both the emperor and the church that were considered heretical by the Byzantine Church.

On the contrary, the reasons for the emperor's Monophysite beliefs are far from obvious.[25] First, not all members of the Armenian clergy and aristocracy shared the official Monophysite belief of the Armenian Church. In the seventh century, there was a strong pro-Chalcedonian party that had political interests in western Armenia. Second, Philippikos-Vardanes' family had been living in the empire for more than a century and was allied with relatives of the emperor Maurice, which renders his Monophysite background or education less probable. In fact, there is no reason to connect Monothelitism (or indeed later Iconoclasm) with a lack of faith in the Chalcedonian doctrine and even less with indulgence in the Eastern churches. This false connection is put forward by Orthodox theologians such as Agatho the Deacon, who lumped together all alleged heresies. The persecution of the Armenian Church during the reign of Philippikos-Vardanes helps to negate such a contrived connection. In fact, far from being an import from the outside world, Monothelitism had roots in the

---

[24] Franz Dölger correctly ascribes the edict to Philippikos. See his *Regesten der Kaiserurkunden des oströmischen Reiches von 565-1453,* vol. 1: *565-1453* (Munich-Berlin: Varlag R. Oldenbourg, 1924), no. 272. John Haldon, *Byzantium*, p. 322n128, finds this attribution erroneous.

[25] The interpretation has been adopted by modern historiography. See, for example, Georgije Ostrogorsky, *Histoire de l'Etat byzantin* (Paris: Payot, 1956, repr. 1996), pp. 180-82; Haldon, *Byzantium*, pp. 321-22; cf. Kaegi, *Byzantine Military Unrest*, p. 205.

same atmosphere of religious anxiety, fueled by the military decline of the empire, as did the Iconoclastic policy of Leo III in 730,
and was in line with the Heraclian policy.

Monothelitism and Caucasian Diplomacy

It is quite possible that the emperor's family connection to the
Armenian nobility placed him in a unique position to strike an
alliance with the Caucasian principalities. In this respect, Monothelitism was also an attempt to put aside religious conflicts and to
strengthen military cooperation, again in keeping with the earlier
policy of Heraclius. In fact, Philippikos-Vardanes took a special
interest in Caucasian affairs, as Movses Daskhurantsi affirms.[26]
The chronicler credits the emperor with the release of the sons of
the prince of Caucasian Albania who had been jailed after having
served in Constantinople as official hostages. He returned the
prisoners with a very distinguished gift, a piece of the True Cross,
for the prince of Albania. Such a display of imperial generosity
perhaps indicates Philippikos-Vardanes' desire to gain Caucasian
support against the Arabs as one of his top diplomatic priorities.

Yet, his attempt to unite the churches, which led to the persecution of the Armenian Church within the borders of the empire, had exactly the opposite effect. In fact, it weakened the
empire, as, according to Michael the Syrian, the people who fled
often became auxiliary troops for the Arabs. It is worth noting that
Michael the Syrian's overall opinion of Philippikos-Vardanes is
diametrically opposed to that of Theophanes. Michael the Syrian
believed that Philippikos-Vardanes was a pious emperor, closer to
the Monophysite faith than the other emperors, and thus looked
upon with favor for his attempt to unite the churches of the
empire.[27] Theophanes, on the other hand, condemned Monothelitism, in keeping with the Sixth Ecumenical Council, and held

---

[26] Movses Daskhurantsi identifies the emperor as a member of the Armenian
nobility but curiously does not mention the name of the house. See *The History of the
Caucasian Albanians by Movsēs Dasxuranc'i*, trans. Charles J.F. Dowsett (London:
Oxford University Press, 1961), p. 203. The omission of such a prestigious family
name calls for an explanation.

[27] Michael the Syrian, *Chronique*, p. 479: "Il était instruit et versé dans les choses
profanes; il voulut abolir le sixième synode et faire disparaître la doctrine de Maxi-
mus."

a negative view of Philippikos-Vardanes. In the chronicle of Michael the Syrian, however, there is a strange contradiction between the positive image of the emperor and the negative view concerning his forced conversion of Monophysite populations attached to the Armenian Church. This discrepancy perhaps offers an indication of a view of the Syriac Church in the eighth century, which was sensitive to attempts at union with both the Armenian Church and Byzantium.[28]

Moreover, the *Narratio de rebus Armeniae*, loosely assigned to the seventh-eighth centuries, which was first written in Armenian and then translated into Greek, was intended to recall the previous attempts at union of the two churches in hopes of convincing members of the Armenian Church to convert to the Chalcedonian faith.[29] The expression "the one who built Saint Sophia" in reference to the emperor Justinian certainly allows us to date the document after Justinian II.[30] It is reasonable to date the *Narratio de rebus Armeniae* to some time during the reign of Philippikos-Vardanes, given his diplomatic efforts to rally the Caucasian princes around Byzantium.[31]

Philippikos-Vardanes adopted two closely related policies, one regarding the Armenians in the empire, while the other concerned the Armenian princes in the Arab-controlled province of Arminya. On the one hand, he demanded that the Armenian population in the empire adhere closely to the Byzantine Church. According to Michael the Syrian, this forcefully imposed policy led to the departure of many Armenians to the Arab province of Arminya. On the other hand, Philippikos-Vardanes wished to cap-

---

[28] The opinion developed by Michael the Syrian on the emperor Philippikos may be the reflection of eighth-century Syriac churchmen, since the Syriac Church was very close to the Armenians at that time and would condemn any attempt at forced conversion of Monophysites in Byzantium. The union of the Armenian and Syriac churches took place in 726 at the synod of Manazkert. See Mahé, "Église arménienne," pp. 481-84.

[29] On the date of composition of the *Narratio*, see Garitte, *Narratio*, pp. 382-94. The date which is most often mentioned is that of the end of the seventh century, because the list of Armenian catholicoi ends with the name of Sahak III Dzoroporetsi (678-703). The religious offensive against the Armenian Church might have been prepared in the first reign of Justinian II and carried out in 689, but its failure was already known to the author of the *Narratio*. See Garitte, *Narratio*, §§144-48, pp. 46-47; Mahé, "L'Eglise arménienne," pp. 476-77.

[30] Garitte, *Narratio*, §78, pp. 37, 189-90; Mahé, "*Narratio*," §78, p. 434.

[31] Haldon, *Byzantium*, p. 321.

italize on his familial relations with the Armenian princes in order
to convince them to ally themselves with the Byzantine Empire.
Philippikos-Vardanes sought a religious compromise, just as Heraclius had attempted between 622 and 641 to reach an agreement
with the Monophysite communities of the empire by proposing a
new religious formula under the decree of the *Ekthesis* in 638.
Philippikos-Vardanes implemented the same political agenda as
Heraclius and his successors by the restoration of Monothelitism,
which in the end proved deleterious to his rule, for the Sixth
Ecumenical Council had already condemned Monothelitism. That
daring choice eventually led to a coup against him and to his death
in 713.

Philippikos-Vardanes was not only the last defender of a policy
of the past, but he was also a precursor of the coming Iconoclastic
policies. The parallel drawn between Monothelitism and Iconoclasm can be supported, since the reversal to Monothelitism was
accompanied by a war of images.[32] Philippikos-Vardanes ordered
the destruction of statues bearing prophetic (pagan) inscriptions,
the removal of the inscriptions and images of the Sixth Ecumenical
Council from the palace precincts, and the restoration to the
Diptychs of Patriarch Sergius I of Constantinople (610-38) and the
other churchmen who had been condemned for their promotion
of Monothelitism.[33]

* * *

The policies adopted by Philippikos-Vardanes reflected the same
religious anxieties that produced Iconoclasm. In the literary production of the seventh and eighth centuries, the Byzantine military defeat at Yarmuk in 636 and the loss of Jerusalem to the
Arabs in 638 were considered the most striking manifestations of
the wrath of God.[34] The religious policies of some of the emperors

---

[32] Dagron, "Le Christianisme byzantin," p. 49; André Grabar, *L'iconoclasme byzantine: Dossier archéologique* (Paris: Collège de France, 1957), p. 48.

[33] Gilbert Dagron, *Constantinople imaginaire: Etudes sur le recueil des Patria*
(Paris: Presses universitaires de France, 1984), pp. 134, 145.

[34] See Stratos, *Byzantium*, vol. 2, pp. 64-72; Fred McGraw Donner, *The Early
Islamic Conquests* (Princeton: Princeton University Press, 1981), pp. 133-46; Walter
E. Kaegi, *Byzantium and the Early Islamic Conquests* (Cambridge: Cambridge Univer-
sity Press, 1992), pp. 112-45; Mikael Nichanian, "Le maître des milices d'Orient Vahan:

at the time must be seen in light of their religious meaning as they were intended to regain the favor of God rather than simply for certain political or diplomatic objectives.[35] In this respect, the Monotheletism of Philippikos-Vardanes represented an endogenous production of the empire rather than the product of foreign influences. In its attempt to unite with the Eastern churches, the decisions of Philippikos-Vardanes may be considered the embodiment or the culmination of the Heraclian policy, but they also heralded the succeeding age of Iconoclasm.

De la bataille de Yarmouk (636) au complot d'Athalaric (637)," in *Armenian Studies in Honor of Dickran Kouymjian* (Costa Mesa, CA: Mazda, 2008), pp. 321-37.

[35] Gilbert Dagron, *Empereur et prêtre: Etude sur le "césaropapisme" byzantin* (Paris: Gallimard, 1995), pp. 192-93.

Coin of Emperor Philippikos-Vardanes

ARMENIAN ELITES IN CONSTANTINOPLE:
EMPEROR BASIL AND PATRIARCH PHOTIUS

Manea Erna Shirinian

The presence of Armenians in the Byzantine Empire was closely related to the complicated history of Armenia. Geographically situated between two rival powers, the Byzantine and Persian empires, Armenia was divided into two parts: Persian Armenia and Byzantine Armenia. Armenian political leaders were obliged to align themselves with their Byzantium or Persia overlords, and those who opposed them were compelled to flee their homeland in fear of persecution. In general, Armenian families seeking refuge in the Byzantine capital of Constantinople came from the higher political strata and were members of prominent families, such as the Mamikonian, Arshakuni, and Kamsarakan.[1] Further, the Byzantine imperial policy of resettling Armenians also led to large population transfers from the Armenian territories. By the ninth century, the number of Armenians in Byzantium, especially in Constantinople, had increased rapidly, and some of the elite families had secured positions of power

---

[1] Hrach Bartikyan, *Kostandin Tsiranatsin* [Constantine VII Porphyrogenitus] (Erevan: Armenian Academy of Sciences, 1970), p. v; Nicolas Adontz [Adonts], *Patmakan usumnasirutiunner* [Historical Studies] (Paris: A. Ghukasian, 1948), p. 484; Stepannos Taronetsi, *Stepannosi Taronetsvoy Asoghikan Patmutiun Tiezerakan* [Universal History of Stepannos of Taron Asoghik] (Saint Petersburg: I.N. Skorokhodov, 1885), p. 85; Hayk G. Melkonyan, *Asorakan aghbyurner: Hovhan Epesatsu "Ekeghetsakan patmutyun"* [Syriac Sources: *Ecclesiastical History* by John of Ephesus] (Erevan: Armenian Academy of Sciences, 1976), vol. 1, ch. 4, pp. 375-76. Adontz discusses how Artavan and Klienes of the Arshakuni family, whose lives were in danger, fled from Armenia to Byzantium in the fifth century (during the reign of Emperor Leo, 457-74); also, the junior Vardan Mamikonian, who had led the insurrection against Persia in 571-72, left Armenia for Constantinople with his family. The same Vardan is mentioned in the letter by Patriarch Photius to Catholicos Zakaria as Kher Vardan—that is, Crooked Vardan.

and status in government and society. Studies have tried to distinguish between those families who were unquestionably of Armenian origin and those whose origins are disputable,[2] a topic of particular import for the purposes of this chapter, especially as pertaining to the emperor Basil I (867-86) and Patriarch Photius I of Constantinople (858-67, 877-86).

Names of Family and Place

The testimonies regarding the origins of Armenian families in ninth-century Constantinople are often contradictory. Although scholars have referred to a family's origins or a person's place of birth, parents, and so forth, certain difficulties nevertheless remain. Many names are so linguistically corrupted (for example, due to transliteration into Greek) that the Armenian root is often unrecognizable, as in the case of Kourkuas derived from Gurgen. The origins of some Armenian surnames are ambiguous, as they are constructed from apparently non-Armenian ethnonyms (as in Kurd or Kurdik, or even Turc, as in the case of General Bardanes Tourkos).[3] Cases such as the brothers Peter the Bulgarian and Leo the Syrian, however, clearly suggest that scholars must be careful not to confuse names and places of origin.[4] Such problems continue to plague medieval Armenian history, but they do not diminish the significance of the fact that beginning in the early ninth century Armenians played an important role in Byzantine affairs and some even sought to capture the imperial throne.

---

[2] For example, see Alexander [Aleksandr] P. Kazhdan, *Armiane v sostave gospodstvuiushchego klassa vizantiiskoi imperii v XI-XII vv.* (Erevan: Armenian Academy of Sciences, 1975). Kazhdan divides Armenians in Byzantium into three categories: 1) Unquestionably Armenian families, 2) Families of mixed origin, and 3) Disputable Armenian families.

[3] John B. Bury, *A History of the Later Roman Empire* (London: Macmillan, 1889), p. 10.

[4] Bartikyan, *Kostandin Tsiranatsin*, p. 262n56. Bartikyan cites this example from Adontz, *Patmakan usumnasirutiunner*, p. 351. Bartikyan in the Armenian translation of Theophanes Continuatus understands the word 't'urk'' as a transliteration of the Armenian word "turk" or "tork"—that is, donation, gift, taxes—and mentions other examples where this word was confused with the word "t'urk." See Hrach Bartikyan, *Teopanesi Sharunakogh* [Theophanes Continuatus] (Erevan: Armenian Academy of Sciences, 1990), pp. 289-90.

Armenians among the Byzantine Political Elite

In the aftermath of a revolt against the emperor Nikephorus (802-11) in 803, Bardanes Tourkos, with the support of his political allies—Michael the Amorian, Leo the Armenian, and Thomas the Slav—tried to usurp the Byzantine throne and proclaimed himself emperor.[5] The struggle for power lasted seven weeks.[6] The first two companions deserted to Emperor Nikephorus, who rewarded them with high political appointments and opulent houses in Constantinople—Michael received the house of Karianos, while Leo received the palace of Zeno with the Dagistheus house.[7] Both men later became emperors. The third companion of Bardanes, Thomas, stood by him and later became the great tyrant.[8] Leo and Thomas are considered Armenian. Leo became the emperor Leo V in 813 and ruled for seven years until his death in 820; there is no disagreement that he was of Armenian origin.[9] As to Thomas, the sources are contradictory: Ioseph Genesios (Joseph Genesius) once makes him out to be an Armenian, and in another place, a Scythian;[10] Theophanes Continuatus considers him to be from Slavonic parentage.[11]

Moreover, when in February 808 "a large number of discontented senators and ecclesiastical dignitaries" attempted once again to depose Nikephorus, "the man who was designated by the conspirators to be the new emperor was also an Armenian,"[12] the patrician and quaestor Arshavir (Arsaber, 750-808),[13] the father of Theodosia, who was the wife of the future Emperor Leo V.

Patriarch Photius I of Constantinople, John the Grammarian,

---

[5] Bury, *History*, pp. 10-14; Paul Lemerle, "Thomas le Slav," *Travaux et Memoires* 1 (1965): 264.

[6] Bury, *History*, p. 11.

[7] Bartikyan, *Teopanesi Sharunakogh*, pp. 4, 291n22-24.

[8] Thomas was originally a military and naval commander. Later, during the reign of Emperor Leo V the Armenian, he was entrusted with high positions. Thomas again turned to rebellion after the death of Leo and the accession of his enemy, Michael the Amorian.

[9] For example, Theophanes Continuatus and Georgius Monachus. See Bartikyan, *Teopanesi Sharunakogh*, pp. 3, 288n10; Bury, *History*, p. 11.

[10] Ioseph Genesios, *Genesii Regum libri quattuor*, ed. Anni Lesmüller-Werner and Hans Thurn (Berlin: de Gruyter, 1978), pp. 8, 32.

[11] Theophanes the Confessor, *Theophanes Continuatus*, ed. Immanuel Bekker (Bonn: E. Weber, 1838), §50.

[12] Bury, *History*, p. 14.

[13] Genesios, *Genesii Regum*, p. 21; Bartikyan, *Teopanesi Sharunakogh*, p. 20.

and Leo the Mathematician were among the most illustrious figures of ninth-century Constantinople. The literature surrounding them is colored by animosity and maledictions. One finds
only maledictions toward and horrible legends about Photius, a
more complicated case than the other two. He was interested in
theological issues as well as in sciences. John the Grammarian
and Leo the Mathematician were iconoclasts. A damaging and
intolerant movement, the iconoclasts also had a positive impact
in that they focused on ancient traditions and in so doing revived
public interest in the study of philosophy.[14] Engagement in theological controversies required sufficient familiarity with philosophy. This interest further flourished in the ninth century under
the influence of John the Grammarian, Leo the Mathematician,
and especially Photius, who "gave an impulse to classical learning"[15] and thanks to whom many works of ancient authors were
preserved.

Patriarch John VII of Constantinople (837-43) was also known
as John the Grammarian and John the Anagnostes. According to
Ioseph Genesios and Photius, he was also a professional
painter.[16] Members of the Orthodox Church gave him derogatory
surnames, and later authors believed he was possessed by a
demon and accused him of practicing black magic. Theophanes
Continuatus states that John the Grammarian was devoid of any
kind of grace.[17] He was detested even after his death; Emperor
Michael III (842-67) went so far as to order his body exhumed
and burned.[18] About his origin, it is believed that he was a son of
Pancratios,[19] from the family of Morocharzamioi.[20] According to

---

[14] Epistolography is an example of the restoration of certain ancient traditions.
This genre was significant in early Byzantine literature in the fourth and fifth
centuries, but remained dormant in the sixth and seventh centuries. Beginning in
the eighth century, epistolography reemerged in Byzantine literature in connection with iconoclasm. For more information, see Tatiana V. Popova, "Vizantiiskaia
epistolografiia" [Byzantine Epistolography], in *Vizantiiskaia literatura* [Byzantine
Literature], ed. Sergei S. Averintsev (Moscow: Nauka, 1974), pp. 181-230.

[15] Bury, *History*, p. 447.

[16] Genesios, *Genesii Regum,* p. 83; Cyril Mango, *The Homilies of Photius Patriarch of Constantinople* (Cambridge, MA: Harvard University Press, 1958), p. 246.

[17] Bartikyan, *Teopanesi Sharunakogh*, p. 18.

[18] Symeonis Magistri ac Logothetae, *Annales*, and Georgii Monachi, *Vitae im-
peratorrum recentiorum*, in *Theophanes Continuatus*, §§681, 834; see also Adontz,
Patmakan usumnasirutiunner, pp. 521-22.

[19] On John the Grammarian, see Bartikyan, *Teopanesi Sharunakogh*, pp. 18,
57-58, 60, 91-93, 113; Symeonis Magistri, *Annales*, p. 606; Georgius Cedrenus,

Theophanes Continuatus, they were a prominent family in Constantinople, and John the Grammarian "was not a foreigner or stranger but a native of Constantinople."[21] Others maintain that he was of Armenian origin, and agree that his father's name Pancratios "seems to conceal the Armenian name Bagrat"[22] or is a transliteration of it.[23] Pancratios was called σκιάστης, which is not so clear.[24] According to Nicolas Adontz, this word, which was one of the surnames of Apollo, should be understood as "pseudo" or "false prophet" because John's father had dealt with the external sciences and was called Astronomer.[25] John's brother had the Armenian name of Arshavir, whose family was likely of Armenian origin. Arshavir was a patrician and the owner of large estates along the Bosphorus.[26]

The ethnic origin of Leo the Mathematician is subject to debate, but scholars agree that he was a cousin of John the Grammarian. Also known as Leo the Philosopher—not to be confused with the emperor Leo the Wise (886-912)—he studied philosophy, rhetoric, grammar, poetry, natural sciences, and especially astrology.[27] His engagement in astrological predictions and classical studies led to the accusation of paganism. He was appointed professor at the great Magnavra university in Constan-

---

Georgius Cedrenus [et] Ioannis Scylitzae ope, ed. Immanuel Bekker (Bonn: E. Weber, 1839), §144; Mango, *Homilies*, pp. 240-41.

[20] Alexander P. Kazhdan read this name as Maurocharzanoi. Kazhdan, *Armiane*, p. 120. See also Bury, *History*, p. 60; Bartikyan, *Teopanesi Sharunakogh*, pp. 92, 325n15; Mango, *Homilies*, p. 242.

[21] Bartikyan, *Teopanesi Sharunakogh*, pp. 91-92.

[22] Mango, *Homilies*, p. 241.

[23] Charles Lebeau, *Histoire du Bas-Empire*, ed. Saint-Martin, 21 vols. (Paris: F. Didot, 1824-1836), vol. 13, p. 14; Bartikyan, *Teopanesi Sharunakogh*, p. 298; Adontz, *Patmakan usumnasirutiunner*, pp. 512-22; Bury, *History*, p. 60.

[24] See Mango, *Homilies*, p. 241.

[25] Adontz, *Patmakan usumnasirutiunner*, p. 520.

[26] See *Theophanes Continuatus*, §§156-57; Bartikyan, *Teopanesi Sharunakogh*, p. 93; *Georgius Cedrenus*, §146. This patrician Arshavir is not to be confused with the aforesaid much earlier patrician and quaestor Arshavir, the father of the Empress Theodosia and with Photius' uncle patrician and magister Arshavir Kamsarakan.

[27] Bartikyan, *Teopanesi Sharunakogh*, p. 114. The name Leo was widespread in Byzantium and sometimes there is confusion among the various Leos who lived in the ninth century. About Leo the Mathematician and this confusion, see Elena E. Lipshitz, "Vizantiiskii uchenyi Lev Matematik" [The Byzantine Scientist Leo the Mathematician] *Vizantiiskii Vremennik* (Moscow) 2 (1949): 106-49.

tinople,[28] which, according to Hrach Bartikyan, was established and sponsored by another Armenian, Caesar Bardas.[29]

The Armenian origin of Bardas seems established beyond doubt.[30] Adontz considered him a powerful person from the Mamikonian family.[31] His paternal uncle was the chief magister Manuel Mamikonian, who was one of the two appointed regents of Michael III to assist his mother, Empress Theodora (the niece of Manuel and the sister of Bardas).[32] Aside from Theodora, Bardas had two more sisters and a brother, Petronas, who was Drungary of the Watch, strategos of Thracessians, and later Domestic of Schools.

Patriarch John VII was the godfather of Empress Theodora, who "belonged to a fairly obscure Paphlagonian family."[33] Herself an image worshipper, she deposed the iconoclast Patriarch John. Theodora had three sisters: Calomaria, Sophia, and Irene. Photius, that great man "who was unequaled by any Greek of the Middle Ages,"[34] was related to Theodora through his mother Irene, who was the sister of Arshavir Magister (Kamsarakan), who in turn was the husband of Calomaria, the sister of Theodora.[35] According to Theophanes Continuatus, the wife of Arshavir was another sister of Theodora, named Irene.[36] Adontz considers this Arshavir to be from the Kamsarakan family.[37]

Among the Byzantine aristocracy in the ninth century, Constantine the Armenian (surname Maniakes)[38] was the Drungary of the Watch under the emperor Michael III, as attested in the writings of his kinsman Ioseph Genesios.[39] According to Gen-

---

[28] See Bury, *History*, pp. 436ff.

[29] Bartikyan, *Teopanesi Sharunakogh*, pp. 110, 114.

[30] See Bartikyan, *Kostandin Tsiranatsin*, p. 110; idem, *Teopanesi Sharunakogh*, pp. 82, 88, 90, 101-04, 109-16, 120-23, 134-47, 218, 322n122; Genesios, *Genesii Regum*, p. 52.

[31] Adontz, *Patmakan usumnasirutiunner*, pp. 320-50.

[32] See Vardan Areveltsi, *Havakumn patmutian Vardanay vardapeti lusabanial* [The Universal History Explained by Vardan Vardapet] (Venice: Mekhitarist Press, 1862), p. 77.

[33] Cf. Bartikyan, *Teopanesi Sharunakogh*, pp. 52-53, 308n11.

[34] Bury, *History*, p. 186.

[35] *Georgius Cedrenus*, §161.

[36] Bartikyan, *Teopanesi Sharunakogh*, p. 104.

[37] Adontz, *Patmakan usumnasirutiunner*, pp. 335-40.

[38] Genesios, *Genesii Regum*, p. 88.

[39] Constantine Maniakes was perhaps the grandfather of Ioseph Genesios. See Adontz, *Patmakan usumnasirutiunner*, p. 446.

esios, Constantine the Armenian was either a relative or a close friend of Bardas.[40] A merciful man in the case connected with the tortures of Patriarch Ignatius by Bardas,[41] Constantine the Armenian was the only senator who did not wish to disgrace Patriarch Ignatius.[42] Along with Leo the Mathematician and Photius, Constantine the Armenian belonged to the circle of Bardas which ruled until another Armenian, Basil, arrived on the scene in Constantinople.

Emperor Basil I the Macedonian

The emperor Basil I (867-86) was the founder of the Macedonian dynasty that ruled the empire for two centuries. Such rapid upward social mobility was not surprising for the Byzantine Empire. Basil was a bright student of politics; he quickly familiarized himself with the techniques of palace intrigues and cultivated close ties with people in power, among whom were many Armenians (for example, Smbat, the Logothete of the Course and son-in-law of Bardas). The founder of the Macedonian dynasty is generally depicted in the literature as a handsome man with a powerful built and athletic strength. There is an apologetic and tendentious work, *Vita Basilii*,[43] by Constantine VII Porphyrogenitus dedicated to his grandfather. The grandson ascribes to Basil a panorama of virtues and maintains that Basil was destined from birth to occupy the Byzantine throne. People were kind toward him and believed that he would become an emperor.[44] His Armenian identity plays an important role in the view that he was destined to become an emperor.

According to John B. Bury, Basil's "Armenian descent is established beyond doubt, and the legend that he was a Slav has no better a foundation than the fiction which claimed Slavonic

---

[40] Genesios, *Genesii Regum*, p. 101.

[41] Bartikyan, *Teopanesi Sharunakogh*, pp. 115-16.

[42] Genesios, *Genesii Regum*, pp. 100-01.

[43] Alexander P. Kazhdan, "Iz istorii vizantiiskoi khronografii X v." [From the History of Byzantine Chronography of the 10th Century], *Vizantiiskii Vremennik* (Moscow), 22 (1961): 84.

[44] *Theophanes Continuatus*, pp. 128-29; Steven Runciman, "The Widow Danielis," in *Études dédiées à la mémoire d'André M. Andréadès*, ed. K. Varvaressos (Athens: Pyrsos, 1940), pp. 425-31.

parentage for the emperor Justinian."[45] Basil used his Armenian
origin to achieve his political ambitions. Alexander Kazhdan
notes that the reign of Basil was peculiar, as it relied heavily on
his relatives and friends.[46] Meanwhile, his ethnicity did not
prevent him from initiating the murder of his political opponent,
Bardas, also an Armenian. His relations with the Patriarch
Photius of Constantinople were tense because the latter belonged
to the circle of Bardas.

Basil forced the removal of Photius as patriarch not only because of tensions in their relations but more important because
of a crisis that involved a complicated political relationship between Constantinople and Rome. Determined to regain its supremacy over the Christian world, Rome increased its resistance
toward Constantinople, and the conflict became particularly
apparent in the early eighth century when Emperor Leo III (717-
41) initiated the attack against images (726). Further, Charle-
magne's efforts in the early ninth century to restore the Roman
Empire of the West, in full accord with the papacy, posed a
serious threat to Byzantium. The strength of the Byzantine
Church was vital to maintain power in the East, which explains
why the regent Bardas in 861 replaced the weak Patriarch of
Constantinople Ignatius (who was obedient to Old Rome) by the
more flexible but strong Photius. Pope Nicholas rejected this replacement and supported Ignatius. In letters to Emperor Michael
and Photius, Nicholas insisted that Ignatius be restored. He also
wrote to the other Eastern patriarchs. In his response (under the
dictation by Photius), the emperor insisted that Nicholas could

---

[45] Bury, *History*, p. 165. "The sole foundation of the Slavonic theory is the fact
that Arab writers consider him a Slav. This is explained by the Arab view that Mace-
donia was Slavonic, 'Slav' being the equivalent of 'Macedonian'." For more ex-
planations on the refutation of the Slavonic theory, see Rach [Hrach] M. Bartikyan,
"K razgadke zagadki o slavianskom proiskhozhdenii osnovatelia Makedonskoi
dinastii Vasiliia I (867-886)" [Concerning the Solution of the Enigma about the
Slavonic Origin of the Founder of the Macedonian Dynasty, Basil I (867-86)],
Lraber hasarakakan gitityunneri 7 (1985): 47-54; See also Alexander Vasiliev,
"Proiskhozhdenie imperatora Vasiliia Makedonianina" [The Origin of the Emperor
Basil the Macedonian], *Vizantiiskii Vremennik* (Saint Petersburg) 12 (1906): 47-54.

[46] Alexander P. Kazhdan, "Sotsial'nye i politicheskie vzgliady Fotiia" [Social
and Political Views of Photius], *Ezhegodnik Muzeia istorii religii i ateizma* 2 (1958):
122. See also Igor S. Chichurov, *Politicheskaia ideologiia srednevekovia. Vizan-
tiia i Rus'* [Political Ideology of the Middle Ages: Byzantium and Russia] (Moscow: Nauka, 1990), p. 54.

do nothing as all of the Eastern patriarchs sided with Photius. In the end, the rulers in Constantinople refused to submit. The renewed claims of Rome to the Illyrian obedience (acknowledgement of the primacy of Rome) met with the encyclical of 867 by Photius, which, in fact, was a declaration of separation—both in ritual and in doctrine—from Old Rome. Such was the strained situation with Rome when in September 867 Michael III was murdered and Basil I ascended the throne. Regional insecurity eventually convinced Basil to improve relations with Rome and to that end he restored the pro-Rome Patriarch Ignatius to the patriarchal throne and exiled Photius.

Patriarch Photius I

Photius, one of the greatest enlightened (φῶς, φωτός) men of his period, was famous as a skillful politician and accomplished author. His encyclopedic knowledge brought forward numerous works on theology, history, philosophy, science, medicine, oratory, romance, and lexicography. One is rightfully amazed how he found time to write so many volumes amid all his cares. His most eminent work, *Myriobiblon* (or *Bibliotheca*), is "a living monument of erudition and criticism," which refers to many lost works by Greek authors.[47]

His name is closely associated with the great church schism between East and West; as a result of this, views of Photius vary greatly from the time of his contemporaries to the present. Yet even those who consider him as the architect of a disastrous schism count him among the greatest scholars and church leaders. Photius himself had announced that as the Patriarch of Constantinople he would not shy away from controversial acts in order to bring to the dyophysite dogma (two distinct natures of Christ as defined at the Council of Chalcedon in 451) various non-Chalcedonians, among them the Armenians. The disagreements arising from seemingly confessional issues between Rome and Constantinople, however, actually served as a pretext for the expansion of political influence over the patriarchates of the Eastern churches.

The confessional problem with the Armenian Church was

---

[47] Eduard Gibbon, *The History of the Decline and Fall of the Roman Empire,* ed. John B. Bury (London, 1898) p. 53.

"one of the essential and hereditary questions of church policy," which became a matter of anxiety for Pope Nicholas I, too, as attested in a collection of documents edited by Jean Mansi.[48] For example, the epistle by Pope Nicholas I to the fourth synod of Constantinople states: "It should become a common business for all of us to return our brothers, I mean the Armenians, to the right path and to assist for their better understanding of God."[49] The importance of this question is underscored as well by the lively correspondence between Patriarch Photius, Catholicos Zakaria I (855-76), and Prince of Princes (*Ishkhanats Ishkhan*) Ashot of Armenia.[50]

Biographical data of Photius appear in the *Annales* of Pseudo-Symeon and in *Vita Ignatii* by Niketas Paphlagon.[51] According to them, Photius descended from a noble Byzantine family. The available information about the origin of Photius from his paternal side is unclear except that his father's name was Sergius, a spatharios (lifeguard).[52] Despite Symeon Magister's legendary stories about Photius' mother, more concrete information is available, as noted above. Her brother was Arshavir Kamsarakan (the husband of Calomaria). The mother of Photius, if Adontz is correct, was from the same Armenian Kamsarakan family. Bartikyan is certain that Photius was an Armenian.[53]

Photius' own letters to Ashot support the view that he was of

---

[48] Fiodor Rosseikin, *Pervoe pravlenie Fotiia, patriarkha konstantinopol'skogo* [The First Reign of Photius, Patriarch of Constantinople] (Sergiev-Posad, 1915), p. 261.

[49] Jean D. Mansi, *Sacrorum conciliorum nova et amplissima collection,* 53 vols. (Paris: Hubert Welter, 1901-1927), vol. 16, p. 303 (2d repr. Graz: Akademische Druck-U. Verlagsanstalt, 1960-1962), 2 vols.

[50] Further information about these correspondences appears in some Armenian sources as well. See, for example, *Samveli kahanayi Ametsvoy Havakmunk i grots patmagrats* [The Priest Samuel of Ani's Collection of the Writings of Historians], ed. Arshak Ter-Mikelian (Vagharshapat: Mother See of Echmiadzin, 1893); Kirakos Gandzaketsi, *Patmutyun Hayots* [History of Armenia], ed. Karapet Melik-Ohanjanyan (Erevan: Armenian Academy of Sciences, 1961), p. 80.

[51] Symeonis Magistri, *Annales,* §§601-760; Niketas Paphlagon, *Vita Ignatii,* Jean-Pierre Migne, *Patrologiae Graecae,* vol. 105 (Turnhout, Belgium: Brepols, 1862).

[52] Symeonis Magistri, *Annales,* §668.

[53] Ibid. Photius was illegitimate and his mother was an escaped nun. Bartikyan, *Teopanesi Sharunakogh,* pp. 58, 329. Concerning the Armenian descent of Photius see also Peter Charanis, *The Armenians in the Byzantine Empire* (Lisbon: Calouste Gulbenkian Foundation, 1963), pp. 27-28; David Marshall Lang, *The Armenians: A People in Exile* (London: Routledge, 1989), p. 54.

Armenian heritage. One of these letters is preserved only in an Armenian translation (No. 298[54]) and the second (No. 284[55]) in Greek original. In an attempt to convince Ashot to accept the Chalcedonian creed and to contribute to the union of Byzantine and Armenian churches, he refers to Ashot as follows: in the first letter *hamasers*[56] (congener) and in the second letter many times (8) συγγενής[57] (relative, kinsman), and once even more definitely συγγενοῦς τοῦ αἵματος (blood relative, relative by descent).[58] With a handful of exceptions, scholars have not made sufficient use of this obvious information about the Armenian origin of Photius.[59] For example, Westerink has noted Photius' reference to Ashot as a kinsman, although in his paper, "The Correspondence between the Patriarch Photius and Ashot V," he merely pointed out these instances but without further elaboration.[60] The suggestion that Photius used the word συγγενής as a literary or figurative expression may be rejected by the fact that he never used the same word in his works to denote such a meaning. In contrast, he uses the word from the same root συγγενικός[61] to mean "relative," as in his Amphilochia No. 45

---

[54] Norayr Pogharian, *Mayr tsutsak dzeragrats Srbots Hakobiants* [Grand Catalogue of Manuscripts in Saint James (Monastery)] (Jerusalem: St. James Press, 1968), pp. 521-25; *Girk tghtots* [Book of Letters], 2d ed. (Jerusalem: St. James Press, 1994), pp. 515-23; *Pravoslavnyi palestinskii sbornik* 2:1 (1892): 210-13. The number of the letter indicated in the text (No. 298) is from Basilius Laourdas and Leendert G. Westerink, *Photius, Epistulae et Ampilochia*, vol. 3 (Leipzig: B.G. Teubner, 1985). The Armenian letter in this edition presented in Latin translation by Bernard Outtier.

[55] Laourdas and Westerink, *Photius*, pp. 1-112; Jean Darrouzès, "Deux lettres inédites de Photius aux Arméniens," *Revue des études byzantines* 29 (1971): 137-81.

[56] Pogharian, *Girk tghtots*, p. 515. As stated, this letter is preserved only in Armenian. If this letter is authentic, it means that Photius knew the story about Vardan Mamikonian.

[57] Laourdas and Westerink, *Photius*, Epistle 284, lines 81-84, 371, 411, 422, 2462, 2857, 3262.

[58] Ibid., p. 6.

[59] For example, Adontz, *Patmakan usumnasirutiunner*, pp. 452-500; Bartikyan, *Teopanesi Sharunakogh*, p. 338.

[60] Laourdas and Westerink, *Photius*, Epistle 284, p. 1; L.G. Westerink, "The Correspondence between Patriarch Photius and Ashot V," International Conference on Armenian Medieval Literature, Erevan, Sept. 15-19, 1986, *Conference Proceedings*, p. 46.

[61] The indexes of the *Vocabula Selecta* (new edition of Westerink) show that the word *suggenikov* was rarely used by Photius; it is indicated in only one particular case (A., 45, 46). See Laourdas and Westerink, *Photius*, vol. 6, pt. 2, p. 124.

under the title "How we shall understand as follows: who is my mother and who are my brothers."[62] Photius, following Christian ideology, considers all Christians brothers and employs the words "father," "mother," or "son" used here figuratively, but at the same time he uses the word συγγενικός in a direct meaning. There is no basis to consider figurative use of the word συγγενικός here, especially when it signifies not just συγγενής (relative) but συγγενοῦς τοῦ αἵματος (blood relative).

The correspondence of Photius with the Bulgarian prince Michael shows a different attitude in his wording.[63] In the letter to Michael, Photius speaks with arrogance and uses a didactic tone, while the letter to Ashot is written in a friendly manner, with epithets of praise and with some knowledge of Armenian history. Photius may have learned this history from a study titled *Narratio de rebus Armeniae* by a Chalcedonian Armenian.[64]

Photius was in exile twice, and both times in Armenia where he spent seventeen years. He is said to have spent his first exile for nine or ten years at a monastery of Skepe. Although such a monastery is unknown in Armenia but it may be the monastery of Holy Mother of God at Skhkev near Lake Van.[65] One can only wonder whether, in addition to writing a large number of letters to his friends and relatives, he established contacts with the local people and whether he spoke and read in the Armenian language. It is possible that he had some knowledge of Armenian, as Byzantine Armenians, especially those in Constantinople, quite likely used the language.[66]

The Armenian background of Patriarch Photius also explains many complicated questions connected with his deposition from and subsequent return to the patriarchal see. These questions

---

[62] Laourdas and Westerink, *Photius*, vol. 4, pp. 185-90.

[63] Ibid., vol. 1, pp. 1-39. For this letter, see also Despina S. White and Joseph R. Berrigan, ed., *The Patriarch and the Prince: The Letter of Patriarch Photios of Constantinople to Khan Boris of Bulgaria* (Brookline, MA: Holy Cross Orthodox Press, 1982).

[64] Gérard Garitte, ed., *La Narratio de rebus Armeniae*, Corpus scriptorum Christianorum orientalium, Subsidia (Louvain: L. Durbecq, 1952), vol. 4, pp. 370-75.

[65] Migne, *Patrologiae Graecae*, vol. 105, 540, col. B; White, *Patriarch*, p. 20. On the monastery of Skhkev, see Gabriella Uluhogian, *Un' antica mappa dell' Armenia: Monasteri e santuari dal I al XVII secolo* (Ravenna: Longo, 2000), no. 336, "Monastero della Madre di Sxkev," pp. 99-100.

[66] Bartikyan, for example, is confident that they knew Armenian. See *Kostandin Tsiranatsin*, p. xi.

are closely linked with the so-called "Genealogy," a forgery he composed to prove the lineage of Emperor Basil to the Armenian royal Arshakuni dynasty. Supposedly this deception convinced Emperor Basil that Photius be allowed to return to the patriarchal see.[67] The "Genealogy" itself was not preserved, but there is a detailed description of it by Niketas David Paphlagon and Symeon Magister.[68] Niketas, the biographer of Photius' rival Patriarch Ignatius, never missed an opportunity to criticize Photius. In *Vita Ignatii*, Niketas Paphlagon notes that even after Photius was deposed as patriarch, after ten years in exile he did everything to win back the favor of the emperor and succeeded.[69] Calling Photius "deceiver," "unworthy," and "malicious," Niketas claims that Photius invented a forged "Genealogy" according to which Basil descended from King Trdat.

The "Genealogy" prophesized that the father of Basil would have a son named "Beclas"[70] who would become emperor. The description of Beclas unmistakably pointed to Basil. Niketas indicates that this is an acronym composed from the first letters of Basil's family—B[asil], E[udocia], C[onstantine], L[eo], A[lexander], S[tephan]. According to that forged document, Basil would be the most blessed emperor; his happy reign would last for a long time, and he would father future emperors.[71] The biographer of Patriarch Ignatius writes: "This invention he wrote by 'Alexandrian letters' on old paper, trying to give to it the shape of old handwriting; he inserted it between the old folios taken from a very ancient book, and placed it in the palace library."[72] The same passage appears in Symeon Magister's work but with slight differences.[73] "Examining his [Basil's] genealogy from the beginning, in accordance with the country and circum-

---

[67] For the Armenian abridged version on this topic, see Mane Shirinian, "Movses Khorenatsu 'Patmutyan' ev Phot patriarki 'Tsnndabanutyan' aghersnere" [The Connections between Movses Khorenatsi's "History" and the "Genealogy" of Patriarch Photius], *Ashtanak* 1 (1995): 85-96.

[68] There are many testimonies about the genealogy or the Armenian origin of Emperor Basil. See, for example, Genesios, *Genesii Regum*; Migne, *Patrologiae Graecae*, vol. 109, p. 1128; *Oraison funèbre de Basile I par son fils Léon VI le sage*, ed., intro., trans. Albert Vogt and Irénée Haussherr (Rome, 1932), pp. 38-79.

[69] Migne, *Patrologiae Graecae*, vol. 105, col. 565C.

[70] On this name, see Bartikyan, "K razgadke."

[71] Migne, *Patrologiae Graecae*, vol. 105, cols. 565D-568A.

[72] Ibid., vol. 105, col. 568A.

[73] Ibid., vol. 109, cols. 749D-752A; Symeonis Magistri, *Annales*, p. 689.

stances, he finished the book and made it appear very ancient and, as it was noted, he placed it in the palace library through Theophanes Sphenodaimonos." According to Mansi, the name of the palace librarian was Phrenodaimonos.[74] Theophanes was in correspondence with Photius, as evidenced in a number of letters.[75]

Theophanes showed this manuscript to the emperor, asserting that although an old and interesting work, no one but the exiled Photius could interpret it. The emperor relayed the manuscript to Photius, who in turn responded that he would dictate the written words only to the emperor himself. Basil recalled Photius from exile, and the latter recited the writing and made a positive impression on the emperor, taking advantage of the emperor's vanity. Basil immediately appointed him as the teacher of his children and soon thereafter restored him to the patriarchal see.[76]

Most scholars agree that this "Genealogy" is a forgery and that Photius authored the manuscript, a fact that appeared to be evident even to his contemporaries. Given its forged character, however, not many experts have considered the reasons and circumstances of this writing, regarding simply as creative legend. The most extensive explanation appears in an article on Basil by Adontz,[77] who in examining the "Genealogy" in detail contends that, contrary to the accepted view, Photius never authored such a forgery and that the only possible truth was that he tried to elucidate the family origins of Basil. Adontz notes that being a nephew of Arshavir Kamsarakan and a friend of the regent Bardas, Photius was close to Armenian circles and could easily discern what was in reality the genealogy of the emperor. Adontz concludes that neither the famous patriarch would have invented something as trivial and silly as the play on words (that is, Beclas), nor was Basil so gullible as to be taken in by such an obvious trick.[78]

Nevertheless, based on the available literature, one may hypothesize that such a forgery with the reference to Beclas did

---

[74] Mansi, *Sacrorum conciliorum*, vol. 16, p. 284, cols. C-D.

[75] Letters, nos. 84, 241, 281, in Laourdas and Westerink, *Photius*, vol. 1, p. 124; vol. 2, pp. 163-67, 232-36.

[76] See testimonies of Niketas Paphlagon and Symeon Magister in Migne, *Patrologiae Graecae*, vol. 105, p. 568, col. B; vol. 109, p. 752.

[77] See, for example, Adontz, *Patmakan usumnasirutiunner*, pp. 479-91.

[78] Ibid., p. 481.

exist, although this view raises a number of questions. If the forgery was the invention of anti-Photian circles, why did other authors repeat it? How did the information, which contained the "Genealogy," enter into Byzantine scholarship? It is noteworthy that the works of contemporary Byzantine authors contain information that could be found only in Armenian sources (for instance, the passage by Theophanes Continuatus regarding Saint Sahak's Vision). The account of that vision about the Arshakuni dynasty is closely related to the information found about the "Genealogy," and scholars agree that this testimony appeared in Byzantine literature thanks to Photius' forged work.[79] The so-called "Genealogy" appears to have wider ramifications for Byzantine and Armenian history than suggested by Byzantine authors and scholars.

Patriarch Photius and Emperor Basil

The friendship that developed rapidly between the two rivals, Photius and Basil, was a significant development, considering, according to Symeon Magister[80] and Georgius Monachus, that when Basil for the first time entered Saint Sophia as an emperor, Photius called him a murderer and a robber and refused him the Eucharist. This had so angered Basil that even after the deposition of the patriarch he twice convened the synods to anathematize him.[81] Years later, by presenting this "Genealogy," Photius now did a great service to Basil as the manuscript provided the illustrious lineage for the emperor. Was this sufficient to receive privileges from the emperor? That question has interested many scholars. The author of a lengthy monograph on the life and activity of Patriarch Photius, Josef Hergenröther,[82] compiled a great deal of essential information about Photius and argued that the hostility between the patriarch and the emperor had ceased thanks to the letter of Theophanes Sphenodaimonos.[83]

---

[79] Bartikyan, *Teopanesi Sharunakogh*, pp. 143, 344; Bartikyan, *Kostandin Tsiranatsin*, pp. 51, 265-66.

[80] Symeonis Magistri, *Annales*, pp. 688-89.

[81] Georgii Monachi, §841.

[82] Josef Hergenröther, *Photius, Patriarch von Konstantinopel: Sein Leben, seine Schriften und das griechische Schisma nach handschriftlichen und gedruckten Quellen*, 3 vols. (Regensburg: Georg Joseph Manz, 1867-1869; repr. Darmstadt, 1966).

[83] Ibid., §§253-54.

Hans-Georg Beck's suggestion that Basil permitted Photius to return to the patriarchal see because he did not want the election of a new patriarch to contribute to the creation of a third party in the already divided Church does not seem convincing because Basil could have elected another candidate of his choice from the two existing parties.[84]

Considering that the relatives and friends of the emperor played leading roles in society, one may assume that Basil supported Photius for other reasons than the forged genealogy.[85] Other factors regarding Photius and the genealogy he presented must be taken into account. Photius composed this forgery while he was in exile in Armenia, and Niketas Paphlagon and Symeon Magister refer to King Trdat. It may be hypothesized that the manuscript was either the *History of the Armenians* by Movses Khorenatsi or a compilation of the works of Armenian historiographers, including Khorenatsi's *History*. Book I of that volume is titled "Genealogy of Greater Armenians." Chapter 87 of Book II might have been of special interest to Photius because it contains a history of the friendship and family ties between Trdat and Kamsar, the founder of the Kamsarakan family: "At that time there came to him his relative and kinsman Kamsar, the eldest son of Perozamat. This Perozamat was the boy whom Burz had rescued and saved when Artashir had slaughtered the Karenian branch of the Pahlav."[86] Khorenatsi further states:

> At the same time there lived another Vzruk Khakan who was an enemy of Kamsar, his [Perozamat's] son. But Kamsar, considering it difficult to live in enmity between two powerful kings, especially because his brothers were not united with him, set out with all his family and entourage and came to Trdat our king, while his brothers went to Shapuh. This Kamsar fought with fearsome bravery in the wars during his father's lifetime.

---

[84] Hans-Georg Beck, *Geschichte der orthodoxen Kirche im byzantinischen Reich* (Göttingen: Vandenhoeck and Ruprecht, 1980), p. 110.

[85] See, for example, Kazhdan, "Sotsial'nye i politicheskie vzgliady," p. 122; Chichurov, *Politicheskaia ideologiia*, p. 54. The fact that Photius considered the bonds between relatives important is attested in his letters; for example, see Letters nos. 92 and 115, in Laourdas and Westerink, *Photius*, vol. 1, pp. 128-29; 152-53.

[86] Moses Khorenats'i, *History of the Armenians*, trans. and comm. Robert W. Thomson (Cambridge, MA: Harvard University Press, 1978), p. 241; cf. Movses Khorenatsi, *Patmutyun Hayots* [History of the Armenians], ed. Manuk Abeghian and Set Harutiunian (repr. Erevan: Armenian Academy of Sciences, 1991), p. 235.

But in [one of] his intrepid assaults he was struck by someone on the head with axe, and a part of the bone of his skull was removed. Although he was cured by medicines, the curve of his head remained incomplete, and for this reason he was called Kamsar.[87]

In addition, Book II, chapter 1, of the same work would also have been of great interest to Patriarch Photius and Emperor Basil. This chapter, among other things, deals with Alexander the Great (from whom Basil descended on his mother's side, according to Theophanes Continuatus[88]) and with Arshakuni, stating:

From then on Arshak the Brave ruled, who was from the seed of Abraham out of the descendants of K'etura, for the fulfillment of the saying of the Lord to Abraham: "Kings of nations will come forth from you."[89]

The following historical event supports the proposition that Photius' work contains material from Movses Khorenatsi's *History*. In 876 Emperor Basil dispatched a delegation to Prince of Princes Ashot Bagratuni of Armenia to request a coronation, since he, Basil, was an Arshakuni and Ashot was "*tagadir aspet Bagratuni*," the Bagratuni coronant knight.[90] Basil's knowledge

---

[87] Khorenats'i, *History*, pp. 241-42; *Patmutyun*, pp. 235-36.

[88] Migne, *Patrologiae Graecae*, vol. 109, p. 232.

[89] Khorenats'i, *History*, p. 130; cf. Khorenatsi, *Patmutyun*, p. 102. The biblical plot regarding "the king of nations" told about the kin of Arshak is present in the passage of the *Vision of Saint Sahak* by Ghazar Parbetsi. See Ghazar Parbetsi, *Patmutyun Hayots* [*History of the Armenians*], ed. Galust Ter-Mkrtchian and Stephan Malkhasiants, modern Armenian trans. and comm., Bagrat Ulubabyan (Erevan: Erevan University Press, 1982), pp. 73-86. The *Vision of Saint Sahak* considered by scholars as a late forged interpolation, was expressed in twelfth century by Nerses Lambronatsi who doubted its authenticity. There is a passage in this *Vision,* which stresses that "the king will rise again from the Arshakuni family and the patriarchal see will be renewed from one of the descendents of Gregory the Illuminator" (ibid., p. 78). Remarkably, it appears also in Byzantium and is attested in the works of Byzantine authors; for example, in Book V, ch. 19, of Theophanes Continuatus, Chronographia is written: "At that time came to reality the foretelling and the prophecy made 350 years ago by Isahak—the most farsighted priest and monk, who was also from the kin of the Arshakuni. He has had the Vision and learned that after [the mentioned] time one of the Arshakuni descendents will bear the scepter of the Roman Empire." See Bartikyan, *Teopanesi*, pp. 143, 344n60; cf. also the same passage in the work by Constantine VII Porphyrogenite, Bartikyan, *Kostandin Tsiranatsin*, p. 51.

[90] *Havakumn patmutian Vardanay*, p. 85.

of this information, which is unusual for an emperor of Byzantium, may be explained by his ethnic or family origin, and it is conceivable that he simply utilized his Armenian origin to achieve political objectives. Basil may have been familiar with Khorenatsi's work or more probably learned of it either through Photius or the "Genealogy" presented by the Patriarch. The fact that Basil asked for the coronation nine years after he ascended the throne also favors the contention that he learned about the hereditary right of the Bagratuni dynasty as coronants from the manuscript presented by Photius.

If the above proposition is valid, a question arises: How did the Patriarch of Constantinople read Khorenatsi's work? Scholars have maintained that Photius did not know any languages except Greek. Yet the argument that he read Khorenatsi in the Armenian language challenges this view and the commonly accepted belief that Byzantine intellectuals of that era did not learn any other language, even Latin, because of the ideology of Roman exclusiveness. The situation was similar in the Latin West; rarely did someone know a foreign language. It was not until the Renaissance that the age of categorized grammar and dictionaries arose. Saint Gregory I (d. 604) had served as an apocrisiary (papal legate) at Constantinople but seemingly did not learn Greek; Pope Vigilius (540-55) spent eight unhappy years there and never knew the language. When Leo IX (1048-54) wrote in Latin to Peter III of Antioch, the latter sent the letter to Constantinople for a translation. Such cases widened the rift between East and West. At various councils, the papal legates addressed the assembled fathers in Latin and no one understood them; the councils deliberated in Greek, and the papal legates wondered what was being said. Failure in communication bred suspicion on both sides, and when translators were called in, questions rose as to whether their versions could be trusted.

The situation was different in the case of Photius, however. He was twice in exile in Armenia (all together for seventeen years), and because of his exceptional abilities, capacity for work, and thirst for knowledge, as well as his Armenian origin, it is plausible that he knew Armenian. During his first exile, deprived of his relatives and friends,[91] he would have time dur-

---

[91] See Laourdas and Westerink, *Photius*, no. 21, vol. 1, p. 21; Photius to Theophanes Sphenodaimonos, no. 84, vol. 1, p. 124; no. 174, vol. 2, pp. 47-61, and no. 188,

ing the nine or ten years, in addition to writing letters to rehabilitate his reputation and post, to learn the local language, if he indeed did not know it prior to his exile. He certainly had the opportunity to read the original works of Armenian historiographers. It might be that in the monastery (which housed many books) he became acquainted with Khorenatsi's *History* and was informed about Basil's ambitions to have a royal lineage. Quite possibly, here in exile Photius envisioned the plan for his own salvation incorporating his forgery into an old manuscript containing the work of Khorenatsi, which was presented to Basil. He was in contact with Theophanes (note the letters written to him), through whom he placed that manuscript sent from Armenia in the palace library.

Another hypothesis confirming the aforementioned issue may be valid. A passage from *Vita Ignatii* contains an interesting but obscure phrase: "Ἀλεξανδρίνοις γράμμασιν" (ALEXANDRINOIC GRAMMASIN).[92] Scholars have debated the meaning of this phrase; some have proposed that it means "by Alexandrian letters." In an article explaining this enigmatic phrase, Guglielmo Cavallo tries to prove that this phrase means Coptic majuscule.[93] This hypothesis, however, does not seem persuasive; the reading of this majuscule does not demand extraordinary abilities from Theophanes Sphenodaimonos (or Phrenodaimonos) whose reputation as a wise and intelligent person is familiar to Byzantine authors.[94] Why then could such an educated man not be able to read this writing and advise the emperor that this manuscript be deciphered only by Photius? It means that the manuscript was written in a language which was incomprehensible for Theophanes but was familiar to Photius. This language could be Armenian. Moreover, the obscure phrase "Ἀλεξανδρίνοις γράμμασιν" could be a contaminated variant of—"Ἀρμενιάκοις γράμμασιν"—that is, "by Armenian letters."[95]

The learned and ambitious Patriarch Photius of Constan-

pp. 87-88.

[92] Victor Gardthausen, *Griechische Paleographie*, vol. 2: *Die Schrift*, 2d ed. (Leipzig: Veit, 1913), §251.

[93] Guglielmo Cavallo, "Γράμματα᾽ Ἀλεξανδρίνα," *Jahrbuch der Österreichischen Byzantinistik* 24 (1975): 23-59.

[94] See, for example, Symeonis Magistri, *Annales*, p. 689.

[95] The adjective Ἀρμενιάκοις was in use by Byzantine historiographers at the time.

tinople was still living in 886 when Emperor Leo the Wise re-established union with the Roman Church. Quite possibly, because of this change in Byzantine policy the emperor obliged Photius to resign and in his stead named his own brother Stephan as the Patriarch of Constantinople. It is also possible that Photius was not particularly favored by the successors of Basil. When another emperor, the grandson of Basil, wrote *Vita Basilii* praising his grandfather, he mentioned the name of Photius only once and then casually.

* * *

Armenians in Constantinople of the ninth century achieved high positions in all spheres of political, ecclesiastical, cultural, and military life. Their strong tendency to be surrounded by relatives is remarkable. Indeed, one can even conclude that they arranged marriages between Armenian families (as, for example, in the case of Leo, son-in-law of Arshavir quaestor; and Smbat, the Logothete of the Course and son-in-law of Bardas). At the same time, despite the strong family bonds, these Armenian figures were susceptible to the influences and callousness characteristic of medieval traditions; being Armenian was not a safeguard against intrigues resulting even in the murder of one's own kin when political or other gain and ambitions were at stake.

❋ 5 ❋

PATTERNS OF CONTACT AND COMMUNICATION: CONSTANTINOPLE AND ARMENIA, 860-976

Tim Greenwood

The eastern frontier of the Byzantine Empire in 860 bordered on the Islamic caliphate and stretched northeastward from Seleucia on the Mediterranean Sea across the Taurus and Anti-Taurus mountains to Trebizond on the Black Sea coast.[1] On the Arab side, a fortified borderland known as the *thughur* had developed from which frequent raids were launched into Byzantine Anatolia. The Byzantine response to such raids was defensive in character, seeking to limit the devastation and to ambush the raiders on their withdrawal rather than trying to prevent the attack in the first place.[2] The strategic advantage lay with the Arabs, as they could choose one or more invasion routes from their bases at Tarsus, Melitene, and Karin/Theodosiopolis.[3] By contrast, the major Byzantine fortresses were located on the northern and western margins of the Anatolian plateau, protecting the fertile coastlands and Constantinople itself rather than the frontier region. This strategic imbalance denied the Byzantine Empire access to, and hence influence across, Armenia. The isolated district of Sper in the Upper Chorokh (Choroh) valley provided the only point of direct contact along this eastern frontier between

---

[1] For a recent history of the Byzantine eastern frontier in the ninth and tenth centuries, see Mark Whittow, *The Making of Orthodox Byzantium, 600-1025* (London: Macmillan Press, 1996), pp. 310-57. For Byzantine interaction with Armenia, see Timothy W. Greenwood, "Armenian Neighbours (600-1045)," in *The Cambridge History of the Byzantine Empire c.500-1492*, ed. Jonathan Shepard (Cambridge: Cambridge University Press, 2008), pp. 333-65.

[2] These tactics are set out in a Byzantine military treatise, titled "On Skirmishing Warfare or De Velitatione Bellica," in *Three Byzantine Military Treatises*, trans. and ed. George T. Dennis (Washington, DC: Dumbarton Oaks, 1985), pp. 144-239.

[3] Modern Erzerum or Erzurum.

the Byzantine Empire and territory held by an Armenian princely family. Even there, the Byzantine influence was intermittent.[4] In
the absence of consistent Byzantine intervention in Armenia, it is
hardly surprising to discover that Armenian princes jostled
among themselves for caliphal favor, with barely a glance towards
Constantinople. From an Armenian perspective, Constantinople
appeared remote, disengaged, and largely irrelevant, at best a
refuge in the event of sustained attack.[5] As recently as 838, prominent Bagratuni and Artsruni princes had participated in an Arab
raid deep into Byzantine territory which had resulted in the sack
of Amorion.[6]

The situation in 976 was radically different. The frontier had
shifted significantly southeastward, running from the Syrian coast
south of Antioch northwest to the Euphrates River, then north
past the headwaters of the Murad Su (Eastern Euphrates) close to
Lake Van and the sources of the Araxes to the east of Theodosiopolis and finally up to the mouth of the Chorokh River on
the Black Sea coast. The thughur had been comprehensively dis-
mantled, replaced by a network of small Byzantine administrative
units known as themes.[7] The Abbasid Caliphate had collapsed
under internal political and religious stresses and the latest regional Arab power to challenge Byzantine supremacy in the east,
the Hamdanid emirate of Aleppo, had been seen off in the previous

---

[4] As recently as 850, Grigor Bagratuni, prince of Sper, had joined forces with the
emir of Melitene and attacked the Byzantine Empire, although he rapidly changed
sides when menaced by the caliph's Turkic general, Bugha al-Kabir. See René
Grousset, *Histoire de l'Arménie des origines à 1071* (Paris: Payot, 1947), p. 366.

[5] Shapuh Amatuni and his son Hamam are reported to have emigrated from Ar-
menia in or around 791. See Ghevond, *Patmutiun Ghevondeay Metsi Vardapeti
Hayots* [History of Ghevond, Great Vardapet of Armenia], ed. Karapet Ezian (St.
Petersburg: I.N. Skorokhodov, 1887), pp. 168-69, trans. Zaven Arzoumanian, *History
of Levond, the Eminent Vardapet of the Armenians* (Wynnewood, PA: St. Sahag and
St. Mesrop Armenian Church, 1982), p. 149.

[6] Josephus Genesius, *Regnum Libri Quattuor Iosephi Genesii*, ed. Anni Lesmüller-
Werner and Hans Thurn (Berlin: de Gruyter, 1978), p. 47, trans. Anthony Kaldellis,
Genesios, On the Reigns of the Emperors (Canberra: Australian Association for Byzantine Studies, 1998), pp. 62-63; Theophanes Continuatus, *Chronographia*, ed. Immanuel Bekker (Bonn: E. Weber, 1838), pp. 126-31.

[7] See Nicolas Oikonomidès, "L'organisation de la frontière orientale de Byzance
aux Xe–XIe siècles et le taktikon de l'Escorial," in *Actes du XIVe Congrès international
des études byzantines*, ed. Mihai Berza and Eugen Stansecu (Bucharest: Editura
Academiei Republicii Socialiste Romania, 1974), pp. 285-302.

decade.[8] Byzantine military tactics were now geared towards offensive warfare.[9] Most pertinently, Byzantium was now actively involved in expanding into Armenian districts, displacing the leading princes who received estates and imperial titles by way of exchange.

This essay will explore just one of these transformations along the eastern frontier in this period, namely the development of relations between successive emperors based in Constantinople and the Armenian elite. First impressions suggest that two phases may be distinguished. The first extended from 860 to approximately 920 and was characterized by seemingly limited contact between the parties, both in terms of scope and frequency. The second lasted from the accession of Romanos I Lecapenus (920-44) as emperor down to the death of John I Tzimisces (969-76) and witnessed an expanded network of diplomatic contacts, with long-term significance for all concerned.

Of course, any periodization is a modern construct, imposed and hence artificial. These phases broadly correspond to the profile of the surviving sources and one should be wary about equating lack of evidence about direct contact with the absence of contact. Nevertheless, it is possible to discern a pattern in Byzantine dealings with individual Armenian princely houses, a progression, from first contact to final annexation of territory by way of concession, accompanied by the displacement and migration of the leading figures. Although the chronology and tempo of relations with Constantinople varied from family to family, the overall Byzantine strategy seems to have been remarkably consistent: attract, engage, and eventually absorb. Whether Byzantine expansion into Armenian-held territory had always been the intended outcome, or whether it came to be so, is hard to determine. However, it is undoubtedly the case that Byzantium fostered tensions within the Armenian noble houses and came to acquire future rights which enabled it to intervene at times of political stress, notably during contested successions. The period 860-976 witnessed the intrusion of Byzantium across western and central Armenia through the gradual acquisition of what

---

[8] For a short introduction to the Hamdanids, see Hugh N. Kennedy, *The Prophet and the Age of the Caliphates* (Harlow: Longman, 2004), pp. 265-82.

[9] See Eric McGeer, *Sowing the Dragon's Teeth: Byzantine Warfare in the Tenth Century* (Washington, DC: Dumbarton Oaks, 1995).

may be termed "Armenian futures," that is rights which were activated and matured only after the death of the grantor. Since the first instance of Byzantine expansion into Armenian-held territory occurred after 920, the two-phase periodization, despite its flaws, will be retained.

Before examining the first phase, it may be useful to offer a brief overview of the principal sources. The four Armenian historical narratives will be familiar to many. The *History of the House of Artsrunik* by Thomas Artsruni records the deeds of the Artsruni princes of Vaspurakan, in southern Armenia.[10] It originally extended to the year 904, and, although a continuator resumed the narrative, his account is focused upon the achievements of the first king of Vaspurakan, Gagik Artsruni, and does not refer to the Byzantine Empire.[11] The *History of the Armenians* by John Catholicos offers greater breadth in that it was not limited to one family; on the other hand, it has very little to offer in the way of information about Byzantine actions or ambitions, other than the exchanges of letters with the patriarch of Constantinople Nicholas I Mystikos.[12] It seems highly likely that the long-standing doctrinal tensions and suspicions between the two churches influenced the scope and content of his composition, which stretched as far as the autumn of 923. The *Universal History* of Stephen of Taron, on the other hand, dates from 1004 and covers the whole period under discussion. However, it offers a Spartan coverage of the first two-thirds of the tenth century, focusing predominantly on monastic foundations and Byzantine military successes against Arab-held fortresses in the thughur.[13] Matthew

---

[10] Thomas Artsruni, *Tovmayi Vardapeti Artsrunvoy Patmutiun Tann Artsruniats* [Thomas Vardapet's History of the House of Artsrunik], ed. Karapet Patkanian/Kerope Patkanov (St. Petersburg: I.N. Skorokhodov, 1887; repr. Tiflis, 1917, and Delmar, NY: Caravan Books, 1991), trans. Robert W. Thomson, *Thomas Artsruni: History of the House of Artsrunik'* (Detroit: Wayne State University Press, 1985).

[11] Thomson, *House of Artsrunik'*, pp. 15-17.

[12] John Catholicos [Hovhannes Katoghikos Draskhanakerttsi], *Patmutiun Hayots* [History of the Armenians], ed. Mkrtich Hovsep Emin (Moscow. 1853; repr. Tiflis: N. Aghaniants, 1912, and Delmar NY: Caravan Books, 1980), pp. 265-84, trans. Krikor H. Maksoudian, *Yovhannēs Drasxanakertc'i, History of Armenia* (Atlanta: Scholar's Press, 1987), pp. 189-97.

[13] The period from the accession of Smbat I in 891 to the death of Ashot III Bagratuni, his grandson, in 977, is covered in less than thirty pages of text. See [Stephen of Taron], *Stepannosi Taronetsvoy Patmutiun tiezerakan* [The Universal

of Edessa's *Chronicle* opens in the year 952 and supplies an intriguing but confused narrative of events, as one might expect from a twelfth-century author attempting to reconstruct the events of two hundred years earlier.[14] While each of these sources has a contribution to make to this essay, their individual characteristics need to be appreciated. It is particularly frustrating that there are no contemporary Armenian historical narratives through which to study the greater Byzantine involvement in Armenian affairs in the second and third quarters of the tenth century and the local reactions to that involvement.

The principal Byzantine source through which to study these contacts is a diplomatic handbook, compiled in about 952 by Emperor Constantine VII Porphyrogenitus (908-59) for his young son Romanos II (959-63), so that he might learn about the various regions, peoples, and princes with whom he would be dealing, their past relations with the empire, and imperial claims to sovereignty over them.[15] This compendium of statecraft, the *De Administrando Imperio*, provides much valuable material about the diplomatic techniques employed on the eastern frontier. It includes a case study on how to develop and maintain contact with several branches of an Armenian princely family and, perhaps more surprisingly, an account of a diplomatic failure that almost jeopardized Byzantine interests to the north of Theodosiopolis.[16] One of the striking features of this text is that it projects the emperor resident in Constantinople retaining personal respon-

---

History of Stephen of Taron], ed. Stepan Malkhasiants (St. Petersburg: I.N. Skorokhodov, 1885), pp. 159-87; trans. Frédéric Macler, *Etienne Asołik de Taron, Histoire universelle* (Paris: Imp. nationale, 1917), pp. 10-49.

[14] Matthew of Edessa, *Patmutiun Matteosi Urhayetsvoy* [History of Matthew of Edessa] (Jerusalem: St. James Press, 1869), pp. 1-40, trans. Ara E. Dostourian, *Armenia and the Crusades Tenth to Twelfth Centuries: The Chronicle of Matthew of Edessa* (Lanham, MD: University Press of America, 1993), pp. 19-36.

[15] Constantine Porphyrogenitus, *De Administrando Imperio*, ed. Gyula Moravcsik and trans. Romilly J.H. Jenkins (Washington, DC: Dumbarton Oaks, 1967); Romilly J.H. Jenkins and Francis Dvornik, *Constantine Porphyrogentius, De Administrando Imperio—Commentary* (London: Athlone Press, 1962). For an invaluable guide, see James Howard-Johnston, "The *De Administrando Imperio:* A Re-examination of the Text and a Re-evaluation of Its Evidence about the Rus," in *Le Centres proto-urbains russes entre Scandinavie, Byzance et Orient*, ed. Michel Kazanski, Anne Nercessian, and Constantin Zuckerman (Paris: P. Lethielleux, 2000), pp. 301-36.

[16] *De Administrando Imperio*, ch. 43 and 46 respectively; Jenkins and Dvornik, *Commentary*, pp. 156-80; Howard-Johnston, "Re-examination," pp. 317-18, 326-27.

sibility for the conduct of diplomacy with neighboring states
and peoples. Successive emperors are presented negotiating with
Armenian princes, both indirectly through envoys and diplomatic
correspondence and occasionally in person, when individuals
were conveyed to Constantinople for a reception or other ceremony in the Great Palace. Emperors are also depicted concluding treaties, interpreting earlier agreements, even determining
the precise location of the frontier.[17] At one level, the degree of
involvement in the operation of policy on the part of the emperor is
not surprising, given the role that Constantine VII has in the composition of the text. But it may also be the case that Constantine
was trying to emphasize to the youthful Romanos the need to
take personal responsibility for future activities in this theater of
the eastern frontier, negotiating directly with local Armenian
elites, to ensure that the emperor was not sidelined or excluded
altogether through the creation of local cross-border networks of
power and authority under the private control of great magnate
families such as the Skleroi or Phokades.[18] In other words, the role
of the emperor in Constantinople as arbiter of relations with the
various noble Armenian houses may be more of a fiction than
has been recognized hitherto, that the *De Administrando Imperio*
is advocating greater imperial engagement along the eastern
frontier rather than simply recording it.

Infrequent Contact, 860-920

Traditionally the year 863 has been heralded as a decisive moment on the eastern frontier, when the tide turned and the era of
Byzantine advance began. It was in this year that the emir of Melitene and his forces were intercepted and annihilated, that the
head of the Tarsus raiding party was surprised and killed, and
that the leader of the Paulicians, a religious sect fiercely antagonistic toward the Byzantines, died. Yet on closer inspection, it is
difficult to detect any sustained attempt to reverse the balance
of power. The series of long-distance raids initiated under Emperor
Basil I (867-86) brought few long-term benefits. After a disas-

---

[17] See *De Administrando Imperio*, ch. 45.

[18] For the great families, see Jean-Claude Cheynet, *The Byzantine Aristocracy and Its Military Function* (Aldershot: Ashgate, 2006), articles 1, 3, 8.

trous attack on Tarsus in 883, it appears that the imperial government decided to close down the eastern frontier, at least as far as offensive operations were concerned. There are several possible explanations for this, not least of which was "the gravitational pull of events in the Islamic world" identified by Mark Whittow, who noted that Byzantine gains tended to coincide with periods of internal crisis within the Abbasid Caliphate.[19] The converse was also true, that the temporary Abbasid revival in the late ninth century coincided with Byzantine quiescence along the eastern frontier. In 883, the Zanj rebellion was finally quashed while Ibn Tulun, the fractious governor of Egypt, died in 884. Under the campaigning caliph, al-Mu'tadid (892-902) and his son al-Muktafi (902-08), the Abbasid regime recovered much of its authority, and this was largely maintained under al-Muqtadir (908-32) until the mid-920s, when significant Qaramita raiding began again.[20] It cannot be merely coincidental that Byzantine activities along the eastern frontier revived in the middle of this decade.

Byzantine actions in the east should also be interpreted in the context of Byzantine relations with the emergent Christian Bulgar state. Emperor Leo VI and his immediate successors were compelled to afford priority to the Balkan theater of operations.[21] The proximity of the Bulgar state to Constantinople, its appeal to the local elites as an alternative source of legitimization and power and, eventually, the imperial pretensions of the Bulgar leader Symeon, all contributed to this redirecting of attention away from the east. It was, however, two catastrophic Byzantine defeats, at Bulgarophygon outside Adrianople in 896 and at Achelous in 917 which determined that the Bulgar threat had to be countered before any sustained initiatives could be undertaken in the east.

From the perspective of the leading Armenian princes, namely Ashot Bagratuni, prince of princes (862-84) and ultimately king (884-890), his son and successor Smbat (890-914), and the several Artsruni princes of Vaspurakan, the second half of the ninth

---

[19] Whittow, *Byzantium*, p. 329.

[20] See Kennedy, *The Prophet and the Age of the Caliphates*, pp. 177-85.

[21] For a recent study, see James Howard-Johnston, "A short piece of narrative history: war and diplomacy in the Balkans 921/2-spring 924," in *Byzantine Style, Religion and Civilization in Honour of Sir Stephen Runciman*, ed. Elizabeth M. Jeffreys (Cambridge: Cambridge University Press, 2006), pp. 340-60.

century was characterized by spasmodic and seemingly ephemeral contact with Constantinople. For them, the principal arbiter of power remained the caliph exercising control through his designated deputy, although the increasingly independent Sadjid emirs of Adharbaydjan (south-southeast of Armenia), Afshin and then Yusuf, strongly influenced Armenia between 890 and 925. Without exception, Armenian princes looked to them first, rather than to the Byzantine emperor, for recognition and support. Thus, for example, in 891, it was only after Smbat had received a crown from the caliph via Afshin that he contacted Emperor Leo VI (886-912).[22] Smbat justified his conduct to an irritated Afshin on the grounds that such contact enabled him to obtain valuable vestments and other ornaments by way of diplomatic exchange for transmission on to the caliph or Afshin himself. Whether or not this was the case, the very fact that John Catholicos reports about Smbat justifying his behavior reveals a good deal about Smbat's own political priorities. As noted, when reading the two main Armenian historical sources for this period, it is striking how little the Byzantine Empire seems to impinge upon the lives of the principal Armenian princes. Rather, it is the Sadjid emirs who intervened in Armenian affairs and with whom Armenian princes entered into agreements. As late as 926, the continuator to Thomas Artsruni records that King Gagik Artsruni of Vaspurakan was temporarily entrusted with responsibility for the countries of Armenia and Georgia by the Sadjid emir Yusuf when the latter was summoned southwards to defend Iraq from attack by the Qaramita.[23]

This is not to argue that Byzantium was entirely excluded. After Ashot I Bagratuni had been crowned king on August 26, 884, the emperor Basil I acknowledged him as his "beloved son," and Leo VI addressed Smbat I Bagratuni in similar terms. In 892, Smbat even sent prisoners who had been captured at Dvin to Leo, although this seems to have been Smbat's own campaign rather than a joint-operation.[24] The *History* of John Catholicos contains a

---

[22] Regarding the crown, see John Catholicos, *Patmutiun,* pp. 146-47; Maksoudian, *Yovhannēs,* p. 132. For contact with Leo VI, see John Catholicos, *Patmutiun,* p. 158; Maksoudian, *Yovhannēs,* pp. 137-38.

[23] Thomas Artsruni, *Patmutiun Tann Artsruniats,* p. 289; Thomson, *House of Artsrunik',* p. 351.

[24] John Catholicos, *Patmutiun,* pp. 160-61; Maksoudian, *Yovhannēs,* pp. 138-39.

well-known exchange of letters between Patriarch Nicholas I of Constantinople and John Catholicos in the immediate aftermath of Yusuf's execution of Smbat Bagratuni in 914, following which Smbat's son, Ashot II Erkat (Iron, 915-28/29), traveled to Constantinople to seek support.[25] But if anything, these letters seem to confirm the irregular nature of such contact. Nicholas wrote that he was at a great distance from John, hardly indicative of close relations.[26]

It is also telling that Nicholas refers back to the endeavors of the patriarch Photius in pursuit of ecclesiastical harmony with the Armenian Church which had broken off over thirty years before; this suggests a lack of meaningful communications on this issue in the intervening period.[27] Although he referred several times to the *curopalate*—by whom he meant the curopalate of Iberia, Atrnerseh—and the leader of Abasgia, Nicholas did not mention any Armenian prince by name, whether Bagratuni, Artsruni, or other. This again implies a degree of separation. Moreover whereas three of Nicholas' extant letters were addressed to the leader (*exousiastes*) of Abasgia and one to the most renowned curopalate of Iberia, none of his letters before 924 were written to Armenian princes.[28]

For his part, John Catholicos was keen to stress the relationship between Ashot and the young emperor Constantine VII, but this very emphasis suggests a revival of contact rather than continuity. Moreover, Ashot's flight to Constantinople and subsequent return at the head of an army falls squarely within a familiar expression of contact, according to which the empire was treated as the last refuge of a fugitive prince.[29] This was the only concrete support that Ashot received from the empire. In the remainder of his *History*, John Catholicos depicts Ashot desperate-

---

[25] John Catholicos, *Patmutiun*, pp. 265-84; Maksoudian, *Yovhannēs*, pp. 189-97.

[26] John Catholicos, *Patmutiun*, p. 266; Maksoudian, *Yovhannēs*, p. 190.

[27] See Igor Dorfman-Lazarev, *Arméniens et byzantins à l'époque de Photius: Deux débats théologiques après le triomphe de l'orthodoxie* (Louvain: Peeters, 2004); Timothy W. Greenwood, "Failure of a Mission? Photius and the Armenian Church," *Le Muséon* 119:1-2 (2006): 123-67.

[28] Nicholas I Mystikos, *Letters*, trans. Romilly J.H. Jenkins and Leendert G. Westerink (Washington, DC: Dumbarton Oaks, 1973), nos. 46, 51, 162 (to the *exousiastes* of Abasgia), and no. 91 (to the *curopalate*).

[29] John Catholicos, *Patmutiun*, pp. 284-86, 292-93; Maksoudian, *Yovhannēs*, pp. 197-98, 201-02.

ly trying to establish himself in various parts of his father's former domains, with only limited success. This lack of Byzantine support should probably be linked to the Byzantine disaster at Achelous in August 917. Nevertheless, when the newly-appointed Byzantine commander John Kourkuas attacked Dvin in 922, he found that it was held by none other than Ashot II who mounted a vigorous and successful defense on behalf of Nasr al-Subuki, the caliph's deputy in Armenia.[30]

If there were only the Armenian sources from which to re-construct relations between Byzantium and Armenia in the period 860-920, the resulting impression would be one of infrequent and superficial contact. Chapter 43 of the *De Administrando Imperio* supplies an important corrective. It records that Leo VI sought to attract several members of the princely family of Taron into relationship with Byzantium through the distribution of hon-ors and presents.[31] Arguably the targeting of Taron as the focus of attention was very deliberate. Taron was the most westerly region of Armenia under direct Armenian control and hence closest to the Byzantine frontier.[32] Moreover, as John Catholicos describes, Taron was briefly the focus of armed hostilities at the very end of the ninth century, when succession problems within the princely family prompted the intervention of neighboring Armenian princes and local emirs.[33]

Leo VI attempted to exploit this instability, pressing the new prince Grigor to travel to Constantinople. Grigor rebuffed the invitation but permitted first his illegitimate son Ashot and then his brother Apoganem to attend upon the emperor. Both were honored with imperial rank, lavishly entertained, and then re-turned. Evidently, this was a confidence-building exercise, de-signed to allay Grigor's suspicions while at the same time demon-strating the material and honorific rewards he could expect. This initiative was helped by the consistent use of the same imperial agent, a *basilikos protospatharios* named Constantine Lips, first to

---

[30] *Stepannosi Taronetsvoy Patmutiun tiezerakan*, p. 170; Macler, *Etienne Asołik*, pp. 24-25.

[31] *De Administrando Imperio*, ch. 43; Jenkins and Dvornik, *Commentary*, pp. 156-64.

[32] Karen N. Yuzbashyan, "L'administration byzantine en Arménie aux Xe-XIe siècles," *Revue des études arméniennes* n.s., 10 (1973-74): 140-44.

[33] John Catholicos, *Patmutiun*, pp. 174-77; Maksoudian, *Yovhannēs*, pp. 145-47.

make contact and then to ferry each of the figures to and from the capital.

Finally, Grigor himself was persuaded to attend the emperor. He was appointed to the high imperial rank of *magistros* and to the office of *strategos* of Taron, although the latter seems to have been little more than a ceremonial post to enable the prince to be paid an annual stipend of ten pounds of gold and ten pounds of miliaresia (silver coins). There is no evidence that he ever fought for the Byzantine army, raised forces, or paid anything resembling taxation or tribute.[34] Since a magistros of Taron was present at a court reception in Constantinople on January 1, 900, it seems that this diplomatic activity occurred in the immediate aftermath of the hostilities, when Grigor was still establishing himself.[35] He was also given the house of Barbaros in Constantinople to use as a residence during this visit and thereafter, anticipating that he would be making further visits. Soon after his brother Apoganem made a second visit and was given the same house of Barbaros, together with an advantageous marriage to the daughter of Constantine Lips.[36] Unfortunately for Byzantine hopes, Grigor died just days after his return to Taron in unknown but undeniably suspicious circumstances. The double grant of the same property in Constantinople had significant repercussions later on.

Chapter 43 therefore confirms that conspicuous efforts were made to attract various members of the princely family of Taron into the sphere of Byzantine influence at the very end of the ninth century. It is not clear, however, whether or to what extent the relationship between Constantinople and the princes of Taron continued after that time, nor indeed how effective it was, at least from a Byzantine perspective. There are several comments at the start of the chapter noting the unreliability of the prince of Taron.[37] These suggest that Grigor judged it advisable to maintain good relations with the neighboring Arab Shaybanid emir in northern

---

[34] It is possible that his elevation to this office may be associated with the creation of the *theme* of Mesopotamia, between 899 and 901, and the appointment of Manuel of Tekis as its first strategos.

[35] *De Ceremoniis*, Bk I, ch. 24, p. 139, line 18.

[36] *De Administrando Imperio*, ch. 43, lines 72-88.

[37] Ibid., lines 7-26: "while in word he pretended to esteem the friendship of the emperor, in fact he acted at the pleasure of the chief prince of the Saracens . . . he was found . . . to prefer the cause of the Saracens."

Syria in preference to the emperor, echoing the stance of Gagik
Artsuni toward the Sadjid emir Yusuf. What is unclear, how-
ever, is whether the frustration over the perfidious conduct of
Grigor, prince of Taron, reflects attitudes from the time of Leo
VI, when the first dossiers were put together, or whether it echoes
the view of the compiler, Constantine VII, looking back over
Grigor's checkered career in imperial service.

Regular Contact, 920-976

If the first phase was characterized by limited diplomatic contact
between Constantinople and Armenia, the years after 920 seem to
have witnessed an expansion in the scope and frequency of these
contacts. This second period also saw the maturing of "Armenian
futures," that is, what happened when the future interests and
rights promised to the Byzantine emperor by an Armenian prince
in return for present recognition or support finally crystallized.
Frustratingly, the contemporary Armenian historical narratives
record almost nothing of this more active phase of Byzantine
policy in the east or Armenian perceptions of it. Instead, it is
necessary to rely on Greek and Arabic sources in order to study
the Armenian elite and their relations with Constantinople during
this fifty-year period. This discussion will focus on two Byzantine
texts before turning to consider one Arabic geographical survey
that supplies a salutary corrective. Deep within a vast and rambling
compendium known as the *De Ceremoniis*, a compilation also
attributed to the emperor Constantine VII, there is a list of
protocols or letter-headings to be used on imperial correspondence
when writing to foreigners.[38] It seems highly likely that it dates
from the 920s. Table 1 presents the relevant extracts:

Table 1
De Ceremoniis, Book II, Chapter 48

To the Prince of Princes of Greater Armenia. A three-solidus
chrysobull. Constantine and Romanos, Autokratores, Augusti,

---

[38] *De Ceremoniis*, Bk II, ch. 48, pp. 687-88. For a thorough study of Chapter 48,
see Bernadette Martin-Hisard, "Constantinople et les Archontes du Monde Caucasien dans le Livre des Cérémonies, II, 48," in *Travaux et Mémoires*, ed. Gilbert
Dagron (Paris: de Boccard, 2000), pp. 357-594.

great Emperors of the Romans, whose faith is in Christ who is God, to X, most famed Leader of Greater Armenia and our Spiritual Son.

To the Prince of Aspurakan or Vasparakan, who now is honored Prince of Princes. A three-solidus chrysobull. Constantine and Romanos, Autokratores, Augusti, Emperors of the Romans, whose faith is in Christ who is God, to X, most famed Prince of Princes.

To the Prince of Kokovit, Armenia; to the Prince of Taro, Armenia; to the Prince of Moex, Armenia; to the Prince of Auzan, Armenia; to the Prince of Sune, Armenia; to the Prince of Vaitzor, Armenia; to the Prince of Chatziene. Armenia; to the 3 princes of the Servotioi, who are called Black Children. Protocol for all those listed above. Command from the Christ-loving despots, to X Prince of Y.

To the Catholicos of Armenia, to the Catholicos of Iberia, to the Catholicos of Albania. Protocol to the 3 Catholicoi. Command from the Christ-loving despots to X most-pious leader of Y.

Several important propositions emerge from this list. The first two protocols attest direct correspondence between the emperor and the principal Bagratuni and Artsruni princes. Evidently there had been a change in designation: the prince of Vaspurakan is described as "now" honored as prince of princes. It is known that the prince in question, Gagik Artsruni, held this rank by 925 because there is a single letter from the Patriarch of Constantinople Nicholas I to the "prince of princes" on the occasion of the death of the Catholicos of Armenia.[39] This must refer to John Catholicos, who died while under the protection of Gagik in either 924 or 925. Intriguingly, therefore, Gagik was elevated to the rank of prince of princes some four years before the death of Ashot II Erkat in 929. This change reflects the supremacy enjoyed by Gagik Artsruni until his death in 943/44, as well as the temporary eclipse in Bagratuni fortunes. This diminution in Bagratuni power can be traced back to the final years of Smbat I Bagratuni and his ignominious death, but it persisted during the era of Ashot II Erkat and his brother and successor Abas I Bagratuni (929-53). The travails of John Catholicos in the last years of his life, shuttling between several princes in search of per-

---

[39] Nicholas, *Letters*, no. 139. For a different interpretation of the identity of the recipient, see Martin-Hisard, "Archontes du Monde Caucasien," pp. 423-25.

sonal security, may be taken as indicative of the rapid changes
in the balance of power within Armenia. Evidently, John became
disillusioned with the ability of Ashot II to protect him, transferring first to latter's cousin and rival, Ashot lord of Bagaran,
the so-called anti-king, and then to Gagik Artsruni.[40] It is not clear
whether Gagik's promotion in rank involved the simultaneous
demotion of Ashot II. The headings are slightly different, notably in respect of the epithet "spiritual son" which is withheld
from Gagik. Significantly the *De Administrando Imperio* titles
Abas not as prince of princes but rather as magistros.[41] This
downgrading is corroborated in a letter composed between 929
and 936 by the imperial secretary Theodore Daphnopates, who
also distinguished the prince of princes Gagik from the magistros
Abas.[42] Whether or not Ashot was himself demoted during his
lifetime, it is clear that his successor held a lesser title.

The earliest instance of contact between an Artsruni prince
and the Byzantine emperor in the tenth century emerges from
Chapter 43 of the *De Administrando Imperio*.[43] Gagik, prince of
Vaspurakan, together with Atrnerseh, curopalate of Iberia, and
Ashot, prince of princes, all complained to Emperor Romanos I
Lecapenus about the *roga* or salary being paid to Grigor, prince
of Taron, arguing that he did nothing more than they did in the
service of the empire.[44] As the curopalate died in 923, this com-
plaint must date from between 920 and 923. Bernadette Martin-
Hisard has argued persuasively for 922, associating the com-
plaint with a Byzantine attack on Dvin in that year.[45] The letter
from Patriarch Nicholas I to Gagik in 925 represents the earliest
extant correspondence with the prince of Vaspurakan. On this
occasion as well, it was Gagik who initiated the exchange, with
the aim of securing the succession of his candidate as Catholicos of
Armenia by means of a ceremony in Constantinople. The letter is

---

[40] John Catholicos, *Patmutiun*, pp. 357-58; Maksoudian, *Yovhannēs*, p. 232.

[41] *De Administrando Imperio*, ch. 44, line 9.

[42] Theodore Daphnopates, *Correspondance Théodore Daphnopatès*, ed. and
trans. Jean Darrouzès and Leendert G. Westerink (Paris: Editions du Centre National
de la Recherche Scientifique, 1978), Letter 4, lines 42-43: *Kakikion archonta ton
archonton*; line 57: *to te Kakikio kai to magistro Apasekio*.

[43] *De Administrando Imperio*, ch. 43, lines 109-14.

[44] This is indirect evidence for the nominal nature of the title of strategos of Taron
that Grigor had previously been granted.

[45] Martin-Hisard, "Archontes du Monde Caucasien," pp. 393-94.

Nicholas' reply to that inquiry. Nicholas was not afraid to raise the divisive issue of doctrinal difference, maintaining that not only would Gagik's candidate have to be instructed accurately in doctrine and ecclesiastical order but also that Gagik himself should be attached to "our Christ-loving Emperor and to our most holy Church of God by the confession of faith and in the spirit of correct doctrine."[46] At the same time, Nicholas referred to the "confession of friendship" by which Gagik was "attached to our Christ-loving Emperor and to our most holy church of God." Although the patriarch was uncompromising in his defense of orthodox belief as he understood it, clearly it was possible to adhere to other doctrinal positions and yet still enjoy a relationship of friendship with the emperor.[47]

Returning to the protocols, the list in *De Ceremoniis* defines no fewer than seven other Armenian princes with whom the emperors Constantine and Romanos were in direct communication. These are described by reference to individual regions or districts in Armenia—specifically Kogovit, Taron, Mokk, Vayots Dzor, Andzevatsik, Siunik, and Khachen—and not in terms of princely house, imperial title, or through ties with other noble families. They comprise middle-ranking figures who rarely feature in the Armenian historical record, and then only in terms of their relationship with one of the leading Bagratuni or Artsruni princes. Yet their presence on this list indicates that the emperors thought it worthwhile to develop a direct relationship with each of them, independently of any influence that might be brought to bear by virtue of their ties with the leading princes. The Armenian historical tradition tends to view the tenth century predominantly in terms of the leading figures, and even then Bagratuni in preference to Artsruni. This list suggests that the principal figures were far more reliant on the support of a network of lords functioning at the level of the district

---

[46] Nicholas, *Letters*, no. 139, lines 43-46.

[47] This was not the end of the matter. A letter purportedly from "Gagik of Vaspurakan, king of Armenia, to the Emperor of the Greeks Romanos" has survived in the *Book of Letters*. Its tone is conciliatory. The author considers himself as a "servant to you, holy and elevated archbishop, patriarch and heir of the Apostles and to you, holy king who preserves the tradition of the heir of the throne of Christ, since we in this country of Armenia, maintained obedience to your imperial throne and to your patriarchal succession, as the books of historians attest." See *Girk tghtots* [Book of Letters], ed. Hovsep Izmiriants (Tiflis: T. Ravtiniants and M. Sharadze, 1901), p. 295.

than the Armenian historical tradition imparts. Despite the re-emergence of the title of "king" in Armenia in 884, the exercise of power still depended to a large extent on the allegiance of local lords and their armed forces.[48] The appearance of these figures in this list suggests that the emperor appreciated their significance.

It is noteworthy that the list includes the prince of Taron, at this time the same figure, Grigor, with whom Leo VI had previously developed ties. Just as Leo VI also met Grigor's brother and il-legitimate son, so, too, did Romanos I Lecapenus encourage con-tacts with both the sons and the nephews of Grigor, and profited from their rivalries. Although the breadth of this list of protocols is impressive, covering the leading figures of nine different princely houses, it does not express the imperial down-reach within each of those families. For that, Chapter 43 of the *De Ad-ministrando Imperio* confirms simultaneous contact with other family members. Collectively the list identifies the principal Armenian princes with whom the emperor was in contact; it does not reflect the true number of Armenian nobles whom Romanos I sought to attract into relationship.

The list refers separately to the Catholicoses of Armenia, Iberia, and Albania, implying individual correspondence with each of them. Again, there are no surviving letters addressed to or received from them. Another letter, however, composed by Theodore Daph-nopates indicates a direct contact with the bishop of Siunik in about 933. This is the first surviving piece of correspondence between Constantinople and Siunik in the tenth century, although it refers to two earlier communications.[49] Theodore severely reprimanded the bishop of Siunik for teaching that Christ had only one nature and hence contrary to the doctrinal position of

---

[48] For the coronation of Ashot I Bagratuni on August 26, 884 as "King of the Ashkenazians," that is, King of Greater Armenia, see John Catholicos, *Patmutiun,* pp. 138-40; Maksoudian, *Yovhannēs,* pp. 128-29, 272-73.

[49] Theodore Daphnopatès, *Correspondance,* Letter 10, pp. 108-41. The start of the letter traces the recent exchange of correspondence, referring to an imperial ordinance on the issue of correct belief sent to the bishop of Siunik and his reply rejecting the emperor's statements. Theodore mentions that the letter from the bishop of Siunik had needed to be translated from Armenian into Greek, thereby confirming that the imperial administration was able to accommodate communications in other languages. Theodore's letter closes by commanding the bishop to read and show it to laymen, monks, and priests in the country of the Armenians, implying that the issue of heterodox belief was not confined to Siunik.

the Greek Church which, following the Council of Chalcedon, maintained two natures. This pressure from Constantinople may have had an impact because some fourteen years later, in 947, the Armenian Catholicos Anania Mokatsi undertook a vigorous defense of the anti-Chalcedonian position in the course of which he was compelled to discipline the metropolitan bishop of Siunik for his pro-Chalcedonian sympathies.[50] The presence of a pro-Chalcedonian party within Siunik is supported by the temporary elevation of Vahan, metropolitan of Siunik, to the rank of Catholicos of Armenia after Anania's death in 967, from where he was expelled because of "the love and agreement" with the Chalcedonians expressed in his letters. It is intriguing to observe that for all his energy in defending the Armenian doctrinal position, even to the extent of countenancing a second baptism for those who had already received baptism in the Chalcedonian tradition, Anania Mokatsi was succeeded, albeit briefly, by someone who professed diametrically opposite views.[51] This suggests that there was substantial support for both confessions across the regions of Armenia. Following his deposition by a synod convened at Ani, Catholicos Vahan I Siunetsi sought refuge with King Apusahl-Hamazasp of Vaspurakan, Gagik's son. This may have reflected the fulfillment of the hopes expressed by Patriarch Nicholas I some forty years earlier that Gagik acknowledge his doctrinal error. The Arstruni association with Byzantine orthodoxy is striking and contrasts with consistent Bagratuni antipathy.

In order to study the subsequent development of the ties between Constantinople and the Armenian elite and the circumstances in which future legal rights were realized, it is necessary to return to the *De Administrando Imperio*. Chapter 43 traces the progress and outcome of the diplomatic contacts between the emperor and various members of the princely house of Taron across two generations. In 923, Prince Grigor of Taron asked Romanos to exchange his interest in the house given him in Constantinople for an estate in Keltzene, a district within the empire. Grigor

---

[50] Jean-Pierre Mahé, "L'Eglise arménienne de 611 à 1066," in *Histoire du Christianisme des origines à nos jours,* vol. 4: *Évêques, Moines et Empereurs 610-1064,* ed. Gilbert Dagron, Pierre Riché, and André Vauchez (Paris: Desclée, 1993), pp. 507-10; Martin-Hisard, "Archontes du Monde Caucasien," p. 405.

[51] *Stepannosi Taronetsvoy Patmutiun tiezerakan,* pp. 178-79, 181; Macler, *Etienne Asołik,* pp. 36, 41.

even requested a specific property, one that had recently been sequestered following Bardas Boilas' failed revolt earlier that year.[52] Evidently, Grigor was very well-informed about recent events inside the empire, to the extent of knowing which estates were available for redistribution. In the end, he was awarded another estate, but this affair antagonized his nephew, Tornikios, the son of Apoganem, who claimed in a letter that his own inherited rights in respect of that house in Constantinople had been violated. Later on, after the death of Grigor, Tornikios returned to this subject, pleading that if he was not entitled to either the original house or the replacement property, both should revert to Emperor Romanos to prevent Tornikios' cousins from getting their hands on them.

This second generation of princes in Taron seems to have been very quick to appeal to the emperor to protect their respective positions, offering major concessions in return. Grigor's elder son Bagarat devised in a will that any children born of his marriage to the sister of a high-ranking official in Constantinople would inherit his entire country; in return, he secured an interest in the same estate in Keltzene, though only for the lifetime of his wife. Grigor's nephew Tornikios went even further, offering his country to the emperor in return for safe-conduct of himself and his family to Constantinople because of the oppression he was experiencing at the hands of his cousins. By the time an imperial agent arrived in Taron to take up the offer, Tornikios was dead, having left a will in similar terms to the proposal he had made when alive.[53] One is left with the distinct impression that Bagarat and Tornikios were competing with one another for imperial favor.

The climax of Chapter 43 is very significant.[54] Although entitled to the whole territory of Tornikios under the terms of his will, Romanos I listened to the arguments of Tornikios' cousins, Bagarat and Ashot, who maintained that they would be unable to live if he occupied that country as his own. They offered to concede a fortress called Oulnoutin and its surrounding land in exchange for the territory of their cousin. It seems highly likely that Tornikios had inherited lands in eastern Taron, while his cousins

---

[52] *De Administrando Imperio*, ch. 43, lines 89-95. The property that Grigor requested had previously belonged to one of the rebels named Tatzates.

[53] Ibid., lines 135-63, 166-77.

[54] Ibid., lines 171-86.

had taken over western Taron. If Romanos were to occupy eastern Taron, Bagarat and Ashot would be effectively cut off from the rest of Armenia and hence "unable to live." Romanos I agreed to their request. Perhaps the most interesting feature of this very involved chapter is that Romanos did not insist on what he was legally entitled to but accepted a compromise. Nevertheless, an important fortress had been secured, a successful outcome from which, one assumes, Emperor Constantine VII intended that his fourteen year old son should learn. This chapter was not intended to provide a complete history of Taron. Instead it was designed to show to the future Emperor Romanos II the importance of developing relations with several members of the same princely family over generations. It was, after all, impossible to second-guess who would emerge as the leading prince in any power-struggle, whether for succession within the family or for survival in violent competition with neighboring houses. It was therefore important to back several figures simultaneously, being careful to secure from each of them rights or interests in return with which to intervene or negotiate in the future.

This essay includes only a cursory discussion of two of the four chapters in the *De Administrando Imperio* which comment most directly upon Armenian affairs. As discussed, Chapter 43 contemplates Byzantine contact and then intervention in the complicated circumstances of the princely house of Taron. Chapter 44 records the succession of Kaysid emirs in Manzikert, a small emirate established to the north of Lake Van. Chapter 45 describes Byzantine operations around the major fortified center of Theodosiopolis, and the challenges of negotiating with local Georgian notables. Finally, Chapter 46 records a failed Byzantine attempt to take control of the commercially vibrant town of Ardanudj, north of Theodosiopolis.

These four chapters are not primarily prosopographical or biographical in focus, despite the plethora of names recorded and the tortuous family situations that are touched upon. Rather, there is a legalistic quality to each of them, concentrating on who enjoyed possession and control of land in each of the theaters, how the dispositions changed over time, and on what basis the emperor could lay claim to sovereignty or ownership of particular fortresses or cities. An important distinction is drawn between what was legally correct, that is, what territory the emperor could legitimately claim was his, and what was practicable, that is, what was politically possible.[55] This is shown clearly in Chapter 43. Although Tornikios made Romanos I the sole heir of all his territory, Romanos heeded the appeals of the sons of Grigor and exchanged his rights for other territory.

Chapter 46 serves as a cautionary example from the recent past, of the dangers of pursuing legal rights without paying sufficient attention to the political realities or consequences. The chapter reports that in 923 Romanos I Lecapenus was unexpectedly offered possession of a key Georgian fortress and thriving commercial center called Ardanudj, well beyond the immediate frontier.[56] He took steps to secure its occupation by Byzantine troops, smuggling them across the intervening territory under the guise of an embassy. When the Byzantine annexation of Ardanudj came to light, however, two of the princes who controlled territory adjacent to Ardanudj threatened to transfer allegiance to the Arabs and campaign with the armies of "Persia," the contemporary term for the Sadjid emirate of Adharbaydjan. Romanos hastily backed down, denying all responsibility, withdrawing his forces, and publicly berating his envoy for exceeding his orders.[57] This placated the princes. In fact, as the chapter makes plain, the envoy was simply following the verbal orders he had received from Romanos. Significantly, this failure did not have a detrimental effect on the envoy's subsequent career under Romanos, indicating that he retained the emperor's confidence. This chastening experience seems to have deterred Romanos from making any further attempts at outright annexation of territory then under Armenian or Georgian control, even if these were of strategic importance and even if he was invited by the prince then in possession, unless it bordered on the empire, as Oulnoutin evidently did. The fact that this final dossier reports a failure after three discrete chapters reporting Byzantine success is most probably not accidental. It was included by Constantine VII as a salutary reminder to the youthful Romanos about the perils of overstretch in a politically fragmented and fluid region.

[55] A similar argument is developed by Jonathan Shepard, "Constantine VII, Caucasian Openings and the Road to Aleppo," in *Eastern Approaches to Byzantium*, ed. Antony Eastmond (Aldershot: Ashgate, 2001), pp. 25-28.

[56] *De Administrando Imperio*, ch. 46, lines 57-62.

[57] Ibid., lines 64-93, 128-48.

It can be seen therefore that a degree of pragmatism colored Byzantine policy toward the Armenian elite in this period. Direct military action against either an Armenian or Georgian prince was ruled out. Armed intervention in support of an individual prince had been shown to be of very limited value. When Zoe's regency council had been unable or unwilling to support Ashot II Erkat Bagratuni consistently after 914, he had turned elsewhere for assistance.[58] Instead, successive emperors sought to engage with as many of the leading figures in each princely house as possible, drawing them into relationship. The outstanding question is: to what purpose? What were Byzantine intentions towards the Armenian elite? This issue of Byzantine motivation along this sector of the eastern frontier is difficult to answer with any degree of confidence. The slow rate of territorial expansion lends some support to the view that Byzantium did not set out to absorb Armenian-held territory, that the empire merely sought to neutralize potential threats and avoid antagonizing Armenian and Georgian princes. On the other hand it is unpersuasive to deduce Byzantine policy solely on the basis of what happened.

To this end, there is value in returning once more to the opening words of Chapter 43, when Constantine VII addresses his son directly.

"It is right that you should not be ignorant of the parts towards the rising sun, for what reasons they became once more subject to the Romans, after they had first fallen away from their control."[59] Tellingly, there is no differentiation between Arab-held and Armenian-held territory. If these chapters are exemplary and if they reflect the particular interest of Constantine VII, then it seems that he had greater ambitions in the east than has perhaps been acknowledged, ambitions that included the annexation of Armenian territory. And in response to the question "why," again the opening lines of this chapter offer a possible answer. These describe the character and conduct of Grigor in singularly unflattering terms. Grigor was found to be unreliable, "double-faced," revealing future plans to the caliph whilst at the same time appear-

---

[58] John Catholicos, *Patmutiun*, p. 321; Maksoudian, *Yovhannēs*, pp. 22, 215, where Ashot obtained recognition and military support from Constantine III of Abasgia.

[59] *De Administrando Imperio*, ch. 43, lines 4-6.

ing to be a loyal Byzantine client.[60] These sentences represent the only substantial biographical passage in these chapters, projecting a particular image of an Armenian prince. Constantine seems to be proposing that all Armenian princes were like this, soliciting favors from both caliph and emperor.

From a Byzantine perspective, given the utter untrustworthiness of the Armenian notables as clients, territorial acquisition was the only alternative. It seems clear that by 952, the date of compilation of the *De Administrando Imperio*, this had become Byzantine policy. It is therefore not surprising to read in the *Universal History* of Stephen of Taron that in 966 the Romans took control of Taron after the death of Ashot.[61] The late eleventh-century Byzantine historian Skylitzes records the same event slightly differently, recording that two brothers, Gregory and Pankratios, ceded their country of Taron to the emperor Nikephoros Phokas in exchange for the titles of *patrikios* and rich, income-generating lands.[62] Skylitzes implies that this concession was suggested by the brothers, but when viewed in the context of the earlier acquisition of rights and claims to territory by testamentary disposition, it appears more likely that this had been negotiated previously by Ashot, namely, that at his death his territory should revert to the emperor.

Although this episode marks the conclusion of Byzantine engagement with an independent Taron, a relationship that had extended across at least three generations, it is important to remember that not every Armenian princely house was at the same stage in terms of its relationship with Byzantium. Each relationship will have developed in different ways and at its own tempo. The agreement of 974 between Emperor John Tzimisces and King Ashot III Bagratuni (952-77), as described by Matthew of Edessa, contained a promise of friendship, by which the emperor probably guaranteed not to advance beyond his borders, in return

---

[60] Ibid., lines 7-26.

[61] *Stepannosi Taronetsvoy Patmutiun tiezerakan*, p. 183; Macler, *Etienne Asołik*, p. 44.

[62] Skylitzes, *Ioannis Scylitzae Synopsis historiarum,* ed. Hans Thurn (Berlin and New York: De Gruyter, 1973), p. 279, trans. and comm. Bernard Flusin and Jean-Claude Cheynet, *Jean Skylitzès Empereurs de Constantinople* (Paris: P. Lethielleux, 2003), pp. 234-35.

for Ashot's supply of men and supplies.[63] There is no evidence to suggest that at this stage Tzimisces acquired, or was looking for, any other rights or claims to intervene in Ashot's kingdom, either immediately or in the future. Such rights were only finally obtained half a century later, when Hovhannes-Smbat III Bagratuni conceded them to Basil II in 1022. The terms of this agreement stipulated that Ani would revert to Byzantium at the death of Hovhannes-Smbat.[64]

There is one final perspective through which to study the relationship between Constantinople and Armenia, namely in terms of the payment of tribute or taxation. In his description of Armenia, Adharbaydjan, and Arran, the Arab geographer Ibn Hawqal records ten figures who were tributaries of the Sallarid emir Marzuban ibn Muhammad in 955. Four of them were clearly Armenian:

> Abul-Qasim Ali ibn Jafar [the vazir of Marzuban] imposed on . . . Abul-Qasim al-Wayzuri, lord of Wayzur, 50,000 dinars plus offerings . . . he imposed on the descendants of al-Dayrani to pay according to the previously agreed (sum), 100,000 dirhems yearly, but exempted them from the payment for four years in recognition of their having yielded up to him Daysam ibn Shadhluya, who had sought their protection but whom they then handed over treacherously. He imposed on the descendants of Sunbat with regard to their districts of Armenia Interior, 2,000,000 dirhems but afterwards remitted 200,000 dirhems for compassionate reasons. He imposed on Sennacharib lord of Khadjin 100,000 dirhems, plus offerings and horses to the value of 50,000 dirhems.[65]

Following Vladimir Minorsky, Wayzur is the Arabic form of Vayots Dzor, a separate principality in Siunik. The Banu Dayrani

---

[63] Matthew of Edessa, *Patmutiun*, pp. 20-21; Dostourian, *Crusades*, pp. 27-28.

[64] Greenwood, "Armenian Neighbours," pp. 360-61.

[65] Ibn Hawqal, *Opus geographicum*, ed. Johannes H. Kramers (Leiden: E.J. Brill, 1938), pp. 354-55, trans. Vladimir F. Minorsky, "Caucasica IV," *Bulletin of the School of Oriental and African Studies* 15 (1953): 519-20. This translation was checked against the Arabic by Andrew Marsham of the University of Edinburgh, whose valuable assistance I gratefully acknowledge. The text specifies dinars rather than dirhems in respect of Vayots Dzor but this looks like a copyist's error. Vayots Dzor is a small mountainous district, and it seems inconceivable that it would be liable for the gold equivalent of 1,500,000 dirhems, an amount in the order of the sum levied on the whole of the Bagratuni lands.

represents the line of Derenik Artsruni, the father of Gagik I Artsruni of Vaspurakan, prince of princes. Likewise the Banu Sunbat comprises the descendants of King Smbat I Bagratuni. Finally, the list refers to Sennacharib or Senekerim, prince of Khachen. One striking feature of this group is that they all appeared in the list of protocols found in the *De Ceremoniis*.

Aside from the striking absence of any ethnic or religious differentiation within the list between Armenian, Albanian, Kurdish, and Arab princes, or the relative amounts levied upon them, several observations should be made. In the first place, the document proves that in 955 Armenian princes were liable for the payment of, considerable sums to an Arab emir of Adharbaydjan. This occurred at a time when Byzantine attention was centered on meeting the military challenge of the Hamdanid emir Sayf al-Dawla of Aleppo and reducing the Arab fortresses in the Taurus and Anti-Taurus, west and south of Armenia. In spite of the pattern of contact and communication with Constantinople outlined above, the emergence of Marzuban ibn Muhammad after 942 prompted most Armenian princes, including the leading Bagratuni and Artsruni families, to pay or at least to agree to pay, tribute. Conversely, there is no evidence to suggest that the emperor ever attempted to levy taxes or extract tribute from Armenian princes, at least while they were in possession of their ancestral lands. Indeed, it is striking that the only persons in the *De Administrando Imperio* who were recorded as paying tribute to the emperor were the three Kaysid emirs of Manzikert, Abu Sawada, Abul Aswad, and Abu Salim, and they were forced to pay only after the raids against them by John Kourkuas in 928 and 931.[66] While developing ties with Constantinople, even the most prominent Armenian princes continued to be mindful of the threat posed by powerful Arab emirs based in Adharbaydjan and the Djazira. Successive Sadjid emirs exerted influence over a thirty-year period (890-925), and the fate of King Smbat I Bagratuni was not easily forgotten by Armenian princes. This helps to explain the swift submission by several Armenian princes, including king Gagik I

---

[66] *De Administrando Imperio*, ch. 44, lines 33-34, 44-45, 58-60, 63-65, 85-91, 110-12. For these campaigns of Kourkuas, see Ibn al-Atir, in Alexandre A. Vasiliev, *Byzance et les Arabes*, vol. 2, pt. 2: *Extraits des sources arabes*, trans. Marius Canard (Brussels: Institut de philologie et d'histoire orientales, 1950), pp. 151-53; *Stepannosi Taronetsvoy Patmutiun tiezerakan*, pp. 169-70; Macler, *Etienne Asolik*, pp. 24-25.

Artsruni, to the Hamdanid Sayf al-Dawla in 940.[67] In the rapidly changing world of Transcaucasia in the tenth century, these princes could not know that Sayf al-Dawla would come under increasing military pressure from the Byzantine Empire and that his dominance of Armenia would be short-lived. Theirs was a decision made on the basis of the contemporary situation and recent experience. It is all too easy to interpret these events with the benefit of hindsight and fail to appreciate the genuine apprehension generated within Armenia by the emergence of emirs like Sayf al-Dawla or Marzuban ibn Muhammad. Although the latter did not impinge directly upon Byzantine ambitions in the east, this does not mean that Marzuban was not a considerable, if ephemeral, figure in Armenia in the middle of the tenth century.

Marzuban died in 957, only two years after the date attached to this list of tributaries, and his successors failed to maintain his political ascendancy. Marzuban's death marked the end of the tribute system articulated by Ibn Hawqal. Whether or not the Bagratuni kings had ever paid the stipulated 2 million dirhems in full or part, after 957 the tax receipts and duties through which this tribute had been collected for onward transmission were now available to Ashot III for expenditure within Armenia. It cannot be coincidental that this period witnessed significant building activity within the kingdom, enabling Ashot III to move his capital from Kars to Ani in 961. Moreover, one may conjecture that it was the control of these resources which enabled the Bagratuni kings of Ani to remain aloof from Byzantium for so long, immune to the attractions of wealth and status within the Byzantine Empire. The extraordinary growth of Ani in the second half of the tenth century must reflect an economic boom, one that the Bagratuni kings were in prime position to exploit. Their steadfast resistance to Byzantine blandishments should be related to their control of the commercial center of Ani.

Conclusions

This essay set out to explore the pattern of contact and communication between Constantinople and the Armenian elite between

---

[67] Ibn al-Azrak, in Vasiliev, *Byzance*, vol. 2, pt. 2, p. 115; Ibn Zafir, in Vasiliev, *Byzance*, vol. 2, pt. 2, pp. 122-23; Whittow, *Byzantium*, pp. 319-20.

860 and 976. Relations were initiated with a range of figures from each princely house, although the surviving sources reveal this only when studied collectively. Moreover the guiding hand behind the single richest source, the *De Administrando Imperio*, namely Constantine VII Porphyrogenitus, shaped his selection of Caucasian material very carefully, stressing to his young son Romanos that he needed to engage directly with the Armenian and Georgian elites and that their loyalty could not be relied upon. In this, Constantine VII was proved to be prescient, as Armenian forces were to play significant roles in the service of Bardas Skleros and Bardas Phokas in the civil wars that characterized the first years of his grandson, Basil II.[68] Indeed one could make a strong case that it was Basil II who heeded his grandfather's advice, persisting with a strategy of obtaining "Armenian futures" which matured at times of greatest political stress, that is times of succession, and presented an opportunity for direct and ostensibly legitimate intervention.

One final issue must be considered. Was this strategy, of territorial annexation and imperial expansion, intended from the outset? Such a notion underpinned the thinking of Emperor Constantine VII in 952, when he penned the introduction to Chapter 43. It was also at play in Taron, when Tornikios named the emperor as the main beneficiary in the event of his death, in return for safe-conduct for his wife and child. The date of Tornikios' death is not securely established; some have argued for 939 as the year when Oulnoutin was transferred into imperial possession although one can make a case for a slightly earlier date in the 930s.[69] Chapter 46 of the *De Administrando Imperio*, however, contains an earlier voluntary concession of territory to the emperor, for Ashot Kiskasis offered to give his city of Ardanudj to the emperor Romanos I in 923, although it is not clear what he expected or hoped to obtain in exchange. Although this affair ended in failure, the very fact that such a concession of territory could be anticipated by an oppressed local lord suggests that such practices may not have been unprecedented. At the very least, it pushes the earliest date for Byzantine territorial ambitions back to 923, but it is conceivable

---

[68] See Catherine Holmes, *Basil II and the Governance of Empire* (Oxford: Oxford University Press, 2005), pp. 311-13, 450-61.

[69] Howard-Johnston, "Re-examination," p. 326n78, in favor of the 939 date.

that such ambitions may have been germinating before this. One feature is clear: Byzantium was content to play a very long game when it came to annexing Armenian-held territory.

Ivory of Emperor Constantine VII Porphyrogenitus Being
Crowned by Christ, 10th Century (Echmiadzin Treasury, now
Pushkin Museum, Moscow)

✽ 6 ✽

INTERSECTION OF SOCIETY, CULTURE, AND RELIGION: THE CONSTANTINOPLE STYLE AND ARMENIAN IDENTITY

Ronald T. Marchese and Marlene R. Breu

The history of a people can be documented by the physical objects they produce and use.[1] Objects communicate social identity and help define societal values and moral principles. They also illustrate artistic accomplishment. The collection of objects in the Armenian Apostolic (Orthodox) churches of Istanbul illustrates the interconnection between material culture, social identity, artisanship, and communal belief. Making objects for the church was a pious act and a confirmation of faith. Contributions from one's own hand instilled a sense of fulfillment and engagement in the spiritual life of the community. Thus, church members commissioned objects of faith as personal and communal expressions to glorify God. Such objects demonstrate a deep attachment to Armenian Christian values and culture in an otherwise Muslim world.

[1] We wish to offer our deepest and sincere gratitude to His Beatitude Mesrob II, Armenian Patriarch of Istanbul and All Turkey for his support and blessing; to Father Krikor Maksoudian of the Armenian Diocese, New York City, who provided translations of the inscriptions; and to His Grace Archbishop Aram Ateshyan for his encouragement, collegiality, and friendship. We also extend sincere appreciation to the church officials, boards of directors, members of the clergy, the staff at the Armenian Patriarchate, and many in the Armenian community of Istanbul for the opportunity to undertake a study of this vital and most personal element of their culture. We acknowledge with thanks financial support from Western Michigan University, especially funds from the Faculty Research and Creative Activities Support Fund; the Graduate School of the University of Minnesota; and the McKnight Foundation.

Faith, however, was more than an abstract expression. Armenian artisans of the Ottoman capital gave physical form to that which was intangible, as they defined an elaborate style of secular and religious art—*the Constantinople style*. From the seventeenth century, the evolution of the Constantinople style reflected the increase in the Armenian population of the city. Continuous Armenian immigration from historic Armenian lands in the east infused the city with regional and sub-regional styles that added bold elements to an otherwise conservative, mostly late Byzantine, urban material culture. In addition, by the eighteenth century, European cultural encroachment into the oriental flavor of Constantinople fostered a more cosmopolitan atmosphere that encouraged experimentation outside the accepted canons of Armenian church art.[2]

Artistic experimentation required patrons, and although the church initially served as the source of such patronage, an Armenian aristocracy, the *amira* class, eventually superseded it. Members of this class possessed not only material wealth but also social status in the Armenian community. They attracted Armenian artisans, who migrated to the city in hopes of gaining valuable commissions and whose talents continuously refreshed the Constantinople style with new ideas. Artistic achievement thus matched the growing opulence and grandeur of the city as the Armenian community came to play an important role in the economic, political, and cultural life of the Ottoman capital.[3]

The Population of Constantinople

Armenians actively participated in the city's rebirth and the level of prosperity it attained in the Ottoman period. Most Armenians were of simple means and occupation, but merchants, entrepreneurs, inventors, craftsmen, clergymen, bureaucrats, fishermen, and porters contributed their talents to its cosmopolitan atmosphere. In many respects, Constantinople became a microcosm of

---

[2] Ronald T. Marchese and Marlene R. Breu, *Splendor and Spectacle: Textile Treasures from the Armenian Orthodox Churches of Istanbul, Turkey* (Istanbul: Çitlembik, 2010); Marchese and Breu, *Treasures of Faith: Sacred Relics and Artifacts from the Armenian Orthodox Churches of Istanbul* (forthcoming).

[3] Marchese and Breu, *Treasures of Faith.*

Anatolia, a mosaic of ethnic groups and cultural traditions.[4] Normally, the best approach in understanding population impact in a region is through census records. The first Ottoman census in the capital and the district north of the Halich or Golden Horn in 1477 registered over 16,300 families, more than 400 of which were Armenian. This placed the Armenian population fourth in rank behind the Muslim, Greek, and the recently arrived Jewish population. Although important as a starting point, the census of Sultan Mehmed II the Conqueror (1444-46, 1451-81) and those of his successors do not provide a complete picture of the ethnic diversity that contributed to the city's renaissance. Immigration not only altered the social and cultural composition of the city; it was "encouraged," especially for those groups and families which possessed wealth, social status, artistic and intellectual competence or were engaged in commerce and industry.

The loyalty such minorities demonstrated contributed to the economic and cultural stability of the city. Although small in number in the fifteenth and sixteenth centuries, the Armenian population was important beyond its numbers since it held a dominant position in the silk trade. After the early seventeenth century, its position and impact on the city's commercial interests further increased relative to a more substantial growth in its population. This increase corresponded to an expanding transit trade with Persia and India.[5] Persian silk, Indian linen, Ankara wool, and Bursa tobacco and silk enriched some Armenian families who came to play a vital role as middlemen and patrons in the prosperity of the Ottoman capital in general and in the religious culture of the Armenian Church in particular. By the eighteenth century, Armenian bankers and entrepreneurs became important sources of wealth and contributed vitally to the process of modernization of the Ottoman state. Such concentration of wealth stimulated the developing artisan classes, especially those associated with precious metal. Armenian craftsmen, many of whom were involved in the *kuyumju* (jeweler) trade, possessed excellent reputations as jewelers, engravers, makers of gold and silver wire, sheet silver,

---

[4] Marchese and Breu, *Splendor and Spectacle.*

[5] Ibid.; Robert Mantran, "Foreign Merchants and the Minorities in Istanbul during the Sixteenth and Seventeenth Centuries," in *Christians and Jews in the Ottoman Empire: The Functioning of a Plural Society*, ed. Benjamin Braude and Bernard Lewis, 2 vols. (New York: Holmes and Meir, 1982), vol. 1, p. 133.

and manufacturers of gold and silver tableware (Fig. 1).[6]

Patriarchal records, though available as a source of data on the Armenian population, add little to the official Ottoman censuses, even though many registered baptisms, marriages, and, in a more restricted context, the number of Armenian households in a *mahalle* or quarter (Map 1). As a result, a total count, either by the number of individuals per household or in the Armenian *millet* or ethno-religious community as a whole, is difficult to determine with any degree of certainty. Since birth/death rates varied among the Muslim and non-Muslim populations, no adequate consensus exists for the city at any given time, and the data indicating increases or decreases were based solely on the ability or the desire of the Ottoman authorities to provide an accurate count. It is safe to assume that the number of Armenian residents steadily increased in the Ottoman capital either by natural increase in the birth rate or by "newcomers" from both the better-established Armenian middle class of the larger urban centers of the empire and the lower-class artisans and peasants from despoiled areas of historic Armenia.[7]

Revitalization of Constantinople

Prior to the Ottoman conquest, Constantinople's population had shrunk to an alarmingly low level from its erstwhile approximately one million inhabitants in the tenth and eleventh centuries to no more than thirty to forty thousand in the mid-fifteenth century.[8] Immediately after the Turkish seizure of the city, the sultan, in order

---

[6] Garo Kürkman, *Ottoman Silver Marks* (Istanbul: Mathusalem, 1996); Hovsep Tokat, *Armenian Master Silversmiths* (Los Angeles: Van Publishing, 2005); Marchese and Breu, *Splendor and Spectacle*; Marchese and Breu, *Treasures of Faith*.

[7] Dickran Kouymjian, "Armenia from the Fall of the Cilician Kingdom (1375) to the Forced Emigration under Shah Abbas (1604)," in *The Armenian People from Ancient to Modern Times,* vol. 1: *The Dynastic Periods: From Antiquity to the Fourteenth Century,* ed. Richard G. Hovannisian (New York: St. Martin's Press, 1997), p. 11; Razmik Panossian, *The Armenians: From Kings and Priests to Merchants and Commissars* (New York: Columbia University Press, 2006), pp. 69, 84. See also J. Semerdjian, "The Armenian Patriarch of Constantinople" (2006), at Hye Etch, the Online Book about the Armenians, http//:www.hyeetch.nareg.com.au/.

[8] Alexander A. Vasiliev, *A History of the Byzantine Empire, 324-1453,* 2 vols. (Madison: University of Wisconsin Press, 1964), vol. 2, pp. 482ff; Halil Inalcik, *The Ottoman Empire: The Classical Age: 1300 -1600,* trans. Norman Itzkowitz and Colin Imber (London: Weidenfeld and Nicolson, 1973), p. 140.

Map 1. Approximate Distribution of Armenian Churches and Armenian Neighborhoods

to rejuvenate the local culture, "invited" educated and professional artisan Greeks from the Morea (Greece), Izmir (Smyrna), and Trebizond, and Armenians from Tokat, Amasia, Bursa, and Kayseri (Caesarea), with offers of free housing, temporary tax exemption, a supply of building materials, and opportunities for employment.[9] When such offers failed, the Ottomans used other methods. Following a well-established Near Eastern tradition that long predates Islam, the early Ottoman rulers had succeeded in transforming their previous capitals of Bursa and Edirne into great metropolises by forced immigration or the *sürgün*. Since many districts in the city as well as outlying villages had been depopulated, Ottoman provincial governors were instructed "to send four thousand families from Rumelia and Anatolia to settle in Istanbul."[10] Nevertheless, opportunities for personal advancement and wealth were stronger incentives for immigration and, over the course of time, these new arrivals prospered.[11]

Further, Christian religious leadership for minority groups was either reconfirmed, as it was for the Greek Orthodox population, or newly established, as it was for the Armenians in the city. Benjamin Braude makes this clear in that the "relative security of Istanbul and the Balkans . . . was reason enough to try to encourage an autonomous see, the so-called Patriarchate of Istanbul, as a focus of loyalty for Armenians within the empire."[12] Armenian Christians from Anatolia were established in different quarters of the city and "within a short time, these new arrivals had constructed remarkable homes and churches."[13]

Encouraging immigration, on the one hand, and forced deportation, on the other, are more than a subtle exercise in terminology. There was a number of such impositions on minority populations in recently conquered districts. This is evident in Mehmed's conquest of Kaffa in the Crimea and in the area of Karaman in Ana-

---

[9] Mantran, "Foreign Merchants," p. 128. More than a thousand years earlier, Constantine the Great had used a similar approach to entice the best families of ancient Rome to immigrate to his new city, Constantinople.

[10] Inalcik, *Ottoman Empire*, p. 140.

[11] Richard Clogg, "The Greek *Millet* in the Ottoman Empire," in Braude and Lewis, *Christians and Jews*, pp. 185-207; Mantran, "Foreign Merchants," pp. 127-37.

[12] Benjamin Braude, "Foundation Myths of the *Millet* System," in Braude and Lewis, *Christians and Jews*, pp. 82ff.

[13] Inalcik, *Ottoman Empire*, p. 141.

tolia. The number of Armenian deportees to the capital, however, is difficult to determine, but in the census of 1477 they appear as the "Armenians from Karamaniya."[14] Resettlement continued in the reign of Sultan Selim I the Grim (1512-20) after his eastern campaigns of 1514-17 when a substantial number of Armenians were deported to the western Ottoman provinces in general and Constantinople in particular. Conquest, famine, and the general anarchy that followed war also stimulated Armenian immigration to more secure areas. This pattern of encouraged or imposed immigration continued throughout the sixteenth century, especially with the addition of Armenian youth to the Janissary military corps of forcibly converted Christians.[15]

A century later, the Polish-Armenian cleric Simeon Lehatsi, a resident of Constantinople for a number of years, wrote that there were 40,000 Armenian emigrant hearths in the city (1604). This most likely referred to individuals and not households. All together, the Armenian population, including Galata (this district possessed only 62 Armenian households at the end of the fifteenth century), was approximately 50,000.[16] After the eighteenth century, "at least in population—Constantinople became the most important Armenian city in the world."[17]

Placed in context, it is quite evident that the Armenian population had increased significantly in size, stature, and wealth since the time of Sultan Mehmed II. This is indicated not only by the greater number of churches in the city but also by the number of Armenian civil servants and administrators who held vital positions at the Ottoman court, especially in the late eighteenth century and throughout the nineteenth century. The increase in Armenian officials was very likely due to the Greek uprising and subsequent Greek war of independence beginning in 1821.[18] Prior to this, the Greek population, empowered by the Greek Patriarchate and providing crucial economic and administrative service, enjoyed a privileged position, including high appointment in the Ottoman bureau-

---

[14] Kouymjian, "Armenia," pp. 13ff.

[15] Panossian, *Armenians*, pp. 70-71.

[16] Kouymjian, "Armenia," pp. 26ff; Mantran, "Foreign Merchants," pp. 128-29.

[17] Kouymjian, "Armenia," p. 26.

[18] George Young, *Constantinople* (New York: Barnes & Noble, 1992), p. 189; Clogg, "Greek *Millet*," pp. 185-207.

cracy.[19] That situation limited the opportunities available to an emerging Armenian elite who had to settle for positions of importance within their own millet in order to display their talent and wealth rather than in the broader arena of Ottoman administration.

After the Greek war of independence, Armenians who were well-placed within their community became active in Ottoman elite circles and the economic milieu, including the imperial mint, gunpowder manufacturing, chief bakers of the court, and privileged architects with valuable commissions—hence the "most reliable Christian group in the state."[20] The change in status to "favored" millet enhanced the social and cultural importance of the Armenian population. This increase in civic prestige of Armenian notables also encouraged further immigration, especially from the outlying districts of the empire.

For the Ottomans, Armenian immigration served two functions: 1) to curtail Greek influence in the city or at least balance such influences; and 2) to meet the growing needs associated with construction in the city and the general administrative requirements of empire. This had already been achieved by the late eighteenth century as Armenian artisans gained widespread acclaim.[21] Armenian craftsmen from Bursa, Sivas, Tokat, Kayseri, Mush, and Malatia found steady employment, with some receiving valuable commissions from churches and the Ottoman court. Consequently, the demands from both church and state fostered an artistic link between the secular and the religious.

Church Foundations as a Reflection of Population

Much of the statistical data in the Ottoman censuses are supported by an alternative method of ascertaining the Armenian population

---

[19] Kemal H. Karpat, *Ottoman Population, 1830-1914: Demographic and Social Characteristics* (Madison: University of Wisconsin Press, 1985), pp. 46ff; Clogg, "Greek *Millet*," pp. 195ff. Forced labor or conscription is clearly seen on an altar standard/*jajanch* from a church in Evereg, in the district of Kayseri. Dated to the late eighteenth century, it states: "This holy radiance is in memory of the boys who are in Istanbul. For the enjoyment of Evereg's Surb Toros [St. Theodore Church]. Amen. In the year 1226 [1777]." Of all the colophons examined, this is the only one that references a group of young men (boys) from any community. A dedication of this nature was made by the community. See Clogg, "Greek *Millet*," pp. 185ff.

[20] Karpat, *Ottoman Population*, p. 51.

[21] Tokat, *Armenian Master Silversmiths*, p. 283.

in the city. The growth of the Armenian community is graphically displayed by the chronological foundation of churches. Their distribution in the greater metropolitan area of Constantinople is shown in Table 1.[22] Church foundations indicate a sustained growth

Table 1
Armenian Churches by Quarter

Quarter	Apostolic	Catholic	Protestant	No Longer in Use
Alemdagh	1			
Bakirkoy	3			2
Balat	1			
Beshiktash	1			
Beykoz		1	1	
Beyoghlu	2	1	1	
Buyukada		1		
Buyukdere	1	1		
Eminonu			1	
Edirnekapu	2			2
Emirghan	1			1
Eyub	2			
Ferikoy	1			
Galata	2	1		1
Gedikpasha	1		1	1[23]
Haskoy	3	1		3[24]
Kadikoy	1	1		
Kandilli	1			
Karagumruk	2			1
Kartal	1			

---

[22] Marchese and Breu, *Splendor and Spectacle*; Pars Tuğlacı, *Armenian Churches of Istanbul* (Istanbul: Pars Yayin, 1991). An increase in the number and size of Armenian families is a reflection of fertility or the size of maturing populations; that is a decrease in the death rate and an increase in the birth rate. Since non-Muslims were not subject to military duty or service, they faired better than their Turkish counterparts, especially in longevity. Karpat (*Ottoman Population*, p. 11) points out that "between 1854 and 1908 the Ottoman state received approximately 5 million Muslim immigrants from Russia (Caucasus, Crimea, Kuban, and Central Asia) and the Balkans; at the same time some 500,000 to 800,000 Greeks, Armenians, and Arabs emigrated, chiefly to Russia and the Americas."

[23] Protestant.

[24] Apostolic.

Kasimpasha	1		1
Kazlicheshme	1		
Kinaliada	1		
Kumkapu	3[25]		
Kurucheshme	1		
Kuzgunjuk	1		
Narlikapu	1		
Ortakoy	1	1	
Pangalti	1	1	1
Rumelihisar	1		
Samatia	2	1	
Sarıyer	1		1
Shishli		1	
Taksim	1	1	
Tarabia	1		
Tersane	1		1
Topkapu	2		1
Uskudar[26]	3		1
Yalova	1		1
Yenikapu	2		2
Yenikoy	1	1	
Yeshilkoy	1		
Zeytinburnu	1		1

in the Armenian population, especially in districts where no previous religious organization existed prior to the establishment of a chapel or church.[27] In this manner it is possible to visualize the ex-

---

[25] Including Surb Astvatsatsin (Holy Mother of God) Cathedral of the Armenian Patriarchate.

[26] Selamiye and Baghlarbashi.

[27] Of the Apostolic churches, 20 percent were founded in the eighteenth century and 47 percent in the nineteenth century. In the period between 1750 and 1850, the percentage of Armenian church foundations was 50 percent and corresponded with the increase in the Armenian population in the city and the emergence of a large number of well-to-do Armenians as an influential group in Ottoman circles. Only 11 percent of the church foundations appeared after 1850. The remaining churches are of earlier date: 11 percent in the seventeenth century, and 15 percent before the seventeenth century, including two dated to the fourteenth century, before the pre-Ottoman conquest of the city. Many churches began as chapels but as the community in a given quarter increased, they were replaced by churches. Both chapels and churches were initially constructed of wood and consequently suffered greatly in the numerous fires

pansion of the Armenian community from the fifteenth to the late nineteenth centuries. This provides a body of data on the concentration of the Armenian population in specific districts, the proximity of Armenian neighborhoods to each other and to the Patriarchate, and their importance as a substantial minority population in the cultural, social, and eventually the political life of the city.[28] This chronological distribution of church foundations in the city and the number of households needed in any given district to support financially a church are a direct result of population growth.

Churches could only be established by an official request to the Ottoman court. Spokesmen for such endeavors were the Armenian notables who represented their community before the Ottoman authorities. The fact that such a large number of churches were founded in the late eighteenth and the first half of the nineteenth century confirms the prestige of the Armenian millet and its influence in the city. It is safe to assume that as the Armenian population increased in any given neighborhood, a specific threshold was reached in order to underwrite the construction and maintenance of a church and the financial obligations necessary to support its clergy.

Constantinople experienced profound change during the nineteenth century because of its shifting demographic composition. In the census of 1830, "which probably included only family heads, the Muslims numbered 45,000, the Armenians 30,000, and the Greeks 20,000."[29] By the middle of the nineteenth century, more than 50 percent of the city was still non-Muslim. This is important since prior to the late nineteenth century the Turkish element held only a plurality, not a majority. It was also in the late eighteenth and especially the early nineteenth century that many new Armenian churches were built outside the Armenian quarters in

---

that devastated the city between 1450 and 1850. Church repairs were also constantly made in order to maintain buildings that simply fell into disrepair over the course of time. In the nineteenth century, many churches were rebuilt in stone. Also, since the establishment and repair or replacement of churches had to be authorized by the Ottoman government, a number of churches periodically dropped out of the registry. This did not necessarily mean that the congregation disappeared but suggests that the community lost the right to have an officially sanctioned religious edifice.

[28] Avedis K. Sanjian, *The Armenian Communities in Syria under Ottoman Dominion* (Cambridge: Harvard University Press), pp. 31ff.

[29] Karpat, *Ottoman Population*, p. 92.

Kumkapu, Yenikapu, and Samatia in the old city, and Beyoghlu and Galata in the new. An increase in the Armenian population in general and destruction caused by catastrophic fire necessitated such construction.[30] The capital suffered seventy-three devastating fires in four centuries, destroying valuable religious and secular records as well as priceless treasures, both Muslim and non-Muslim. As church collections as well as objects that graced the households of the wealthy had to be replaced, Armenian artisans in woodworking, construction, and precious metals found a ready market for their labor. In this way, they enhanced their collective reputation as some of the best artisans in the city.[31]

As Constantinople gained political and cultural significance, the Armenian community in "the city gradually became the center of Armenian ecclesiastical and national life."[32] By the middle of the nineteenth century, the Armenian population in the city numbered between 162,000 and 200,000 and perhaps as high as 300,000.[33] The increase in the number of churches in the first five decades of the nineteenth century not only confirms the growth of the Armenian population but also higher socioeconomic levels attained by influential families and the community in general. The pace of construction, however, slowed in the later half of the century when only six additional churches were founded for a number of reasons: 1) pre-existing churches adequately met the needs of the Armenian population; 2) there was a decline in Armenian immigration to the capital; 3) the city's Armenian population became less mobile; 4) the renewed Greek preeminence in the affairs of the Ottoman state minimized opportunities for Armenians; 5) the Ottoman authorities denied *firmans* for new church construction; and 6) political and social unrest increased, much of which was aimed at minority populations. Clearly, the reasons were multifaceted and involved the "democratization" of the Armenian community in its ecclesiastical and civil affairs, the establishment of an Armenian national constitution, and Ottoman mistrust of Armenian motives. No doubt Armenians began to feel less secure under the watchful eye of the imperial court at the end of the nineteenth century than they had earlier. The forced "Ottomanization" of minor-

---

[30] Ibid., p. 90.

[31] Kürkman, *Ottoman Silver Marks*; Marchese and Breu, *Treasures of Faith*.

[32] Sanjian, *Armenian Communities*, p. 34.

[33] Ibid.; Kouymjian, "Armenia," p. 26; Karpat, *Ottoman Population,* p. 104.

ities also increased violence against the Armenians. Such actions hindered, if not curtailed, immigration.[34] As a result, the advantages Constantinople possessed were countered by a general increase in hostility toward minority groups.

Nevertheless, 47 percent of all Armenian Apostolic churches in the city were built in the nineteenth century. A number of older churches were also renovated and enlarged. As in the past, when funds were lacking, well-to-do families accepted the financial burden associated with such endeavors. This included prominent individuals such as Harutiun Amira Bezjian (Fig. 2), Sarkis Balian, Garabed Balian, Hovhannes Dadian and his sons Arakel and Artin, Harutiun Amira Nevruzian, Hagop Noradoungian (Jacob Nora-dunkian), Hovhannes Duzian and his son Hagop Chelebi Duzian, Shnork Amira Mihranian, Mgrdich Amira Jesayirlian, Sarkis Kalfa, Garabed Amira Manugian, Hovsep Chelebi, and Mateos and Apik Unjuyan. Renovation and new construction also offered ample opportunity for renowned goldsmiths and silversmiths to exhibit their talents (Fig. 3). Artisans such as Aznavur, Nargileji Yeghiozar Agha, the official goldsmith of the palace during the reign of Sultan Abdul Mejid (1839-61), Mikayel Kurian, Chamichoghlu Boghos Agha, the son of Chamich Hovhannes Effendi, Chobanian Hovhannes Agha, Ghazar Effendi, Krikor Keyisian Agha, Chaylak Khachadur Agha, Zorayan and Gabriel Mgrdich Agha, Baba Atam, who made the silver plated door handles for the Dolmabahche Palace, Garabed Arifian, and Levon Mazlumian to name a few, possessed substantial reputations with few equals.[35] Many of these men, well-respected in Ottoman circles, included imperial architects, the head of the imperial gun powder mill, directors of the Imperial mint and financiers. Individuals of stature also absorbed the cost for the building of schools and hospitals. Such donations were part of the religious life of the lay community in general with many artisans and lay people alike contributing to the wealth of their respective churches.

At the beginning of the twentieth century, 72 Armenian Ap-

---

[34] Tuğlacı, *Armenian Churches of Istanbul*; Clogg, "Greek *Millet*," p. 199.

[35] Hagop Barsoumian, "The Dual Role of the Armenian *Amira* Class within the Ottoman Government and the Armenian *Millet* (1750-1850)," in Braude and Lewis, *Christians and Jews in the Ottoman Empire*, pp. 175ff; Tokat, *Armenian Master Silversmiths*, pp. 282-84; Tuğlacı, *Armenian Churches of Istanbul*, pp. 80-206 and 250ff.

ostolic, Catholic, and Evangelical churches existed in the city, 55 of them affiliated with the Apostolic rite.[36] The Armenian community also supported five daily newspapers and eight weekly gazettes.[37] From modest beginnings, the city's Armenian population accounted for 17 to 22 percent (perhaps as high as 30 percent) of its more than 900,000 inhabitants at the end of the nineteenth century.[38] The Armenian Patriarch of Constantinople thus came to symbolize the totality of Armenian life, ecclesiastical as well as secular, for the Armenians in the capital and for those across the vast reaches of the Ottoman state.[39]

Armenian Culture and Constantinople

During the nineteenth century, Constantinople underwent a remarkable transformation. This stimulated further change in the interior of the country, which in turn subjected the city to a variety of new pressures. The capital was a micro-model of the demographic, social, and economic change in the entire country. Like the Ottoman state as a whole, it received a flood of new immigrants, and it, too, fell under the growing influence of the capitalism and the liberal political thought of Europe, even adopting European architectural styles and patterns of urban organization and administration in the course of altering itself under the impact of these outside influences.

Despite these changes, Constantinople was still composed of four main groups, defined by religion, who resided in mostly segregated neighborhoods (mahalle). The Greeks were located in Fener, Samatia, Jibali, and a number of villages along the Bosphorus. The Armenians lived in high concentrations in Kumkapu, Yenikapu, Samatia, Bakirkoy, and in smaller numbers in other quarters both within and outside the confines of the city's ancient walls. A large and prosperous community existed on the Asian side at Uskudar with other Armenian communities located along the shores of the Bosphorus and the Sea of Marmara. The Jewish population was concentrated in mixed neighborhoods with the

---

[36] Tuğlacı, *Armenian Churches of Istanbul.*
[37] Karpat, *Ottoman Population*, p. 96.
[38] Ibid., pp. 95-106; Panossian, *Armenians*, p. 84.
[39] Panossian, *Armenians*, p. 84; Thierry, *Armenian Art*, pp. 305ff.

Armenians in Balat, Haskoy (Khaskoy), and Kasimpasha. Galata and Beyoghlu also had mixed populations including Europeans, the latter mostly settled in the area referred to as Pera.[40] It is significant that the majority of Armenian Catholic churches and the Catholic Patriarchate are located in the area of Galata/Beyoghlu.

Although common ground existed in the numerous bazaars, most of the population in the city did not mix. As the economic structure changed in the nineteenth century, in many respects reflecting the capitalistic tendencies of the modern era, manufacturing processes changed as well. The old artisan/tradesmen (*esnaf*) system, controlled by guild masters (*subashi*), in existence before the Ottoman conquest in the mid-fifteenth century, was abolished.[41] It was replaced by new economic institutions and large-scale industrial systems, many under the supervision of state officials and administrators. Commerce, traditionally localized in a number of bazaars, however, spilled out into the surrounding districts and streets where competition was keen. Kemal Karpat states:

> Turkish merchants specialized in the sale of hides, furs, clothing, books, perfumes, and engravings; the Greeks sold cotton goods and worked as tailors and leather workers; the Armenians dealt in jewelry, watches, and embroideries; and Jews were engaged in a variety of other occupations.[42]

Occupations varied among all groups, and all millets offered a variety of goods and services in order to meet the needs of their own constituents. Some groups, however, were better known for specific goods of higher quality; for example, Armenian jewelers

---

[40] Karpat, *Ottoman Population*, pp. 86ff. As late as 1880, more than 50 percent of the city's inhabitants were non-Muslim, excluding the resident foreign population. This changed by 1885 when the Muslim population reportedly reached 54 percent, and in 1900, 70 percent.

[41] See Tokat, *Armenian Master Silversmiths*, p. 282. Although many artisans came from the east, especially from the region of Lake Van, local techniques found wider dissemination in the cosmopolitan environment of Constantinople. Van artisans were noted for fine *niello* work in silver, but this unique technique of silver enhancement does not appear to have been widely used on objects donated to the Church. This does not mean that niello was not utilized or was not in favor in the capital but rather may have been considered inappropriate for religious objects of high symbolic significance. Niello, however, was very popular in the secular market where such objects appeared in abundance.

[42] Karpat, *Ottoman Population*, p. 94.

and Greek and Armenian embroiderers possessed a high reputation, many of whom gained valuable commissions in both Ottoman
and European circles.[43]

Those of the non-artisan class were primarily unskilled labor,
most of whom were from rural districts. Others formed a class of
vendors: "they worked as *hamallar* (porters), *saka* (carriers of
water in big leather bags), *helvaji* (makers and sellers of helva),
shekerji (candy makers and sellers), *jigherji* (sellers of fried liver),
and in other occupations."[44] Porters were primarily Turks and
Armenians. A good number of Armenians also were employed as
*kayikji*s (boatmen) and *balikji*s (fishermen). The well-to-do, however, dominated the uppermost stratum of Armenian economic life
as capitalists, entrepreneurs, and bankers. All contributed their
talent, energy, and wealth in order to underwrite a unique material
culture that was both Western and Eastern in its physical manifestation (Table 2; Map 2).[45]

The available data indicate that a social and economic balance
existed in the early nineteenth century between Muslim and non-
Muslim groups. This situation, however, changed drastically after
1838 when cheap European machine-made goods, especially from
England, began to flood the market. According to Karpat, the
ability to maintain an economic balance between the millets
faltered and "in a matter of years the Muslim Ottoman middle
class, which had consisted of craftsmen and small shopkeepers,
was wiped out." A new Greek and Armenian middle class emerged,
which distributed the cheaper, manufactured goods of Europe.[46]
Economic processes, commercial ties with distant political states
in the West as well as in the East, and the Greek war of independence, reinforced the position of the Armenian millet and empowered a number of Armenian families who appeared in a variety
of influential positions, including regional administrators, diplomats, financiers, entrepreneurs, artisans, craftsmen, inventors,
and food vendors.[47]

---

[43] Kürkman, *Ottoman Silver Marks*, p. 71; Marchese and Breu, *Splendor and Spectacle*; Marchese and Breu, *Treasures of Faith*.

[44] Karpat, *Ottoman Population,* pp. 94-95.

[45] Kouymjian, Personal correspondence, 2007; Marchese and Breu, *Splendor and Spectacle*; Marchese and Breu, *Treasures of Faith*.

[46] Karpat, *Ottoman Population*, p. 95.

[47] Tuğlacı, *Armenian Churches of Istanbul*; Roderic Davison, "The *Millet*s as

Table 2

Distribution of Armenian Jewelers, Silversmiths, Gilders, and Engravers in Constantinople by Quarter[48]

Quarter	Jewelers	Silver-smiths	Gilders	Engravers	Others
Balat	5	1	1		
Beshiktash	18	1	1	1	
Eyub		3		1	
Haskoy		9			
Kadikoy	3				1
Kandilli		1			
Karagomruk		4			
Kumkapu	33	1		1	
Kurucheshme		5			
Kuzgunjuk		7		1	
Narlikapu		1			
Ortakoy		3			
Pera/Beyoghlu		9			
Rumelihisar		1			
Samatia		31			2
Samatia/ Yenimahalle		4			
Topkapu		6			
Uskudar Baghlarbashi/ Yenimahalle		2			
Uskudar Selamiye		11		1	
Yenikapu		16	1	1	2
Yenikoy		1			

Agents of Change in the Nineteenth Century Ottoman Empire," in Braude and Lewis, *Christians and Jews*, p. 327; Karpat, *Ottoman Population,* pp. 86ff; Barsoumian, "Dual Role," pp. 171ff.

[48] Kürkman, *Ottoman Silver Marks*, pp. 288-89, provides a list of silversmiths, goldsmiths, gilders, engravers, metal casters, designers, ring makers, stone setters, precious metal thread makers, etc. who paid a tax to the Armenian Patriarchate in 1872. All are listed by specialty and profession and are generally associated with the jeweler craft.

118

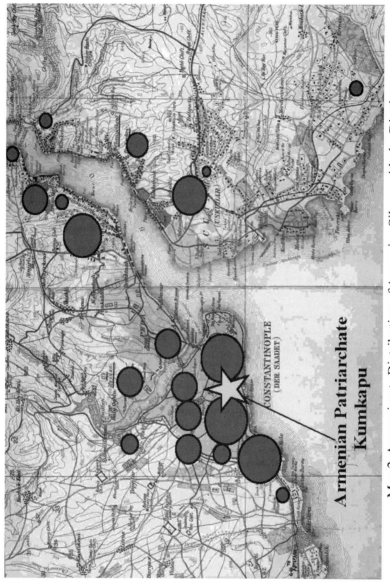

Map 2. Approximate Distribution of Armenian Silversmiths by District

The Constantinople Style

Political leadership, economic prowess, and artistic talent came together in a unique style of art, the Constantinople style.[49] Multiform in nature, the Constantinople style was defined by a variety of ornate objects of exceptional quality produced in the city between the late seventeenth and the late nineteenth century. Such objects attained a wide distribution as indicated by donations of Constantinople origin in the patriarchal treasuries at Echmiadzin, Jerusalem, and Sis (later housed at Antelias, Lebanon).[50] The Constantinople style was rooted in indigenous Armenian material culture, although external influences that initially defined the "modern Armenian renaissance" were also evident. Kevork Bardakjian comments:

> [I]nitiated by the Mekhitarist Congregation of Venice . . . the Mekhitarist monks revived Armenian literature, language and history, set up an extensive network of schools and transmitted Western thought to their fellow countrymen in Armenia proper and elsewhere in the [Ottoman] empire. But Constantinople, not Venice, was eventually to assume leadership of the Armenians of the empire. The individual efforts of Patriarch Yovhannes Kolot [Hovhannes IX Golod] marked the beginning of a cultural revival in Constantinople which, under formative influence of the Mekhitarists, was to flourish into the nineteenth century. The renaissance wrought profound changes in the community, the most significant of which was perhaps the sense of unity it stirred among the Armenians. The patriarchate came to be regarded as the very symbol of this unity, thus assuming such recognition and

---

[49] Hermann Göltz and Klaus E. Göltz, eds., *Rescued Armenian Treasures from Cilicia: Sacred Art of the Kilikia Museum, Antelias, Lebanon* (Wiesbaden: Reichert, 2000); Kouymjian, Personal correspondence, 2007; Marchese and Breu, *Splendor and Spectacle*; Marchese and Breu, *Treasures of Faith*.

[50] V. Ghazarian, "Miniatures," and S. Davtian, "Needlework," in Karageuzian, *Treasures of Echmiadzin*; Göltz and Göltz, *Rescued Armenian Treasures*; Bezalel Narkiss, "Early Illuminated Manuscripts," in *Armenian Art Treasures of Jerusalem*, ed. Bezalel Narkiss (New Rochelle, NY: Caratzas, 1979), pp. 29-40; Dikran Kouymjian, *The Art of Armenia* (Lisbon, Calouste Gulbenkian Foundation, 1992), p. 53; Jannic Durand, Ioanna Rapti, and Dorota Giovannoni, *Armenia sacra: Mémoire chrétienne des Arméniens (IVe-VIIIe siècle)* (Paris: Musée du Louvre, 2007), pp. 418ff; Tokat, *Armenian Master Silversmiths*, pp. 282ff.

authority as never before.[51]

The Mekhitarists served as a bridge between the West and the East "in the dissemination of many European ideas and approaches (particularly in cultural, historical, linguistic and of course religious matters) into Armenian thinking."[52]

This is especially evident in material culture after the middle of the eighteenth century with the adaptation of the European Baroque, Rococo, and the Neo-Classical movement in church art and architecture in Constantinople. By the middle of the nineteenth century, the Imperial style of the French court of Louis XVI was also well-represented. Hovsep Tokat states that "however unique the style realized by the Armenian goldsmiths and silversmiths of Istanbul, sometimes their works revealed the influence of France of Louis XVI, but this has more to do with adaptation than imitation, otherwise the tradition of Istanbul-Armenian craftsmen [remained] wholly distinctive."[53]

Ottoman political and cultural alignment with the Western world, the abandonment of the Oriental style (as summarized by the sumptuous *saray* or palace tradition of the Topkapu Palace) for the architectural grandeur and opulence of the European inspired Dolmabahche Palace, the adaptation of European dress and culture, all reflected the changing conditions in secular taste of the nineteenth century.[54] These changes included substantial architectural

---

[51] Kevork B. Bardakjian, "The Rise of the Armenian Patriarchate of Constantinople," in Braude and Lewis, *Christians and Jews*, p. 96. The order was founded in 1712 by the Catholic monk Mekhitar and later relocated to Venice in 1717 where the cultural environment of the early Enlightenment affected both humanistic as well as religious thought. This monastic order had a significant impact on the re-awakening Armenian spirit. See Panossian, *Armenians*, p. 102.

[52] Panossian, *Armenians*, p. 109.

[53] Tokat, *Armenian Master Silversmiths*, p. 283.

[54] The French Imperial style developed out of the Neo-Classical tradition of the early nineteenth century. It influenced all aspects of material culture: architecture, furniture, painting, and the decorative arts. This is clearly seen in a number of religious objects in the church collections that feature more graceful curvilinear designs beyond the more ornate Rococo of the eighteenth century. The Imperial style is associated with Napoleon I and continues to the reign of Napoleon III. This latter phase is usually defined as the Second Imperial style and is viewed by some as gaudy and ostentatious. In cosmopolitan Constantinople the adaptation of the French Imperial style was part of the modernization of the Ottoman world which began to abandon Oriental taste in architecture and

enhancement in the secular and the religious realms. Both Muslim and non-Muslim structures graced the city as physical examples of the shift in material culture, especially architectural splendor. This is clearly seen in the adaptation of European inspired interior space in Armenian church architecture which emphasized the clean lines and palette of muted colors associated with the Neo-Classical school.

As the taste of the patrons changed, religious enhancement was modified in order to replicate the general changes taking place in secular material culture. Not quite European in style, yet removed from the Oriental taste in favor at the Ottoman court of the previous centuries, the Constantinople style adhered to well-established Armenian norms that echoed both worlds—East and West—in a sumptuous palette of color, pattern, and distinctively unique form. The Constantinople style after the middle of the eighteenth century matured into an elaborate artistic movement that mirrored the social and cultural transformation taking place in the city. It was based on a lavish display of pictorial scenes, intricate floral patterns, interconnected composition, a commitment to detail, and an extravagant use of precious metals, pearls, and gem stones (Figs. 4-14). In many respects, the cosmopolitan atmosphere of Constantinople, its diverse population and culture, and the assimilation of Armenian immigrant craftsmen from the east amalgamated a number of regional traditions that created a unique and uniform style that was recognized for its artistic flair and elaborate decoration (Figs. 15-17b). The Constantinople style reflected the success of the cultural heterogeneity of the Ottoman capital in that the "sumptuary arts depended on an atmosphere of opulence and wealthy patronage in which to thrive . . . a society where piety went hand in hand with a love of luxury and display and men sought insurance for the welfare of their souls in eternity by lavish gifts to churches here on earth."[55] A rich use of foliage appears on a

---

interior design in the late eighteenth century. Ottoman architectural design and decoration, however, appears to have rejected the simpler style and clean lines associated with the Neo-Classical tradition in favor of the more ornate Baroque and Rococo. Although Armenian church architecture, especially in the design of interior space, reflects a Neo-Classical convention, the portable material culture exhibits a movement to the French Imperial style with lingering Rococo influences.

[55] Pauline Johnstone, *The Byzantine Tradition in Church Embroidery* (Chicago:

number of pieces in the collections and is evident on liturgical garments, altar curtains, and metal objects (Figs. 18-37).

The Constantinople style, however, did not develop in an artistic vacuum. It was part of a well-established and mature Christian culture that predated the Armenian Patriarchate of Constantinople by a thousand years. Each of its elements connected the laity and the clergy to the living context of ritual.[56] The Constantinople style 1) involved the community, both individually and collectively, as direct participants in religious celebration; 2) connected the laity to the saints and martyrs of the church and to the previous generations of the faithful through consecrated sacred objects; 3) reinforced the prestige of the church through rich donations and embellishments; 4) encouraged the production and donation of material culture as being essential to the liturgy and oral traditions of the church, thereby intensifying the community's religious commitment to Christian doctrine; and 5) used many objects to invoke a desire to attain eternal life, since donations to the church reinforced the image of personal piety and individual salvation.

In many respects, mobile elements of sacred art made the religious ceremony a more intimate and personal experience that transcended time and space. They became symbols of faith in the process of honoring God. The faithful of one Armenian Christian generation recognized their forbearers' existence and eternal life in Christ. Objects donated to the Church were vested with divine omnipotence by the act of anointing, and through the process of blessing physical objects transcended the material from which they were produced—parchment and paper, plaster, stone, wood, metal,

---

Argonaut, 1967), p. 74. Johnstone (p. 46) points out that "the seventeenth and early eighteenth centuries saw a revival of the arabesque background pattern in a highly ornamental form. The embroidered leaves of the classic pattern are enlarged to luxuriant foliage, the scrolling is elaborate and prolific, and every kind of flower blossoms in the encircling stems. This kind of ornament ranges from scrolling carnation firmly rooted in Asia Minor, to a less naturalistic, purely decorative European rococo style." Floral borders were quite popular throughout the seventeenth century and more so in the eighteenth and nineteenth centuries. This is clearly seen in the varied use of the rose, carnation, lily, and tulip in a number of embroideries and cast metal objects of Armenian origin.

[56] Torkom Saraydarian, *The Symbolism of the Ecclesiastical Vestments and Vessels of the Armenian Apostolic Church* (Van Nuys, CA: Holy Martyrs Armenian Church, 1967).

and cloth. Those associated directly with the sacrifice of Christ, especially illuminated manuscripts, chalices, reliquaries, and crosses, possessed higher religious significance. Images of the Divine also enhanced the importance of specific objects over those of lesser significance.

The Context of Use

The production of religious objects can be attributed to several factors: 1) the number of feast days, requiring the manufacture and use of physical objects as part of religious celebration; 2) periodic destruction of church treasuries by fire, necessitating replacements; 3) confiscation by the Ottoman state of precious metals and the subsequent destruction of reliquaries, but not relics; 4) the natural wear of items, especially textiles, through continuous use; and 5) the personal piety and the desire of the maker and donor to honor God. In this manner, there was a conscious effort to glorify God through gifts from one generation to the next and to link them in order to support and reinforce the identity of the community. It is through the Divine Liturgy that Armenian identity and heritage were displayed. It is this process of identity that enabled the Armenians of Constantinople to maintain a national spirit without traditional political representation of their own. As a result, much of Armenian material and religious culture could be expressed through the work of devout artisans who labored to fashion spectacular objects for the Church. Master artisans created objects that graced churches and enhanced the spiritual meaning of Christian belief.[57]

Religious Objects and the State

Since many objects were made with some kind of precious metal, the Ottoman state guaranteed the quality of the metal and actually intervened in the process of donating valuable items to either individual churches or the Patriarchate by placing an official tughra or stamp on objects where possible.[58] Such stamps not only guar-

---

[57] Levon Abrahamian and Nancy Sweezy, eds., *Armenian Folk Arts, Culture, and Identity* (Bloomington: Indiana University Press, 2001), p. vii.
[58] Kürkman, *Ottoman Silver Marks*, p. 64.

anteed the quality of the precious metal in question, which was primarily silver (900 karat), but also provided the state with information about the wealth of the artisan community and individual manufacturers (especially jewelers) as well as about the general wealth of minority communities and their secular and religious leaders.

Purity of metal was very important. It was considered a capital offense to counterfeit marks or stamp items with a sultan's tughra on lesser quality objects. Tughra dies were engraved before witnesses and stored in sealed cases prior to transport to the state mint. A signed receipt was necessary upon transferring the die to the mint officials. Punishment for fraud, failure to follow the law, or violation of security measures to insure the safety of the official tughra was severe, including the cutting off of hands and even beheading.[59] Fraud, however, appears to have been common in the market place, especially when silver was scarce. The Ottoman authorities, through edicts issued from the *Divan*, made a conscious effort to minimize fraud and questionable practices in the bullion market, particularly for those goods sold in the private sector.

State guarantees on the purity of silver were also reinforced by patriarchal concerns about the quality of precious metals since artisans paid a tax to the patriarchate.[60] No doubt artisans used lower grade silver, especially in times of scarcity, to meet the needs of those who wished to make donations to the Church. Such a concern by-passed Ottoman regulations and offered some guarantee for the survival of objects since the purity of the object would not measure up to the official standard. The vast majority of work was not signed and where inscriptions appear, they emphasize the donor and not the craftsman commissioned for the work. Ottoman registers rarely list the names of craftsmen, although a number of them do appear in later patriarchal records.

The vast majority of silversmiths were from the minority millets. The names and place of origin for the Armenian silversmiths indicate that many came from the east—Aleppo, Damascus, Bitlis, Diarbekir, Van, Erzinjan, Malatia, Sivas, Trebizond, and Yozgat[61]—as indicated in their logos.[62] Drawn to the capital for a

---

[59] Ibid., p. 68.

[60] Ibid., pp. 288ff.

[61] Ibid., pp. 71ff; Tokat, *Armenian Master Silversmiths*, pp. 81ff.

[62] Since religious objects achieved some form of standardization, especially in

number of reasons, many families possessed extended lineages and familial relations that made assimilation easier, especially since many of the trades associated with precious metals were organized around families in specific occupations such as silversmiths, jewelers, engravers, gilders, casters, metal thread makers, ring makers, and silver and gold sheet and plate makers. Many served a number of years as apprentices and master craftsmen prior to recognition or appointment as head master. All enjoyed high prestige.[63]

Survivability and Date

Unlike objects made of non-valuable material such as fiber, base metal, and wood, those in the church collections of Constantinople made from precious metal possessed value beyond religious symbolism. Gold and silver metal objects were luxury items, as were textiles, especially those enhanced with silk and with gold and silver wire.[64] The manufacture of thin wire, added to many religious textiles as well as secular garments and apparel, was an Armenian specialty. For the Ottoman rulers, such objects possessed value as bullion and were easily converted into currency in times of economic and civil distress. Garo Kürkman raises a question that is significant in the analysis of the sacred artifacts from the Armenian churches: "Why has so little of the ware produced by . . . goldsmiths and silversmiths . . . survived?"[65] Tens of thousands of gold and silver objects were produced during the Ottoman period and the number of goldsmiths and silversmiths throughout the empire certainly numbered in the thousands, many of whom were non-Turkish. This question may have a rather simple answer. From the very beginning of the Ottoman state, the government lacked a comprehensive and stable monetary policy. As more "silver, whether in the form of foreign coins, bars or artifacts . . . left Turkey than entered the country, a stable silver market was never

---

precious metal where a specific shape is primarily known in silver (for example, censers), similar items manufactured in base metal were marked with a stamp denoting a *taklit* or imitation. Murat Bilir, personal correspondence, 2008.

[63] Kürkman, *Ottoman Silver Marks*, p. 73.

[64] Kouymjian, *The Art of Armenia*, p. 51.

[65] Kürkman, *Ottoman Silver Marks*, p. 37.

achieved, and this undermined the currency."[66] The scarcity of silver meant rationing to artisans, but this did not reverse the drain of silver coins to pay for foreign goods.

Furthermore, illegal hoarding and the smuggling of silver made it difficult for the Ottoman treasury to meet its monetary obligations. The government therefore resorted to periodic confiscation of silver to be melted down and reused as coinage. Silver plate, gold and silver containers, and textiles were collected for reprocessing. Textiles were stripped of their precious stones, including pearls, and were burned in order to collect the metal. Objects that were of pure silver or enhanced with gilded silver and gold were simply melted. This explains why the majority of Armenian sacred objects date primarily to the late eighteenth and more so the early nineteenth century with few examples of earlier date. Thierry also argues that in the seventeenth and eighteenth centuries "Armenian communities were growing rich, and religious ceremonial objects were a form of investment appreciated both by clerics and laymen. Numerous reliquaries were [previously stripped of their silver enhancement] . . . restored."[67]

This view of a revival in donations is supported by the church collections of Constantinople. Objects with the dates of manufacture and donation, especially from the middle to late eighteenth century, are from affluent families and individuals who eagerly contributed to their churches and to the Patriarchate. Some made donations during pilgrimage to various sites in Armenian Christendom.[68] Consequently, the disappearance of religious objects from various churches in Constantinople may be explained in the context of Ottoman domestic policy and international relations. Armenians residing in the city and the Church were vulnerable to the state's "requests" for silver donations, and this periodic "calling in" of gold and silver had a profound effect on the survivability of church art.[69] Many objects were melted to meet the demands of state officials who exercised their authority through the Patriarch as the *milletbashi* or head of the ethno-religious community. Our

---

[66] Ibid.

[67] Jean-Michel Thierry, *Les arts Arméniens* (Paris: Editions Mazenod, 1987), trans. Célestine Dars, *Armenian Art* (New York: Harry N. Abrams, 1989), pp. 314-15.

[68] Narkiss, "Early Illuminated Manuscripts," pp. 29-40.

[69] Nancy Netzer, *A Catalogue of Medieval Objects: Metalwork* (Boston: Museum of Fine Arts, 1991), p. 11.

understanding of the Constantinople style, therefore, has come to rely on 1) objects that still exist at the Patriarchate and in various churches throughout the city, and 2) donations to the treasury of Saint James in Jerusalem, to the Monastery of Saint Sophia of the Catholicosate of Cilicia at Sis, and to the Mother See at Echmiadzin. All confirm the artistic flare of the Constantinople style and the extraordinary craftsmanship of Armenian artisans in the city.

Summation

Armenian religious material culture waned with the disappearance of the last autonomous Armenian principalities after the conquest of Armenia by Selim I in the sixteenth century, as it was detached from secular patronage and sources of wealth. A number of factors contributed to the revival of Armenian religious art in Constantinople. First, over the course of five centuries, the Armenian millet evolved from a small and numerically insignificant entity to one of the largest and most influential groups in the city at the close of the nineteenth century. The increasing Armenian population in the capital led to the growth in the number of Armenian entrepreneurs of high social status. This in turn strengthened the position of the Patriarch, particularly as the amira class augmented the cultural significance and ecclesiastical authority of the Patriarchate.[70] With the additional ability to preserve monasteries and churches, the Patriarchate possessed considerable clout in stimulating a revival in church art.[71]

Furthermore, secular and religious patronage enhanced the prestige of the Church. The latter had initially acted as a patron but came to rely on wealthy individuals who not only supported the

---

[70] Father K.H. Maksoudian, "The Religion of Armenia," in Mathews and Wieck, *Treasures in Heaven,* p. 34; Vrej Nersessian, *Treasures from the Ark: 1700 Years of Armenian Christian Art* (London: The British Library, 2001), pp. 59-60. Cf, Kouymjian, "Armenia," p. 48; Panossian, *Armenians*, p. 85. Although theoretically the Patriarch held legal authority as head of his community with absolute power over the Armenian millet, including the administration of churches, schools, charitable organizations, and prisons, those that controlled the selection of the Patriarch in reality controlled the Armenian community internally within Constantinople as well as externally in the Ottoman domains. See Panossian, *Armenians*, pp. 87, 90ff, 149.

[71] Thierry, *Armenian Art*, p. 306.

personal authority of the Patriarch but who also invested substantial sums into religious material culture as an obligation to the
community, as indicated by the inscriptions on many objects in the
church collections. A vast assortment of objects was commissioned
or donated to individual churches as a statement of personal faith.
The Patriarchate therefore became the focal point in defining a
unique religious material culture that was cosmopolitan in form
and content.

It is also not surprising that the rise of a wealthy class of Armenian entrepreneurs and church patrons in the eighteenth and
nineteenth centuries facilitated artistic creativity by financing religious enterprises, especially in the commission and donation of
ceremonial objects. Such objects were not only an open expression
of personal piety, but they also became a form of investment
appreciated by clerics and laymen alike. In essence, "it was [the
well-to-do] who met the expenses of the Patriarchate and the
ecclesiastical and national institutions and this in turn earned them
the right to dictate their will upon the community,"[72] including the
selection of the patriarch.[73] At times overbearing in civil matters,
especially in their conservative concern of maintaining the political status quo, their substantial incomes and their position in the
Ottoman state as loyal subjects provided not only the necessary
capital for religious investment but also prestige for the Armenian
community. Such prestige for some time also helped insulate the
Armenian community from the dictates and harsh treatment by
state officials. The consolidation of wealth and high social status
established a sense of unity within the Armenian community. The
Patriarchate "came to be regarded as the very symbol of this unity,
thus assuming such recognition and authority as never before."[74]

In this manner the Armenian community achieved a sense of
unity with a unique combination of society, culture, and religion
which intersected in forming the foundation and development of
the Constantinople style in Armenian art. Collective pride ce-
mented national identity.[75] Many Armenians were proud of the

---

[72] Sanjian, *Armenian Communities*, p. 36.

[73] Barsoumian, "Dual Role," p. 179; Davison, "The *Millets* as Agents of Change,"
pp. 319-38; Clogg, "Greek *Millet*," pp. 185-207.

[74] Bardakjian, "Rise," p. 96.

[75] Ronald T. Marchese and Marlene R. Breu, "Social Identity and Sacred Art from
the Armenian Orthodox Churches of Istanbul," *International Journal of the Arts in*

contributions they made to the city. Through their efforts the city prospered as a diverse expression of human culture not duplicated elsewhere in the Ottoman world.

Society 1:6 (2007): 41-54.

Appendix

Catalogue of Objects

Fig. 1.
Chandelier ornament/*chah*. Holy Resurrection (Surb Harutiun) Church, Kumkapu.
Early nineteenth century.
Silver, 41 centimeters from point of chandelier attachment to chandelier to bottom of fish.
Inscription:
Aram of Istanbul.

Fig. 2.
Seal stamps from the textile workshop of Harutiun Amira Bezjian, 1833.
Inscription:
This is a memorial gift from Harutiun Bezjian, 1833.

Fig. 3.
Altar Ark/*debank* (altar ornamentation/*seghani zard*). Holy Cross (Surb Khach) Church, Uskudar.
Dated 1831.
Silver, gilded silver, 93 x 52 x 13 centimeters.
Inscription:
Memorial gift from Harutiun Bezjian, 1831.

Fig. 4.
Mitre/*khoyr*. St. John the Precursor (Surb Karapet) Church, Baghlarbashi/ Uskudar.
Late eighteenth century.
44½ x 37 centimeters.

Figs. 5A-5B.
Mitre/*khoyr*. Patriarchal Museum, Kumkapu.
Early to mid-seventeenth century.
Gold, silver, silk thread, and silk floss embroidery on unknown ground, couching, brick stitch, garnets, peridots, 35 x 32 centimeters.
Inscription:
[This] *is* [a gift] *from hocha Margare and his brother Melkon.*

Figs. 6A-6B.
Mitre/*khoyr*. Holy Mother of God (Surb Astvatsatsin) Church, Beshiktash.
Late eighteenth century.

Gold, silver and silk thread embroidery on red silk velvet ground for background and silk satin, fresh water pearls, diamonds, 45 x 37 centimeters.

Fig. 7.
Mitre/*khoyr*. Holy Mother of God Cathedral, Kumkapu.
Dated 1779.
45 x 38 centimeters.
Inscription:
> *This crown* [mitre] *is for the enjoyment of Zakaria of Kaghzuan* [Kagizman], *Patriarch of Constantinople* [and] *Second Legate of Holy Echmiadzin in the year 1128* [1779], *June 1.*

Figs. 8A-8D.
Mitre/*khoyr*. Holy Trinity (Surb Errordutiun) Church, Beyoghlu. Patriarchal Museum, Kumkapu.
Dated 1800.
Gold and silver thread embroidery on dark teal blue silk satin; pearls, emeralds, rubies, 44½ x 34 centimeters.
Inscription:
> *For the enjoyment of Poghos*, vardapet [educator] *who gave* [this] *as a memorial* [gift] *to the Holy Mother of God Church of Bursa, 1249* [1800].

Fig. 9.
Crown/*saghavart*. Holy Mother of God Church, Yenikoy. Patriarchal Museum, Kumkapu.
Late eighteenth–early nineteenth century.
Silver, gilded silver and cloth over metal frame, 28 x 18 centimeters.

Fig. 10.
Crown/*saghavart*. Holy Mother of God Church, Yenikoy. Patriarchal Museum, Kumkapu.
Silver, gilded silver and cloth over metal base, 29 x 20 centimeters.

Figs. 11A-11C.
Collar and Lappet Set. Holy Mother of God Church, Beshiktash.
16 x 62 centimeters (collar).

Fig. 12.
Chalice Cover/*skihi tsatskots*. Holy Mother of God Cathedral, Kumkapu.
Dated by stamp 1829.

Silver and silk thread embroidery on coral wool twill, chain stitch, 107
centimeters square.

Fig. 13.
Chalice Cover/*skihi tsatskots*. Holy Mother of God Cathedral, Kumkapu.
Dated 1813 (1829 acquisition date stamped on back).
Gold and silk thread and silk floss embroidery on red wool twill, silk back-
ing, sequins, couching, outline stitch, 83 centimeters square.
Inscription:
> *This veil* [cover] *is in memory of Apraham, Samuel, Noemzar, Ham-
> pasiur, and Aslik. Palasan and Abraham and his father Samuel and
> Mariam, Kendnets Gaspar, Brapeon and Mariam of Blessed Memory,
> from Ter* [Father] *Aristakes, 1262* [1813].

Fig. 14.
Chalice Cover/*skihi tsatskots*. Holy Cross Church, Uskudar.
Late eighteenth century.
Gold, silver, and silk thread, and silk floss embroidery, on green silk 2/2
twill, chenille yarn, pearls, coiled wire, couching, satin stitch, French
knots, bullion stitch, 105 x 112 centimeters.

Fig. 15.
Table Censers/*khnkanots*. Holy Cross Church, Uskudar.
Dated 1867 and tughra of the Ottoman Sultan Mahmud II (1861–76).
Artisan's mark in Armenian script.
Silver and gilded silver, 24 x 13 centimeters.

Fig. 16.
Table Censers/*khnkaman*. St. Nicholas (Surb Nikoghos) Church, Beykoz.
Patriarchal Museum, Kumkapu.
Mid-nineteenth century.
Gilded Silver, 25 x 12.5 centimeters.
Inscription:
> *Taklit* (Imitation).

Figs. 17A-17B.
Altar Standard/*jajanch*. Holy Cross Church, Uskudar.
Dated 1831.
Silver and gilded silver, 56 x 29 centimeters.
Inscription:
> *This is* [a gift in] *remembrance from Harutiun Bezjian, 1831.*

Fig. 18.
Patriarchal Staff/*patriarkakan* (*kathoghikosakan*) *asa*. Patriarchate, Kum-

kapu. Patriarchal Museum, Kumkapu.

Belonging to Patriarch Balatli Garabed (Karapet, 1823–31).

Wood, gold, gilded silver, brass, precious and semi-precious stones, and enamel, 162 x 6 centimeters (3 centimeters at the top of staff).

Inscription:

John 1:1—*That which was from the beginning, which we have heard, which we have seen with our eyes, which we have looked upon, and our hands have handled, of the Word of Life.*

Fig. 19.

Processional/Altar Cross/*tapori mets khach* (currently used as a hand cross/ *dzerats khach*). Holy Cross Church, Uskudar.

Dated 1780.

Silver, gilded silver and enamel, 21 x 8.5 centimeters.

Inscription:

This Holy Cross is in memory of usda Ghazar's wife Tiruhi, at the gate of the Holy Cross [Church] *in Uskudar, 1229* [1780].

Fig. 20.

Processional Cross with relics/*tapori mets khach masunkov*. Holy Cross Church, Uskudar.

Late eighteenth or early nineteenth century.

Gold, gilded silver, precious and semi-precious stones, 26 x 11 centimeters.

Inscription:

In this are the relics of Pantaleon the physician, Hermolaos the priest and Eupraxia [Euphrasia] *the virgin.*

Fig. 21.

Miuron Vessel, Dove for the Holy Miuron/*Miuronatap Aghavni*. Holy Mother of God Church, Beshiktash.

Early nineteenth century.

Silver and gilded silver, 39 x 26 centimeters.

Fig. 22.

Incense Arks/*khnkaman debank*. Holy Mother of God Cathedral, Kumkapu.

Early nineteenth century.

Silver and gilded silver, 8 x 23 x 31 centimeters.

Fig. 23A.

Vardapet staff/*gavazan vardapetakan*. St. Gregory the Illuminator (Surb Grigor Lusavorich) Church, Karakoy. Patriarchal Museum, Kumkapu.

Dated 1715–41, belonging to Patriarch Hovhannes Golod (Kolot).

Brass, mother-of-pearl, marble, precious and semi-precious stones, 170 x
10 centimeters.

Fig. 23B.
Vardapet staff/*gavazan vardapetakan*. St. John the Precursor Church,
Baghlarbashi/Uskudar. Patriarchal Museum, Kumkapu.
Dated 1886.
Silver, gilded silver, brass shaft (originally silver) with inscription, wood,
jade, precious stones, 170 x 14.5 centimeters.
Inscription:
Memorial gift to Lord Matteos, Bishop Izmirlian, St. Karapet Church,
Nor-tagh [new quarter]*, Uskudar, February 16, 1886.*

Fig. 24.
Ewer/*parch* and basin/*gonk*. St. Stephen (Surb Stepanos) Church, Yeshil-
koy. Patriarchal Museum, Kumkapu.
Mid-nineteenth century.
Silver, Ewer 28 x 18 centimeters, and Basin diameter 31 centimeters.

Fig. 25.
Central Plaque, Gospel Cover/*kantagvadz ardzatapat goghk* for illumi-
nated Gospel/*avetaran*. St. Gregory the Illuminator Church, Karakoy.
Patriarchal Museum, Kumkapu.
Early nineteenth century.
Brass and gilded silver, 34 x 24 centimeters.
Inscription:
Blessing of God.

Fig. 26.
Chalice/*skih*. Holy Archangels (Surb Hreshtakapet) Church, Balat.
Patriarchal Museum, Kumkapu.
Early nineteenth century.
Silver and gilded silver, 19 x 15 centimeters.
Inscription:
In memoriam archangel [?] *Tamam hanum for Chohar Hay usteayn*
Mikayel for kuyumju Sargis' soul, this chalice I donate to the Church
of the Holy Archangels in the tenth year.

Fig. 27.
Chalice/*skih* with paten/*maghsma*. Apparition of the Holy Cross Church,
Kurucheshme. Patriarchal Museum, Kumkapu.
Dated 1837.
Gold, silver and gilded silver, 36.5 x 19.5 centimeters; paten 21.5
diameter.

Inscription:

O celebrant holy priest, remember before the Lamb of God me, Gohar Aristakesian who gave this memorial [gift], *together with my daughters who are asleep* [in Christ], *Tiruhi, Marta with her family, and Hripsime, 1286* [1837].

Fig. 28.

Chalice/*skih*. Holy Mother of God Church, Beshiktash. Patriarchal
    Museum, Kumkapu.

Dated 1818.

Silver and gilded silver, 32 x 22 centimeters.

Inscription:

This is a [gift] *to the Holy Mother of God Church in memory of mahtesi Sima and* [his] *wife Mariam and sons Asatur and Arif, 1267* [1818].

Figs. 29A-29B.

Chalice/*skih*. Holy Cross Church, Uskudar.

Early nineteenth century.

Silver, gilded silver and enamel, 36 x 23.5 centimeters.

Fig. 30.

Reliquary Ark/*masunkov debank*. St. Gregory the Illuminator Church,
    Karakoy. Patriarchal Museum, Kumkapu.

Dated 1745.

Silver, 15 x 11 x 5 centimeters.

Inscription:

In this Holy reliquary are the beneficent relics of the saints, [namely] *the blessed Apostle Thaddeus, the Holy Virgin Hripsime and the Patriarch Aristakes; they are intercessors before the Lord. May the Lord be reconciled with me, a sinner, on the day of the Great Judgment. I, sinful Lelina, am the daughter of Oskan. O Holy children of Holy Sion, o clerics, pray for mercy at the feet of the saints for my sinful self, for my parents Oskan and Sultan pasha, my brothers and my entire family and you shall receive what you seek. In the year 1194* [1745].

Fig. 31.

Altar Ark/*masunkov debank*. Holy Archangels Church, Balat; Patriarchal
    Museum, Kumkapu.

Dated 1787.

Silver, gilded silver, wood and cloth, 71 x 127 centimeters.

Inscription:

This vestry is in memory of the soul of the late Minas Amira of the

Musheghka village of Akn and [in memory] *of the soul of his wife Anna who is alive and their living and asleep* [family members], *at the gate of St. Hreshtakapet* [Holy Archangels] *in Balat, 1236* [1787].

Fig. 32A.
Belt/*goti*. Patriarchate, Kumkapu. Patriarchal Museum, Kumkapu.
Late eighteenth or early nineteenth century.
Silver and gilded silver, 11 x 24 centimeters.

Fig. 32B.
Buckle/*jarmand*. Holy Mother of God Cathedral, Kumkapu. Patriarchal
    Museum, Kumkapu.
Dated 1715–41 belonging to Patriarch Hovhannes Golod.
Silver and gilded silver, 10 x 6.5 centimeters.
Inscription:
    John 16:33—*Be of good cheer* [for] *I have overcome the world.*

Fig. 33A.
Belt/*goti*. Holy Cross Church, Uskudar.
Early nineteenth century.
Gilded silver, jade, and semi-precious stone, 19.25 x 9 centimeters.

Fig. 33B.
Belt/*goti* and buckle/*jarmand*. Holy Cross Church Selamiye/Uskudar.
Late eighteenth or early nineteenth century.
Gilded silver and gold, 77 x 3.5 centimeters (belt), 8 x 8 centimeters
    (buckle).

Fig. 33C.
Belt/*goti* and buckle/*jarmand*. Apparition of the Holy Cross Church,
    Kurucheshme.
Late eighteenth or early nineteenth century.
Silver, gilded silver and cloth, 149 x 6 centimeters (belt), 30 centimeters.
The belt has a woven pattern of leaves and berries and a geometric zig-zag
    pattern representing the flowing river of life. The buckle is cast with
    elaborate filigree on the surface.

Fig. 34.
Personal cross/*khach veghari masunkov*. Holy Mother of God Cathedral,
    Kumkapu. Patriarchal Museum, Kumkapu.
Dated 1743.
Gold, jade, enamel, precious and semi-precious stones, 10 x 8 centimeters.
Inscription:
    This Holy Sign [of the Cross] [was] *granted by Cardinal Pelu-*

kye [Cardinal Luis Antonio Belluga y Moncada] *to the late Patriarch Hovhannes vardapet and* [was] *ornamented with gems and gold by Patriarch Hakob, a memorial to St. James which* [is in] *Jerusalem in the year of the Lord 1743.*

Fig. 35.
Writing table with pen and ink set. Patriarchate, Kumkapu. Patriarchal
  Museum, Kumkapu.
Dated 1896–1908 belonging to Patriarch Maghakia Ormanian.
Silver, gilded silver and gold, 23 x 21 x 19 centimeters.

Figs. 36A-36B.
Cope. Holy Mother of God Cathedral, Kumkapu. Patriarchal Museum,
  Kumkapu.

Fig. 37.
Embroidered cope/*shurchar*. Holy Mother of God Cathedral, Kumkapu.
  Patriarchal Museum, Kumkapu.
Dated 1834.
Metal and silk thread embroidery on green silk satin, chenille yarns, cotton
  yarns, pearls, sequins, coiled wire, coiled wire knots, couching, 340
  centimeters; along the straight edge, 158 centimeters long at the center
  back.
Inscription:
  This Holy and costly sacerdotal [set of] *vestments is a memorial* [gift] *to the Holy Cross Church of the village of Apuchekh in* [the region of] *Akn. [They are] embroidered with diamond crosses, pearls and silver [thread]—namely the crown, the amice, the cope, the stole, the maniple [s], the girdle, the slippers—through the provision and subsidy of the God-living Hovhannes Agha, son of the senior father Stepan Ter [Father] Poghosian, and his spouse, the humble Mrs. Eva, and his son Stepan Agha and his daughter-in-law Desnof hanum, and his daughter, Sinemeshah hanum, and may our memory not be forgotten before the immortal Lamb of God. And let Him save [us] with all [our] relatives from visible and invisible tribulations. It was [donated] in the year 1834.*

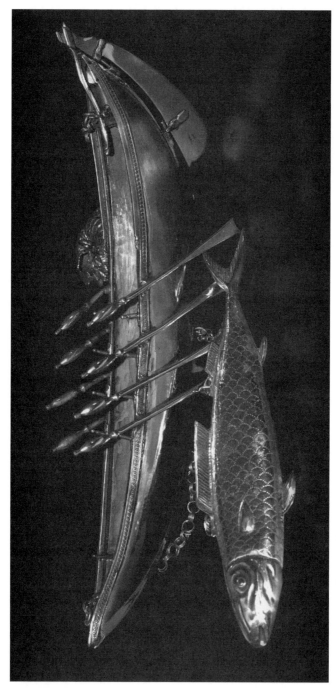

Fig. 1. Chandelier Ornament, Holy Resurrection (Surb Harutiun) Church, Kumkapu

Fig. 2. Seal Stamp from the Textile Workshop of Harutiun
Amira Bezjian, 1833

Fig. 3. Altar Ark, Holy Cross (Surb Khach) Church, Uskudar

Fig. 4A. Mitre, Saint John the Precursor (Surb Karapet) Church,
Baghlarbashi/Uskudar

Fig. 4B. Detail, Mitre, St. John the Precursor Church,
Baghlarbashi/Uskudar

Fig. 5A. Mitre, Patriarchal Museum, Kumkapu

Fig. 5B. Reverse, Mitre, Patriarchal Museum, Kumkapu

Fig. 6A. Mitre, Holy Mother of God (Surb Astvatsatsin) Church, Beshiktash

146

Fig. 6B. Reverse, Mitre, Holy Mother of God Church,
Beshiktash

Fig. 7. Mitre, Holy Mother of God Cathedral, Kumkapu

Fig. 8A. Mitre, Holy Trinity (Surb Errordutiun) Church, Beyoghlu

Fig. 8B. Detail, Mitre, Holy Trinity Church, Beyoghlu

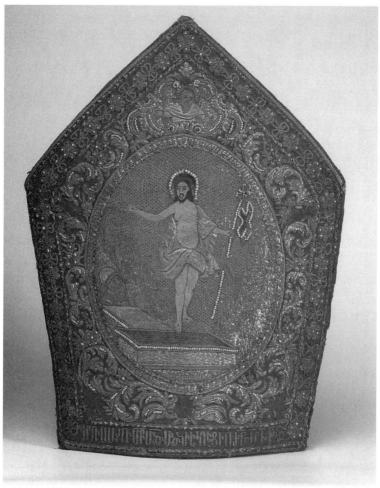

Fig. 8C. Reverse, Mitre, Holy Trinity Church, Beyoghlu

Fig. 8D. Detail, Mitre, Holy Trinity Church, Beyoghlu

152

Figs. 9-10. Crowns, Holy Mother of God Church, Yenikoy

Fig. 11A. Collar and Lappet Set, Holy Mother of God Church,
Beshiktash

154

Figs. 11B-11C. Detail, Collar and Lappet Set, Holy Mother of God Church, Beshiktash

Fig. 12. Chalice Cover, Holy Mother of God Cathedral, Kumkapu

Fig. 13. Chalice Cover, Holy Mother of God Cathedral,
Kumkapu

Fig. 14. Chalice Cover, Holy Cross Church, Uskudar

Fig. 15. Table Censers, Holy Cross Church, Uskudar

Fig. 16. Table Censers, Saint Nicholas (Surb Nikoghos)
Church, Beykoz

Fig. 17A. Altar Standard, Holy Cross Church, Uskudar

Fig. 17B. Detail, Altar Standard, Holy Cross Church, Uskudar

Fig. 18. Patriarchal Staff, Patriarchate, Kumkapu

Fig. 19. Processional/Altar Cross, Holy Cross Church, Uskudar

Fig. 20. Processional Cross, Holy Cross Church, Uskudar

Fig. 21. Miuron Vessel, Dove for the Holy Miuron/*Miuronatap Aghavni*, Holy Mother of God Church, Beshiktash

Fig. 22. Incense Arks, Holy Mother of God Cathedral, Kumkapu

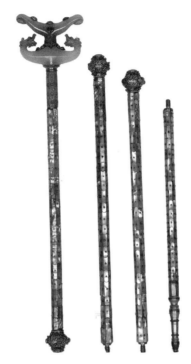

Fig. 23A. Vardapet Staff, Saint Gregory the Illuminator
(Surb Grigor Lusavorich) Church, Karakoy

Fig. 23B. Detail, Vardapet Staff, Saint John the Precursor
Church, Baghlarbashi/Uskudar

Fig. 24. Ewer and Basin, Saint Stephen (Surb Stepanos)
Church, Yeshilkoy

Fig. 25. Gospel Cover, Saint Gregory the Illuminator
Church, Karakoy

Fig. 26. Chalice, Holy Archangels (Surb Hreshtakapet) Church,
Balat

Fig. 27. Chalice, Apparition of the Holy Cross Church,
Kurucheshme

172

Fig. 28. Chalice, Holy Mother of God Church, Beshiktash

Fig. 29A. Chalice, Holy Cross Church, Uskudar

Fig. 29B. Detail, Chalice, Holy Cross
Church, Uskudar

174

Fig. 30. Reliquary, Saint Gregory the Illuminator Church, Karakoy

Fig. 31. Altar Ark, Holy Archangels Church, Balat

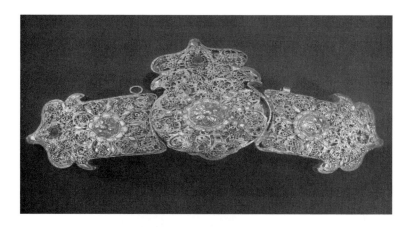

Figs. 32A-32B. Belts, Holy Mother of God Cathedral, Kumkapu

Figs. 33A-33B. Belts, Holy Cross Church, Uskudar

178

Fig. 33C. Belt, Apparition of the Holy Cross Church, Kurucheshme

Fig. 34. Personal Cross, Holy Mother of God Cathedral,
Kumkapu

Fig. 35. Writing Table, Patriarchate, Kumkapu

Fig. 36A. Cope, Holy Mother of God Cathedral, Kumkapu

Fig. 36B. Detail, Cope, Holy Mother of God Cathedral, Kumkapu

182

Fig. 37. Cope, Holy Mother of God Cathedral, Kumkapu

❋ 7 ❋

THE ARMENIAN BIBLE OF 1623
AND THE MERCHANT COMMUNITIES
OF CONSTANTINOPLE AND NEW JULFA

Ina Baghdiantz McCabe

Relations between the Armenian merchants in New Julfa, Iran, and their counterparts in Constantinople have rarely been a subject of scholarly examination. The Constantinople Armenian Bible of 1623 (Gulbenkian Collection, Ms L.A. 152) serves as a concrete example of the contacts between the two cities, which had emerged as the main centers of the Armenian Diaspora by the seventeenth century.[1] The superior quality of the illuminations of this Bible represents the craftsmanship of the Armenians in Constantinople and is of interest to historians of art and of merchant networks.

This Armenian Bible was commissioned by Khwaja (Khoja) Nazar, the leader of the merchant community of New Julfa, and it was copied in a Constantinople workshop in 1623.[2] It arrived in New Julfa in 1629, as is recorded in one of its three colophons. New Julfa was an entirely Armenian suburb of Isfahan. It became a new settlement of Armenians who had previously lived in the city of Julfa on the banks of the Araxes River in Nakhichevan, a region presently in the Republic of Azerbaijan. The *khachkar*s (cross-

---

[1] In January 2000, this beautifully illuminated 1623 Armenian Bible was displayed at the exhibition of the Gulbenkian Collection at the Metropolitan Museum of Art in New York. See Katharine Baetjer and James David Draper, eds., *Only the Best: Masterpieces of the Calouste Gulbenkian Museum* (Lisbon: Metropolitan Museum of Art, 1999).

[2] After the exhibition, Sylvie Merian of The Pierpont Morgan Library in New York was given permission to study the Bible for details. At the end of her examination, the colophon was deciphered, confirming her translation of a reference to the two wives of Nazar. I am most grateful to her, for in the process, she read Nazar's title to me, unaware what and how much her communication meant to me. The notes by Sirarpie Der Nersessian were generously made available by the Gulbenkian Museum.

stones) that marked the tombs of the silk merchants of old Julfa were wantonly destroyed with bulldozers by the Azeri authorities in three major stages, in 1998, 2003, and 2005.[3]

The control of the major silk-growing regions by the Safavids at the beginning of the seventeenth century, namely the provinces of Gilan, Mazendaran, Karabagh, and later Shirvan, which were previously under Ottoman control, opened an era of prosperity for Iran. Unlike Constantinople, Isfahan had not been an important long-time capital city.[4] The profits of the silk trade were crucial to building Isfahan by Shah Abbas (1587-1629). One may wonder if the deportations of the Armenians of Tabriz by the Ottomans to Constantinople in earlier times had not inspired the shah's decision to have wealthy Armenian silk merchants forcibly transferred to live in his new capital.

A little over a decade after Isfahan became the new capital of Safavid Iran in 1590, a wealthy new suburb was constructed south of the river Zayandeh Rud, which flowed through the city's best neighborhoods. Having resettled thousands of Armenians from Julfa on the Araxes to New Julfa in 1605, Shah Abbas I, in a 1619 edict, ceded the royal land of the suburb as *a'nam* (a land grant without rent) to a group of prominent Armenian silk merchants.[5] In this all-Armenian suburb, named after its original town of Julfa, the residents most probably had to pay a 10 percent fee on its value upon receipt of the gift. All such gifts, both those to and from the shah, were taxed.[6] Nevertheless, the prosperous Armenian community enjoyed a highly privileged political status in Iran. Although the Armenians had been important silk traders in the Otto-

---

[3] Some of these khachkars have been documented. See Kéram Kevonian, "La société reconstituée," in *Les Arméniens dans le commerce asiatique au début de l'ère moderne*, ed. Sushil Chaudhury and Kéram Kévonian (Paris: Maison des sciences de l'homme, 2007), pp. 371-89.

[4] Sussan Babaie, Kathryn Babayan, Ina Baghdiantz-McCabe, and Massumeh Farhad, *Slaves of the Shah: New Elites of Safavid Isfahan* (London: I.B. Tauris, 2004), pp. 49-80.

[5] See Ina Baghdiantz McCabe, *The Shah's Silk for Europe's Silver: The Eurasian Silk Trade of the Julfan Armenians in Safavid Iran and India (1590-1750)* (Atlanta: Scholars Press, 1999), note 187; Harutiun Ter Hovhaniants, *Patmutiun Nor Jughayi (Spahan)* [History of New Julfa (Isfahan)] (New Julfa: All Savior's Cathedral, 1980), vol. 1, pp. 44-47.

[6] *Tadhkirat al-mulūk* [A Manual of Safavid Administration] (Tehran: Amir Kabir, 1368 [1990]), p. 156.

man Empire prior to their resettlement in New Julfa, it was under Safavid political protection that they perfected their international network. An organized group of Armenian merchant families operated a worldwide commercial network of Iranian silk in exchange for silver and European manufactured goods. Merchant patronage financed Armenian printing presses and scriptoria even when the Church appeared directly as the patron, since the Church itself depended on financing from merchant families.[7] New Julfa soon emerged as the hub of Iran's international silk trade and the center of a vast commercial organization covering half the world, from Amsterdam to the Philippines, from Arkhangelsk and Narva to the coast of Coromandel in India, the Moluccas, and Siam.

The seventeenth century witnessed a renaissance of manuscript illumination in Constantinople, in the Crimea, and later in Isfahan, but the Ottoman capital had not only served as a model for the Armenians of New Julfa in the arts and in the local scriptoria as several art historians have argued, but also for the Safavids themselves in planning their new capital. In the 1620s, about a decade after its first constructions and its earliest church, New Julfa had not yet established any scriptoria of its own. Bibles were commissioned from the well-known scriptoria in Constantinople and then exported to New Julfa.[8] Vrej Nersessian has shown that many of their compositions were repeated with slight differences in three Bibles copied in New Julfa. The Armenian Bible of 1623, or of 1629 as it is sometimes described, was copied in *bolorgir* script, an Armenian script in minuscule, by the copyist Hakob.[9]

Silk merchants and bankers in the Ottoman Empire and Iran supported Armenian life in the Diaspora beyond their own communities by providing finances for the churches, the clergy, the scriptoria, and the printing presses founded in Venice, Amsterdam, and Marseilles. They financed major institutions that defined and propagated Armenian religious culture and the new secular culture. Publications included Armenian handbooks for merchants,

---

[7] On the role of Julfan money in establishing printing presses as far away as Amsterdam, see Ina Baghdiantz McCabe "Merchant Capital and Knowledge: The Financing of Early Armenian Printing Presses by the Eurasian Silk Trade," in *Treasures in Heaven: Armenian Art* (New York: Pierpont Morgan Library, 1998), pp. 58-73.

[8] Baetjer and Draper, *Only the Best*, p. 22.

[9] Vrej Nersessian, *Treasures from the Ark: 1700 Years of Armenian Christian Art* (London: British Library, 2001); Nersessian, p. 188, gives 1629 as the date.

dictionaries, and even world maps, and many of them printed in Europe found their main market in Constantinople and from there were shipped to New Julfa.[10] Despite the fact that for years the Constantinople community did not have a printing press of its own, the city not only remained the intellectual center but also served as the distribution center for books to the rest of the Diaspora. The New Julfans looked to the workshops in Constantinople for models to imitate, and the parallel development of printing and scriptoria continued well into the nineteenth century.[11] As the presses in Europe and Iran failed at the end of the seventeenth century, Constantinople emerged as the main center for Armenian book distribution. However, it became a center for book printing and production only later—in the nineteenth century. In the seventeenth century, the Armenian Church and merchants of Constantinople financed the books produced in the local Armenian scriptoria.

It is difficult to speak of merchants as a class in the Ottoman Empire because of the structure of Ottoman society. Islamic law and Ottoman practice did not recognize Constantinopolitan or Aleppine merchants, Muslims and Christians alike, as a separate corporate body. Merchants seldom acted as a unified group, although they did have some form of organized leadership under prominent figures who were usually urban notables, often referred to as the *a'yan*.[12] In Iran, the absence of a bourgeoisie has long been a subject of debate, even though the Armenians of New Julfa have often been perceived as a "bourgeoisie" under Safavid rule.[13]

Numerous studies have maintained that no merchant middle class existed in Iran until the end of the nineteenth century. A central difficulty here is the concept of bourgeoisie or mercantile class, which in the case of Europe is an urban middle class distinct from the landowning nobility. This distinction is essential in these

---

[10] Raymond H. Kévorkian, *Catalogue des "incunables" arméniens (1511/1695), ou, Chronique de l'imprimerie arménienne* (Geneva: P. Cramer, 1986).

[11] "Rethinking Categories: Armenian Manuscript Art within an East-West Context," Thirtieth International Congress of the History of Art, London, September 3-8, 2000. For details of the similarities between the two communities, see Nersessian, *Treasures*, pp. 188-89.

[12] Bruce Masters, *The Origins of Western Economic Dominance in the Middle East* (New York: New York University Press, 1988), p. 48.

[13] See the introduction to *Tadhkirat al-mulūk: A Manual of Safavid Administration (circa 1137/1725)*, Persian text in facsimile (British Museum, Or. 9496), trans. and annotated, Vladimir Minorsky (London: Luzac, 1943).

theoretical models, the most fundamental being Karl Marx's analysis of European political economy and definition of the bourgeoisie as an urban middle class.[14] In Iran, the richest merchants, including the Armenians, accumulated vast amounts of capital and were rich landowners; the shah himself was a merchant.[15] The problem was similar in the Ottoman Empire with the urban a'yan. There was no separate class of merchants, and in both cases the wealthy became part of local structures and land-owning elites. The Julfans, however, became an integral part of the palace. Their ruler, the *kalantar* or provost, ruled an autonomous city-state under Safavid rule. They were not strictly middle class, both because of the immense fortunes they amassed and because of their inclusion in the *khassa* (royal household), which made them part of the royal administrative system and gave them a political and administrative role within the palace. Their inclusion in the royal household and their association with the converted Caucasian deportees called *ghulams* (royal slaves) open a window that helps explore the structure of the Safavid household. Many Armenians (Christians and ghulams) rose through the hierarchy of the Safavid political world, and some Armenian ghulams even attained the post of grand vizier.[16]

In contrast, there were no Armenian merchant city-states formed in the Ottoman Empire, and the Constantinopolitan and Aleppine merchants did not form a governing body that exercised political power. New Julfa emerged in Iran as an Armenian city-state not because of a specific structure that offered a special corporation (much like the Ottoman case), but perhaps because of the political structure of the Safavid royal household.[17] The city-state of New Julfa became possible because the Armenian elite played a unique political role in seventeenth-century Iran.[18] New Julfa was the only Armenian autonomous protected city, with its churches and mer-

---

[14] Ahmad Ashraf, "Historical Obstacles to the Formation of a Bourgeoisie in Iran," in *Studies in the Economic History of the Middle East*, ed. M.A. Cook (London: Oxford University Press, 1970), pp. 308-33.

[15] Jean Aubin, "La propriété foncière en Azerbaydjan," *Le Monde Iranien et l'Islam: Sociétés et Cultures* 4 (1976-77): 79-132.

[16] Baghdiantz McCabe, *Shah's Silk*, chs. 3, 5, 7 *passim*.

[17] Ina Baghdiantz, "The Merchants of New Julfa: Some Aspects of their International Trade in the late Seventeenth Century," Ph.D. diss., Columbia University, 1993.

[18] See Baghdiantz McCabe, *Shah's Silk*, pp. 123-64.

chant houses now still standing. Although the city's preservation is at stake, the Iranian government has protected it from the fate of the cemetery at old Julfa and has taken great care in classifying the area and its historic monuments. The Bible examined here was commissioned by the most important ruler of New Julfa and it offers unprecedented information about him.

Khwaja Nazar was the third to rule the New Julfans after the deportation of the Julfans to Iran, and their second formal kalantar/ provost. According to the historian Arakel of Tavriz, negotiations and an agreement between Shah Abbas and the leaders of the Armenian Church, who were crushed in debt to the Ottomans, were a prelude to the deportation of the Armenians of Julfa.[19] Although Arakel does not say that the leaders of old Julfa participated in these initial negotiations, he does write of the ruler of the town of Julfa receiving the shah by feasting with him for three days and giving him the key to the city. The Julfan deportation was headed by Khwaja Khachik of the Shafrazian family, Khwaja Nazar's father. The initial agreement was revisited and altered, however, in the shah's visit to Julfa in 1603, resulting in the Julfan exodus with generalized massive and tragic deportations. Although this cannot be viewed as a voluntary move, there were negotiations for special circumstances amid a more brutal reality of forced circumcision, castration, and conversion and slavery in the arena of war. Until his death in 1605, Khwaja Khachik remained the leader of the deported Armenians as they settled in Isfahan. His son, Khwaja Safar, served as the first kalantar of New Julfa from 1605 to 1618 and was succeeded by his brother Nazar from 1618 to 1636. According to Safavid royal edicts, both Shah Abbas I and Shah Safi I (1629-42) referred to this second ruler of New Julfa, Khwaja Nazar, as "shah."

The provost of the suburb formally bore the Iranian title of shah, as documented in a Safavid royal edict. Some travelers called him a prince, but no other source that confirmed this information had been noticed until the Bible of 1623 came to New York in a Metropolitan Museum exhibit of Calouste Gulbenkian's collec-

---

[19] For the agreement between the shah and the church leadership, see the English version of *The History of Vardapet Arak'el of Tabriz /Patmut'iwn Arak'el Vardapeti Dawrizhets'woy,* intro. and trans. George A. Bournoutian (Costa Mesa, CA: Mazda Publishers, 1995), pp. 18-21.

tions. Gulbenkian had not only purchased one of the finest Bibles, but he had also helped preserve a source that recorded the title of Khwaja Nazar. Three colophons appear at the end of the Bible, the last entered in 1796 in Tiflis. In the first and longest colophon of 1629 (pages 1208-10) lies the Armenian version of the title held by "shah" Khwaja Nazar of Julfa. The pertinent passage reads: "*Paron paronats patvial ev metsarial i TGRTs* [*Tagavorats*]," abbreviated without vowels and with a long line above "*Jughayi khojay Nazarn*" (Khwaja Nazar of Julfa). The classical Armenian meaning of the word is given in the dictionary *Nor Bargirk*, which explains its origins in a medieval Latin title and defines it as *ishkhan* or prince.[20] Who chose Khwaja Nazar's Armenian title of *paron paronats*? Who bestowed it on him? The colophon dates, at the earliest, in the first year of the reign of Shah Safi, 1629. The text of the colophon confirms that although the Bible was completed in Constantinople in 1623 (year 1072 of the Armenian era), it was taken to New Julfa a few years later in 1629 (year 1078). It is in New Julfa that the first colophon, one that spans nearly four pages, was written to describe the circumstances of the Julfan exile. It clearly states that the manuscript was copied by the scribe Hakob for the "prince of princes" Khwaja Nazar and his sons Sarfrabek, Eliaz, and Haykaz. That the most powerful ruling family of New Julfa commissioned its Bible in Constantinople remains rich in political significance.

The silk trade from Iran had to cross the Ottoman domains to get to Europe. There is no doubt there must have been collaboration between the Ottoman and Iranian merchants of Armenian origin, yet little is known about this collaboration. The silk trade was a source of tremendous wealth for Iran, but its transit certainly created profits for the Ottomans, as Suraiya Faroqhi has argued. European consumption of silk was around 200,000 to 250,000 kilograms per year. Of this, 86 percent came from Safavid Iran, while some of the rest came from Syria.[21] The silk trade did not benefit Iran or the Julfan Armenians alone but undoubtedly also

---

[20] The title in full would read: "Prince of princes honored and exalted by kings: the Julfan Khwaja Nazar." The Gulbenkian Museum holds the description notes left for this Bible by Sirarpie Der Nersessian, who translated the title as "prince of princes."

[21] Suraiya Faroqhi et al., *An Economic and Social History of the Ottoman Empire*, vol. 2: *1600-1914* (Cambridge: Cambridge University Press, 1997), p. 503.

benefited Ottoman Armenian merchants on the roads to the markets across the empire.

The Armenian Merchants
of New Julfa and the Ottoman Empire

There were differences between the Armenian merchants living under Ottoman rule and the New Julfans. Ottoman Armenians were subjected to more rules. There were differences in vestments between the Armenian merchants living under Ottoman rule and the New Julfans. Ottoman Armenians wore a white turban tinged with blue and purple, but they were not allowed the white turban of the Turks.[22] No distinction of dress appeared in Iran. Iranian Armenians often wore a red turban like their Iranian merchant counterparts, but never the red *taj*, a head dress reserved for the spiritual followers of the Safavids. Julfan Armenians were even allowed by the shahs to wear the color green, a color otherwise strictly reserved for the descendants of the Prophet and one that was prohibited to the Armenians in the Ottoman Empire. Their privileges in Iran were exceptional.[23]

Julfan commercial success long predated the Iranian monarch's interest in the Armenians in the early seventeenth century. The Armenian silk merchants of old Julfa had emerged as successful traders in the mid-sixteenth century in competition with the Europeans and made their fortunes first in the Ottoman Empire prior to their deportation to Iran. The success of this group of Armenians in the Ottoman markets of Aleppo, Bursa/Brusa, Smyrna/Izmir, and Constantinople requires a closer examination than has been available in the literature thus far.[24]

The fall of Tabriz to the Ottomans in 1514 after the battle of Chaldiran, at the very early stages of Safavid rise to power, marked the beginning of nearly a century of Ottoman control of the silk

---

[22] Roberto Gulbenkian, "L'habit Arménien laissez passer oriental pour les missionnaires marchands et voyageurs Européens aux XVIIème et XVIIIème siècles," *Revue des études arméniennes*, n.s., 25 (1994-95): 369-88.

[23] See Francis Richard, ed., *Raphaël du Mans, missionnaire en Perse au XVIIe siècle*, vol. 2: *Estat de la Perse, 1600* (Paris: L'Harmattan, 1995), for their similitude of dress, p. 33; for the color green, p. 329.

[24] Edmund Herzig, "The Rise of the Julfa Merchants in the Late Sixteenth Century," in Melville, *Safavid Persia*, pp. 305-22.

markets and the silk-producing regions in Iran. It brought the Ottomans vast profits. Although areas of silk production such as Kashan, Yazd, Shiraz, and Khorasan escaped Ottoman control, Iranian merchants had trouble supplying silk to the other centers because of the Ottoman presence. As a result, India became a major export destination for Iranian merchants, and the Kandahar land route, presently in Afghanistan, served as the primary road for the caravans to India.[25] Not only was Tabriz in Ottoman hands but a local dynasty in Gilan, the main silk-producing region, asked to come under Ottoman protection.[26] This situation did not change until the reign of Shah Abbas I, when the Safavids deprived the Ottomans of their control over the silk trade. That the Julfans continued to serve as merchants during the contested century of Ottoman rule could not have been insignificant for their future commercial ties.

Wars and unrest frequently interrupted the traffic of raw silk. Having imposed a blockade against Iranian goods after the victory of 1514, the Ottomans raided Tabriz and transferred many merchants, among them Armenians, to Constantinople.[27] It is clear that the Genoese controlled the western end of this silk trade to Europe, from Bursa on, and the Armenian merchants of Tabriz having been moved to Constantinople, one might reasonably assume that Iranian merchants were transporting the silk from Tabriz to Bursa and other markets. However, save for a few theoretical expositions, the Iranian merchants have not been studied. No information has been uncovered to date from Iranian sources on the role of Iranian merchants in the silk trade. Ottoman sources may compensate for this gap to some degree. For example, evidence found in the Bursa archives shows that during the second half of the fifteenth century Muslim Iranian merchants, mostly Azeris, transported Iranian raw silk to Bursa and exchanged it for Western goods imported by Italians into the Ottoman Empire. The other market was Aleppo where, again, Iranian caravans brought their silk via the Bitlis-

---

[25] Ronald W. Ferrier, "An English View of the Persian Trade in 1618," *Journal of the Economic and Social History of the Orient* 19 (1976): 203.

[26] Halil Inalcik, "Bursa and the Silk Trade," in *An Economic and Social History of the Ottoman Empire,* vol. 1: *1300-1600,* ed. Halil Inalcik with Donald Quataert (Cambridge: Cambridge University Press, 1997), pp. 218-55.

[27] Vartan Gregorian, "Minorities of Isfahan: The Armenian Community of Isfahan, 1587-1722," *Iranian Studies* 7:2 (1974): 658.

Diarbekir-Mardin route.[28] Julfan Armenians virtually controlled the Iranian silk trade in the city[29] and were major players in the Aleppine market.[30]

Throughout the fifteenth and sixteenth centuries, unlike in the case of Aleppo, the merchants who came to Bursa to sell to the Italians were overwhelmingly Muslims (Iranian and Azeri) mostly merchants from Iran, called *azemi* in the Genoese records. They controlled the eastern leg of the raw silk trade. The Iranians either sold to the Italians in Bursa directly or sent their own agents to the Balkans and into Italy. Armenians as importers of silk are mentioned at this time, albeit very rarely, in the Bursa records. However, they replaced the Muslim Iranians as importers in the Bursa records from the reign of Shah Abbas in the early seventeenth century.[31]

Shah Abbas consolidated his monopoly over the silk trade by confiscating silk purchased by private merchants. This royal monopoly made him the chief capitalist in Safavid Iran in 1617-19 and was the means through which the Armenians became a crucial element in his state-building policies. Yet, government policy alone did not enable their success; even before the reign of Shah Abbas, the Julfans had long established elaborate networks based on family associations. Since few Europeans visited Iran before Shah Abbas' reign, however, the misperception has arisen that the Iranian silk trade was born *ex nihilo* during his reign and along with it the Armenian participation within it. Armenian silk producers and silk merchants assumed a prominent role in Safavid economy at this new juncture largely because of their knowledge of the Ottoman markets and their relationship with other merchants in Aleppo, Constantinople, Bursa, and later Smyrna. Further, they had settlements and trading houses in the market cities of the Ottoman Empire and in the ports of the Mediterranean, such as Marseilles, Livorno, and Venice.[32] A *farmân* by Shah Abbas, dated Rabi' al-Thani 1014/1605, attests to the Julfans' prior prosperity under the Ottomans. The shah states that more than 2,000 *tumans*

---

[28] Inalcik, "Bursa," p. 224.

[29] Avedis K. Sanjian, *The Armenian Community in Syria under Ottoman Dominion* (Cambridge, MA: Harvard University Press, 1965), pp. 48-49.

[30] Masters, *Origins*, pp. 48-49.

[31] Inalcik, "Bursa," p. 227.

[32] Ferrier, "English View," p. 203.

were spent on some of old Julfa's houses in Nakhichevan ("*dar julâ khâne bûd ki dû hazâr tumân kharj ân kardah bûdand*"). He adds: "They had them torn down in order to come here [Isfahan] with their households."[33] Their success reached its zenith in Iran, but the roots of their success rested in their continuous contacts with Armenians and markets in the Ottoman Empire.

Like the Julfans, other groups were also forcibly moved during the sixteenth and seventeenth centuries. The Safavid and Ottoman rulers considered the local inhabitants of the Caucasus, Muslim and Christian alike, subjects of the opposing forces during their frequent wars, and the victors deported many prisoners to the major cities. As stated, when Sultan Selim conquered the city of Tabriz in 1514, he deported many of the inhabitants, including 3,000 Armenian Christians, to Constantinople.[34]

There were other cases of mobility and contact. Several Armenian *melik*s or princes had come to Iran requesting the shah's protection and had stayed in Iran a short while. In the decrees translated by Hakob Papazyan, one finds the privileges granted to a few of them, such as lordships and the right to collect taxes in their regions.[35]

Constantinople and New Julfa

Constantinople was the most important city in the region in the seventeenth century, both politically and as a major market, and it served the Safavids as a model for building the new Iranian capital of Isfahan (established in 1589). Information about the population of the Ottoman capital is at best vague. The English traveler George Sandys wrote of 700,000 inhabitants; in 1640, the Venetian Alviso Contarini mentioned a million inhabitants, as did Evliya Chelebi; Pietro Civrano placed the number at 800,000 in 1681. Robert Mantran and Suraiya Faroqhi have accepted between

---

[33] This *farmân* has been translated into Armenian on page 46 in Harutiun Ter Hovhaniants, *Patmutiun Nor Jughayi* (Julfa, 1880; New Julfa: All Savior's Cathedral, 1980), vol. 1. The original is at New Julfa's All Savior's Museum. I thank Mr. Levon Minassian, conservator of the museum, for providing copies of the *farmân*s.

[34] Gregorian, "Minorities," p. 658.

[35] A.D. Papazyan, *Persidskiye dokumenty Matenadarana: Ukazy* [Persian Documents of the Matenadaran: Edicts] (Erevan: Armenian Academy of Sciences, 1956), pp. 89-90, 99-100.

600,000 and 700,000 as a reasonable estimate.[36] In his description of Constantinople in the middle of the seventeenth century, Evliya Chelebi counts 9,990 Muslim neighborhoods (*mahalle*), 304 Greek neighborhoods, 657 Jewish, and 27 Armenian, and 17 neighborhoods inhabited by the Franks. Mantran has cautioned against taking this proportion of a thousand Muslim mahalle for a thousand non-Muslim ones seriously. There are more precise figures in the documents of 1690-91, which record the non-Muslim populations of Galata, Stambul, and Eyub who had to pay the *jeziya* head tax and which allow for the estimate of 62,000 non-Muslim households in the city. Mantran uses the conservative figure of 4 to 5 inhabitants per household to arrive at a figure of 250,000 to 300,000 non-Muslim inhabitants in the Ottoman capital. One could argue that those small households were non-existent in the Middle East in the seventeenth century and are a modern European model. If one chose a more realistic model for the Jewish, Armenian, Greek, or Genoese extended families of the seventeenth century, this number would be considerably higher. As it stands, the Christian and Jewish households represented roughly a quarter of the population.

The Armenian population in the Ottoman capital consisted of three groups at this time: a small community that had established residence in the city prior to the Ottoman conquest; those who had immigrated voluntarily from war-torn Anatolia, the Armenian plateau, and the Caucasus; and those who had been forced out of their towns, such as the Armenians of Tabriz in 1514. A French missionary provides a rare figure for the Armenian population in Constantinople. The French were exceptionally well informed about the Christians of the Ottoman Empire in this period. Their missionaries sought to convert the Armenians to Catholicism, and in one case of a failed attempt they were so zealous as to kidnap the Armenian Patriarch of Constantinople, Avetik I, and hold him prisoner in the Bastille. According to the Capuchins in the year 1700, the Armenians had 40 churches in the city of Constantinople with about 40,000 adherents.[37] This figure does not include the

---

[36] Robert Mantran, *Histoire d'Istanbul* (Paris: Fayard, 1996), p. 253; Faroqhi, *Economic and Social History*, p. 493.

[37] See Raymond Kévorkian, "Document d'archives français sur le patriarcat de Constantinople," *Revue des études arméniennes*, n.s., 19 (1985): 333-71, and his "L'imprimerie Surb Ejmiacin at Surb Sarkis Zoravar et le conflit entre Arméniens et Catholiques à Constantinople," *Revue des études arméniennes*, n.s.,15 (1981): 401-02.

Catholic Armenians who migrated to Constantinople from the strongly Catholicized region of Nakhichevan.

Everywhere except in New Julfa, the Armenians remained a classical trading diaspora as defined by Curtin and discussed by Bruce Masters and Sanjay Subrahmanyam.[38] One criterion for a classical trade diaspora is to be excluded from political power in the host society. Unlike Armenians in Safavid Iran, those in the broader diaspora did not wield political power in other governments, although they did have political influence because of their financial role as bankers or financiers. It would not be an exaggeration to call Nazar the ruler of this city-state, albeit one under the protection of the Safavid monarch. There was also a form of Armenian state within the Safavid state, headed by a ruler with a title of "shah." The revelations in the colophon in the 1623 Bible reiterate what the royal edicts pointed to, namely that Khwaja Nazar, the ruler of Julfa, had been bestowed political power within Safavid Iran and exercised a form of kingship. And it was he who commissioned the most important object of his household, the Bible from Constantinople.

The powerful families of Constantinople have been less explored than those in New Julfa. It seems clear that the Armenian merchant class in Constantinople was a classical trading diaspora, although further research on the amira class in the Ottoman Empire and its proximity to political power might yield some surprising results in the future.[39] The Armenian merchants of Constantinople have been little studied, and then mostly from the eighteenth century onward. The late Hagop Barsoumian and Araxe Shahiner have been the only ones who have examined this group to a considerable extent. Shahiner's conclusions are integrated in Edhem Eldem's recent work on Istanbul.[40] In addition, Onik Jamkochian

---

[38] Ina Baghdiantz McCabe, "A 'Trade Diaspora' Redefined: State Building, National Interest, and Colonial Settlement in Early Modern Trading Groups," paper presented at "Interactions" conference, Library of Congress, Washington, DC, March 2001; Ina Baghdiantz McCabe, Gelina Harlaftis, and Ionna Minoglu, eds., *Diaspora Entrepreneurial Networks: Four Centuries of History* (Oxford: Berg, 2005), ch. 2.

[39] See Hagop L. Barsoumian, "The Armenian *Amira* Class of Istanbul," Ph.D. Diss., Columbia University, 1980, which, however, does not extend to this early period.

[40] See Edhem Eldem, "Istanbul: From Imperial to Peripheralized Capital," in *The Ottoman City between East and West: Aleppo, Izmir, and Istanbul*, ed. Edhem Eldem, Daniel Goffman, and Bruce Masters (Cambridge and New York: Cambridge University Press, 1999), pp. 135-206.

has demonstrated the trading ties between the Shahrimanians, one of the four major families of New Julfa, and the amiras of Constantinople.[41] One of the wealthy and influential families of the Ottoman capital, the Dadian, has been studied to some extent, but many others also held key posts as political advisors, bankers, jewelers, and in the mint and production of artillery.[42] Writing about the wealthy notables of Constantinople has become politically sensitive because of the subsequent fate of the Constantinopolitan elite in 1915. Yet it is clear that the wealth of the *amira* class was instrumental in making the Ottoman capital a center of cultural life in early modern and modern times. Further examination of the relations between different groups in Constantinople and between them and their compatriots in New Julfa is likely to shed more light on their ties and permit a real comparison of their positions in the two capitals.

The argument has been made in the catalog of the Gulbenkian exhibition at the Metropolitan Museum that the Constantinople Bibles served as a model for those produced later in New Julfa.[43] To support this point, Vrej Nersessian has argued that the Constantinople Bible arrived in New Julfa in 1629 and served as a model for three Bibles illustrated in New Julfa: that of 1639; that of Saint James, 1645; and that of All Savior's, 1662.[44] Constantinople would have been the cultural model for New Julfa's scriptoria, but there is one known example of artistic talent and influence traveling in the other direction, a mirror case of the 1623 Bible discussed here, with patron and artist changing places. For a Bible commissioned by a Constantinople patron, whose name is now erased, a certain Khachatur Isfahani traveled from New Julfa to Constantinople.[45]

Often relations between the two cities remained unbroken, even

---

[41] Onik Jamkochian, paper presented at the conference on Asian trade, Maison des Sciences de l'Homme, Paris, 1998. The conference papers were published in Sushil Chaudhury and Kéram Kévonian, eds., *Les Arméniens dans le commerce asiatique* (note 3 above) but Jamkochian's paper is not included.

[42] See Pars Tuğlaci, *The Role of the Dadian Family in Ottoman Social, Economic and Political Life/Dadyan ailesi'nin Osmanli toplum, ekonomi ve siyaset hayatındaki rolü* (Istanbul: Pars Yayın, 1993).

[43] Baetjer and Draper, *Only the Best*, p. 22.

[44] Nersessian, *Treasures*, pp. 188-89.

[45] Bezazel Narkiss, ed., *Armenian Art Treasures of Jerusalem* (New Rochelle, NY: Caratzas Bros., 1979), p. 95.

through war and political upheaval. That the ties between them assumed extraordinary importance in the cultural lives of the Armenians is unquestionable. Helen Evans and Sylvie Merian have argued, however, that the different political and cultural situation of the two capitals led to two different styles. Since the New Julfans were deported from the Nakhichevan region, the artists attached to this tradition came from the Siunik region and Lake Van, especially Khizan. Particular to this tradition are vivid color contrasts and dynamic compositions that characterize the late medieval style of Greater Armenia.

The Constantinople workshops were for wealthy Armenian patrons who were architects and businessmen as well as government functionaries and were influenced by a different palette, the pastels of Cilicia, a more realistic figure style and a delicacy of execution. When the Armenian kingdom of Cilicia fell in 1375, the Armenians fled, bringing their manuscripts with them to Constantinople and the Crimea. In the Crimea, a mingling with a Greek and Russian population brought about a new "Byzantinizing" style. The article by Evans and Merian argues, based on Siarpie Der Nersessian's pioneering studies, that the Constantinople style arrived in New Julfa as is clearly evident through a manuscript commissioned by Khwaja Safar in 1658-59.[46]

* * *

The Armenian Bible of 1623 demonstrates the interwoven nature of the history of two cultural and economic capitals. It is a history of networks in contact, as Constantinople and New Julfa were in constant dialogue. Constantinople was an older capital and its influence is unquestionable, but the history of these two centers of Armenian life was interdependent and richly informed by their mutual interaction. The head of New Julfa, a prince of princes, a "shah," even in Safavid eyes, turned to Constantinople to commission a family Bible in order to record his kingly title and the names of his family for posterity. To date, this crucial exchange between two powerful centers of Armenian life in the early modern

---

[46] Helen Evans and Sylvie Merian, "The Final Centuries: Armenian Manuscripts of the Diaspora," in *Treasures in Heaven: Armenian Illuminated Manuscripts*, ed. Thomas F. Mathews and Roger S. Wieck (New York: Pierpont Morgan Library, 1994), pp. 105-07.

period has remained a missing link. The cultural exchange explored through the 1623 Bible is a rare and faint echo of a past rich in commercial exchanges and intellectual contacts.

❋ 8 ❋

CYRUS HAMLIN AND AMERICAN EDUCATION FOR ARMENIANS IN CONSTANTINOPLE

Barbara J. Merguerian

American missionaries entered the Middle East in the early decades of the nineteenth century with the grandiose purpose to Christianize the nations but with little in the way of concrete plans to accomplish their ends. It was clear from the beginning that education was to be an integral part of the work. But questions about the nature of that education, its level of achievement, its potential beneficiaries, and even the language of instruction were yet to be determined and in time became subjects of fierce controversy. One of the most outspoken participants in the debates over education, a man who was credited even by his strongest opponents as an exceptionally talented missionary teacher, was Cyrus Hamlin, who was assigned to Constantinople in 1838 specifically to establish a high school for Armenian youth. A towering figure of driving energy and multiple talents, Hamlin is best remembered as the founder and president of the first American institution of higher learning established abroad, Robert College (today, Boğaziçi University) in Constantinople. Hamlin's firm conviction that "the gospel of Christ could be better preached by deeds rather than words"[1] placed him at odds with his most of his colleagues, who believed that missionaries should confine their efforts to preaching. At the same time Hamlin's concern for the general welfare of the people and his advocacy of higher education with strict standards made him one of the most popular American missionaries among the Armenians.

---

[1] The quotation is from the memoirs of a subsequent president of Robert College, Caleb Frank Gates, *Not To Me Only* (Princeton: Princeton University Press, 1940), p. 161.

The first American missionary station in Turkey was founded in Constantinople in 1831, one year after the United States established diplomatic relations with the Ottoman Empire. Through their earlier work in the Middle East, beginning in 1819 in Smyrna (Izmir) and then in Jerusalem and Beirut, the Americans had encountered social and legal barriers to their work among the Muslim peoples of the empire; they therefore turned their attention instead to the minority populations.

The first two missionaries accordingly had been instructed to work with the Greeks, Armenians, and Jews. Both men were somewhat familiar with the Armenians. The Reverend William Goodell had written a paper while still a student at Andover Theological Seminary on "Armenia as a Mission Field," in which he stressed the potential of the Armenians as co-workers in the missionary work, once their Church had been returned to what he believed to be its original and authentic state.[2] Later, he counted the Armenians among his most interested clients during the years he had spent as a missionary in Beirut. The junior missionary, the Reverend Harrison Gray Otis Dwight, had just returned from a sixteen-month exploratory trip surveying Armenian communities throughout Asia Minor, Russia, and Iran. Along with his fellow missionary Eli Smith, he published a fascinating account of their travels.[3]

Objectives of the American Mission to the Armenians

The missionary ideals were the apostles of the New Testament, and their motto was the biblical imperative to "go into all the world, and preach the gospel to every creature" (Mark: 16:15). Such a romantic and utopian vision, however inspiring, was not very helpful for two well-educated Americans arriving in the mixture of peoples, cultures, and religions in the Ottoman capital, a situation made more difficult by the despotic and arbitrary government whose attitude was ambiguous at best. Goodell and Dwight contacted the Patriarch of the Armenian Church, met

---

[2] Goodell's paper was subsequently printed in the *Boston Recorder*, vol. 4, no. 10 (March 6, 1919).

[3] Eli Smith, *Researches of the Rev. E. Smith and Rev. H.G.O. Dwight in Armenia, Including a Journey through Asia Minor and into Georgia and Persia* (Boston: Crocker and Brewster, 1833), 2 vols.

with him and other leaders, and discovered a reform movement that emphasized the need to raise the educational level of the clergy. The Americans enjoyed cordial relations with Armenian Church leaders at first. They concentrated on learning the local languages—for Goodell, Turkish (or more precisely Armeno-Turkish, the Turkish language written with Armenian letters) and for Dwight, Armenian. Their work was divided into two separate but related areas: publication of religious material in the local languages and educational programs for the native populations. Discovering that their educational efforts were meeting with a favorable response among the Armenians, the two missionaries petitioned their headquarters in Boston, the American Board of Commissioners for Foreign Missions (ABCFM), to send out an educator capable of establishing a high school for Armenian youth. The Board responded by assigning the task to Cyrus Hamlin.[4]

In common with most of the missionaries, Hamlin came from a well-respected but not particularly wealthy family. Born in 1811 in Waterford, Maine, he lost his father when he was only a few months old and therefore was compelled, beginning at an early age, along with his older brother Hannibal, to help his mother run the family farm. The farm was almost entirely self-sufficient, so Cyrus and his brother had to learn how to perform all of the necessary chores. When Cyrus reached the age of sixteen, his mother decided to apprentice him to a silversmith in Portland, Maine, where he remained for two years, until one of the elders in the local Congregational Church, observing his debating skills, suggested that he enter the ministry. Upon reflection, Hamlin determined to pursue this course, but given his lack of a regular education, he had first to attend preparatory school

---

[4] On the establishment of the Constantinople mission, see Rufus Anderson, *History of the Missions of the American Board of Commissioners for Foreign Missions to the Oriental Churches* (Boston: Congregational Publishing Society, 1872), 2 vols.; William E. Strong, *The Story of the American Board: An Account of the First Hundred Years of the American Board of Commissioners for Foreign Missions* (Boston: Pilgrim Press, 1910). Among the published memoirs of early missionaries, see *Forty Years in the Turkish Empire: or, Memoirs of Rev. William Goodell, D.D.*, ed. E.D.G. Prime (New York: Robert Carter, 1877); H.G.O. Dwight, *Christianity Revived in the East; or, A Narrative of the Word of God Among the Armenians of Turkey* (New York: Baker and Scribner, 1850); John B. Adger, *My Life and Times, 1810-1899* (Richmond: Presbyterian Committee of Publication, 1899).

before completing his studies at Bowdoin College and the Bangor Theological Seminary, both in Maine. He excelled in academic pursuits but retained for the rest of his life an interest and an ability in mechanical labor which he had acquired on the farm and during his apprenticeship. During his final year at the Seminary, 1836-37, Hamlin volunteered his services to the most prominent American missionary organization at the time, the American Board of Commissioners for Foreign Missions. He imagined himself going to Africa, chose China as his second destination, but was not disappointed to find himself assigned to Turkey as a missionary to the Armenians. The next year he was married, ordained, and sent with his bride to the Ottoman capital.

The Hamlins arrived in Constantinople early in the year 1839, a particularly turbulent time for the Americans.[5] The Patriarch had issued an order banning his flock from the reading of evangelical literature or association with the missionaries, and the early cordial relations between the Americans and the leadership of the Armenian Church became transformed into intense hostility.[6] At first, Hamlin devoted his energies to learning the Armenian language. During his first months in Turkey, he had to engage three successive Armenian teachers: the first disappeared after several young men were arrested and thrown into jail upon the orders of the Patriarch because they had associated with the missionaries; the second was an Armenian who was banished to his native Russia but with Hamlin's help managed to escape to India; and the third was working with Hamlin when unexpectedly the American missionaries were ordered by the Ottoman government to leave the country.[7] While they awaited a response

---

[5] See Cyrus Hamlin, *My Life and Times* (Boston: Pilgrim Press, 1893); Marcia and Malcolm Stevens, *Against the Devil's Current: The Life and Times of Cyrus Hamlin* (Lanham, MD: University Press of America, 1988). Cyrus Hamlin's first cousin, Hannibal Hamlin, became vice president of the United States during the first term of Abraham Lincoln (1861-1865).

[6] The religious ferment of this period is captured in G.H. Chopourian, *The Armenian Evangelical Reformation: Causes and Effects* (New York: Armenian Missionary Association of America, 1972). A more general discussion is in Leon Arpee, *The Armenian Awakening* (Chicago: University of Chicago Press, 1908).

[7] Cyrus Hamlin, *Among the Turks* (New York: Robert Carter and Bros., 1878), pp. 30-39; Hamlin, *My Life*, pp. 184-88, 196-200. The best qualified of Hamlin's teachers, by far, was the second one, Mesrob Taliatine (also Talatyan or Taghiatiants), a Russian subject who had studied for the priesthood at the Holy See of Echmiadzin, then attended for six years Bishop's College in Calcutta, before coming to

to their appeal to the U.S. Department of State to clarify their status, the missionaries saw the situation in Turkey change abruptly: the Ottoman navy surrendered to Mohammed Ali of Egypt, the Ottoman army suffered a major defeat in Syria at the hands of the Egyptian army, and Sultan Mahmud II died. Distracted by these events, the government of the new young sultan, Abdul Mejid, did not enforce the expulsion of the Americans.[8] But the experience demonstrated the precarious position of the missionaries in Turkey.

After a lengthy search, Hamlin settled on a site for the boys' high school in the suburb of Bebek, about 5 miles out of the center of the city, on the European side of the Bosphorus. The boarding school, known as Bebek Seminary, was opened in 1840, and housed between twenty and fifty students, the majority of whom were Armenians. At times, there was a Greek section, and occasionally a Turkish or Jewish student would be admitted. Hamlin's repeated proposals to expand the school, up to a hundred students, were turned down by economy-minded superiors in Boston. Local circumstances forced the school to close on several occasions, as during the events associated with excommunication of the evangelicals by the Armenian Church in 1846, but Hamlin waited for the storm to pass and quietly reopened the school.[9]

Constantinople to participate in the Armenian reform movement. Following his escape from Turkey in 1839, Taliatine returned to India, where he had an outstanding career as a journalist and educator. See *Sovetakan Haykakan Hanragitaran* [Soviet Armenian Encyclopedia], vol. 4 (Erevan: Armenian Academy of Sciences, 1978), p. 131, which does not, however, mention Taliatine's brief association with the American missionaries. See also Khachig Tölölyan's article about Taliatine, "Textual Nation: Poetry and Nationalism in Armenian Political Culture," in *Intellectuals and the Articulation of the Nation*, ed. Ronald Grigor Suny and Michael D. Kennedy (Ann Arbor: University of Michigan Press, 1999), pp. 79-102.

[8] The American minister in Constantinople, Commodore David Porter, was of the opinion that since the treaty between the United States and the Ottoman Empire was a commercial one, therefore the missionaries did not enjoy any particular right to protection. At the insistence of the missionaries, this opinion was appealed to Washington, where Secretary of State Daniel Webster issued a strong statement affirming the rights of the American missionaries to protection equal to that of the European Catholic missionaries, under the "most favored nation" provision of the treaty. Hamlin, *Among the Turks*, pp. 37-40; Hamlin, *My Life*, pp. 196-99.

[9] Frank Andrews Stone, *Academies for Anatolia: A Study of the Rationale, Program and Impact of the Educational Institutions Sponsored by the American Board in Turkey* (Lanham: University Press of America, 1984), pp. 54-55.

Educational Philosophy and Unintended Consequences

Hamlin modeled the curriculum of the seminary on American college-preparatory schools but with some modifications; for example, instead of teaching classical Latin and Greek, he stressed modern and classical Armenian, Turkish, and English. Initially the aim of the school was to provide a Protestant education and to prepare teachers for the rapidly growing number of missionary schools in the capital and the provinces. With the establishment of the Armenian Evangelical Church in 1846, a major goal became the preparation of preachers and pastors for the new parishes.[10] The principles of education that the American missionaries stressed evolved from their basic religious philosophy: that the only road to salvation was to read the Bible, particularly the Gospels, and to live according to its precepts. Knowledge of the Bible was the duty of every person, who stood in a direct relationship with the Creator; in this view there was no one—no clergyman, no bishop, no person in authority—standing between the individual and God.

This philosophy demanded, first of all, that copies of the Bible and religious literature be available to all, in a language easily read and understood. A fundamental precept of the ABCFM was that its missionaries were to work in the local languages. This posed a problem for the Armenian programs. Up to this time, the literary language among the Armenians was the classical *grabar* (*krapar*), and its use was limited to a small educated elite consisting mainly of the higher clergy.[11] Such a situation was unacceptable to the Americans, and their immediate goal became the transformation of the vernacular Armenian spoken in Constantinople into a literary language. Reporting to his missionary sponsors at home in 1840, Hamlin asserted that modern Armenian had "neither dictionary, grammar, nor law" and summarized the linguistic situation as follows:

---

[10] Annual reports of Bebek Seminary can be found in the Archives of the ABCFM at Houghton Library, Harvard University. See ABC 16.7.1, Mission to the Armenians, vols. 3-5, 8-9.

[11] Vahé Oshagan, "Modern Armenian Literature and Intellectual History from 1700 to 1915," in *The Armenian People from Ancient to Modern Times,* Richard G. Hovannisian, ed. (New York: St. Martin's Press, 1997), pp. 152-56; Crosby H. Wheeler, *Ten Years on the Euphrates, or Primitive Missionary Policy Illustrated* (Boston: American Tract Society, 1868), pp. 114-15.

The modern Armenian has entirely lost its ancient beautiful and philosophical structure. Its idioms and its collocations of words are entirely Turkish. Its grammatical structure is broken up and marred by the introduction of Turkish and Persian peculiarities. Its use of tenses, cases, prepositions and other particles is completely Turkish, and the opposite of what the genius of the language demands. Many of the words in common use are borrowed from the Turkish. . . . But it is not only necessary to study the Turkish, it is equally necessary to study the ancient Armenian, which contains nearly all the literature of the nation, and from which the modern tongue must be enriched and improved.[12]

Hamlin and the other missionaries intensified their efforts to translate and publish material in modern Armenian, beginning with the Bible. Working with Armenian assistants, they purged the language of foreign words and made every effort to develop the grammar in a regular fashion. Some of the earliest published works in modern Western Armenian came from the missionary presses. The literary development of the vernacular, or spoken, language became an issue of great contention among Armenian intellectuals during the nineteenth century, and the missionaries were not its only advocates.[13] However, they were among the earliest to promote Western Armenian as a literary language and remained always its strong supporters. Looking back in 1893, Hamlin observed how rapidly the Western Armenian had developed: "The modern Armenian is now wholly transformed; it has become a beautiful and cultivated language. The books and translations presented fifty years ago are considered obsolete unless they have been carefully reedited. The Bible has gone through repeated revisions to keep it up with the growth of the lan-

---

[12] ABCFM, *Annual Report of the ABCFM Presented at the 31st Annual Meeting Held in the City of Providence, R. I. September 9, 10, and 11, 1840* (Boston: Crocker & Brewster, 1840), p. 90.

[13] The first literary work published in Western Armenian was a translation by Minas Pzhshkian of *Robinson Crusoe*, printed in 1817. See Marc Nichanian, "Minas Pzhshkian and the 'History of Pontus'," paper presented at the Conference on the Armenian Communities of the Black Sea-Pontus Region, UCLA, May 4-5, 2002. Pzhshkian's publication was useful for the early missionaries studying the Armenian language. Abbott Mekhitar had earlier published a small grammar of Western Armenian, and in 1828 Hovhannes Zohrabian had published a Western Armenian version of the New Testament under the auspices of the British and Foreign Bible Society.

guage."[14] Summarizing his views on the subject (and indirectly answering those who criticized his advocacy of using the English language in secondary and higher education), Hamlin asserts in his memoirs:

> One's native language, his mother tongue, must be his chief instrument of thought and expression. Our course gave a great impulse to the cultivation of the Armenian language. We found it clay and iron, and we left it gold. I only claim that the seminary at Bebek had a part and an honorable part in the renaissance of the language. The entire influence of the mission went in that direction.[15]

The missionary support for the development of modern Western Armenian contributed to the rise of Armenian nationalism, but this was an unintended consequence. The motivation of the missionaries came from their conviction that one's religion should be expressed in one's native language. Indeed, in those areas where most Armenians spoke Turkish (for example, in the Cilician centers of Marash and Aintab), missionary programs were carried out primarily in Armeno-Turkish. The insistence on instruction in the student's native language was a first principle of American education in the Ottoman Empire, as in all mission stations at that time.

The second distinguishing feature of American evangelical education was again based on religious principles: that everyone should reach an elementary level of knowledge sufficient to study the Bible with comprehension. The required skills were reading, writing, arithmetic, and a basic understanding of the natural laws of the universe. Through their classrooms and instructional material for students of all ages, the missionaries supported universal education. Indeed, as most of their clients came from the middle class or the poorer members of the community, who had nothing to lose by associating with the Americans, the missionary programs had tremendous political and social implications. The goal may have been to make the Bible accessible to all people, but the effect was to create a large, educated Armenian reading public that could benefit not only from the new religious texts but also from the secular literature

---

[14] Hamlin, *My Life*, p. 211.
[15] Ibid., p. 250.

that was appearing in the community. The idea that everyone is equal before God, the emphasis on reading and interpreting the Bible for oneself and not accepting authority blindly, the attention paid to the lower classes, all are consistent with democratic ideals. This is not to suggest that the missionaries had a monopoly on these concepts. There were many other forces at work to democratize Armenian society, but the missionary programs contributed to these trends. The decade of the 1840s was a period of turmoil when the Armenian middle classes rebelled against the authority in the community exercised by the wealthy bankers and imperial office holders known as *amiras*. Speaking of the dissention within the Armenian community at the time, Hamlin explained:

> The people had begun to be restive under the rule of the bankers and the ecclesiastical primates. A very excited contest had arisen, in which the people had gained certain rights, which had been seized by this ruling party. This democratic spirit of freedom was extravagantly attributed to the influence of the missionaries, who had nothing directly to do with it.[16]

Writing in 1878 about the adoption of the Armenian constitution in the Ottoman Empire, Hamlin made a greater claim for Protestant influence: "From such movements as these, helped forward, incited and guided by some hundreds of Protestant organizations in the empire, a large amount of democratic freedom is enjoyed under a very despotic government."[17]

A third distinguishing feature of American missionary education was the inclusion of women. The missionaries believed female students should also have access to elementary education, for the ability to read and to interpret the Bible was just as important for girls as it was for boys. Indeed, it might even be more important because women were responsible for the religious upbringing of the children. The missionaries emphasized the higher education of women in order to train them as teachers. The educated men could be freed to become preachers and

---

[16] Ibid., pp. 283-84. The indirect influence of missionaries on the development of Armenian democratic and constitutional thought is described by Vartan Artinian, *The Armenian Constitutional System in the Ottoman Empire, 1839-1863: A Study of Its Historical Development* (Istanbul, 1988), pp. 43-44.

[17] Hamlin, *Among the Turks,* p. 68.

pastors, while the women could teach in the classroom. Educated women were also needed to be proper wives for pastors and to serve as role models for the community. There was, however, a great deal of resistance at first in the Armenian communities to the idea of female teachers, particularly in rural areas, but gradually it gained acceptance.[18]

Cyrus Hamlin was interested in the Armenian Girls' Seminary in Constantinople, which opened in 1845, and for a few years it was located in Bebek, alongside the Boys' Seminary. Hamlin opposed the closing of the Girls' Seminary in the capital in 1862; years later, he strongly supported the establishment of its successor, the Constantinople College for Women, which opened its doors in 1871.[19]

The fourth distinguishing feature of missionary education for the Armenians was the introduction of the sciences, especially chemistry, physics, astronomy, geology, and botany. This was a novelty for educational establishments in the Near East where there had previously been little interest in these subjects. Elementary education in the sciences was important, the missionaries believed, in order to understand and appreciate God's creation. The Americans also used science for the practical purpose of attracting attention as well as students. Even before Hamlin's arrival in Turkey, Reverend Dwight was writing home for scientific apparatus—telescopes, microscopes, and the like.[20] Hamlin with his scientific bent carried such studies even further, and one can imagine him presenting scientific demonstrations before a curious public. One popular practice of the missionary schools was the examination held at the end of the year, during which parents and the public were invited to observe students giving talks, reciting poetry, performing experiments, and generally showing what they had learned.[21]

Within these broad parameters of educational principles, there were areas of disagreement. Hamlin was a firm advocate of what

[18] On education for women, see Stone, *Academies,* pp. 54-55.

[19] Keith M. Greenwood, *Robert College: The American Founders* (Istanbul: Boğaziçi University Press, 2000), pp. 175-77.

[20] Describing the early visitors to the American mission, Hamlin later wrote: "Many came from curiosity to see noted experiments in physics and chemistry." *My Life,* p. 228.

[21] John Freely, *A History of Robert College, the American College for Girls, and Boğaziçi University* (Istanbul: Yapi Kredi Yayinlari, 2000), vol. 1, p. 71.

is called today "vocational education." He believed that every student should learn a trade and that time spent by students in vocational education helped their overall academic performance. From a practical point of view, exercising a trade could also help students defray the cost of their education. As noted, it was mainly the poorer Armenians who took advantage of the missionary programs. Most students who attended Bebek Seminary did not pay tuition or board, but they were expected to provide their own clothes. Even this was too onerous for most students. As a result, Hamlin initiated a series of small businesses. Enlisting investment by some of his English acquaintances, he acquired equipment to teach the students how to make stove pipes and stoves, lasts and mousetraps, and he then became more ambitious with a bread-making business which was successful with the outbreak of the Crimean War in 1853. It was on a visit to a British hospital that Hamlin realized that men were suffering more from the Crimean lice than from their military wounds, and he began a laundry business, in the process of which, using beer kegs, he developed a prototype washing machine.[22]

All these endeavors, however, met with hostility from the other missionaries, who argued that such "secular" pursuits distracted the mission and encouraged the students to engage in business activities upon leaving school, rather than teaching and preaching. Hamlin's protests that this was the only way he could support and clothe the students fell on deaf ears. He claimed that he could not understand why his opponents considered it preferable for his students to wear tattered clothes and to beg rather than to work to earn an honest wage:

I became fully convinced that two or three hours' work every day, leaving Saturday afternoon free for recreation, was promotive of studious habits, of good morals, and manly character. This industry went on very successfully for a few years, but it was an innovation, and like all innovations, whether good or bad, had to meet with opposition.[23]

At one point, the mission station voted that Hamlin should end all entrepreneurial activities. Hamlin replied that he would

---

[22] Hamlin, *Among the Turks*, pp. 212-14, 218-43.
[23] Hamlin, *My Life*, p. 265.

be pleased to do so, but that he would therefore have to give the responsibility for the clothing of his students to the station. His colleagues "agreed that Brother Hamlin take his own way to keep out rags."[24] Hamlin's motive in establishing these businesses was not only to aid the students but also to provide employment for Protestant families, whose excommunication by the Armenian Church often took away their sources of livelihood as well.

The end of the Crimean War in 1856 eased somewhat the situation of the Armenians. A new reform decree by the government, the *Hatt-i Humayun*, promised equality to all Ottoman subjects irrespective of their ethnicity or religion. Moreover, the war economy had provided an impetus to the economy and the availability of jobs. Hamlin now strategically retreated and disbanded his businesses or handed them over to his Armenian associates. When he came to balance his books, he found he had realized a profit of $25,000, a considerable sum in those days. The missionary society refused to accept the money, and therefore Hamlin set up a special church-building fund. Over subsequent decades, the money in this fund helped Evangelical Armenians living in various parts of the empire to acquire thirteen churches with attached schoolrooms.[25]

New Controversies about Education

More serious debates now emerged concerning the level of education to be provided and the use of English as a language of instruction in the higher academic levels. Rufus Anderson, the foreign secretary of the American Board, from his office in Boston developed in the 1850s a philosophy of missions according to which education should be limited to elementary instruction in the vernacular and provided only to the children of those parents who had already converted to the evangelical faith; English would not be taught under any circumstances. To Hamlin, all of this was nonsensical. He argued in vain that it would

---

[24] Ibid., p. 280.

[25] Ibid., pp. 280, 372. For example, according to Gates, *Not to Me Only*, pp. 138, 150, 168, Protestant churches in the Ottoman Empire had already been built or repaired earlier, out of the profits from Hamlin's industries, and proceeds from the bakery had provided the funds for purchase of the land on which Euphrates College was subsequently erected.

be impossible to provide a higher Western education without teaching students English and thereby opening to them the vast array of Christian literature. To be considered legitimate, Armenian pastors needed an education comparable to that of ministers in the United States, he argued. He himself had been responsible for the translation into Armenian of two basic textbooks, but he saw it as impossibly ambitious in the foreseeable future to translate all the necessary textbooks into the vernacular Armenian. Hamlin also realized that the educational programs represented a major instrument for attracting Armenians to the Protestant cause and that their curtailment would be extremely unpopular with the local population:

> In our field, and the same is true of every field where the gospel is preached to intelligent beings, we need disciplined and educated men. A general reformation has a tendency to produce them. This tendency should be aided, not repressed, and by the blessing of God we may raise up men more able and better qualified than ourselves to enter into the widening fields and reap the thickening harvests. In no other way can the reformation take root in the soil itself and spread its shadow over the land.[26]

Anderson's views prevailed at the time.[27] As Hamlin expressed it in his memoirs: "Dr. Anderson was a man of great power, and his errors were proportionably injurious."[28]

On one point both his supporters and opponents agreed: that Hamlin was a superb educator, dedicated to the welfare of his students. He spent a great deal of time with his young scholars (for example he regularly joined them for lunch) and established high educational standards, while at the same time taking into account individual differences. Graduates of Bebek Seminary became the pastors in the newly formed Evangelical churches as well as teachers; many others went on to distinguished careers in the

---

[26] Hamlin to Anderson, March 12, 1847, ABC: 16.7.1, Mission to the Armenians, vol. 12, "Letters from Constantinople Station" (Hamlin, no. 202).

[27] The curriculum debate of the 1850s is described in the ABCFM histories. See also the introduction by editor R Pierce Beaver to *To Advance the Gospel: Selection from the Writings of Rufus Anderson* (Grand Rapids, MI: Wm. B. Erdmans, 1967), pp. 3-38; Greenwood, *Robert College*, pp. 70-73; Robert Alan Schneider, "The Senior Secretary: Rufus Anderson and the American Board of Commissioners for Foreign Missions," Ph.D. Diss., Harvard University, 1980.

[28] Hamlin, *My Life*, p. 414.

professions, in business, or in government service. Throughout the 1850s, however, criticism was leveled at the Bebek Seminary by the other missionaries for providing too high a level of education and for the fact that a significant number of its graduates traveled abroad for professional education, obtained jobs as interpreters, or went into business. In vain did Hamlin point out that no theological seminary produces all of its graduates for the ministry and that his seminary was the chief supplier of pastors for the evangelical churches in the interior, as well as a number of teachers and preachers.

Finally Hamlin realized that it had been decided in Boston to close both the male and female seminaries at Constantinople and to open them in the interior, on an entirely different basis. Weary of constant criticism and fully convinced that the educational system being developed was, in his words, "erroneous in principle, and must be disastrous in effect,"[29] Hamlin began to consider his options. Fortuitously, he found a new pursuit worthy of his talents and experiences. The New York businessman and philanthropist Christopher R. Robert had visited Constantinople in the late 1850s and met Hamlin. The two began a lively correspondence in which they explored the possibility of establishing an American college in Constantinople. Hamlin accordingly submitted his resignation to the American Board, effective in 1860, in order to turn his attention to the new project.

Cyrus Hamlin now had amassed more than two decades of experience as an educator in the Ottoman Empire. Although his work had been primarily among the Armenians, he had been in contact with other Christians, Muslims, and Jews and had become convinced that most of the problems in the society were the result of ignorance, superstition, and prejudice, all of which could be overcome by providing a liberal education to the new generation. In a lengthy paper written at this time, Hamlin argued that circumstances were driving the country to modernize. Though belonging to the past and clinging to tradition, Turkey was surrounded and penetrated by modern influences and found itself compelled to adopt European principles and modes of art, government, war, "and even its religious notions are being shaken out of their place." The previous year alone, 200 Turkish students had gone to Paris to study, and one steamer carried forty

---

[29] Hamlin, *Among the Turks*, pp. 283-84.

young Armenians abroad, all seeking a European education.

A new era was dawning in Turkey, and the practical question arose as to the role of the Protestant world in these new circumstances. Hamlin's answer was clear: "The first and at present the most important demand is a good Christian institution for general education—an institution bearing the character of a New England college." Many parents could not or would not send their children abroad, yet would welcome a Western institution in which they could have confidence. To support this contention, Hamlin argued that: 1) such an institution would find a rich pool of potential students in the large, diverse, multicultural population of the capital and could also attract students from other cities; 2) the "numerous and richly endowed Jesuit institutions of education" could not meet the demands of the country because their system "cramps and destroys rather than educates the mind"; 3) the schools established by the government were "wholly destitute of the requisite religious and moral elements" and would not for a long time "supercede the necessity of institutions conducted by men of European training and habits of teaching"; 4) an institution of learning which combined "sound mental discipline" with science and Christianity would not only accomplish a great good on its own, but would provide a model to be widely emulated, even as missionary schools had exerted a significant influence on the general development of education; and 5) it was the duty of Protestant Christianity to provide such an institution to Turkey. Using mainly the English, French, and Turkish languages, this institution would be open to Turks, Bulgarians, Greeks, Armenians, Romanians, Kurds, and Jews. Hamlin concluded:

> Such a Christian educational institution as we propose would be a constant and steady light to thousands of minds, in regard to the true nature of Christianity, which the missionary cannot at present approach. Its secular constitution would give it a weight and an authority in certain minds which would be armed with suspicion against any missionary institution. It would be a new demonstration of what our faith is, which the Oriental world greatly needs. It would be a new ally in the work, a new force common to the field of battle in the midst of the conflict, fresh and unwearied, to choose it position and decide the day.[30]

---

[30] "Educational Institutions and English Literature for Turkey," ABC: 16.7.1, vol. 12, "Letters from Constantinople Station" (Hamlin, #269). The document is

The idea of establishing an American college in Turkey was not original with Hamlin. It had been first suggested by the Reverend Dwight's two sons, James and William, who had grown up in Constantinople and received their higher education in the United States. They had discussed the idea with Christopher Robert, who was intrigued with the plan but put off by their suggestion that the institution be secular in nature. Robert also doubted that the Dwight brothers possessed the necessary experience.[31] On the other hand, Hamlin appeared perfectly qualified for the task, and his concept of a Christian institution which would be independent and non-sectarian appealed to Robert. Once free from his ABCFM duties, Hamlin threw himself into the new project with his customary vigor and enthusiasm. The first step was to find an appropriate site for the college, and this proved to be much more difficult than anticipated. Hamlin discovered the ideal spot high on a hill just above the historic Rumeli Hisar fortress, only about half a mile from the Bebek Seminary—a magnificent site with an unsurpassed view of the Bosphorus, the narrow strait that connects the Black Sea with the Sea of Marmara. Convinced that this site was not available, he examined twenty-four possible locations, according to his memoirs, before property was purchased at Kurucheshme.[32]

Hamlin now returned to the United States to raise money for the new institution. The timing was unfortunate, however, for he arrived in Boston in September 1860, when the turbulent conditions that were to lead to the Civil War made serious fundraising impossible. Robert, however, unwilling to give up so quickly, placed additional funds at Hamlin's disposal to begin construction of the college. On his return to Constantinople, Hamlin found the situation changed: Sultan Abdul Mejid had died, and as a result of the ensuing political changes the owner of the Hisar land found himself in dire financial straits and was anxious to sell. Hamlin quickly agreed to purchase what he had considered the perfect site, and a few months later obtained

---

not dated, but it was received in Boston on May 30, 1857.

[31] Hamlin's biographers, Marcia and Malcolm Stevens, suggest that it was an Armenian graduate of Bebek Seminary, Christopher Der Seropian, who had convinced the Dwights to make the college a secular one and to exclude religious exercises. Seropian was a classmate of the Dwights at Yale University. Stevens, *Against the Devil's Current*, pp. 243-44.

[32] Hamlin, *My Life*, p. 415.

official permission from the Ottoman Ministry of Education to found a college.[33]

Now, however, another obstacle appeared; despite his efforts, he could not obtain the necessary building permit. Frustrated by being so close to achieving his goal yet unable to proceed, Hamlin now took advantage of his many years of experience in Turkey. Bebek Seminary, which he had founded and directed for so many years, had been moved to Marsovan, and its former building was left vacant. Hamlin reached an arrangement with the ABCFM to use this building temporarily for the college, and the basic principle of *adet* or custom in Ottoman law worked in his favor: since an American institution had been functioning on that site for so many years, the government could not legally prevent its continued use for that same purpose. In the fall of 1863, with a program printed in five languages and a freshman class of four members, the new college opened. Unable to settle on a name for the new institution, Hamlin had come up with Robert College, in honor of the establishment's chief sponsor, and the name was adopted over Robert's protests. By the end of the academic year, the student body had grown to 20; by the end of the second academic year, there were 28 students (including 4 Greeks, 1 Armenian, and 1 Bulgarian); and at the end of the third academic year, the 51 students included 20 Armenians, 9 Bulgarians, and 6 Greeks; the fourth year enrollment of 96 students was made up of 19 Armenians, 9 Bulgarians, and 6 Greeks. The fifth academic year saw the first two graduates: the Armenian Hagopos Djedjizian, who went on to a long and distinguished teaching career at the college, and the Bulgarian Petco Gorbanoff, who subsequently enjoyed a prominent political career in Bulgaria.[34]

The Building of a New Campus

Soon after the first graduation exercises, a seemingly unrelated event took place that had an impact on the fate of the college. The U.S. European naval squadron, commanded by Admiral David Farragut, arrived at the Turkish capital in August 1868. At the

---

[33] Ibid., pp. 425-31.
[34] George Washburn, *Fifty Years in Constantinople* (Boston: Houghton Mifflin, 1909), p. 305; Freely, *History*, p. 71.

urging of his young son Alfred, Hamlin visited the admiral and
spoke with him about his difficulties concerning the college,
following which Farragut apparently raised the issue in his meetings with Turkish officials. Three months later, Hamlin was
astonished to learn that not only had official authorization been
granted to build the college on the Hisar site but also that permission had come in the form of an imperial *irade*, which granted
the right of extraterritoriality to the land, so that Robert College
was allowed to fly the American flag and enjoyed diplomatic
immunities. Apparently the Turkish officials viewed this as a
small concession to the United States to ensure its good offices
in the empire's foreign policy problems, particularly with Greece
over the issue of Crete. Hamlin was to encounter no further
obstacles from the government during construction. In the spring
of 1869 excavations for the college building began; on July 5 of
that year the cornerstone was laid; in May 1871 students occupied the building; and on July 4 of that year the official opening
took place, with former American Secretary of State William E.
Seward as the featured speaker.[35]

During the construction, Hamlin was not limited to the role
of college president but also assumed the responsibilities of
architect, engineer, and contractor. Stories abound in the literature about his activities in this period, which are well summarized
in the description provided by his son-in-law, George Washburn,
who had been drafted to help administer the college and was
soon to succeed Hamlin as president:

> During those years, while the work of construction was going
> on, Dr. Hamlin was always at Hisar, but one never knew where
> to find him. He might be in the water at the bottom of the well
> mending the force pump, or at the top of the building standing
> on an iron girder with forty feet of empty space below him. He
> might be setting up a steam-engine or doctoring a horse or
> teaching his masons how to lay stone. He might be entertaining
> some Turkish gentleman or using his rich vocabulary of in-
> vective on some wild Kurdish laborer. He made a sort of hut for
> himself in a pile of lumber near the building, and you might
> find him there taking a five minutes' nap in his chair or sharing
> his meager lunch with a tailless green lizard which had made
> friends with him. If you came at the right time, you might be

---

[35] Hamlin, *My Life*, pp. 435-52, 468-78.

treated to a delicious cup of coffee made by himself. You might see him . . . tenderly dressing the wounds of some unfortunate workman. Wherever you found him, you saw that his whole mind and heart was concentrated upon the building. He had endless difficulties, but was never discouraged and never daunted by any new and unthought-of problem which presented itself in the building. I think that those were the happiest days of his life.[36]

Constructing the building proved to be an easier task than developing the curriculum. Students came from various backgrounds and with different levels of preparation: Hamlin divided them between a preparatory department and the college proper but did not have a set list of courses to be taken every year. In the fall, he would sit down with the staff and determine which students were to be prepared for graduation that year. It was the system Hamlin had always used, and it was appropriate for a small student body. The college directors in the United States, however, including most importantly Robert, were distressed by the lack of organization. Washburn complained in letters to the Trustees about Hamlin's seemingly haphazard administration, but later in his memoirs he admitted that "we have no graduates who have distinguished themselves in later life more than those who were under Dr. Hamlin's personal influence." Hamlin had, according to Washburn, "a marvelous power of impressing his own personality on his students," he "lived with the students, ate at the same table, and managed, in spite of the variety of his occupations, to see much of them."[37] Language issues were ever-present. Hamlin believed that the basic language of instruction should be English, supplemented by the native languages (mainly Turkish, Greek, Armenian, and Bulgarian).[38] This left no space in the curriculum for the classical languages of Latin and

---

[36] Washburn, *Fifty Years*, pp. 28-29.

[37] Ibid., p. 37.

[38] On this question, Hamlin disagreed with his colleague, Dr. Daniel Bliss, who founded Syrian Protestant College (later the American University of Beirut) in 1866 and at first used the missionary model of teaching in the native languages. Washburn visited Beirut in 1874 and was severely critical of the use of Arabic, reporting to Robert that "all the professors believe that this is a mistake and a calamity." Robert conceded in reply that he had been critical of Hamlin on the language issue but now he was "becoming reconciled to our multiplicity of tongues." Correspondence quoted in Greenwood, *Robert College*, pp. 150-51.

Greek. The college trustees in the United States, on the other hand, dominated by chairman Robert, insisted on following the American models and including the classics in the curriculum.

Another series of disagreements between Hamlin and the college trustees revolved around attitudes toward the native peoples and the degree of responsibility given them. This was a serious issue in the American missionary movement in general, and particularly among the Armenians. Although the avowed rationale of the Americans for working among the Christian peoples in the Ottoman Empire was to train co-workers for the long-term goal of converting (they would use the term "saving") Muslims and Jews, they were remarkably reluctant to assign responsibility to the native helpers. Armenians resented this policy and became increasingly restive under the control exercised by the Americans. The gradual replacement of the first experienced generation of American missionaries in Turkey by newer recruits exacerbated the problem. Hamlin stood out among his colleagues for his willingness to assign responsibility to local leaders. Earlier, in 1854, Hamlin's name had been conspicuously absent from a petition submitted to Boston by members of the Constantinople mission, protesting against the rumored assignment to their mission of an Ottoman Armenian then completing his higher education in the United States; the petitioners expressed alarm that an Armenian might have equal status with the Americans or be paid the same salary.[39]

A similar situation arose in 1872 when Hagopos Djedjizian was named adjunct professor of ancient and modern Armenian. One of the first two graduates of the college in 1868, Djedjizian became the first local person to be appointed professor. Robert had initially opposed Hamlin on this appointment but finally acquiesced, probably for financial reasons, since American faculty members were considerably more expensive.[40]

---

[39] This remarkable petition concludes with the recommendation that the Armenian be assigned instead to India, where "he will undoubtedly do much good." Greenwood, *Robert College*, pp. 73-75.

[40] The views of Robert on the subject of Hagopos Djedjizian's appointment display a remarkably negative attitude toward the individuals being educated at the college:

> I never had any idea that the native teachers would take part in the government of the college. Perhaps 50 or 100 years hence, they may take part in the administration but even then the objectionable elements of their character

Another aspect of this problem appears in financial issues. Hamlin strongly advocated a self-supporting institution whose costs would be covered by tuition, fees, and local fund-raising. This not only satisfied his New England sense of frugality, but it also insured that the local population would embrace the institution as its own. The trustees proposed establishing an endowment in the United States that would provide the income for three professors. Hamlin argued that such an arrangement would make the college too independent and isolated from its environment. It was a problem the missionaries were encountering in Constantinople over the question of who was to control the Protestant churches, a dispute that ended up in the courts. In Hamlin's mind, the problem came from trying to impose from above what ought to have come from below:

> I have a great horror of that independence which the younger missionaries contend for as the only condition of having a Christian college. This independence allowed them to trample with impunity upon those laws of human nature which will in some way or another finally avenge themselves. They have seen the missionary cause finally in the grave here and are now fighting in the courts and in the public newspapers causing public astonishment and scandal. Well, they have abstract right on their side but they have sacrificed all the sympathies of the people. . . . The entire Protestant body . . . would vote the missionaries away if they could. . . . Now manage a college so as to sacrifice the sympathies of the scholars and parents and trample upon their prejudices, despise requests which to the petitioners seem reasonable, rebuke them with anger and lofty disdain, threaten them with expulsion if they don't think and act just as you do, and you will empty any college very soon.[41]

---

will, I fear, not be so diminished as not to render a large share of American brains necessary, but that is too far in the future for profitable discussion. As to how long native teachers should be retained, I cannot of course tell, but my impression is that . . . it will not be wise to keep them over 3 or 4 years. Men who are so sensitive as to their honor so as to always be on the alert lest their associate encroach upon their dignity, are always troublesome and often so occupied in guarding their honor as to neglect important duties to others.
Letter to Washburn, Feb. 19, 1872, quoted in Greenwood, *Robert College*, p. 173.

[41] Hamlin to Robert, May 15, 1869, quoted in Greenwood, *Robert College*, pp. 126-27.

Protestant Christian or Non-Sectarian?

The confidence of the Constantinople Armenian community in Robert College was severely shaken as a result of disputes over religious policy. Hamlin had placed great importance on the college's independence from the sectarianism represented by the ABCFM, but he was adamant that it should be Christian in character. A controversy over the religious nature of the college arose during its first years. Two young American professors, the Reverends Henry A. Schauffler and George A. Perkins, had been appointed to the faculty, and after one year of teaching under Hamlin's direction, they mounted a major attack on his capability as college president. At the heart of their displeasure was what they described as an anti-missionary policy, but what we might consider today Hamlin's religious toleration. The college constitution stipulated that "all the students shall attend religious services unless for special and imperative reasons some are excused by the faculty and teachers." The two faculty members had discovered, however, that Hamlin was permitting students to absent themselves from religious services at the college in order to attend their own churches or synagogues (There were no Muslim students at this time, and therefore no mention was made of mosques). Hamlin had done this arbitrarily, without consulting them, they charged, and he was violating the basic evangelizing mission of the college. Hamlin had gone too far in disassociating the college from the mission, they argued:

> When the *Levant Herald* spoke of the college as the representative of the American mission, Dr. Hamlin was greatly disturbed and wrote the Herald strongly disavowing any connection with any mission society. This was well enough. But he closed by saying that although Robert College was a Christian rather than a Mohammedan institution, it was entirely non sectarian in character and principle. We felt that instead of covering up our Protestant character . . . that we ought rather . . . to reveal that our aim . . . is the same as that of the missionaries, viz, the evangelization of Turkey.[42]

How many students were involved or to what faiths they

---

[42] Letter, H.A. Schauffler to Robert, Nov. 29, 1864, quoted in Greenwood, *Robert College*, p. 88.

belonged is not mentioned. This dispute ended when Robert expressed his complete confidence in Hamlin as college president, and Schauffler and Perkins resigned. Apparently, Hamlin continued to exhibit a tolerant attitude toward other religions, and the college gained a reputation as a place that afforded students from the disparate national groups of the Ottoman Empire a neutral ground. Regardless of their religious and national affiliations, they came together in the common pursuit of knowledge. The tenth academic year had closed in the spring of 1873 with a total enrollment of 257, of which by far the largest group, 98, consisted of Armenians, with 48 Greeks, 38 Bulgarians, and 73 of various other minorities.

No sooner had Hamlin left Constantinople in September 1873, ostensibly to try to raise an endowment in the United States, than George Washburn, who had been left in charge, faced a major crisis on the religious front. In October 1873, Washburn received a letter signed by eleven Armenian students who refused to attend Bible classes, "considering that the commentaries on the Bible will not be in strict conformity with the especial doctrines of the Armenian church." Seeing this as a direct attack on the religious program of the college, Washburn refused to permit exemption since such a move "would involve the cessation of all moral instruction in the college without which we believe no institution of learning can secure the favor of God or man." The result was the departure of twenty-six Armenian students, which was serious enough, but also led to a great commotion in the community. The students did not hesitate to explain their position in the Armenian press, asserting that the college curriculum was designed to "make them Protestants" and calling upon parents "who feel any interest in their own church" to "remove their sons to our national schools." The students asserted: "It was impossible for us to believe that so celebrated an American institution in Turkey would ever be the means of violating the freedom of conscience." As one historian of Robert College has pointed out, these students demonstrated that they had learned their lessons well. "To be required, as communicants of the Armenian Orthodox church, to participate in the prayers of the American Congregationalists, struck them as a violation of the very religious liberties they were hearing about from their teachers." Nine of the twenty-six students returned after petitioning Washburn. The next year, in 1874, there were only thirty-two

Armenian students, and it took several years before they attained their earlier percentage of the student body.[43]

The numbers of Bulgarian students increased after 1872 with the appointment to the faculty of Albert Long, who had been for many years a missionary in Bulgaria. The college became associated with efforts to publicize Muslim "atrocities" in Bulgaria, particularly in the British press. This led to a political crisis in Turkey in 1877-78. Hamlin, who had returned to the United States by this time, was distressed by the situation and insisted that the college must remain aloof from any subversive political activity. As a missionary, Hamlin had been a strong advocate of programs among the Bulgarians, describing this as a most promising field of service, but he now cautioned against any political involvement by the college. Individuals who wished to work for Bulgarian independence were free to do so, he argued, but the college as an institution chartered by the Turkish government must make every effort to separate itself from politics in general and from support for Bulgarian separatism in particular.[44]

Always antagonistic to Russia, Hamlin did not believe that the break-up of the Ottoman Empire would serve any useful purpose. In one letter, he expressed astonishment that any missionary could "make such an ass of himself as to wish Russia in Constantinople." He made fun of the oratory of the Liberal Prime Minister William E. Gladstone in England. "War cannot heal the diseases of Turkey," which were identified as "ignorance, superstition, bigotry, and fanaticism" in a letter Hamlin wrote to Robert in 1875. By this time, however, Washburn was in control of the college. He and Long (along with prominent Bulgarian graduates of the college) were generally recognized as the prime movers in the campaign that culminated in the autonomy of an enlarged Bulgaria by the Treaty of San Stefano in 1878 and, although somewhat smaller in area, confirmed by the Congress of Berlin later that same year.[45] Fortunately for the col-

---

[43] The controversy is described in Greenwood, *Robert College*, pp. 183-88.

[44] Ibid., pp. 203-06.

[45] The debate is discussed in Greenwood, *Robert College*, pp. 192-208, 216-22; Stevens, *Against the Devil's Current*, pp. 381-406. Years later, Washburn was to deny his role: "I did not create Bulgaria . . . and never encouraged the Bulgarians . . . to rebel against the Turkish government." In contrast, British Ambassador Sir Edwin Pears commented: "I know of no other instance in history where a single institution has so powerfully affected the life of a nation as Robert College has affected

lege, the government did not retaliate after the dust of war had settled. These circumstances, however, branded Robert College as a distinctly Christian institution and hindered it from playing the kind of enlightening role for the Muslim or Turkish population that Hamlin had envisioned. There were no Turkish students enrolled until the early twentieth century.

Against his wishes, in 1873 Hamlin had been brought home to the United States by Robert to raise funds for a college endowment. Little did he realize that he would be prevented from returning to Turkey and forced to resign as president four years later. Hamlin did not like raising money (which he compared to "begging") and did not think he was good at it. He had failed in fund-raising before, once in 1860 on the eve of the Civil War and again in 1871. As Robert increasingly exhibited a tendency to place more responsibility for running the college in the hands of the methodical Washburn rather than the unpredictable Hamlin, the latter proposed undertaking a new project, the establishment of a women's college, only to be brushed aside by an impatient Robert. As he had predicted, Hamlin was not able to raise the necessary funds to place the college on a solid financial footing, and while he crisscrossed the country on speaking tours, Washburn was consolidating his position in Constantinople.[46] To calm Washburn's apprehensions about the financial future of the college, Robert assured him confidentially that he would continue to fund the college for as long as he lived whether an endowment was raised or not and that he would provide for the college generously in his will; at the same time Robert cautioned Washburn not to divulge this to anyone, for fear of undermining Hamlin's fund-raising efforts. Finally, in a bitter showdown in Robert's New York City office in the fall of 1875, Robert informed Hamlin that he was not to return to Constantinople.[47]

---

the life of Bulgaria" (both quotations from Stevens, p. 405).

[46] Washburn later argued that the failure to raise an endowment at this time could be explained by the fact that the institution was named after Robert, and people therefore expected Robert to fund it. Moreover, "no man in New York was more universally respected nor more universally admired than Mr. Robert but he was not a popular man." Washburn also pointed out that the frequently stated argument of Robert and Hamlin that the college could and should be self-supporting was self-defeating. If the college was to be self-supporting, what was the rationale for an endowment? Washburn, *Fifty Years*, pp. 59-60.

[47] Hamlin, *My Life*, pp. 502-04.

Hamlin was bitterly disappointed that he could not realize his dream of continuing the work in Turkey and ending his life there, to be buried next to his first wife and two deceased children. He had to earn a living to support himself and his family. Throughout his missionary career he had always taken a minimal salary and never thought about saving for his retirement. Hamlin now accepted preaching invitations and began to write his memoir, *Among the Turks*, which enjoyed a modest success. In the fall of 1877, he accepted a position as professor of theology at his alma mater, Bangor Seminary, for three years, and then served as president of Middlebury College in Vermont for five years. His success in transforming Middlebury College from an almost bankrupt establishment with falling enrollments, an obsolete curriculum, and decaying plant into a prosperous and highly regarded institution provides a vindication of his abilities as a college administrator. "There is no question that Middlebury's gain was a profound loss for Robert College," writes Hamlin's biographer.[48] Hamlin then retired to Lexington, Massachusetts, where he continued his writing, public speaking, and preaching until his death, in 1900, at the age of 89. At his funeral, two of the four speakers were Armenians (Hagop Arakelyan and Dr. M.A. Melcon) and six Armenian men served as pallbearers. Engraved on Hamlin's tombstone in the Lexington cemetery are the following words: "This monument of granite from Maine, his native state, is erected by his Armenian friends in gratitude for his enduring and devoted services to their people."[49]

* * *

Cyrus Hamlin lost the argument in the mid-nineteenth century over the importance of higher education in missions and over including economic and social programs for the betterment of the people. But he lived long enough to see his ideas triumph; indeed, he himself helped those ideas triumph by the success of his initiative to establish an American college in the Near East, an effort that inspired the establishment of the American Univer-

---

[48] Stevens, *Against the Devil's Current*, pp. 434-53. Given Hamlin's strong advocacy of higher education for women in the Ottoman Empire, it is not surprising that during his presidency women were first admitted to Middlebury College.

[49] Ibid., pp. 473-78.

sity of Beirut only four years later and of a network of American higher educational institutions in the Ottoman Empire, including Euphrates College, Anatolia College, Central Turkey College, and Tarsus Institute. Perhaps an analogous missionary impulse remains today in American activities abroad, now almost completely devoid of religious content (which Hamlin would have regretted) and focused on economic, social, and democratic reform (which Hamlin would have applauded). This missionary who spent more than thirty years of his life in Constantinople as an educator working mainly with the Armenians left an indelible mark on the development of American activism abroad dedicated to creating opportunities to achieve a better life for the peoples of the Near East and around the world.

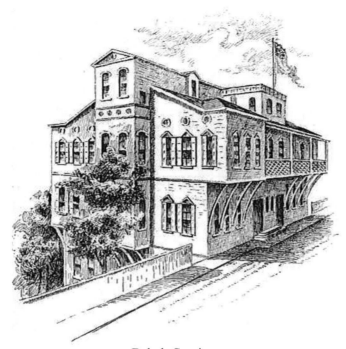

Bebek Seminary

Robert College and Hamlin Hall, 1870s

Christopher Robert

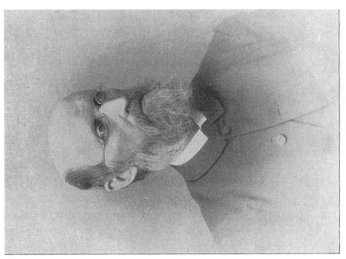

Cyrus Hamlin

George Washburn

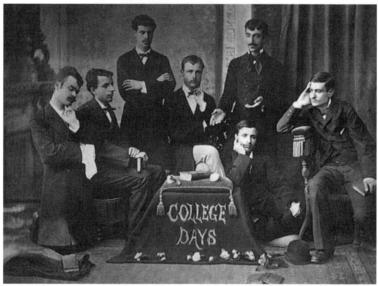

Robert College Seniors, 1880s

�֍ 9 ✣

THE ARMENIAN COMMUNITY OF CONSTANTINOPLE IN THE LATE OTTOMAN EMPIRE

Ohannes Kılıçdağı

This study utilizes a small sample of Armenian sources to explore the social and political characteristics of the Armenian community in Constantinople in the late nineteenth and early twentieth centuries, with particular attention to the structure of the community and its relations with the Armenian compatriots living in the provinces. The primary sources include 1) the first twenty-six issues of the Armenian periodical, *Jamanag* (*Zhamanak*; Times), published between 1863 and 1869, initially as a biweekly and later as a monthly under the editorship of Stepan Boghos Papazian;[1] 2) the works of satirist Hagop Baronian (Hakob Paronian, 1842-1891), especially *Ptoyt me Polsoy tagherun mej* (A Stroll through the Neighborhoods of Constantinople) and *Metsapativ muratskanner* (The Honorable Beggars), which offer vivid descriptions of local customs and traditions in the 1870s;[2] 3) a collection of short stories written between 1909 and 1911 by Krikor Zohrab (Grigor Zohrap, 1861-1915);[3] 4) and the novel, *Amirayin aghjike: Polsakan gianki drvakner* (The Amira's Daughter:

---

[1] Another newspaper of the same name has been published in Constantinople/ Istanbul since 1908.

[2] Hakob Paronian, *Ptoyt me Polsoy tagherun mej* (Istanbul: Aramian Sanuts Miutiun, 1962); *Metsapativ muratskanner* (Istanbul: Aramian Sanuts Miutian, 1961).

[3] Krikor Zohrab was a member of the Ottoman Parliament and one of the leading intellectuals in Ottoman society. As a lawyer, he contributed to the famous Dreyfus case in France by submitting a petition to the court. He authored many short stories and several novels in which he advanced his progressive ideas. He was murdered on the road from Aleppo to Diarbekir on orders of the Young Turk/ Ittihadist government in 1915.

Episodes of Constantinopolitan Life), authored by journalist and teacher Erukhan (Ervand Srmakeshkhanlian, 1870-1915) and first published in 1904.[4] Although these sources offer no more than impressionistic glimpses into the Armenian community, as they are neither quantitatively nor qualitatively sufficient to provide "solid facts,"[5] they nonetheless shed some light on the contemporary community.

The Armenian Constitution of 1863 and Its Administrative System

After the Reform Edict of 1856 during the so-called *Tanzimat* restructuring period in the Ottoman Empire (1839-76), each non-Muslim community was authorized to prepare a statute on the administration of its internal affairs. The document prepared by the Armenian community, which the Ottoman government accepted with modifications in 1863 under the title of Regulations (*Nizamname*), has since been referred to somewhat misleadingly as the "Armenian National Constitution" (*Sahmanadrutiun*). It established a National Assembly consisting of 140 members, 20 of whom were to be clergymen elected by the clergy, 40 were to represent the Armenians of the interior provinces, while the remaining 80 were to be elected by the Armenians of Constantinople.[6] This Assembly was to elect the Armenian patriarchs of Constantinople and Jerusalem. It was to convene, except in emergencies, once every two years for two months to hear and examine reports concerning administrative affairs, supervise the budget, and elect members of the Religious Council and the Civic Council, which were to oversee the political and social affairs of the empire's Armenian community (*millet*). The Religious Council consisting of 14 clergymen was to manage the religious affairs of the Armenian Apostolic Church, while the Civic Council, consisting of 20 members was responsible for

---

[4] Erukhan, *Amirayin aghjike: Polsakan gianki drvakner*, in *Erker* [Works] (Antelias: Catholicosate of Cilicia, 1993; first ed. 1904).

[5] For example, no sources from the period of the 1880s to 1900 are included in this overview.

[6] Here the inequality in representation is obvious since a few thousand people in the capital city were allowed to elect 80 deputies, whereas more than one million people in the provinces were represented by only 40 deputies.

"worldly" issues. In matters pertaining to both councils, a joint body could be constituted. The Civic Council conducted much of its affairs through a number of committees and subcommittees (educational, judicial, economic, monastic properties, financial, inheritance, and hospital administration). In sum, this statute created, at least on paper, quite a detailed bureaucracy with its specialized and hierarchical units.

Organizational Unit of the Community: The Neighborhood

In the cities of the Ottoman Empire in the late nineteenth and early twentieth centuries, communities, including the Armenian community in Constantinople, were organized around the neighborhood as the smallest unit of communal organization. For the Armenians, the *tagh* (quarter or neighborhood), was a vital aspect of city life and defined their sense of belonging and identity. Although each neighborhood had its own unique characteristics, all of them maintained similar practices and organizational structures. Each neighborhood was governed by a council, whose members were elected by the male adult residents every four years and the number of whose members, according to the Constitution, ranged between five and twelve. In August 1863, for example, *Jamanag* reported the results of new elections for the twenty-six neighborhood councils.[7] According to proposed regulations prepared for the neighborhood council of Pera in 1861 and published in *Jamanag*, each council was to be responsible for several services, including maintaining the churches, cemetery, and schools within the tagh; caring for the poor; governing movable and immovable possessions and income; and settling disputes between Armenian residents. Additionally, the council was to serve as a mediator between the neighborhood residents and the Armenian Patriarchate. Although it is not clear whether this proposal was actually implemented for all of the councils in the capital, the descriptions in *Jamanag* of their various administrative functions provide insights with respect to their influence and public expectations in the

---

[7] *Jamanag* [*Zhamanak*], no. 17 (Aug. 17, 1863), pp. 129-31.

Armenian neighborhoods.[8] In July 1863, the journal reported:

> When we seek to understand why people of Ortakiugh[9] feel so much sympathy to their neighborhood council, we find that the council not only settled every dispute in the neighborhood peaceably but also was able to pay off the former debt of the neighborhood which is 70,000 *kurush*, and additionally the council is enthusiastically involved with the two neighborhood schools.[10]

The selection of committees, their policies, and their practices generated considerable political debate and tension. For instance, a committee responsible for care of the neighborhood poor was required to conduct a detailed survey concerning the financial situation of every family in order to determine whether one was "poor" and therefore eligible to receive assistance. In *Amirayin aghjike*, Erukhan describes such a committee member: "Because of his responsibility this man knows everybody living in the neighborhood and their material conditions; he even has some information about family secrets. From time to time, people request information from him about the moral and material conditions of a certain family. People come to him for information concerning a girl whom they wish to have as a bride."[11] Although seemingly invasive, in a sense such committee members may have contributed to the continuity and maintenance of order in the neighborhood.

At times, however, these committees and the neighborhood councils may have also contributed to instability. For example, in his *Ptoyt me Polsoy tagherun mej*, Hagop Baronian frequently refers to arguments or "fights" taking place within the councils or because of the councils, particularly during election time. In fact, although officially a member of council was elected for a four-year term, often he or the entire council would be forced out of office by their opponents only a few months after the

---

[8] *Jamanag*, no. 24 (Nov. 24, 1863), pp. 190-91; no. 25 (Dec. 7, 1863), pp. 198-200; no. 26 (Dec. 21, 1863), pp. 206-07.

[9] Turkish: Ortaköy, meaning Middle Village, a neighborhood on the western shore of the Bosphorus.

[10] *Jamanag*, no. 15 (July 20, 1863), p. 114.

[11] Erukhan, *Amirayin aghjike*, pp. 241-42.

elections. Regarding the Karagumruk tagh, Baronian writes: "If a man is elected to the neighborhood council, he either resigns after six months or he carries his bed to the council of-fice."[12] Similarly, in the case of the Selamsiz tagh, he observes: "After the promulgation of the Constitution, there has not been any council that completed a full term in office."[13] The residents of Pera "are never happy with their council, so they are always skirmishing."[14] Networks of patronage further complicated local politics. During elections, for example, every businessman voted for his favorite customer and in return relied on his private ties with those in office to secure tangible material benefits from the council's decisions.[15]

Disputes and struggles for power occurred not only within the neighborhood but also between neighborhoods. A dispute between Karagumruk tagh and Balat tagh, both on the western side of the Golden Horn, entailed the matter of their unification into a single neighborhood. Karagumruk tagh wished to remain a separate neighborhood, whereas Balat hoped to bring Karagumruk under its jurisdiction. "Balat does not want to let its prey escape," reported *Jamanag*.[16] In the end, the quarrel was resolved by maintaining the two as separate neighborhoods.[17] This case implies that being a distinct neighborhood was advantageous and most probably revolved around the taxes collected from the residents by the neighborhood councils.[18]

Beyond providing local governance, neighborhood life also established moral norms for individuals and families. In this sense, the Armenian community with its emphasis on traditional values and customs was not so different from its Muslim neigh-

---

[12] Paronian, *Ptoyt me*, p. 283.

[13] Ibid., p. 302.

[14] Ibid., p. 330.

[15] Paronian, *Metsapativ muratskanner*, p. 79.

[16] *Jamanag*, no. 22 (Oct. 26, 1863), p. 175.

[17] Ibid., no. 26 (Dec. 21, 1863), p. 204.

[18] The national ("agzgayin") tax is covered in articles 90-93 of the 1863 Constitution. According to this regulation, every adult (that is, male adult) was obliged to contribute to "the expenses of the nation" by an annual tax. This tax was divided into two parts. The first was collected by the Patriarchate of Constantinople for the central expenses, while the second part was collected by the neighborhood councils to meet local expenses. Moreover, these councils were authorized to decide how the local tax would be levied and collected.

bors, as both refused to recognize the existence of an individual morality independent of the collective. Although it is usually believed that Armenians in the latter part of the Ottoman era were closer to European values and were more "modern" than Muslims, contemporary sources show that Armenians held unfavorable attitudes toward individual independence and moral standard vis-à-vis the community. For example, Krikor Zohrab, in his story "Deceased," paints an unflattering picture of the residents of a conservative neighborhood who scorn a widow and her two daughters because of the absence of a male in charge of the family. Zohrab exposes the cruelty of the tagh by chronicling its obsession with respectability as it launches an inquisition into the background of the widow and her family.[19] Zohrab also describes a brother who refuses to marry before his two younger sisters because a traditional moral rule dictated that an older brother could not marry before his sisters had done so.[20]

Among the Armenians of Constantinople in late nineteenth and early twentieth centuries, as in other communities of the empire, there was a tension between the traditional and the modern, between the values and way of life they represented. A speech, made in an awards ceremony at the Amenaprkich Varzharan (All Savior's School) in the Galata neighborhood and published in *Jamanag*, reflected this tension. Mgrditch Hagopian, one of the students of the school, wrote that if Armenians hoped to develop as a nation, they would have to adopt Western technology and especially Western methods of education. Yet he also emphasized that Armenian values and Christianity should not be forgotten but be taught to the school children.[21] This was a familiar argument heard not only among Armenians but also Muslim Ottoman intellectuals in the nineteenth century—that on the way to modernity with Western methods it was essential to maintain a people's own moral values. Preserving the moral norms and values of the Armenian community represented one of the most pressing issues for the neighborhood councils.

---

[19] Krikor Zohrab, *Hekiatner* [Fables] (Istanbul: Agos, 1998), p. 55.

[20] Ibid., p. 53.

[21] *Jamanag*, no. 17 (Aug. 17, 1863), p. 134.

Armenian Societies

The Armenians of Constantinople created, besides the neighborhood councils, many organizations or clubs (Armenian: *miutiun*) which brought together likeminded members of the community. Baronian's *Ptoyt me Polsoy tagherun mej* depicts a society in the Ortakiugh tagh, which taught various crafts to the unemployed youth, while another in the Balat tagh distributed money and various presents to the poor during the Christmas season and at Easter. A miutiun in the Salmatomruk tagh sought to encourage reading among the residents and organized discussion sessions about literature. Similarly, an organization in the Selamsiz tagh aimed to contribute to the improvement of education and Armenian schools.[22]

Jamanag frequently announced the formation of such societies. For example, Varzhabedagan Engerutiun Hayots (The Armenian Teachers' Society) was established to standardize the methods of education in Armenian schools and to enhance the living standards of the teachers and their communities.[23] Another society, the Haygazian Engerutiun in Beshiktash published books to foster literacy among the Armenians.[24] In addition, Andznanver Engerutiun (Altruistic Society) taught reading and writing to Armenians who had migrated to Constantinople from the provinces to earn money.[25] In a similar vein, the graduates of the Samatia School founded a society to improve the quality of education at that same institution.[26] As long as this society and the neighborhood were united, *Jamanag* commented, the residents could work harmoniously together, demonstrating the extent to which societies could be influential among the Armenian people.

The Ergrakordzagan Engerutiun (Agricultural Society), established in Constantinople by migrants from the twin towns of Everek and Fenese in Gesaria (Kayseri) deserves special mention. The society purchased lands near Everek-Fenese to conduct

---

[22] Paronian, *Ptoyt me*, pp. 258, 280, 303, 334, 363.

[23] *Jamanag*, no. 1 (Jan. 2, 1863), pp. 3-4.

[24] Ibid., no. 7 (March 30, 1863), p. 54.

[25] Ibid., no. 13 (June 22, 1863), p. 103.

[26] Ibid., no. 15 (July 20, 1863), pp. 118-19.

agricultural experiments. The society focused on cash crops like silk and cotton. According to *Jamanag*, there were between 600 and 700 shareholders who paid 5 kurushes each to generate the capital needed for the enterprise. Although the principal motivation was not profit, the shareholders could receive their principal with dividends five years later. The society accumulated 150,000 kurushes and apparently distributed a part of that amount to its shareholders and reinvested the remainder in the project. Further, this society also provided a solidarity network among the migrants by creating a communication line with Everek-Fenese. In the 1860s, because of the primitive transportation infrastructure, normally months would pass before a letter reached its destination. As a service for the migrants and their families back home, the Ergrakordzagan Engerutiun, through a special agreement with the public post office, collected and dispatched the letters securely and quickly to Everek-Fenese and received letters in return as expeditiously as possible. The society also collected letters from non-members and even from non-Armenians for a fee.[27]

These societies, along with the neighborhood councils, performed various social functions and strengthened the structural foundations of the Armenian communities in Constantinople. The Armenians of the capital were clearly organized and mobilized around specific projects such as philanthropy, education, and entrepreneurship.

Education of Armenian Girls

If the level of women's education represents an indicator of the degree of a society's "modernity," then the Armenian community in Constantinople in the late nineteenth and early twentieth centuries appeared to be relatively advanced. Many Armenian parents decided to send their daughters to school. In his *Ptoyt me Polsoy tagherun mej*, Baronian often mentions the existence of separate schools for girls and, albeit rarely, coeducational schools. Each tagh usually operated separate schools for boys and girls. There was one school for girls (Hripsimiants Varzharan) in Ortakiugh, Salmatomruk, Eyup, Kadikoy, Topkapu (60

---

[27] *Jamanag*, no. 19 (Sept. 14, 1863), pp. 150-51.

students), Balat (80 students), Yenikapu, and Ijadiye; two schools in Kumkapu (more than 100 students); and a coeducational school in Kinaliada.[28] Thus, in the 1870s there were at least eleven Armenian girls' schools in Constantinople for an estimated 500 students.

Despite the persistence of traditional values in the Armenian communities, these schools for girls played an important role in enhancing the influence of women in social circles in the Ottoman capital. In Ortakiugh, the Hripsimiants Varzharan had been operating for three years in 1863. An anonymous correspondent in *Jamanag* praised the improvements shown during those three years.[29] In addition, the Nazarian School for girls in Yenikapu, with its primary (three year) and secondary (two year) divisions, was opened in February 1863.[30] According to its founder and principal, Toros Nazarian, the school aimed at improving intellectual skills and handicrafts of its girls.[31] *Jamanag* encouraged families to enroll their daughters in this school: "Send your daughters to school in exchange for a small sum; instead of buying luxurious clothing for them, contribute to the development of their hearts and minds."[32] The Nazarian School was a private institution that charged a tuition, but poor girls were admitted for 50 percent of the tuition if the neighborhood councils could confirm their financial status.[33]

The importance attached to the education of girls in the Constitution of 1863 is captured by the third clause of its introduction. It explicitly declares that the "nation is responsible to provide the necessary education for both boys and girls equally." Similarly, some literary works emphasized the significance of education for women for the advancement of the individual

---

[28] Paronian, *Ptoyt me*, pp. 256, 265-66, 281, 286, 291, 308, 333, 338, 358, 370.

[29] *Jamanag*, no. 15 (July 20, 1863), p. 115.

[30] The school was divided into two sections: primary and secondary. The founder and principal of the school stated that it would accept girls of all ages. The primary level offered courses in reading, writing, religion, history, grammar, morality, mathematics, geography, French, painting, and sewing; the secondary level, in addition to the above courses, included literature, economics, and music. *Jamanag*, no. 6 (March 16, 1863), p. 47.

[31] Ibid., no. 5 (March 2, 1863), p. 40.

[32] "Tbrots Nazarian," in *Jamanag*, no. 6 (March 16, 1863), p. 46.

[33] Ibid.

and of society. For instance, Arshak, one of the protagonists in Erukhan's *Amirayin aghjike*, says to his lover: "I do not want you to be ignorant; on the contrary, you should be educated. All my books are at your disposal. I will do everything to make you an enlightened girl."[34]

Constantinople Armenians Discussing
Their "Brothers" in the Interior

Armenians who had come to Constantinople from the interior provinces remained attached to their hometowns, and many Armenians in general showed a strong interest in events in the interior provinces. The social, economic, and political situation of their struggling compatriots emerged as one of the most urgent issues for Armenians in the capital. *Jamanag* is replete with news and complaints reported from various parts of the empire. Many Armenians directed their complaints to Constantinople in hopes of attracting the attention of the Armenian Patriarchate and the Constantinopolitan community in order to solve the problems and daily injustices. Comments appearing in *Jamanag* clearly indicated that the grievances could not be addressed effectively. For example, just before the first elections for the Armenian National Assembly in 1863, *Jamanag* wrote:

> Regarding the extreme misery of the provincial villages and the incompetence of the administrative body in Constantinople, we would foresee an unfortunate future for our nation if we were not on the eve of the formation of a constitutional administration.[35]

Some of the major problems in the provinces involved the conversion of Armenians to Catholicism, deepening poverty, recurring Kurdish assaults on the Armenian villages, rampant corruption by officials, and unceasing exploitation of the Armenian peasantry. For instance, *Jamanag* reported that Armenians in Ovajigh (Chankiri) began to adopt Roman Catholicism

---

[34] Erukhan, *Amirayin aghjike*, p. 192.
[35] "Verjin antskere" [The Latest Developments], in *Jamanag*, no. 17 (Aug. 17, 1863), p. 135.

because the Patriarchate of Constantinople failed to provide the care and attention required to solve their problems. The journal described this situation as a "moral fire."[36] There was the "danger" of Catholicism also in Zeitun, a region of social and political unrest because of frequent tension between the Armenians and the government. According to *Jamanag*, Catholic clergymen, "who have the habit of fishing in muddy waters," visited Zeitun and promised the Armenians to solve their problems if they converted to Catholicism.[37] Similarly, *Jamanag* announced in equally alarmist terms that in Bilejik (Urfa district) some 100 Armenians had already converted to Catholicism.[38]

News coming from the interior was not limited to conversions to Catholicism. *Jamanag*'s pages frequently reported on the murder and abduction of Armenians. For instance, letters from Van complained that "one of the important figures of the Armenian community in Van (M. Akribas) was killed on his way to Arshak village, but the criminals could not be caught."[39] On June 22, 1863, *Jamanag* published an article titled "Sad News from Mush," which relayed from the local *Taroni artzvik* (Eagle of Taron) newspaper that seven assaults had occurred against Armenians in different villages of Mush between April 21 and May 22. The victims were either killed or wounded and their properties seized. In most cases, the perpetrators, identified simply as "Kurds,"[40] were never apprehended or else were released after spending two or three days in prison. A petition presented to the Patriarch in Constantinople by a group of neighborhood councils indicated that other places in the interior— Kharpert (Harput), Palu, Marash—experienced similar crises. The petition stated that Armenians in the provinces, who constituted the majority of the Armenian nation, were in urgent need of a solution to the serious problems that grew worse day by day. Their only hope was the Patriarchate and their Armenian brothers in the capital. Such disturbing events created dis-

---

[36] *Jamanag*, no. 5 (March 2, 1863), pp. 36-37.

[37] "Konstantinapolso mej mard gtnelu dzhvarutiune" [The Difficulties of Finding a Man in Constantinople], *Jamanag*, no. 21 (Oct. 12, 1863), p. 166.

[38] The details of this news are not given. *Jamanag*, no. 6 (March 16, 1863), p. 47.

[39] Ibid., no. 13 (June 22, 1863), p. 101.

[40] Ibid., "Mushen tsavali lurer," p. 104.

content in those regions and within the Armenian community of Constantinople. Yet the petitioners apparently were also cognizant of the fact that many Armenians in Constantinople were not closely interested in their plight, as they warned that "if necessary solutions are not found, only the Armenian community of Bolis will be left as the sole remaining Lusavorchakan [Apostolic] one."[41]

The difficulties involved in addressing these problems notwithstanding, the Civil Council of the Armenian National Assembly created a special body, *kavaragan hantsnazhoghov* (Provincial Commission), to review the complaints and to seek means to address the problems. The commission, consisting of four members,[42] was expected to meet once a week to discuss the questions related to the situation in the interior and to prepare weekly reports to the Civic Council.[43] While further research is necessary to determine the extent of its activities, the commission submitted petitions to the Ottoman government to demand the dismissal of some state officials because of their poor treatment of Armenian peasants.[44] As some Armenians converted to Catholicism or Protestantism or fled to the Russian Empire, *Jamanag* urged the villagers affected by such crises to be patient and to discuss their cases with inspectors being sent by the central government to the provinces.[45]

As it happened, news about the deteriorating situation in the interior had a mixed reception among Constantinopolitan Armenians. Many were clearly concerned about their compatriots, while others showed little interest in such matters. In the final analysis, however, the Armenian community was unable to provide any real solutions.

Conclusion

The Armenian community in the Ottoman capital in the late

---

[41] Ibid., no. 22 (Oct. 26, 1863), pp. 174-75.

[42] *Jamanag* gives the following names: Hagop Burunsuzian, Varteres Misakian, Harutiun Sarughanian, and Mardiros Muhendisian.

[43] *Jamanag*, no. 24 (Nov. 23, 1863), p. 189.

[44] Ibid., no. 25 (Dec. 7, 1863), p. 195.

[45] Ibid., no. 18 (Aug. 31, 1863), p. 141.

Ottoman Empire was organized around certain collective bodies such as the tagh/neighborhood councils and various societies that helped to maintain a functioning society and contributed to its well-being. This did not mean, however, that Armenians always worked harmoniously or efficiently. On the contrary, the institutions of stability at times became a source of dissension and conflict. Still, the Armenian neighborhood communities enjoyed a vibrant social existence and were active, for example, in matters pertaining to the education of girls and to the worsening conditions in the eastern provinces. Future studies would profit greatly by a closer examination of the relationship between the Armenians of Constantinople and the interior. While the picture presented here is far from complete, it may perhaps be regarded as a starting point.

Hagop Baronian

THREE LITERARY VIEWS OF ARMENIAN CONSTANTINOPLE AND ITS INHABITANTS

Victoria Rowe

Constantinople was the center of the *Zartonk* (Awakening) of the Western Armenians, home to numerous literary journals, great poets, dramatists, and prose writers. The educational opportunities and cultural contacts, the salons, journals, and Armenian cultural associations available to aspiring writers made that city the center of Western Armenian intellectual and artistic life. As Rosemary Betterton has noted in the nineteenth-century European context, the modern city offered unique opportunities for aspiring artists in "education and training, as well as the possibility of economic independence and a range of cultural contacts that were less available in a provincial or rural setting."[1] The expansion of education in the Armenian language and greater educational opportunities for male and female students of various social classes in Constantinople contributed to the cultivation of the talents of a wide range of people and created a vibrant cultural life.

One of the most significant results of the new educational system was the participation of Armenian women in the literature of the metropolis. By the late nineteenth and early twentieth century, a circle of Armenian women writers had begun to publish poetry, short stories, novels, and plays in the Armenian journals and publishing houses of the capital. These authors included Srpuhi Diusap (Srbuhi Tiusab), Sibyl (pen name of Zabel Asadur), Isguhi Minasian, Anayis, Zabel Yesayan (Zapel Esayan), and Hayganush (Haykanush) Mark. Largely forgotten today (with the possible exception of Zabel Yesayan), at the time these women writers

---

[1] Rosemary Betterton, "Women Artists, Modernity and Suffrage Cultures in Britain and Germany 1890-1920," in *Women Artists and Modernism*, ed. Katy Deepwell (Manchester: Manchester University Press, 1998), p. 19.

attracted both the criticism and praise of the Armenian literary
elite. Some, like Srpuhi Diusap, were criticized for their radical
ideas and excessive romanticism, while others like Zabel Yesayan,
were praised as talented and intelligent. This chapter focuses on
Srpuhi Diusap (1841-1901), Sibyl (1863-1934), and Zabel Yesayan
(1878-1943), three prominent literary figures whose works offer
insights into the urban environment of Constantinople, where Armenian women published their works, and specifically into Armenian life at the time when social change and the idea of modernity
became one of the main preoccupations of the Constantinople
literary scene.

The more "open, complex and mobile social relations" of city
life in the Ottoman capital "gave women a degree of freedom,
which they could not experience within the confines of a more
traditional environment."[2] Boghos Levon Zekiyan has noted that
"changes in habits and customs," in "social life and behaviour" and
in the modern "conception of human and social values,"[3] characterized the Zartonk period. Contemporary Armenian observers
were conscious of the novelty of women's social position and the
emergence of women writers in the Armenian literary milieu. The
sense of the novel is clearly demonstrated in an article about Armenian women writers, which appeared in the New York based
journal *Arakadz* in 1911. The author of the article, Yenovk Armen,
remarks on the fact that the existence of Armenian women writers
is so recent that its origins are within living memory and his sense
that this was a new but important development is revealed by his
desire to record the beginnings of this phenomenon.[4]

It is clear that the advent of women writers in the Armenian
literary scene was connected to social changes in Armenian society
in Constantinople, especially changes in social behavior and education. By the end of the nineteenth century, Armenian women in
Constantinople had greater mobility than their rural counterparts or
even their "Bolsetsi" grandmothers had experienced. One of the
most obvious examples of this change was in terms of the clothing

---

[2] Ibid.

[3] Boghos Levon Zekiyan, "Modern Armenian Culture: Some Basic Trends between
Continuity and Change, Specificity and Universality," in *Armenian Perspectives*, ed.
Nicholas Awade (Surrey, UK: Curzon Press, 1997), p. 345.

[4] Yenovk Armen, "Hay kin groghnere" [Armenian Women Writers], *Arakadz*
(*Aragats*) (June 22, 1911): 68.

and seclusion of Armenian women. Lucy Garnett, visiting the Ottoman Empire in the early 1890s, noted that Armenian women in Smyrna and Constantinople no longer wore the "native Armenian costume" and instead favored European dress.[5] Contemporary Armenian accounts also confirm the change. For example, in his portrayal of Ottoman social life, Krikor Basmajian states that when he was a boy in the 1850s, Armenian women wore the *yashmak* (veil) and *fereje* (cloak)[6] but by the 1890s, urban Armenian women wore European dress.[7] Zabel Yesayan's account of her youth in Constantinople confirms Basmajian's observation. Yesayan states that while her grandmother's generation had worn the yashmak, which was associated with Islamic rather than Armenian culture, her generation wore European clothes.[8] In the past the veil and the confinement of Armenian women of Constantinople in the home had been to protect women from attracting the attentions of the Janissaries of the capital and possibly being abducted.[9] Many Armenian women in the provinces continued to wear the veil and were kept indoors because of concerns for their physical safety so long as abduction by Kurds and Turks remained a threat.[10] In an article written in 1903, Zabel Yesayan, commenting on the changes

---

[5] Lucy Garnett, *The Women of Turkey and Their Folklore* (London: David Nutt, 1893), p. 211.

[6] The yashmak was a veil, which covered the face; the feradje was a type of cloak wore outdoors. See Jennifer Scarce, *Women's Costume of the Near and Middle East* (London: Unwin Hyman, 1987), pp. 49, 85.

[7] Krikor H. Basmajian, *Social and Religious Life in the Orient* (New York: American Tract Society, 1890), p. 166.

[8] Zapel Esayan, "Silihtari parteznere" [Gardens of Silihdar], in *Erker* [Works] (Erevan: Haypethrat, 1959), p. 399.

[9] Ibid., pp. 399-400. Here Esayan describes how as a young girl, her grandmother was kept indoors for protection and only left her home heavily veiled to attend her confirmation. Upon leaving the church, her veil was torn from her head by Janissaries. As a consequence, the family feared that she would be abducted and immediately married her to prevent possible abduction by Janissaries.

[10] The problem of the physical insecurity of the Armenian population was reflected in various aspects of Armenian material culture, including domestic architecture. Garnett (*Women of Turkey*, p. 197) comments on the fortress-like appearance of Armenian houses designed to protect the occupants. Susie Hoogasian Villa and Mary Kilbourne Matosian, *Armenian Village Life before 1914* (Detroit: Wayne State University Press, 1982), p. 29, note the connection between domestic architecture and security and explain that in the villages of Western Armenia houses, stables, and neighboring dwellings were often interconnected, creating a "semiunderground warren in which people could hide themselves and their valuables."

in material culture and social customs and behavior, states that if the Armenian women of Constantinople could "change places with our grandmothers for a minute, it seems to me that we would feel different from each other, in terms of customs and progress, and we would find ourselves in an unfamiliar environment."[11]

Yesayan identified the expansion of female education as being one of the primary factors in the social changes affecting the status of women.[12] The proliferation of foreign missionary schools in the nineteenth century provided some of the earliest education for Armenian girls. Roman Catholic nuns administered a secondary school for girls as early as 1839 in addition to primary schools for girls.[13] Education sponsored by American Protestants for Armenian girls also increased in the latter half of the nineteenth century as a result of the formation in 1868 of the Women's Board of Missions.[14]

A comparison of the education received by the three writers discussed here reveals the opportunities provided by the city to Armenian women writers and the growing accessibility of educational institutions beyond the privileged elite. For example, Srpuhi Diusap, the daughter of a wealthy Constantinopolitan family, received private education with instruction in French, the natural sciences, and history, and is said to have mastered Greek and Italian, and read ancient Greek philosophy and the modern European Romantics. She studied Armenian language and literature under the Romantic poet Mgrdich Beshigtashlian (Mkrtich Peshiktashlian, 1828-1868).[15] Initially Sibyl, too, attended a French primary school but was not skilled in written Armenian.[16] Later Sibyl described the problems she encountered when transferring from the French school to the well-known Armenian primary school of Surp Khach (Holy Cross). She noted particularly her ignorance of Armenian history and language. For example, in the following exchange she

---

[11] Zapel Esayan, "Mer kinere" [Our Women], *Tsaghik* (April 26, 1903): 150.

[12] Ibid., p. 150.

[13] Barbara Merguerian, "The Beginnings of Secondary Education for Armenian Women: The Armenian Female Seminary in Constantinople," *Journal for the Society of Armenian Studies* 5 (1990-91): 108.

[14] Ibid., pp. 116, 121.

[15] A.S. Sharuryan, *Srbuhi Tyusab: Kyanke ev steghtsagortsutyune* [Srpuhi Diusap: Her Life and Creative Work] (Erevan: Erevan State University, 1963), pp. 9-11, 17.

[16] Sibyl, "Dzriner" [Charity Cases], in *Erker* [Works] (Erevan: Hayastan, 1965), p. 150.

reveals the Armenian school's expectations and her own limitations:

Have you read [Armenian] Christian books? No.
Grammar? No.
Geography? No.
History? No.[17]

Sibyl was placed in a class of younger children in order to learn to read and write Armenian.[18] In contrast with her older female relatives, Yesayan was literate and she was educated in the Armenian schools which had proliferated by the 1880s when she began to attend school. Unlike Srpuhi Diusap and Sibyl, Yesayan received her primary school education entirely in Armenian institutions, first attending a private school in her neighborhood and then the Surp Khach School.

By 1883 when Yesayan enrolled in primary school at the age of five, Constantinople had eleven Armenian girls' schools. Armenian schools of the 1880s faced problems of censorship as the Ottoman government routinely confiscated books on Armenian history and geography, and the Armenian press complained of the lack of standardization in the administering of these schools. Nevertheless, the schools were successful in teaching the Armenian language and instilling in a generation of students a sense of Armenian identity.[19] For example, the education Yesayan received at Surp Khach consisted of instruction in history, French, Armenian, and arithmetic.[20] When Yesayan was twelve years old, her teacher of Armenian language was the author Hrant (Melkon Giurjian/Kiurchian, 1859-1915), who frequently spoke of the conditions of Armenians living in the provinces and secretly gave the pupils books by the patriotic author Raffi (Hakob Melik-Hakobian, 1835-1888). Yesayan noted that reading Raffi's novels *Davit Pek, Samvel,* and especially *Khente* (The Madman) captivated her imagination, making her dream of living in the provinces and helping the Armenians there. Hrant early recognized Yesayan's literary talent and encouraged

---

[17] Ibid., p. 150.
[18] Ibid., p. 151.
[19] Sharuryan, *Srbuhi Tyusab,* pp. 41-43.
[20] Zapel Esayan, "Inknakensagrutyun" [Autobiography], *Sovetakan grakanutyun* (1979): 53.

it.[21] As a result, although Yesayan was not a member of a very wealthy family like Diusap, public schooling enabled her to attain an education in Armenian and prepare for a literary career that would have been unavailable to her a generation earlier.

In addition to greater educational opportunities, cultural networks such as the salon and Armenian national agencies facilitated women's writing in Armenian. The salon was one of the few public spaces in the Ottoman Empire where Armenian women and men could meet together to discuss the pressing intellectual, political, social, and literary matters of the period. Both Srpuhi Diusap and Zabel Yesayan participated in contemporary intellectual debates in the salon. In fact, it was at Mrs. Gayane Matakian's salon that Yesayan first encountered Armenian intellectuals, including the renowned Arshag Chobanian (Arshak Chopanian), founder of the journal *Tsaghik* (Flower), where her early fiction and nonfiction articles on women's rights were published.[22]

The Armenian national societies, especially charitable organizations devoted to education or social work, also encouraged Armenian women's writing by creating a legitimate place for Armenian women to engage in public work and provided funds to open schools for girls. Both Srpuhi Diusap and Sibyl began their careers as heads of charitable organizations devoted to women's education. Diusap was head of Philomathic Armenian Women's Association (Tbrotsaser Dignants Engerutiun), which trained Armenian women to become teachers in Armenian schools outside of Constantinople. Sibyl was founder of the Patriotic Armenian Women's Association (Azkanver Hayuhiats Engerutiun), which established Armenian girls' schools in the provinces. Their work and philosophies concerning these associations were articulated in their subsequent fiction writing. For example, Diusap's novels discuss the need for female education and the importance of women's employment,

---

[21] Ibid., pp. 56-57.

[22] Gayane Matakian (1852-1900), educator and philanthropist, was born in Tiflis, educated in pedagogy in Switzerland, and founded kindergartens for Armenian children in Tiflis, Erevan, and Constantinople, where she had relocated in 1886. She organized teacher training courses for young Armenian women and was instrumental in sending several young women to France for further training. Matakian held salons in her home attended by prominent intellectuals, such as Krikor Zohrab (Grigor Zohrap), Yervant Odian (Ervand Otian), Arpiar Arpiarian, and Sibyl. See Anahit Harutyunyan, *Ereveli tiknants dare* [The Age of Notable Women] (Erevan: Hogevor Hayastan, 2005), p. 85.

goals which she had tried actively to put into practice during her involvement in the Philomathic Armenian Women's Association.

In Constantinople, Armenian women could contribute to current discourses on modernity and social issues preoccupying the Armenian intelligentsia of the period and they were involved in Armenian public life through schooling, the formation of charitable organizations, and participation in mixed literary gatherings.[23] Armenian women writers, like their male counterparts, viewed social issues as important topics in their literary texts. Western Armenian writers of this period believed that the writer should use the pen to benefit the Armenian people; accordingly, they wrote about the problems Armenians experienced, both in rural areas and in the capital. Here, however, the concentration is on texts pertaining to Constantinople and its Armenian inhabitants.

Armenian women writers of Constantinople display varying degrees of talent, employ different writing styles, and follow either the romantic or realist literary school dominant in the city literary scene. They share with each other, however, an urban sensibility and a concern with the problems facing the Armenian women and men of Constantinople. The literary texts to be discussed include: Srpuhi Diusap's novel *Siranush* (1884), Zabel Yesayan's novel *Erb aylevs chen sirer* (When They No Longer Love, 1914), and Sibyl's play *Harse* (The Daughter-in-Law, 1918). Each of these literary texts reveals a different aspect of the Constantinopolitan social reality and the role of modernity in Armenian society in the late nineteenth and early twentieth century. Modernity here refers to the definition of *modernité* as articulated in 1863 by Charles Baudelaire (who was certainly well-known to the Western Armenian intelligentsia), meaning a "sense of difference from the past and to describe a peculiarly modern identity."[24] In the Armenian milieu, especially in the theories of Armenian women writers, modernity explores the character of modern social relations—

---

[23] The introduction of mixed gatherings among Armenians of the capital was a recent phenomenon at the beginning of the twentieth century. The writer Anayis (Yevpime Avedisian) (1872-1950) notes that her grandfather was one of the first Armenians to host mixed gatherings in his home in Constantinople. See Anayis, *Hushers* [My Memoirs] (Paris: n.p., 1949), p. 13.

[24] Baudelaire's statement appears in Francis Frascina et al., *Modernity and Modernism in French Painting in the Nineteenth Century* (New Haven: Yale University Press, 1993), p. 9.

particularly those pertaining to men and women, the family and social classes.

Siranush

Srpuhi Diusap had made her debut in Armenian letters with the publication of three articles addressing Armenian women's education and employment, published in 1880 and 1881. Her first novel *Mayda*, published in 1883, unleashed a storm of controversy about the status of women in Armenian society. Diusap has been called a "feminist," and it is indeed true that her three novels are concerned with the amelioration of the position of women in Armenian society. In her second novel, *Siranush*, however, Diusap addressed the question of women from a complex perspective of the role of social class and the impact of modernity on Armenian women and men of Constantinople.

In the novel *Siranush*, the heroine, the daughter of a wealthy *amira*, falls in love with Yervant (Ervand), the son of a poor artisan, but is forbidden to marry him; instead, she is forced to marry a wealthy amira.[25] Despite the banality of the plot, Diusap uses this theme to address contemporary political and social issues, including the conflict between the amira and other classes for control of the Armenian *millet* or religious community, the conflict between traditional and modern values, and the status and role of women in Armenian society. Diusap describes the contemporary Armenian ruling elite as being divided into three competing groups: the amiras, bureaucratic officials, and the intellectuals. She states:

> Eventually the bureaucratic official gained prominence over the amiras and this resulted in a new elite, based on the bureaucracy, which competed for influence with the wealthy merchant class. And the third class, the intellectual class, competed for existence

---

[25] The amiras usually acted as bankers or moneylenders in the Ottoman taxation system. They were permitted to wear clothes reserved for Ottoman officials and ride horses, privileges denied to non-Muslims in the Ottoman Empire. Because of their power at court, the amiras exercised great authority in the Armenian community, including the election of the patriarch. See Hagop Barsoumian, "The Dual Role of the Armenian Amira Class within the Ottoman Government and the Armenian Millet (1750-1850)," in *Christians and Jews in the Ottoman Empire*, ed. Benjamin Braude and Bernard Lewis, 2 vols. (New York: Holmes and Meier Publishers, 1982), vol. 1, p. 171.

with the other two classes. This was a struggle over position, wealth, and enlightenment.[26]

Diusap characterizes the bureaucratic class as dependent, the amira class as independent, and the intellectuals as progressive, adding, however, that while the intellectual class had some strength, it was not as powerful as the other two groups.[27]

Diusap's description of the struggle for control over the Armenian millet reflects the political situation of the period. From 1810 to 1845, the amiras dominated the Armenian millet through their control of the Armenian patriarch, the spiritual and civic leader of the Armenians of the Ottoman Empire. The amiras were frequently generous patrons of schools, hospitals, and churches, and thus facilitated the cultural revival of the nineteenth century. The source of their wealth and prestige, however, was dependent upon their role as intermediaries between the Ottoman state and the Armenian millet. By the mid-nineteenth century, an increasingly vocal group of Armenians saw the amiras as being concerned with protecting their position within the Ottoman state rather than the interests of the Armenian population.[28] Liberal Armenians and members of the guilds demanded a voice in the government of the community, and this conflict led to the creation in 1860-63 of the Armenian National Constitution, which governed the internal affairs of the community. The new semi-representative assembly was composed of lay and religious members, who sought to curtail some of the power of the clergy and the amira class.[29]

In *Siranush*, Diusap reveals how the political conflict between the amiras and the intelligentsia was manifested on a personal, gendered level. She depicts the tensions between the amira class, represented by Siranush's father, Haynur, and her husband, Tarehian, on the one hand, and the new intellectual class, represented by Siranush, on the other, as a family conflict between father and daughter and husband and wife. Siranush's education and way of thinking is contrasted with her father, the son of a wealthy amira

---

[26] Srbuhi Tiusab, *Siranush*, in *Erker* [Works] (Erevan: Sovetakan Grogh, 1981), p. 155.

[27] Ibid., p. 155.

[28] Barsoumian, "Dual Role," pp. 179, 181.

[29] George Bournoutian, *A History of the Armenian People*, 2 vols. (Costa Mesa, CA: Mazda Publishers, 1994), vol. 2, pp. 22-23.

family, who is uncultured and shows little concern toward those without wealth or position in the bureaucracy. Siranush's future husband, too, is from a wealthy family, a high ranking official who "possesses a pride which is the product of having inherited wealth." Although he is also known to behave "immorally" by consorting with prostitutes, Siranush's father and other wealthy families consider him to be a good match for their young daughters because of his wealth.[30]

While she emphasized the differences between Siranush and Haynur and Tarehian to illustrate the tensions between the intellectuals and the amiras, she never lost sight of the category of gender and its relationship with class and demonstrated that the position of women in the amira class also divided Siranush from Haynur and Tarehian. As the daughter and wife of amiras, Siranush can be considered part of the amira class and yet she is not; Diusap firmly allies her heroine with the intellectual class. Both Siranush and her mother experience alienation and powerlessness. The author questions the extent to which women belong to any social class when they lack the same power as men. The conflict over Mr. Haynur's decision to marry Siranush to Mr. Tarehian demonstrates the inequality of women. Without asking for either Siranush's or his wife's consent, Haynur agrees to Tarehian's proposal. At this point Diusap interjects into the text in a mocking tone: "After all, isn't he the father? Doesn't he have absolute authority over his child's fate, particularly in this sort of illustrious case?" When Haynur finally informs his wife of his decision, he is surprised to discover that she is not pleased, as she argues that the groom's debauched lifestyle is not in harmony with her daughter's innocence.[31]

Siranush's mother speaks in favor of marriage based on mutual love and respect rather than an arranged marriage, while Mr. Haynur represents traditional expectations of male and female behavior in marriage among members of the amira class, particularly the subordination of women. The tragedy is that while Siranush and her mother argue against the idea of marriage as an economic transaction, their protests remain unheeded. Haynur is unmoved and bullies his wife to such a degree that Siranush feels

---

[30] Tiusab, *Siranush*, pp. 155, 178.
[31] Ibid., p. 180.

compelled to marry Tarehian in order to protect her mother. After her marriage, Siranush's situation worsens; she is virtually a prisoner in her home, spied upon by servants and subject to her husband's jealousies while he is free to visit his mistress.[32] Siranush and her mother are not compliant; they protest, but because they are women they lack wealth and public position—the hallmarks of amira power and status. Women are regarded as possessions to be exchanged between amira families through marriage, and they are powerless and cannot ameliorate their situation despite belonging to the same powerful amira class. Diusap did not attempt to conceal her contempt for that class, specifically its customs and mores which she identified as harmful to women. In her preface to *Siranush*, Diusap criticized the amiras saying, they "live in a sordid [moral] atmosphere and at the same time demand to be loved and respected by their wives. Love! Respect! What an astonishing ambition, a foolish dream. To be loved it is necessary to love and to respect."[33]

In contrast with the amiras' devaluation of women, Diusap saw the intellectual class as being the locus of progress in terms of class hierarchy and women's emancipation. She portrays the intellectual class as being much more fluid, in sharp contrast with the amira class. In her novels, admittance into the intellectual class was not achieved through the possession of wealth or social standing but rather through the world of art, intellectual accomplishments, and commitment to progress and to the Armenian nation. The intellectual class therefore was not restricted to men or a single social class. She saw the new standards of the intelligentsia as having the potential to undermine the traditional amira evaluation of human worth. In the novel, Siranush's beau, Yervant, decides to go to Rome to develop his talent in painting but also to improve his social position in order to be considered worthy of marrying Siranush in the eyes of her father. Yervant believes that "intelligence is the highest equality"—a belief that can potentially subvert the old structures and hierarchies as determined by wealth, social position, and gender.[34] The emphasis of the intellectual class on knowledge as the basis of merit and value rather than gender and birth was

---

[32] Ibid., pp. 279, 281.

[33] Ibid., p. 146.

[34] Ibid., p. 172.

inclusive of women and the artisan class. Siranush could be a member of the intellectual class because of her education and interests:

> To study was a beloved dream of Siranush's, particularly the study of ancient and modern national [Armenian] history and the literature of other nations, too. She loved to study the causes of national progress and decline, and she wisely noted that the intellectuals gave people life, while vice and ignorance brought only death.[35]

Diusap portrays Siranush as a young woman who studies history and literature and desires to participate in the task of improving the condition of her people. This portrait not only demonstrates that Diusap viewed it as the responsibility of the intellectual class to work for the good of the nation rather than for personal profit but also is indicative of the emancipation she believed was offered to women by the intellectual class. As an intelligent young woman with intellectual interests Siranush could and clearly desires to participate in the movement for national progress. The fact that she is prevented from doing so is the result of her weak position as a woman within her upper-class Constantinople family. The novel, *Siranush,* reveals the revolutionary potential of modernity on social values and structures, especially in the categories of gender and social class, but portrays such values as weak and unable to overthrow the power of existing gender and class hierarchies.

Harse

Srpuhi Diusap's interest in modernity and its impact on Armenian society in Constantinople were continued by Sibyl, who greatly admired Diusap's works. In her play *Harse*, Sibyl continues the discussion of the role of modernity in Armenian society from the perspective of its advent into the extended family structure.[36] The play explores changing social relations by examining how the

---

[35] Ibid., p. 156.

[36] The Armenian title of the play "Harse" means bride or daughter-in-law in English usage. It has been translated as "The Daughter-in-Law" instead of "Bride" as the former better captures Sibyl's emphasis on the relationships within the extended family rather than the relationship between husband and wife. There is some deliberate irony in Sibyl's choice of this title as Arusiag turns out to be a rather untraditional daughter-in-law.

relationships within the extended family alter when the idea of romantic love enters the equation. As in Diusap's *Siranush*, romantic love in these texts is a signifier of marriage as a union of companionship between a man and a woman and conflicts with the older vision of marriage as an alliance between families.[37] Sibyl explores this theme through the relationship between the daughter-in-law, the son/husband, the mother-in-law, and sister-in-law in a middle-class Constantinopolitan family.

In the play, the daughter-in-law, Arusiag, lives with her husband, Arshag, his widowed mother, Digin (Mrs.) Diruhi, and his unmarried sister, Hanumig. The extended family is represented in this case by the inclusion of Hanumig, the sister-in-law, in the story. Although Arusiag and Hanumig are close in age, Hanumig constantly criticizes Arusiag's style of dress, behavior, and sewing and encourages her mother to exercise her traditional authority as a mother-in-law in order to curtail Arusiag's liberty. Traditionally, the daughter-in-law had the least power in the extended family, sisters-in-law could exercise power over a brother's young wife, while the mother-in-law had great authority over her children, especially her daughters-in-law, giving the younger women orders on how to perform chores and how to rear their children.[38] In Sibyl's play, the mother-in-law views Arusiag as a hostile stranger. According to Digin Diruhi, "A daughter-in-law is not one's own child. She's an enemy"[39] who must be treated as such: "Now, we have a stranger in our house, so let's not act dishonorably toward her."[40] The tension of this play revolves around the fact that Arusiag is always polite and good-natured, in contrast with the hostility and ill-temper shown by her mother-in-law and sister-in-law, Hanumig. The traditional subordination of the daughter-in-law, however, has been subverted because the marriage between Arusiag and Arshag is a love match rather than an arranged marriage, and the daughter-in-law does not have to fear her husband's family—thereby rendering traditional rules governing the status of

---

[37] For example, Villa and Matosian, *Armenian Village Life*, p. 72. state that among Armenians a marriage was "an alliance not just between individuals, but also between groups."

[38] Florence Mazian, "The Patriarchal Armenian Family System: 1914," *Armenian Review* 36 (Winter 1983): 20.

[39] Sibyl, *Harse* [The Daughter-in-Law] (Boston: Hairenik, 1938), p. 6.

[40] Ibid., p. 17.

the daughter-in-law meaningless. Arusiag's mother-in-law states: "Akh, what can I say to my Arshag now, since he didn't even ask for my permission but simply went out and hastily got married? If I had been there, I wouldn't have given permission!"[41]

Digin Diruhi's lament demonstrates the perception that love threatens the traditional authority of the family and by extension the structures of power in society. Armenian culture traditionally regarded the overt expression of love between husband and wife as shameful, and a newly married bride was forbidden to talk to her husband in front of his parents.[42] Zabel Yesayan commented that in the Constantinopolitan Armenian community of the 1890s the concept of a "love match" was regarded as shameful, and couples who married "for love" met "with disapproval."[43] In this context, Diruhi expresses outrage at Arusiag's expression of love for her husband because her conduct corrodes Diruhi's authority as her mother-in-law. She complains:

> "I love my Arshag," she brazenly says to me! I've also been married and looked after a husband but never once did such shameful words pass my lips.[44]

Further, Arusiag wishes that she and her husband live separate from his family, a clear sign of a threat to the extended family:

> I would have preferred a small apartment of my own, decorated according to my tastes, with lots of plants and flowers, and every-thing prepared by my own hands. They threaten me with having to work in the kitchen but to me it would be a pleasure if I could be alone with my beloved husband, without being endlessly attacked by those two critics.[45]

This wish is one, which Arusiag can only express to herself and makes no plans to separate her husband and herself from his family.

In the course of the play, the mother-in-law attempts to regain her authority by emphasizing her position as a Constantinopolitan Armenian. She taunts her daughter-in-law about her lack of breed-

---

[41] Ibid., p. 10.
[42] Villa and Matosian, *Armenian Village Life*, p. 92.
[43] Esayan, *Silihtari parteznere*, p. 405.
[44] Sibyl, *Harse*, p. 8.
[45] Ibid., p. 33.

ing because she is an "outsider" (that is, not from Constantinople), and in one scene she jeers at Arusiag for not being a member of the city's elite. Their exchange also alludes to the rivalry between Smyrna and Constantinople, the latter claiming to represent the cultural and intellectual center of the Western Armenians:

> *Digin Diruhi*: What could you have learned from your family or friends in the Anatolian mountains?
> *Arusiag*: The city of Smyrna is not the Anatolian mountains, Mama. It's a city just like this one. And furthermore, as you know, my parents are originally from Bolis!
> *Digin Diruhi*: Oh well, there are Bolsetsi and then there are Bolsetsi! The upper classes, like us, are different.
> *Arusiag*: (To herself) She's starting again! I'll put a stop to it. (Aloud) You're right! *Il y a cordonnier et cordonnier* [There are shoemakers and then there are shoemakers!][46]

The pretentious mother-in-law is confident of her superiority as a Constantinopolitan. Yet, ironically, we learn in the play that she is actually from a small provincial town and has only recently migrated to the capital. In many ways the character of Digin Diruhi is reminiscent of the figure of the "Bolis snob" found in Western Armenian literature of this period, especially in the plays of Hagop Baronian (Hakob Paronian, 1842-1891). Ultimately, however, the daughter-in-law prevails against the manipulations of her mother-in-law and sister-in-law by espousing ethical principles and by being a true companion to her husband, something which was viewed by the author as being representative of modern social values.

The character of Arusiag, as constructed by Sibyl, represents the modern, "new woman" who wears bright clothing, sings, plays the piano for guests, writes novels, and frequently goes visiting. On the other hand, her sister-in-law, Hanumig, follows tradition and customs, stays home, and hems tablecloths.[47] The author, however, takes great pains to present the "new woman" pressing for modern values as a positive, ethical character, in contrast with the negative images found in plays of Hagop Baronian.[48] Arusiag espouses

---

[46] Ibid., p. 14.

[47] Sibyl, *Harse*, pp. 7-8, 25.

[48] See, for example, Paronian, "Paghtasar aghbar," in *Erker* [Works] (Erevan: Loys, 1987). The new woman in this play is an adulterous woman.

ethical principles, unlike her deceptive and conniving mother-in-
law and sister-in-law. For instance, when Arshag tells his mother
and sister that he is in financial difficulties, they refuse to help
him, responding that "We're women, we can't interfere in business
matters."[49] Arusiag, on the other hand, agrees to help her husband
with her own money. She questions the custom that dictates that
men financially support women, while women are not allowed to
work for pay. She says: "How horrible social customs are! A man
works, tires himself, and struggles to earn a living, while we three
women sit comfortably at home, without a care. Why? Because
that's the custom! The senseless, absurd custom!"[50]

For Sibyl, Arusiag's rejection of oppressive customs and her
desire to act as a responsible partner in her marriage pointed to the
changes required in Armenian society and represented modern
relations between men and women within the family. Rather than
destroying the family, as critics sometimes charged, Armenian
women writers constructed a vision of marriage wherein the
partners were mutually responsible and devoted to maintaining an
equitable and honest union. Sibyl's *Harse*, like Diusap's *Siranush*,
presents modernity as an ethical social force righting the oppres-
sions of the past. This is not to say, however, that they rejected all
traditions. For example, both Diusap and Sibyl depict their ideal
Armenian women as obedient to and respectful of parents even
when the latter are clearly in the wrong.[51] The vision of modernity
found in the texts of Diusap and Sibyl reflects a synthesis of what
the authors identified as the best in both traditional and modern
social values.[52]

---

[49] Sibyl, *Harse*, p. 24.

[50] Ibid., p. 37.

[51] Diusap's advocacy of respect for parents is found in her novel, *Siranush*, when
she marries in order to be obedient to her father and out of filial devotion to her
mother. Tyusab, *Siranush*, pp. 191, 194. In Sibyl's play, respect for parents is shown
by both Arshag's and Arusiag's respect for Digin Diruhi, even when she has revealed
herself to be less than honorable.

[52] Zekiyan, "Modern Armenian Culture," p. 352, states that Armenians did not
simply copy their models but rather "integrated and harmonized them" in new synthe-
ses. He identifies women's emancipation as one of the areas in which this process of
"harmonization" occurred. Armenian women's theories of women's emancipation
sought to integrate feminist concepts with their social and political reality in the Ottoman
state. See Victoria Rowe, *A History of Armenian Women's Writing, 1880-1922* (London: Gomidas Institute, 2009), and "Armenian Writers and Women's Rights Discourse
in Turn-of-the-Century Constantinople," *Aspasia* 2 (2008): 44-69.

Erb Aylevs Chen Sirer

Zabel Yesayan's novel *Erb aylevs chen sirer* (When They No Longer Love) presents another view of the Armenian inhabitants of Constantinople. This novel introduces the reader to a world far from the upper and middle classes, and, unlike the other two literary texts discussed above, it considers the modern, particularly the modern economic system, as a negative force. The story takes place among the inhabitants of a small quarter in Constantinople who earn their livelihood by dyeing cloth for commercial use. Stressing the psychological impact of economic oppression, Yesayan presents the plight of the workers caught in a cycle of poverty, exploitation, and alcoholism. This novel, like her other works—for example, *Krake shapik* (Shirt of Fire, 1934)—emphasizes that poverty strips people of finer feelings and causes them to be cruel in order to escape relentless and miserable poverty. When the workers in the cloth-dyeing factory are laid off because of cuts in production, they must borrow money to feed their families, which in turn results in their being heavily in debt. Yesayan skillfully portrays the vulnerability of the workers to exploitation, as unskilled men and women enter the workforce, in debt, and desperate to support themselves and their children. The novel also depicts a working-class woman's attempt to ameliorate her situation by marrying the powerful boss of the cloth-dyeing factory.

Their boss, Hagopjan Agha (*agha* is an honorific title and its use in the text serves to demonstrate his higher position vis-à-vis the people in his employ) is a cruel man, widely suspected of cheating his workers:

> His workers don't like him, but they respect him because he is the person who provides them with the work they need in order to live. He is cold and unbending in hard times, declining to offer help. He never misses the chance to cut costs, and they even suspect that he deliberately falsified the accounts of money owing to the ignorant and illiterate female workers.[53]

Yesayan's portrayal in this novel of the working conditions and dishonesty of the boss is based on the experiences of her maternal

---

[53] Zapel Esayan, *Erb aylevs chen sirer* (Beirut: Shirak, 1972), pp. 29-30.

aunts. In her autobiography *Silihtari parteznere* (Gardens of Silihdar, 1935), Yesayan describes her maternal aunts' work in the textile industry and their conviction that their boss cheated them and the illiterate women workers by paying them less than he should have for their piece work when he came to their houses to collect their handiwork.[54]

As in several short stories by Krikor Zohrab (Grigor Zohrap) (1861-1915),[55] Yesayan paid close attention to sexual exploitation of women workers. For instance, one day when the boss Hagopjan Agha is visiting Yeranik Hanim and Yevpime, he sees Yevpime washing the cloth at the fountain in the courtyard. While Yevpime is washing her dress becomes wet and her clinging clothes reveal the contours of her body. Hagopjan Agha is attracted by this sight and fantasizes about what it would be like to be married to a healthy, young woman like Yevpime in contrast with his own sickly wife who is dying. He indicates his interest in Yevpime by commenting on her beauty to her mother Yeranik Hanim and demanding a chair to sit in the courtyard to watch the girl work. Ultimately, all the power in the relationship between Yevpime and Hagopjan Agha rests in his hands. He tells Yeranik Hanim that because he likes Yevpime, he insists on giving her some extra work, despite being aware of the fact that she prefers not to do the work.[56]

More than her job, Yevpime's reputation is also at stake. Hagopjan Agha can and does compromise the women's reputation in the neighborhood when he visits them in their home without promising to marry Yevpime. As a result, Yevpime's reputation is ruined in the neighborhood. No other man will marry her.[57] As Yeranik Hanim states: "We have the man in our hands but at the expense of our neighbor's goodwill."[58] Yesayan shows, however, that Yeranik Hanim and Yevpime do not entirely blame their neighbors for their disapproval; in similar circumstances, they, too,

---

[54] Esayan, *Silihtari parteznere*, p. 432.

[55] See, for example, Krikor Zohrab's tale of the sexual exploitation of domestic workers in wealthy homes in Constantinople in the short story "Postal." See Grigor Zohrap, "Postal" [Whore], *Erkeri zhoghovatsu* [Collected Works], 2 vols. (Erevan: Haypethrat, 1962), vol. 1, pp. 3-9.

[56] Zapel Esayan, *Erb aylevs chen sirer*, pp. 29-30.

[57] Ibid., p. 58.

[58] Ibid., p. 61.

would be disapproving. Nevertheless, they have compromised their reputations and gone into debt to provide Hagopjan Agha's evening entertainment to such a degree that they cannot turn back.[59] The difference between the women and the boss in the novel is that if he chooses not to marry Yevpime he will have lost nothing. Yevpime must marry Hagopjan Agha or she will have lost everything, reputation and money. The women's plight is not resolved by the end of the story as the reader never conclusively learns whether Hagopjan Agha will marry Yevpime.

Yesayan's portrait of female employment in *Erb aylevs chen sirer* is quite different from her portrayal of women and work in her *Hogis aksorial* (My Soul in Exile, 1922). In the latter novel Yesayan portrayed a woman's joy in her work. The main character of this novel, Emma, is an artist who has lived abroad but returns to Constantinople to exhibit her paintings. This positive portrayal in *Hogis aksorial* reveals that Yesayan did advocate female employment but recognized that what distinguishes women's experience of work is affected by social class. Emma enjoys her work because she freely chose to enter into it, and her job enables her to exercise her talents and thereby increases her self-confidence. For the working-class Yevpime, on the other hand, work is simply a necessary evil and contributes to her victimization.

Yesayan's *Erb aylevs chen sirer* portrays working-class men and women as having no alternatives to oppressive economic structures. The novel does not offer solutions; instead, through the story of Yevpime's life, Yesayan illustrates how oppressive structures converge to limit poor and uneducated people's options. Yesayan's fictional portrayal of oppression in this novel resembles Marilyn Frye's discussion of how oppression works. Frye states:

> The experience of oppressed people is that the living of one's life is confined and shaped by forces and barriers which are not accidental or occasional and hence avoidable but are systematically related to each other in such a way as to catch one between and among them and to restrict or penalize motion in any direction.[60]

In *Erb aylevs chen sirer,* Yevpime's life is shaped by forces

---

[59] Ibid., pp. 58-60.
[60] Marilyn Frye, "Oppression," in *Feminist Frontiers III*, ed. Laurel Richardson and Verta Taylor (New York: McGraw-Hill, 1993), p. 8.

beyond her control, such as poverty and her father's alcoholism, which in turn are part of an economic system which controls laborers by paying them little. This is "systematically related to" a hierarchical structure of gender relations, both in the place of work and at home. While working-class men are subordinated to upper-class men, the former nevertheless dominate women of their own class by exercising direct control over women in decisions pertaining to relations, marriage, job, wages, and even dowries. The main women characters, however, are not portrayed as saints anymore than the men are. Yesayan describes Yeranik's and Yevpime's callousness as they daily discuss Hagopjan Agha's dying wife and feel no shame about making plans for marrying her husband after her death. They even display anger toward the dying woman, believing that she is clinging to life in order to spite them. When Yeranik Hanim goes to visit the dying woman, she realizes her suspicions are untrue. Hagopjan Agha's wife is in absolute agony, and Yeranik is confronted by the grief of the dying woman's mother. At this point Yeranik Hanim momentarily realizes that there are kinds of spiritual or physical pain that are as bad as or worse than poverty. After leaving the woman's sickbed, however, Yeranik forgets this flash of insight and upon her arrival home plots with Yevpime about her future marriage once the wife is dead. Yesayan attributes the callousness that Yeranik and Yevpime display, like the men who frequent the tavern for solace, as being unconsciously cruel because they fear for their very survival and seek any means available to escape or forget their circumstances.

Yevpime's situation is portrayed by the author as hopeless. In part Yesayan offers no solutions to Yevpime's situation because Yesayan apparently wrote *Erb aylevs chen sirer* under the influence of the naturalist school in literature. Naturalism, as articulated by the French author Emile Zola (1840-1902), whom Yesayan had read, emphasized the author's impartiality and viewed people's attitudes and behaviors as determined by hereditary, social and cultural milieu, and the circumstances of the moment.[61] In this novel, Yesayan, while attempting to remain impartial, portrayed the psychological consequences of Yevpime's experience of alcoholism and poverty. Yesayan believed that the structures of oppression

---

[61] Lilian R. Furst and Peter N. Skrine, *Naturalism* (London: Methuen, 1971), p. 42.

could not be altered without wider social and economic changes.

* * *

The views of Constantinople and its inhabitants presented in the three literary works reveal the possibilities offered by the intellectual milieu that facilitated women's writing. They also depict the three authors' search for answers to contemporary urban social issues, including the advent of modernity and especially its effects on women in the family and in the workforce. Diusap's *Siranush* and Sibyl's *Harse* portray modernity as a positive force in social customs, while Zabel Yesayan's *Erb aylevs chen sirer* portrays the negative impact of modern economic relations on working-class urban Armenians. Thus, these texts demonstrate the complexity of modernity in its positive and negative aspects. Although modernity in the context of these three literary pieces implies a break with the past, it does not mean a total rejection of all traditional Armenian customs. Each author saw past practices as containing values worthy of protection but also sought to blend traditional and modern values in such a way as to ensure that the talents of large numbers of Armenians could blossom and at the same time preserve and cultivate Armenian culture.

Sibyl (Zabel Asadur)

Zabel Yesayan

Srpuhi Diusap

❦ 11 ❦

The Balian Dynasty of Architects

Sarkis Balmanoukian

Remnants of obliterated monuments and churches scattered across the landscape of historic Armenia are a testament to the region's rich architectural past.[1] Ancient fortresses, palaces, churches, and residential buildings bear the imprint of Armenian architectural style developed over centuries, but only a handful of the names of the architects who built them have survived. These include Manvel (tenth century), who built the Surp/Surb Khach (Holy Cross) Church on the island of Akhtamar in the province of Van/Vaspurakan; Trdat (tenth-eleventh centuries), the architect of the cathedral in the Bagratuni capital Ani, whom the Byzantine Emperor Basil II invited to Constantinople in 989 to repair the dome of Hagia Sophia; and Momik (thirteenth-fourteenth centuries), the architect of Amaghu Noravank in the province of Siunik. The loss of Greater Armenia in the middle ages resulted in the migration of a large number of skilled artisans and architects to foreign shores. Those who remained behind contributed greatly to the architectural development of their successive conquerors: the Arabs, Seljuks, Mongols, and Ottoman Turks.

Armenians had settled in Constantinople as early as the fourth century. After the Turkish conquest of Constantinople in 1453, the Islamization of the city was accompanied by the construction of mosques and minarets which came to dominate its landscape. Architects of Armenian descent contributed significantly

---

[1] This chapter relies heavily on Pars Tuğlacı's *The Role of the Balian Family in Ottoman Architecture* (Istanbul: Yeni Çığır Bookstore, 1990). Other consulted sources include the following: Pars Tuğlacı, *The Armenian Churches of Istanbul* (Istanbul: P. Tuğlacı, 1991); Chris Hellier and Francesco Venturi, *Splendors of Istanbul: Houses and Palaces along the Bosporus* (New York: Abbeville Press, 1993); Philip Mansel, *Constantinople: City of the World's Desire, 1453-1924* (London: John Murray, 1995); *Istanbul* (Travel Guides) (New York: DK, 1998).

to this process as they were employed to build the mosques and palaces for the sultans. One such architect and an early convert to Islam was the Great Sinan (1491-1588), an Armenian from Aghernas, a village in Caesarea (Kesaria/Kayseri).

Under Suleiman the Magnificent, Sinan, one of the most prolific architects in history, held the title of Royal Architect and was commissioned to build the Suleimanye Mosque (1550-57). Hovsep Aznavurian, Mgrdich Charekian, Mihran Azarian, Bedros Nemtse, Hovhannes Serverian, and Kapriel Mgrdichian bore the title of Royal Architect and were employed by the crown to build palaces and municipal buildings in the city.[2] In the meantime, a number of Armenian families, such as the Balian, Dadian, and Duzian, rose to prominence and gained acceptance into Ottoman social circles.

The Balians of Constantinople

The most famous of the Armenian architects in Constantinople were the nine members of the Balian family. Four generations of Balians worked for six different sultans for more than a century. They built palaces, pavilions, mansions, mosques, churches, and military barracks in the Ottoman capital, a city already renowned for its multitude of magnificent palaces, cathedrals, and public buildings. Pre-Balian architecture in Constantinople had been influenced by Arabic, Persian, and other Islamic styles. In the nineteenth century, the city witnessed an influx of architects from France, Germany, and Italy, many of whom held the prestigious title of Royal Architect. The Balians, for their part, gave the local architecture a Western accent that fused different styles. Influenced by the French Renaissance, Neo-Classical, Greek Revival, Baroque, Rococo, and Art Nouveaux, the Balians adapted these architectural styles to a predominantly Oriental and Islamic culture. This successful juxtaposition produced a rather grandiose and formidable style of high artistic value.

Bali Khalfa (?-1800) was the first of the Balian architects and, like the great Sinan, came from a village of Caesarea— Derevenk. Little is known of Bali Khalfa. He arrived in Constantinople in the first half of the eighteenth century and began his career remodeling and renovating old buildings. Quickly gaining

---

[2] Tuğlacı, *The Role of the Balian*, p. 1.

popularity as a talented architect, he was appointed Royal Architect by the sultan. An inscription on the tombstone of one of his sons, Bedros, reads "Son of the Imperial Architect Bali."[3]

Bali Khalfa's son, Krikor Balian (Grigor Palian, 1764-1831), continued in his father's footsteps and was the first to use the family's Armenian surname. Krikor became Royal Architect under Sultan Selim III and continued under Sultan Mustafa IV and Sultan Mahmud II. Krikor had a large workshop and was known to be a philanthropist.[4] Among the many palaces he built for the sultans were Akintiburnu, Beshiktash, and Defterdarburnu, as well as the Aynalikavak and Chaghlayan *Kasir*s or summer palaces (Figs. 1-2). Krikor is also credited with building five military barracks, among them the barracks of Davud Pasha, Selimiye, and Taksim. Perhaps the most noted of his accomplishments was the Nusretiye Mosque (1826, Fig. 3). He also built several Armenian churches, including the Holy Mother of God (Surp Asdvadzadzin/Astvatsatsin) Cathedral in Kumkapu (1828, Fig. 4) and the Surp Stepannos in Khaskoy (1831). The government also commissioned him to build several pavilions, kiosks, two reservoirs, and the Tower of the War Ministry. Most of these edifices bear Krikor's distinctive Baroque signature, perhaps his greatest contribution to the development of native Ottoman architecture. The audience chamber of Aynalikavak Kasir and the front facade of Taksim Artillery Barracks are masterpieces of Ottoman Baroque architecture. Krikor's brother Senekerim (?-1833) was another talented architect. He worked with Krikor and built only one building, the Beyazid Fire Tower. He died at a young age while on a pilgrimage to the Holy City and was buried in the cemetery of Holy Savior (Surp Prgich/Prkich) Church in Jerusalem.[5]

Garabed Balian

The most outstanding and prolific member of the Balian family of architects was Garabed Balian (Karapet Palian, 1800-1866), the son of Krikor Balian. Under the careful tutelage of his father, Garabed mastered the art of architecture. He visited the medieval

---

[3] Ibid., p. 4.
[4] Ibid., p. 5.
[5] Ibid., pp. 84-87.

Armenian capital of Ani, which influenced his designs. Appointed as Royal Architect by Sultan Mahmud II, Garabed Balian built four palaces: the Bayildim and Izmid imperial kasirs, and the Dolmabahche (Figs. 5-6) and Old Chiraghan (Fig. 7) palaces. His other works include two military barracks, several factories, reservoirs, and schools. Garabed, an expert on the construction of domes, was originally commissioned to renovate the dome of the Hagia Sophia; the commission, however, fell through and he was replaced by the Italian architect Kaspar Fossati.[6] He nonetheless did repair the famous Dome of the Rock in Jerusalem in 1853, where he was also commissioned to repair and decorate the interior of the mosque.[7]

Garabed often had to adapt his designs to the more Westernized tastes of the sultans he served—Mahmud II, Abdul Mejid, and Abdul Aziz. Garabed's most famous work was the Palace of Dolmabahche (Filled Garden) on the European shore of the Bosphorus. This three-storey, 300 meter (984 foot) long building comprised 285 private rooms, two-thirds of which were for the sultan's harem, and 46 reception rooms, each uniquely designed and decorated. To construct the facades, Garabed borrowed many elements from Classical Greek and Greek Revival architecture. This was the first palace built in Western style. He also constructed a four-story 27 meter (89 foot) clock tower with his son Nigoghos (Nikoghos) in 1895 (Fig. 8). The architectural details of the clock tower (molded cornices, columns and imposts in the two lower stories, and pilasters in the top half) resemble closely those of Dolmabahche Palace.

Garabed also built six Armenian churches. He used the traditional cruciform plan for Surp Asdvadzadzin (Astvatsatsin) Church in Beshiktash (Fig. 9) but was prohibited by the Ottoman government from adding the dome. The church was more Neo-Classical and Western than Armenian in style, yet it was richly decorated with pilasters, interior frescoes, and an altar. The same Neo-Classical elements appear in another of his churches, Surp Khach in Kuruchesme. Among his works is an Armenian hospital in Yedikule (1834), which he built in collaboration with

---

[6] Ibid., p. 87.

[7] *A Brief Guide to the Dome of The Rock and Haram Al Sharif* (Jerusalem: Supreme Awqaf Council, 1955), p. 89.

his brother-in-law, Hovhannes Serverian. Garabed also built the church within the Surp Prgich Hospital's compound (Fig. 10).

Of Garabed's nine children, four became architects and attained the title of Royal Architect. Nigoghos, Sarkis (Sargis), Hagop (Hakob), and Simon all studied at Collège Sainte-Barbe in Paris. Nigoghos proved to be the most talented, but like his brother Hagop, he suffered an untimely death. Yet despite their short professional careers, the two brothers contributed greatly to the rich heritage of the Balian dynasty of architects.

Nigoghos Balian

Nigoghos (1826-1858) was the first Balian to receive a professional degree at Collège Sainte-Barbe. Among his first architectural accomplishments was the Western style library in the Old Chiraghan Palace. Upon the completion of the project, Sultan Abdul Mejid appointed him Royal Architect and artistic advisor.[8] The Audience Hall in Dolmabahche Palace (Fig. 11) stands as the most notable work of Nigoghos, which, with its Baroque style, to this day remains the most beautiful section of the palace. This large ceremonial hall, blending in with the rest of the palace complex, measures at 44 meters (144 feet) by 46 meters (151 feet) and 36 meters (118 feet) high, and has 56 columns. Its richly decorated walls, exuberant *trompe l'oeil* ceiling, and the dome are masterpieces of European architecture. Another addition to the palace attributed to Nigoghos is the palace theater (1857), which burned down and was demolished in 1937. Inspired by Italian theaters, Nigoghos embellished the interior of the palace theater with fluted columns, gold, marble, velvet, and highly ornate balcony boxes, reminiscent of the splendor of the Opera de Versailles. He was also responsible for designing the monumental ceremonial portals of the Dolmabahche Palace. Designed in the Baroque style and inspired by Roman triumphal arches, these portals were extravagantly carved to satisfy the Ottoman tastes of the time.

Continuing the legacy of building magnificent palaces, Nigoghos designed the Ihlamur Palace (1848-53), the Adile Sultan Kasir (1853), the Beykoz Palace (1854), and the Kuchuksu Palace

---

[8] Tuğlacı, *The Balian Family*, p. 303.

(1856). The Kuchuksu and Ihlamur palaces (Figs. 12-13), built on the Asian shore of the Bosphorus, exhibit a Neo-Baroque style with extensive decorative reliefs covering their facades and ornate spiral exterior staircases leading to the main entrance.

Another uniquely styled building designed by Nigoghos for Sultan Abdul Aziz was the New Chiraghan Palace (1864-71, Fig. 14), a much more opulent and exotic construction than the Dolmabahche. The magnificent ceremonial hall and other reception halls are in Ottoman-Arabic style. (This palace burned down in 1910; in later years it was restored and reopened as a luxury hotel). Nigoghos also submitted many drawings in various competitions. These pieces demonstrate an amazing talent in the sphere of Oriental interiors. His drawings of the facades, halls (Figs. 15-16), gates, and staircases of the New Chiraghan Palace show a great appreciation for the different styles, including Baroque, Islamic, and Moorish, which were often fused together in Balian architecture. He also built a number of mosques, among them the Ortakoy (Fig. 17) and Bezmialem Valide Sultan's mosques and the mosques within the Dolmabahche and the Chiraghan palaces. At Nigoghos' untimely death, Sultan Abdul Mejid declared three days of mourning at the Dolmabahche Palace.[9]

The Succeeding Balians

Like his brother Nigoghos, Hagop Balian (1837-1875) graduated from Collège Sainte-Barbe in Paris and received further training in Vienna and Venice. Upon Nigoghos' death, Hagop (Portrait 1) returned to Constantinople and collaborated with his father and brothers. Hagop's creative genius was evident early on in his design of the Beylerbey Palace on the Asian shore of the Bosphorus (Figs. 18-19). While the exterior facades of the palace are in French style, the interior walls and ceilings are largely Oriental in design. The most splendid rooms are the luxurious Blue Room with its artificial blue columns; the Pool Room with its magnificent staircase, marble fountain, and painted frescoes embellished with Arabesque patterns and Arabic calligraphy; and the Admiral's and the Mother of Pearl rooms (Fig. 20). Hagop

---

[9] Ibid.

also designed two identical waterfront kiosks on both sides of
the Beylerbey Palace, with colonnaded gallery, ornate facades,
and pointed roofs. He also designed several pavilions, palaces,
mansions, and a mosque. Grief-stricken after his young wife's
sudden death in 1873, Hagop left for Paris, where he, too, died at
a young age two years later and was buried in the Père Lachaise
Cemetery.[10]

Sarkis Balian (1831-1899) was the most influential of Garabed's sons. In Paris, he studied architecture at Sainte-Barbe,
broadened his horizons at the Academy of Fine Arts, and developed his talent in mechanical engineering. Upon returning to
Constantinople, he worked with his father and brother Nigoghos,
while pursuing his interests in engineering, scientific research,
and business on the side. Sarkis was a natural innovator and
inventor, a painter and a pianist (Portrait 2). Highly decorated by
sultans and foreign monarchs, he built more than fifty buildings,
including six palaces, fifteen pavilions, three mosques, four
barracks, two schools, and various other edifices.[11] Sarkis also
completed the construction of many unfinished projects begun
by his father and brothers. His career as an architect coincided
with the reigns of sultans Abdul Aziz and Abdul Hamid II, the
latter of whom bestowed on Sarkis the title of Chief Architect of
the State.

As a Royal Architect, Sarkis built the New Chiraghan and Bey-
lerbey palaces (designed respectively by Nigoghos and Hagop),
the Yildiz Palace complex (1861-76), which included the Great
Mabeyn (Fig. 21), Chadir, and the luxurious Shale pavilion; the
Adile Sultan Palace in Kandilli; and the Mejidiye Palace in the
Topkapu complex (Fig. 22). Today, his Mejidiye Barracks (1863-
64) house the architectural and engineering faculties of Istanbul
Technical University. He built the Aziziye Mosque in Machka,
the Chaghlayan Mosque, and the Pertevniyal Valide Sultan
Mosque in Aksaray (Fig. 23), as well as the Ministry of War
building, most noted for its highly decorated entrance hall (Fig.
24), the Naval Ministry, and several hunting lodges. Most of his
buildings have survived a number of earthquakes.[12]

---

[10] Ibid., p. 395.
[11] Ibid., pp. 429, 434.
[12] Ibid., p. 438.

Simon Balian (1864-1894), like two of his brothers, died young at the age of thirty. An architect and a miniaturist, he decorated many of the walls and ceilings in various palaces and pavilions in Constantinople and earned the appointment of Second Degree Royal Architect. Simon designed the Machka Armory and Police Station (both buildings now housing several faculties of Istanbul Technical University) and the Yildiz Pavilion. Sarkis Balian completed all of these projects after Simon's death.[13]

The last Balian architect in Constantinople was Nigoghos' son, Levon Balian (1855-1925). He graduated from the Ecole des Beaux Arts in Paris and spent his career assisting his uncle Sarkis in his practice.[14]

The Balians and the Armenian Community

The Balian family was considered a part of the Armenian nobility. Aside from their contribution to the Islamic and Ottoman culture in Constantinople, they were actively involved in the community's religious, social, and cultural life. Their houses were often a gathering place for Armenian intellectuals. Unfortunately, no additional records about their residences have been discovered. Being highly philanthropic, the family contributed to the Armenian community by building churches, schools, and hospitals. Krikor Balian constructed two churches, Surp Asdvadzadzin in Kumkapu (1828) and Surp Stepannos in Khaskoy (1831). He also took an active role in religious affairs and attempted to unite the Apostolic and Catholic Armenian communities.

Garabed helped to establish an Armenian Supreme National Assembly (Azkayin Kerakoyn Zhoghov) in 1847 and was elected a member of that body in 1853. He built six Armenian churches: Surp Sarkis (Sargis) in Banderma, Surp Mariam Asdvadzadzin in Beshiktash, Surp Khach in Kurucheshme, Surp Errortutiun (Holy Trinity) in Galatasaray, Surp Hagop in Zeytinburnu, and a church in distant Baiburt. Garabed built and financed the Surp Prgich Hospital (1832-34) founded by Kazaz Artin Amira (Harutiun Amira Bezjian). Along with his brother-in-law, Hovhannes Serverian, Garabed also established the Armenian Jemaran (College)

---

[13] Ibid., p. 662.
[14] Ibid., p. 667.

in Uskudar in 1838 and financed most of the building expenses. In 1858, he and Boghos Dadian founded the Surp Hagop Monastery and Seminary to educate clerics. He also donated property in Yalova to finance the renowned Armash Seminary near Ismid.[15]

Nigoghos Balian was one of the initiators of the Armenian National Constitution (Hayots Azkayin Sahmanatrutiun), which was ratified in 1863.[16] He was buried in the Beshiktash Armenian cemetery, which was destroyed during the construction of the New Yildiz road.

Hagop's home in Ortakoy was a cultural center for contemporary Armenian intellectuals, some of whom received his patronage. He also financed the construction of the Armenian Theater in Constantinople and attempted to establish an Armenian Language Academy for the study and enhancement of his native language. Similarly, Sarkis' home became a gathering place for the Armenian elite. He once received the world famous Russian-Armenian marine painter Ivan (Hovhannes) Aivazovsky, whom he introduced to Sultan Abdul Aziz.[17] As a patron of Armenian arts and education, Sarkis financed and built the Makruhian School (1866) in memory of his wife Makruhi, and constructed the Arshaguniats School in Dolabdere in 1875. A painter and a pianist, he is also credited with setting to music the most popular Armenian song dedicated to the Arax River (Mayr Arax).[18]

* * *

The contribution of the Balian dynasty to Ottoman architecture is an inextricable part of the history of Constantinople in the nineteenth century, which was called the Era of Balian Architecture. Their works reflect the Westernization and reforming spirit that was introduced into the capital. They were the pride of Ottoman architecture as well as the pride of the Armenian community.

---

[15] Ibid., p. 88.

[16] Ibid., p. 303.

[17] Ibid., pp. 395, 434.

[18] Hakob Paronian [Hagop Baronian], "Azgayin jojer" [National Bigwigs], in *Erker* [Works], vol. 1 (Erevan: Sovetakan Grogh, 1979), p. 182.

Fig. 1. Aynalikavak Kasir. Architect, Krikor Balian

Fig. 2. Chaghlayan Kasir. Architect, Krikor Balian

Fig. 3. Nusretiye Mosque. Architect, Krikor Balian

Fig. 4. Surp Asdvadzadzin (Holy Mother of God)
Cathedral, Kumkapu, Interior.
Architect, Krikor Balian

276

Fig. 5. Dolmabahche Palace, From the Bosphorus.
Architect, Garabed Balian

Fig. 6. Dolmabahche Palace, Side Facade

Fig. 7. Old Chiraghan Palace. Architect, Garabed Balian

Fig. 8. Dolmabahche Palace,
Clock Tower. Architects,
Garabed and Nigoghos Balian

Fig. 9. Surp Asdvadzadzin Church, Beshiktash, Interior.
Architect, Garabed Balian

Fig. 10. Church of Surp Prgich Hospital.
Architect, Garabed Balian

Fig. 11. Dolmabahche Palace, Audience Hall.
Architect, Nigoghos Balian

Fig. 12. Kuchuksu Palace, Main Facade.
Architect, Nigoghos Balian

280

Fig. 13. Ilhamur Palace. Architect, Nigoghos Balian

Fig. 14. New Chiraghan Palace. Architect, Nigoghos Balian

Fig. 15. New Chiraghan Palace, Ceremonial Hall.
Watercolor by Nigoghos Balian

Fig. 16. New Chiraghan Palace, Council Chamber.
Architect, Nigoghos Balian

Fig. 17. Ortakoy Mosque. Architect, Nigoghos Balian

Fig. 18. Beylerbey Palace. Architect, Hagop Balian

Fig. 19. Beylerbey Palace, Facade

Fig. 20. Beylerbey Palace, Mother of Pearl Room

Fig. 21. Yildiz Palace, Imperial Mabeyn. Architect, Sarkis Balian

Fig. 22. Mejidiye Palace. Architect, Sarkis Balian

Fig. 23. Pertevniyal Mosque, Main Entrance.
Architect, Sarkis Balian

Fig. 24. Ministry of War, Main Entrance
(now Istanbul University). Architect, Sarkis Balian

286

Sarkis Balian, Royal Architect

Hagop Balian, Royal Architect

❊ 12 ❊

THE MUSICAL WORLD
OF ARMENIANS IN CONSTANTINOPLE

Lucina Agbabian Hubbard

For the most part, the sultans of the Ottoman Empire determined the music that disseminated through all levels of Constantinople's multi-ethnic and multi-religious society. This trend began with the first sultans, who adopted the formalized medieval Persian-Arabic *maqam* (or *makam*)[1] as the official form of music for their vast empire. Musicians who followed the other musical traditions of the city still used the maqam, the classical music of the time, for instructional purposes.[2] In the employ of the sultans in the seventeenth century, court musicians and pedagogues belonging

---

[1] A highly developed form of Eastern oral musical tradition, *maqam* in Arabic refers to a standardized suite of improvised vocal and instrumental pieces expressed with melodic and rhythmic variations. It is also referred to as "Islamic maqam" because of its mystical character and possibly because it was performed in gatherings of religious people.

[2] A textbook in the late nineteenth century, for example, explained the fundamental characteristics of Armenian sacred songs with terminology used in Ottoman Turkish music. See Nikoghos Tahmizian, *Hakobos Ayvazyane ev nra arevelyan erazhshtutyan dzernarke* [Hagobos Ayvazian and His Manual on Eastern Music] (Erevan: Armenian Academy of Sciences, 1990), in Russian. Beyond the mere use of musical terminology, there was also an inclination to "correct" the medieval modal structure of Armenian sacred music to fit the Turkish tonal system. These two systems are incongruous since in Turkish music the octave is divided into 24 unequal intervals with complex ratios, whereas Armenian modes are built on the untempered diatonic scale, with dovetailed major tetrachords in various combinations of whole and half tone intervals, adding up to a decachord that avoids the tonic. Additionally, the slightly shortened first interval of the Phrygian tetrachord (EFGA) in a scale thus constructed creates narrowed and widened intervals, giving the Armenian modal structure its distinctive sound characteristics. The tempered scale has been in use since the middle of the nineteenth century. For illustrations, see Margarit Brudyan, *Hay zhoghovrdakan erazhshtakan steghtsagortsutyun* [Creativity in Armenian Folk Music] (Erevan: Loys, 1983), pp. 16-22.

mainly to the Mevlevi order of Sufi mysticism[3] modified the adopted maqam, with rhythms, modes, and melodies rooted in Turkish and ancient Anatolian folk music. Further, new musical ideas and styles found their way into Ottoman courts as the sultans expanded their reach through military conquest and international relations. As a result, by the eighteenth century, the maqam had taken distinctly Ottoman Turkish characteristics in both style and form.[4] Thus, until the middle of the nineteenth century, the original and evolved versions of the maqam, coupled with the exclusive use of the Turkish language as mandated by the imperial government, defined the boundaries of all music in Constantinople.

The small émigré community of Armenian artisans in Constantinople had grown from its humble beginnings in the middle of the fifteenth century into the largest Armenian society outside the homeland, numbering up to a quarter million by the late nineteenth century.[5] The Ottoman capital city eventually became the Western Armenian cultural and financial center. The upper and middle classes enjoyed refined lifestyles and an active cultural life, with numerous Armenian associations, publications, schools, churches, theaters, and concert halls. While the Armenian *zartonk* or cultural renaissance was in full bloom with impassioned nationalistic poetry and songs, Armenian music had not yet been cultivated. Even the intellectual and cultural elite heading the enlightenment movement were unaware of their own musical legacy: an oral tradition of secular and sacred songs, woven from distinctive threads of Armenian poetry, rituals, and social customs. Total immersion in the dominant Ottoman musical culture for four centuries had caused the loss of Armenian national musical identity. Thus they consumed westernized Turkish songs, Turkified Armenian sacred songs, French salon music, Italian opera arias, and the chamber music of Western instrumental ensembles.[6] From a historical perspective,

---

[3] The Mevlevis are an ascetic Muslim sect (also referred to as "whirling dervishes") whose rituals in their monasteries are accompanied with vocal and instrumental music of the classical maqam.

[4] For a history of Ottoman music, see Kurt and Ursula Reinhard, *Die Musik der Türkei* (Paris: Buchet-Chastel, 1969).

[5] See Maghakia Ormanian, *Hayots ekeghetsin* [The Church of Armenia], 6th ed. (Beirut: Sevan Press, 1960), p. 69.

[6] Matevos H. Muradyan, *Urvagits arevmtahay erazhshtutyan patmutyan (XIX dar ev XX daraskizb)* [Historical Outline of Western Armenian Music (19th Century and Early 20th Century)] (Erevan: Armenian Academy of Sciences, 1989), pp. 21-22.

the nineteenth century was a critical period in the evolution of Armenian music. Armenian musicians educated in the West returned to Constantinople with renewed creative energy and began to search for their own national musical roots—a process that ended abruptly in April 1915 with the arrest and deportation of the city's Armenian intelligentsia, including the famous musicologist Gomidas Vartabed (Komitas Vardapet).[7] This essay provides an overview of the Armenian musical environment in Constantinople in the nineteenth and early twentieth century.

The growing popularity of Western music coincided with the decline of the Ottoman Empire and the *Tanzimat* reform period (1839-76).[8] European music, at first reserved for performance in the sultan's palace, gradually became the preferred music for nearly the entire ruling class; and by the 1870s complemented the secularized Turkish *sharki, turki, peshref, semayi,* and *taksim,* which represented individual vocal and instrumental pieces included in a maqam. These were consumed by the city's upper economic class, Turks as well as other Ottoman nationalities, including Armenians, Greeks, and Jews. Nevertheless, the traditional Mevlevi order of Sufi mystics continued to teach and develop classical Ottoman Turkish music.

The Armenian *Ashugh*

Serving all levels of Constantinople society were Turkish-speaking Armenian *ashughs*[9]—poet-singer-instrumentalist-storytellers who,

---

[7] Gomidas Vartabed (1869-1935) was an ordained celibate priest who learned the basics of music at the Gevorgian Seminary of Echmiadzin. He furthered his music education in the private conservatory of Richard Schmid in Berlin, where he received his doctorate in music theory after presenting his thesis on Kurdish music. He is the most prominent scholarly ethnomusicologist in Armenian musical history. His approach integrated both Eastern and Western musical traditions. Many of his findings were scattered or lost while he was tormented in a Turkish prison, followed by wasted years in Turkish and French sanatoriums. Only some of his works have survived. These include his presentations at musicological conferences in Berlin and Paris, material he presented at the International Musical Society of Europe, short articles intended for Armenian newspapers, and reports of his lectures by others.

[8] On the Tanzimat period, see Hagop Barsoumian, "The Eastern Question and the Tanzimat Era," in *The Armenian People from Ancient to Modern Times*, vol. 2: *Foreign Dominion to Statehood: The Fifteenth Century to the Twentieth Century*, ed. Richard G. Hovannisian (New York: St. Martin's Press, 1997), pp. 175-201.

[9] The Armenian *ashugh*s, successors to medieval Armenian *gusan*s, were profes-

having spent years of apprenticeship with a master ashugh to sharpen their individual skills, entertained audiences in various settings. They accompanied their vocal improvisations and virtuoso performances on Eastern stringed instruments, including the *saz, tar, oud, kamancha, kemani, kanon, santur, zurna, ney,* and *tambur.* Each ashugh came to be identified by his favorite instrument, often made by himself; for example, Kemani Tateos, Lavoutaji Ovrig, Oudi Arshag, Kanoni Nubar were prominent ashughs in Constantinople.[10] They translated their repertoire into Turkish, and at times composed in that same language and style.[11] Being multilingual and adept at local dialects, they had the agility to satisfy the ever-changing popular tastes in Turkey, Azerbaijan, Georgia, and Armenia.

The most professional among the ashughs were often invited to perform and teach in the palaces of the sultan[12] and the mansions of the moneyed class of Armenian *amiras.*[13] At times, the latter competed among themselves for the services of these celebrities. Their audiences included the wealthiest and most influential members in the capital. The ashughs entertained them with secular themes, although in some instances religious melodies did find their way into the sultan's palace. The favorite *hijaz*[14] of Abdul Aziz (1861-76) was the "Sird im sasani," the elaborate *dagh*-aria from *votenlva,*[15] which Kemani Sepuh often played for him on his

sional performers in the oral tradition common to Eastern cultures. See Robert A. Atayan et al. eds., *Komitasakan,* 2 vols. (Erevan: Armenian Academy of Sciences, 1969, 1981), vol. 2: Manuk Manukyan, *Komitase ev hay ashughakan-gusanakan ergarvesti harazatutyan hartse* [Gomidas and the Question Regarding the Authenticity of the Ashugh-Gusan Vocal Art], pp. 231-32.

[10] See "Arevelyan hay erazhishtner ev nvagatsuner 1768-1930 shrjanin" [Eastern Armenian Musicians and Instrumentalists in the 1768-1930 Period], *Surb Prkich,* monthly periodical of the Armenian National Hospital, Istanbul (March 2000): 23-31.

[11] Nikoghos Tahmizian, *Sayat Novan ev hay gusana-ashughakan erg-erazhshtutiune* [Sayat Nova and the Armenian Gusan-Ashugh Song-Music] (Pasadena, CA: Drazark Press, 1995), p. 59.

[12] Ibid., p. 34.

[13] Amiras were heads of wealthy dynastic families. They enjoyed great prestige as bankers and financial advisors to Turkish officials and held important positions in the government. Some prominent names associated with musical developments in Constantinople included the Dadian, Duzian, and Balian families.

[14] Hijaz is a traditional Eastern melody built on a mode that is associated with a certain mood. The melody is developed with prescribed principles in improvisation.

[15] This is a ritual in the Armenian Church, which reenacts the scene in which

violin.[16] Ashughs who lacked advanced training served the migrant working classes congregated in the poor quarters of the city. These included the Armenian émigré community of Constantinople, which had fled Turkish and Kurdish exploiters in the interior provinces in hopes of finding better living and working conditions. Unnoticed by society, the members of this minority group within the Armenian community in the capital at first sang their songs in their regional dialects, heavily mixed with Turkish and Arabic words, but in time they adapted to the cultural environment and popular tastes of Constantinople.[17]

Unlike the professional ashughs discussed earlier, the ashughs performing for the migrant working class played multiple roles as priest, philosopher, and compatriot. They addressed the daily concerns of their listeners, protested the injustices of class distinctions by ridiculing the rich, inspired hope for social reforms, and preached self-reliance and patriotism, though in veiled language. They sang snatches of Armenian folk melodies in regional dialects familiar to their audiences, and while their repertoire included foreign epics they abridged them and Armenianized them with versification styles of Armenian poetry.

In the nineteenth century, there were about 300 Turkish-speaking Armenian ashughs in Turkey,[18] attesting to their popularity across the Ottoman Empire. Nevertheless, their lower social status, as defined by the city's intelligentsia and upper socioeconomic classes, did not improve with the increasing demand for their services. It is possible that the religious segments of both Armenian and Turkish society did not approve of the ashughs' preoccupation with secular music and poetry. Furthermore, the Armenians had reservations about the Islamic origin of the repertoire, not to mention its "tasteless" performance style, which included nasal vocalization, sliding microtones, chromaticism, and excessive ornamentation of melodies. Despite the apparent popularity enjoyed by the ashughs, neither Turkish nor Armenian scholars have undertaken a comprehensive study of their contributions to Constantinopolitan music. Hundreds of Turkish language manuscripts exist that have been transcribed by ashughs in Armenian characters

---

Jesus washes the feet of his disciples as a symbolic act of humility.

[16] See *Arevelyan hay erazhishtner*, p. 30.

[17] Muradyan, *Urvagits*, p. 186.

[18] Ibid., p. 81.

and signed with Turkish, Persian, or Arabic pseudonyms.[19]

Armenian Folk Songs and Liturgical Music

Noticeably absent from Constantinople, however, were strains of Armenian folk song melodies, developed centuries earlier in the historic Armenian homeland and in Cilicia. These were songs improvised in the poetic style of the oral tradition in the regional dialect and the musical idiom of villages, distinguishable by their melodic, modal, and stylistic content. They were passed on from one generation to the next, repeated and modified social events and traditional rituals. Beyond their artistic merit, these indigenous songs contained invaluable bits of ethnographic information. These folk songs were distinctively Armenian, once etched into the memory of the émigrés, but now virtually neglected by the urbanized Armenian society of Constantinople.

The liturgical music of the Armenian Church in Constantinople could be heard not only in churches but also in the adjoining schools and occasionally in the mansions of the amiras. In all three settings, the medieval mystic songs of Armenian composers were performed in the secular style of Turkish popular music. Melodies were embellished with extraneous *fiorituras*, exaggerated emotive *melisma*, chromatic passages, excessive *portamenti*, and dragging tempi. In fact, these indulgences were carried to such extremes that the hymns (*sharagan*s), sacred arias (*dagh*s), and chants in the divine liturgy (*patarag*; *badarak*) performed in nasal vocalization reminded the worshipers of Turkish coffeehouses and casinos. Nothing different could reasonably be expected since those who took on the role of *diratsu*[20] in the church on Sundays were the same musicians who performed in the courts of the sultan and the amiras and in the casino and nightclubs during the week. Their admiring supporters, who often included Turkish officials, Mevlevi musicians and members of the city's religious minorities, followed them to church for the sheer pleasure of listening to their vocal improvisations.

Decrying the Armenian Church's tolerance for such indis-

---

[19] Ibid., p. 17.

[20] *Diratsu* (*tiratsu*) is a church musician who assists the priest in conducting the Armenian Divine Liturgy.

criminate distortions of the original sacred chants, Hampardzum Limonjian,[21] an early nineteenth century musician, complained that the beautiful sharagans had become the playthings of conceited church musicians who sang them improperly but acted as though the melodies had been passed on to them directly from Catholicos Nerses Shnorhali in the twelfth century: "They ignore the fact that our church music is beautiful and sublime in its simplicity. Why is it necessary to introduce in them inappropriate trills in imitation of this or that singer?"[22] Witnessing this same abuse of Armenian liturgical music half a century later in "all locations of Turkish-Armenian churches, starting from the capital to the remote village churches," Gomidas was equally critical of the diratsus: "They entered a race to surpass each other with arbitrary gurgles and trills, which contributed a great deal to the deterioration of the melody."[23]

Equally aggravating was the fact that these same diratsu-ashughs were entrusted with the musical education of prospective deacons and choristers. Gomidas complained that the "self-appointed musicians" imposed their "individual tastes" on their successors with "numerous *daghs*, *Der voghormia*s . . . in short rites of the badarak, in Turkish *sharki, turki, mani, nani* melodies, which were carefully inscribed in notebooks . . . with ornate letterings, and passed on to their students as priceless treasures, heritage. . . ."[24] Gomidas was even more scathing in his review of a new badarak submitted to him by a diratsu, calling it "a pile of notes with no musical vitality, not to mention the complete disagreement between the melody and the central meaning of the text."[25] At one

[21] Hampardzum Limonjian (1768-1830) studied church music with Zenne Boghos Tbir. He entered the circle of Duzian Palace which was a meeting place for musicians. He became a protégé of Hovhannes Chalabi and studied Greek music with Vonoprios Psalti. His connection with the Sufi Dervish musicians was Hamami Zade Ismail Dede, from whom he learned the music of their rituals. Limonjian was considered the best performer of the *tambur* (a string instrument). See Muradyan, *Urvagits*, pp. 32-35.

[22] Kristofor S. Kushnaryan et al., *Aknark hay erazhshtutyan patmutyan* [A Survey of the History of Armenian Music], Pt. 2: Matevos H. Muradyan, *Hay erazhshtutyune XIX darum ev xx dari sgzbum*, [Armenian Musi,c in the 19th Century and Beginning of the 20th Century] (Erevan: Armenian Academy of Sciences, 1963), pp. 73-217.

[23] Komitas, *Hodvatsner ev usumnasirutyunner* [Articles and Studies], ed. Ruben Terlemezyan (Erevan: Haypethrat, 1941), pp. 111-12.

[24] Ibid., pp. 131-32.

[25] Ibid., p. 134.

point in his tirade against such practices, Gomidas stated: "This licentious period lasted from 1864 to 1873."[26] It is hard to tell if this was stated with a groan of distress or a sigh of relief. Thus, with the tacit approval of the Church in Constantinople, the vocal virtuosity of a secular foreign style had taken precedence over the established norms of chanting Armenian liturgical music—a norm that had been perpetuated for its ability to put the Christian Armenian faithful into a spiritual, introspective mood conducive to communication with God.

Secular and foreign musical styles had influenced Armenian sacred music throughout the centuries of its development, but they had always been tested against the established traditions, under the critical supervision of church authorities, and remained within the artistic boundaries set by a musically literate clergy. By the nineteenth century, however, the Armenian Church was denied the benefit of its monastic educational centers, once spread all over Armenia and Cilicia, and it had essentially lost its economic independence. As a result, the church could no longer maintain its own standards, which had once been achieved by the command the church leaders exercised on both the composition and the performance of hymns.[27]

In Constantinople, the Armenian Church was left to its own devices. As the officially recognized Armenian religious institution in the Ottoman Empire, the Armenian Church was delegated the awesome responsibility of overseeing not only the religious but also the cultural, educational, social, and legal matters that related to the Armenian *millet* (confessional community).[28] Eventually unable to meet the challenges of the times, the Church had yielded much of its traditional leadership role to the secular segments of society. The most influential individuals were the Armenian amiras, who patronized religious, social, and cultural projects in the city. They even determined the aesthetic standards for liturgical music by appointing their favorite ashughs to the coveted posts of diratsu. Some nonetheless also supported a project to devise a new

---

[26] Ibid., p. 135.

[27] Egon Wellesz, "Music of the Eastern Churches," in *New Oxford History of Music,* vol. 2: *Early Medieval Music up to 1300,* ed. Don Anselm Hughes (London: Oxford University Press, 1954), p. 52.

[28] The Patriarchate in Constantinople had jurisdiction over Armenians throughout the Ottoman Empire. See Ormanian, *Hayots ekeghetsin*, p. 70.

notation system to transcribe sacred melodies.

In the first half of the nineteenth century, a small group of scholarly Armenian musicians had alerted the amiras and the church to the glaring incompatibility between the style of singing and the spirit of the sacred texts. Prominent among these musicologists were Hampardzum Limonjian, Nigoghos Tashjian[29] and Yeghia Dndesian.[30] They occupied prestigious posts in the sultan's court and the Mevlevi lodge as composers, pedagogues, and music theoreticians. As protégés of the amiras, they also served in the church as diratsus and were distinguished from other musicians by their broad knowledge of sacred music, the canons of the Armenian and Byzantine churches, the chants of the local synagogue, the Greek neumes, and the European notation system. They were in contact with their counterparts in non-Armenian religious institutions and occasionally attended each other's sacred rituals and exchanged observations about the fundamental characteristics of their music. Backed by their experience, knowledge, research, and the support of like-minded musicians, these musicologists set out to remove foreign musical elements from the traditional Armenian spiritual melodies. Oral transmission had failed to preserve the character of the Armenian liturgical chants and hymns, and the practice of singing melodies off the *khaz* notations found in medieval manuscripts needed to be reinstituted.[31] Yet, nobody had been able to read the khaz symbols since the eighteenth century

---

[29] Nigoghos Tashjian (1836-1885) studied with Mevlevi Ismail Dede Efendi (1778-1846) and enrolled in the Imperial Music School patronized by Grand Vizier Ali Pasha. He was an authority on Mevlevi ritual and even taught dervish ceremonies in their lodge. Nigoghos and his brother published the Armenian journal *Ottoman Music* in 1875. Sixty-three of his *sharki* compositions have survived. He was active as teacher, diratzu, composer, editor, and contributor to Armenian journals. He is noted mainly for his expertise in the Armenian khaz notation. See Muradyan, *Aknark*, pp. 97-98.

[30] Yeghia Dndesian (1834-1881), a talented and prolific Church musician, was one of the earliest to transcribe church music in Armenian and European notations, some of which were published as early as 1864.

[31] *Khaz* is the term used for notation symbols written above the text of Armenian liturgical chants, to guide the singing and secure the performance standard endorsed by the Armenian Church authorities. They appear mostly in manuscripts from the eighth through the fourteenth century, ranging from simple to complex symbols, indicating the evolutionary process in the composition and performance of Armenian sacred music. For a thorough discussion on medieval khaz notations, see Robert A. Atayan, *Haykakan khazayin notagrutyune* [Armenian Khaz Notation] (Erevan: Armenian Academy of Sciences, 1959), pp. 1-287.

due to the pillaging of monastic universities in Armenia and Cilicia and the subsequent collapse of the educational structure. In fact, no medieval textbook on the subject could be found, rendering any plans to decode the medieval notation system virtually impossible.

After much deliberation[32] and dedicated effort, a committee of musicians headed by Limonjian devised a substitute notation system for both Armenian sacred hymns and the monophonic music of the region.[33] Mindful of national tradition, they lifted khaz symbols from medieval manuscripts and gave them new meanings borrowed from the European system of notation.[34] After testing its usefulness and in the process refining the symbols,[35] Nigoghos Tashjian employed the new khaz system to transcribe the chants in *Zhamakirk* (breviary), *Sharaganots* (hymnal), and *Badarak* (Divine Liturgy) in three volumes, relying on the vocal renditions of Catholicos Gevorg IV of Echmiadzin, formerly of Constantinople, as his primary source.[36] While Yeghia Dndesian's compilation of notated sharagans was still under consideration, Tashjian published all three volumes (1874-78) in Vagharshapat and received the approval of the Catholicos for their use in all Armenian churches. This decision promised to ensure a uniform performance standard for Armenian churches worldwide, but the church in Constantinople rejected it, preferring instead to use the familiar style. Dndesian's volume, published posthumously in 1934, is valued for its scholarly approach to selecting melodic variants believed to reflect more closely the original intent of the medieval composers.[37]

---

[32] Topics for deliberations were whether existing Greek neumes should be adopted or new khaz symbols designed for the purpose of serving the monodic music of Eastern cultures as well and whether the new khaz should be reserved expressly for Armenian sacred songs or whether the European notations should be adopted, their being accessible internationally and preferable for possible homophonic arrangement of Armenian sacred songs. See Mouradian, *Aknark*, p. 82.

[33] Members in this committee were: Aristages Hovhannesian, Yeghia Dndesian, Hampardzum Cherchian, Gabriel Yeranian, and Nigoghos Tashjian. They were among the first to use the New Notation System. See Aleksandr Shahverdyan, *Hay erazhshtutyan patmutyan aknarkner, XIX-XX dar* [Survey of the History of Armenian Music, 19th-20th Centuries], ed. Robert A. Atayan (Erevan: Haypethrat, 1959), pp. 336-37.

[34] Komitas, *Hodvatsner ev usumnasirutyunner*, p. 128.

[35] For the interpretation and practical usage of these symbols, see Muradyan, *Urvagits*, pp. 34-41.

[36] See Tahmizian, *Sayat Novan*, p. 63n78.

[37] Muradyan, *Urvagits*, pp. 107-08.

Some considered these developments as interim measures. In many ways the forerunner of Gomidas, Dndesian devoted his life to the study of medieval khaz notations in the libraries of the Jerusalem, Echmiadzin, and Mekhitrarist monasteries. Gomidas gave serious consideration to Dndesian's writings on the subject,[38] while he conducted his own research for twenty years.[39] Both made substantial advances toward decoding the khaz, but neither musicologist was able to publish his findings.[40] Dndesian was arrested for nationalistic sentiments in his publications and met an untimely end in a Turkish prison in 1881.[41] Gomidas lost the will to pursue a creative and scholarly life soon after his traumatic experiences during the Armenian Genocide. But before their tragic ends, their exhaustive pursuit of the key to the mystic medieval past of Armenian music was motivated by a conviction that the recovered music would show the intrinsic beauty of these chants and would reveal the distinguishing features of what may be defined as truly Armenian sacred music. Khaz-notated medieval manuscripts were considered the only dependable source of reference in scholarly research and analysis concerning Armenian music and musicology, and they contained the unquestionably authentic style of singing the Armenian Divine Liturgy.

All these concerns and achievements related to sacred music were of no interest to the younger generation of Western educated Armenian musicians. Expectations that Armenian musicology could be defined on the basis of orally transmitted hymns, only recently transcribed with newly devised khaz symbols, must have seemed unconvincing if not unrealistic; yet they knew of no alternative to suggest.

Unlike their contemporaries in literature, who used their newly found freedom of speech to delve into the roots of Armenian pagan

---

[38] Ibid., p. 114.

[39] In a short article in response to a question raised about the result of his research on khaz, Gomidas writes: "It is true, I have found the key to the Armenian khaz and am even reading the simple examples, but I have not reached the final point." *Tajar*, no. 10 (1914), p. 311. Komitas, *Hodvatsner ev usumnasirutyunner*, p. 166. See also Atayan, *Haykakan khazayin notagrutyune*, pp. 143-49.

[40] Gomidas reported certain aspects of his findings in musicological journals and conferences. See Komitas, *Hodvatsner ev usumnasirutyunner*, pp. 153-65.

[41] The Ottoman government harassed Dndesian for having published patriotic and religious songs in a collection titled *Nvagk Haykakan* [Armenian Music]. See Atayan, *Haykakan khazayin notagrutyune*, p. 127.

and medieval literature and found expression with a modified literary language, musicians of all generations in Constantinople (except for the select few discussed above) were not familiar with the oral tradition of Armenian folk music, which predated and later developed in parallel with the Christian music. So, some among them declared, privately and in the press as late as 1913 that "there exists no such thing as Armenian music, in the real sense of the word, . . . and whatever exists, bears Assyrian-Byzantine or Indian-Persian influences."[42]

Gomidas responded to such claims with a scathing article titled "Yes, Armenians Have Their Own Music." He proceeded to defend his case with arguments based on his research as an ethno-musicologist and concluded that "a music is as true and national, as authentic and unique to itself as are its language and literature, because the music of each nation emerges and develops from the intonations of its language. The Armenian language has its partic-ular intonation and therefore its corresponding music."[43] Gomidas had in mind a new source of inspiration for Armenian music, namely, the Armenian folk songs, which he had already compiled and categorized during the twenty years of his ethno-musicological research in Armenian villages of the Araratian region.

In the mid-1800s, young musicians turned their attention to the contemporary sounds and forms of European vocal-instrumental music. Salon music of mostly piano and guitar became fashionable in the homes of the upper classes. European performers of classical music introduced the *bel canto* singing style and the rich tonal qualities of Western classical instruments. Homophonic choral and orchestral arrangements of marches, dances, romances, and lights and colors of stage sets provided an exciting contrast to the mono-phonic expressions of Eastern music and folk instruments. The urban society was fascinated with the technical achievements of European music.

East and West met in Constantinople. With a window opened to the outside world, the population was freed from their cultural isolation. Musically inclined young men were eager to study at the music conservatories in Europe. The prospect of being at the forefront of a new order of aesthetic sounds was not only refreshing

---

[42] Komitas, *Hodvatsner ev usumnasirutyunner*, p. 47.
[43] Ibid., p. 49.

but also liberating. Between 1843 and 1848 alone, Armenian amiras interested in the intellectual progress of the nation sent about thirty promising young students to European (mostly French) universities.[44] Other youth went independently to Italian and Belgian music conservatories. Some of them preferred to stay in Europe and eventually enjoyed brilliant careers as performers and pedagogues.[45] Others returned home, energized with progressive musical ideas and placed their talents and expertise at the service of their fellow Armenians. Young musicians joined forces with poets and writers in a variety of cultural activities to enlighten the Armenian community and to cultivate a sense of national identity and unity.

In their rush to catch up with the West, the young musicians adopted Western forms and styles entirely in their original state: melodies intact with homophonic arrangements. They translated French and Italian lyrics on patriotic themes directly into the Armenian vernacular *ashkharhabar*, which became the modern Armenian literary language.[46] They paired their melodies with the impassioned calls of Armenian poets for national emancipation, disregarding the fact that the phrases and accents of the lyrics did not match the melodies. An examination of songbooks from this era reveals the mechanical application of Western harmonies in close imitation of European nationalistic songs. Additionally, foreign and Armenian translators, musicians, and poets are either unnamed or incorrectly credited.

Thus, European-educated musicians wittingly or unwittingly misled Armenian society into believing that these nationalistic songs, to which they were attached emotionally, were Armenian in text and melody.[47] Aware of the dominance of European music, Dndesian observed: "We can have national songs because we have national poetry; however, unless we instill good taste in music by

---

[44] Vahé Oshagan, "Modern Armenian Literature and Intellectual History from 1700 to 1915," in Hovannisian, ed., *Armenian People*, vol. 2, p. 151.

[45] For an impression of this scene, see the biographical sketch of one violin virtuoso, Kisag Vrooyr (1884-1973), who was born in Constantinople, educated in Europe, and earned his living as first violinist in Metro Goldwyn Studios in Los Angeles. See Anahit Tsitsikyan, *Haykakan agheghnayin arveste* [The Art of Armenian Strings] (Erevan: Sovetakan Grogh, 1997), pp. 94-103.

[46] Muradyan, *Urvagits*, p. 14.

[47] Ibid., pp. 82-96.

educating the public, we can never have national music."[48] There were exceptions, however, and some composers did create original works by synthesizing European music with the more traditional urban music of Constantinople. Notably, Dikran Chukhajian (1836-1898) emphasized national awareness in his compositions of vocal-instrumental pieces, which included the patriotic march "Zeytuntsineru kaylerke," the romance "Karun," the lyric song "Tsmern antsav" from the operetta *Leplepiji hor-hor*, and the libretto of the opera *Arshak II*.[49] His works reveal themes that suggest Armenia's heroic past as the nation fought for its freedom and sought independence from foreign domination. Chukhajian became noted in Europe and in the Middle East as the "Armenian Verdi" and "Turkey's Offenbach."[50] He was the first composer in Turkey to compose his own Italian-style operas and French-style operettas.[51] Gabriel Yeranyan, a colleague of Chukhajian, was also distinguished for the successful fusion of Eastern and Western musical traditions in his songs about the Armenian struggle for national freedom. Most familiar to the contemporary public are "Arik Haygazunk," "Giligia," and "Hayastan."[52]

No doubt the spirit behind the efforts of the Europeanized Armenian musicians was patriotic, but their music had no organic connection to the nation's music. Despite the profusion and variety of their activities, Armenian musicians at this time were far removed from creating original works. Separated from the musical roots and poetic traditions of the homeland, they were wandering in the East-West musical world of Constantinople without a clear sense of an artistic direction, reaching for what was new and accessible. As composers, choral conductors, lecturers, music teachers, and cultural activists, this generation of Armenian musicians in Constantinople laid the groundwork for the next wave of professional composers. They established several musical journals and

---

[48] Ibid., p 121.

[49] See Nikoghos K. Tahmizian, *Tigran Chukhachian: Kianke ev steghtsagortsutine* [Dikran Chukhajian: His Life and Works] (Pasadena, CA: Drazarg, 1999).

[50] Muradyan, *Urvagits*, p. 187.

[51] *Arshak II* and *Zemireh* operas, *Arif*, *Kyose-kehya* and *Leplepiji hor-hor*, operettas (in Italian, French, Turkish, and Armenian), among others, whose manuscripts have not survived.

[52] For additional information and musical examples, see Muradyan, *Urvagits*, pp. 96-106.

associations and created a printing press to publish Armenian and Western notation systems, which they introduced serially in their journals.[53] They also introduced their patrons to Western music theory. Their choral, instrumental, and solo pieces were integrated into the productions of Armenian theater companies.[54] Chamber and symphonic pieces were composed for European instrumental ensembles and presented live on concert stages and in the salons of the amiras.

The new generation thus played a significant role in expanding the base of listeners. Young Armenian musicians active in Constantinople enriched the musical world of the capital by introducing European musicological principles and techniques. For the first time in the history of the Constantinopolitan music world, the ashughs no longer dominated the music scene in the higher echelons of the city's society, although Turkish music and folk instruments remained popular among the masses.

Gomidas

This was the state of Armenian music in Constantinople when Gomidas entered the cultural life of the city at the end of September 1910.[55] Gomidas—the consummate musician in the humble cloth of a celibate priest—had already achieved international fame as an ethnomusicologist, composer, conductor, and lecturer. He had accepted an enthusiastic invitation from the Armenian intellectual elite of Constantinople to establish his residence in the city.[56] Members of the community had been following reports of his

---

[53] *Knar arevelyan* (1858) was a monthly that published Eastern and Armenian melodies in European notation. *Knar haykakan* (1862) was an association and a journal by the same name that published popular and nationalistic songs. *Nvagk haykakan* was another such journal. See Anna A. Parsamyan and Markarit K. Harutyunyan, *Hay erazhshtutyan patmutyun* [History of Armenian Music] (Erevan: Loys, 1968), p. 80. See also Muradyan, *Urvagits*, pp. 44, 93-96.

[54] These included the Arevelian Tadron, Ottoman Opera Theater, Vartovyan, and Benglian theatrical companies, which presented both European and Armenian plays and musicals and for which they had in-house vocalists and choral and instrumental musical ensembles. See Parsamyan and Harutyunyan, *Hay erazhshtutyan patmutyun*, p. 81.

[55] Gaspar N. Gasparyan, ed., *Zhamanakakitsnere Komitasi masin* [Contemporaries about Gomidas] (Erevan: Haypethrat, 1960), p. 21.

[56] Muradyan, *Aknark*, pp. 168-69.

activities in the fields of music theory and performance and had read about his lectures on comparative analysis of Armenian, Turkish, Persian, and Kurdish music, which he had delivered (personally singing examples of each style) at musicological conferences in Berlin and Paris.[57] They knew of his vast collection of Armenian folk and sacred music, which he had selected for their musical value and authentic indigenous Armenian origins. They had heard that a select compilation of songs, cultivated with polyphonic arrangements for a cappella choral singing was being readied for publication,[58] and they had read rave reviews of his performance as conductor of this music before packed concert halls in the capitals of Europe and the Middle East.[59] His friends and members of the literary and musical community, therefore, wanted him to bring his talents to Constantinople. They eagerly sought his cooperation, to join hands in their common cause of awakening fellow Armenians to their collective cultural identity, of enlightening the minds and spirits of society, of unchaining them from their apathy, despair, and frustration at having to bear their own subjugation for so long.

Gomidas believed that all of these goals were within reach. The native sounds of Armenian songs, which he valued as miniature gems, could restore the bruised psyche of his people. But he needed a cadre of committed workers. To this end, he had developed a comprehensive music education program and the necessary teaching materials,[60] which might, at last, find receptive audiences in the small but forward-looking group of musicians and writers in Constantinople. The city elite assured Gomidas that he would receive the solid support of a committee organized expressly to advance his most cherished project—a music conservatory for the

---

[57] See reviews and letters from European musicologists attending the first conference of this newly instituted society. Gomidas was a founding member and in 1899 presented a paper on "The Sacred and Secular Music of the Armenians." Gasparyan, *Zhamanakakitsnere Komitasi masin*, pp. 11-13.

[58] Ibid., pp. 115, 121-22, 126.

[59] Prior to his stay in Constantinople, he gave concerts in Tiflis (1905), Paris (1906), Baku, Zurich, Lausanne, Berne, and Geneva (1908), and in the Armenian provinces.

[60] Gomidas had presented these in a letter addressed to Catholicos Madteos II in May 1910, seven months prior to arriving in Constantinople. See Komitas, *Hodvatsner ev usumnasirutyunner*, p. 51.

young generation of Armenians.[61] This promise was like a salve for the humiliation and bitter disappointment he was feeling at the time. Catholicos Matteos Izmirlian at Echmiadzin had just dismissed his earnest request for financial support for a professional approach to the music education of the young seminarians in the monastery where he was the choir-master.[62] Besides, he yearned to move away from the oppressive environment of Echmiadzin,[63] where incessant gossip, criticism, and condemnation of his involvement with musical activities outside the monastery hounded him at every turn. He missed the sense of freedom that he had experienced in Europe, the freedom to imagine, to create, and to interact with brilliant musicologists and composers.[64] The thought of living and working among independent thinkers and enlightened minds in a large cosmopolitan city, like Constantinople, appealed to him, especially with the kind of moral and financial backing that he had been promised.

Gomidas' first success in the city was a full concert program of Armenian songs in two sections: first, sacred hymns of the Armenian Church, followed by lyric folk songs of the Armenian peasants. This concert was presented in Bdi Shan theater on November 21, 1910. The audience heard beautiful shades of polyphonic music from a hastily assembled chorus of 300 talented, albeit inexperienced, young singers. The power of his conductor's baton and his baritone solos transported the audience to the mystic past of an Armenian monastery and to the beautiful landscapes of the Armenian countryside.[65] His talent for imaginative interpretations of the sharagans, erks, elaborate dagh-arias, and the Armenian peasant's intuitive gift for the seemingly simple yet inventive melodies touched and excited his listeners beyond their expectations. The international press praised the program and its repeat performances in superlative tones. Gomidas became the

---

[61] See Gasparyan, *Zhamanakakitsnere Komitasi masin*, p. 127, for Gomidas' letter from Constantinople to Marguerite Papayan in 1909. See also Muradyan, *Urvagits*, p. 251, for details on Gomidas' plans for a conservatory in Constantinople.

[62] Ruben Terlemezyan, *Komitas* (Erevan: Armenian Academy of Sciences, 1992), pp. 51-52.

[63] See Gasparyan, *Zhamanakakitsnere Komitasi masin*, p. 123, for Gomidas' letter from Echmiadzin in 1909 to Marguerite Papayan.

[64] Ibid., p. 118.

[65] See comments and reviews, Muradyan, *Urvagits*, p. 248; Gasparyan, *Zhamanakakitsnere Komitasi masin*, p. 22.

envy of non-Armenians attending these concerts. At least one article in the Greek press in Alexandria, Egypt, asked: "When will God create a Gomidas among the Greeks who will save the ancient Hellenic music from loss?"[66]

Yet, to the Armenian Church in the Ottoman capital, Gomidas was a constant embarrassment. He was simply a priest who was investing an improper amount of interest and time in secular music. In fact, this concert of Armenian indigenous music, heard in Constantinople for the very first time, had met with fierce objections from the Armenian patriarch.[67] He had requested that Gomidas omit the Armenian sacred songs in the first section of the program because, the patriarch argued, it was sacrilegious to present them in the secular environment of a theater. Gomidas impatiently replied that he had in his pocket a written approval from Catholicos Mgrdich (Mkrtich) Khrimian "Hayrig" for the program.[68] Having registered a major success in Constantinople, Gomidas charged into the musical life of the city. With a great burst of energy and good humor, he dashed from choral rehearsals to children's music classes, from delivering talks to conducting concerts, from lectures and concert tours around Constantinople, in cities of Europe, and the Middle East, back to Constantinople to periods set aside for research and composition.[69] He also joined heated discussions in the press, with insightful observations and sharp-witted prose. He hoped to shed some light on the uninformed and insecure posture of the composers and clergy toward their own musical heritage, their indigenous Armenian songs. He was occasionally relieved and encouraged by visits from his artist friends.[70]

As a Turkish speaking Armenian until the age of twelve, Gomidas had not been raised with Armenian folk songs. He had heard them

---

[66] Ibid., p. 25.

[67] Muradyan, *Urvagits*, pp. 244-50; Samson G. Gasparyan, *Komitas: Kianke, gortsuneyutyune, steghtsagortsutyune* [Gomidas: Life, Activities, Creations] (Erevan: Haypethrat, 1961), p. 84.

[68] Gomidas was referring to a letter of recommendation that Catholicos Mgrdich I (1892-1906) had given him on a previous occasion.

[69] In a letter addressed to the famous poet Hovhannes Tumanian in 1913, Gomidas wrote: "I am already settled in Bolis, and started my work. I have my private school where I am preparing choral directors and singers. I have a 300-member group of mixed voices, named 'Gusan.' I am preparing concerts and giving lessons; here it is, my new life."

[70] Shahverdyan, *Hay erazhshtutyan patmutyan aknarkner*, pp. 446-47.

for the first time as a teenager on a summer vacation to his friend's village of Keorpalu.[71] He must have been deeply touched by this experience because he began searching for additional examples of this Armenian village music. Gomidas meticulously transcribed countless songs on the spot as they were being improvised spontaneously during the daily experiences of Armenian village life. These were beautifully crafted melodies and poetic verses created and re-created by the Armenian peasantry up to the twentieth century.

His comparative analysis of Persian, Turkish, Arabic, Kurdish, and Armenian songs identified the distinguishing features of a developed Armenian musical vocabulary: its modal system, melodic turns and phrases, rhythmic patterns, metric structures, and emotive expressive styles.[72] Combined, these aesthetic elements created a musical idiom that was intimately connected with the structure of the Armenian language, traditions, and customs. He was convinced that by making the music and its theoretical analysis available, he would lay a foundation upon which future composers could build new interpretations of the traditional, could revitalize the sacred and the secular traditions of Armenian music. Such accomplishments, he hoped, would also boost the national self-image of the present and future generations of Armenians. His goal, however, was not fully realized during his lifetime, although the survivors of the genocide, scattered around the globe, turned to this music as a source of comfort and inspiration.

Thanks to Gomidas, the ethnomusicologist, the composer, the conductor, and the educator, the folk songs of the unassuming Armenian peasant and the sacred hymns of the obscure Armenian monk were, for the first time, brought out from the villages and monasteries of historic Armenia and Cilicia to the concert stages of Constantinople, among other capitals. The final polyphonic version of the badarak for male voices, on which Gomidas had worked intermittently for many years, was scheduled for performance at the patriarchal church in the Kumkapu quarter on Easter morning of 1915. Instead, he and more than two hundred other Armenian intellectuals were arrested and exiled into the

---

[71] Izabella R. Yolyan, *Komitas* (Erevan: Armenian Academy of Sciences, 1969), pp. 17-18.

[72] V. Korganov, *Caucasian Music* (Tiflis, 1908), p. 82, cited by Gasparyan, *Komitas*, p. 20.

interior, where most of them were murdered.[73]

Gomidas left a great deal of work unfinished. Foremost on his list of projects was the publication of his conclusive findings on the medieval khaz symbols. This would have provided a definitive picture of Armenian musicology, formulated in academic terminology, which could be appreciated universally. Still, Gomidas accomplished much and received a level of recognition well above what most artists could hope to attain. The public appreciation accorded to Gomidas was especially noteworthy, for he achieved his objectives without the backing of the state, an institution, or even an established music conservatory, which, though promised to him, never materialized.[74] Perhaps had it not been for the adversarial attitude of the Armenian clergy,[75] the indifference of economically powerful classes, and the devastation of the Genocide, Gomidas would have witnessed Armenian music among the most advanced and universally appreciated musical cultures of the world. It is worth noting that, even after having experienced the horrors and misery of the Armenians during the deportations and massacres, he persevered briefly upon returning to Constantinople. Just before he lost his creative drive and sank into a severe depression, he put the final touches on his composition of "Armenian Dance Miniatures for Piano."[76]

Conclusion

After four centuries of Persian-Arabic maqams, Ottoman Turkish music of the sufis, Turkish popular songs of ashughs, and Turkified church songs of Armenian deacons, the musical world of the Armenians in Constantinople finally experienced a revival. It was invigorated by the new sounds and sights of musical performances

---

[73] The horror which he experienced during the Armenian Genocide led to a severe depression, and he was committed to a sanatorium in France for the rest of his life.

[74] Obstacles to this project included insufficient funding and delays because of the sultan's wish to establish a state conservatory in Constantinople; in fact, the sultan asked Gomidas to head up that project. See Matevos Muradyan, "Azgayin erazhshtakan uzheri patrastman Komitasyan tsragirnere" [Gomidas' Plans for the Preparation of National Musical Forces], in *Komitasakan*, ed. Robert A. Atayan et al. (Erevan: Armenian Academy of Sciences, 1981), vol. 1, p. 238.

[75] See Gasparyan, *Zhamanakakitsnere Komitasi masin*, pp. 116-17, 123-24, 126.

[76] Ibid., p. 40.

coming from Western Europe. Armenian musicians educated in Western conservatories began to use the more developed and refined European instruments. They borrowed salon music and patriotic melodies as they composed new forms for instrumental and vocal ensembles. They experimented with creating a fusion of the Eastern with the Western musical traditions in their compositions for the theater, opera house, and concert hall. They were successful in introducing polyphony to Armenian sacred chants and to indigenous folk melodies. Music education, publications, performances of a varied repertoire and musical styles appealed to the larger part of the Armenian society in the Ottoman capital. Thus, forward-looking, dedicated Armenian musicians and musicologists in Constantinople enriched and expanded the musical world of all Armenians in the Great City.

Gomidas (Komitas)

❊ 13 ❊

DANIEL VAROUJAN
AND LITERARY HEATHENISM

Souren Danielyan

Modern Armenian literary heathenism in Constantinople represented a philosophical current, which having originated in the
early nineteenth century sought to combine new aesthetic values
with national struggles for freedom. Literary heathenism is
found in the works of Daniel Varoujan (Taniel Chbugkiarian,
1884-1915), Siamanto (Atom Yarchanian, 1878-1915), Levon
Shant (Levon Seghposian, 1869-1951), Vahan Tekeyan (1878-
1945), and Hakob Siruni (Hagop Chololian, 1890-1973). This
movement searched for a national credo and for a heroic past in
the deep sources of pre-Christian Armenian culture and propagated the worship of nature and beauty.

Daniel Varoujan placed particular emphasis on pre-Christian
Armenian culture and maintained that human strength and
struggle are essential for cultural revival, "the new dawn." He
advocated a return to heathen values for an Armenian renaissance and renewal. The creation of the national ideal of strength
in the 1910s had political implications, for the revival of the
memory of ancient times would enable the desperate hero to
retrieve the lost beauty and power and to recall the lost homeland. In efforts to escape from the existing harsh reality, he set
out to search for the perfection and harmony of beauty.

In February 1908, Varoujan confessed to Arshag Chobanian
(Arshak Chopanian, 1872-1954): "The heathen life grips me day
by day. If it were possible today to change religion, I would
eagerly adopt poetic heathenism."[1] During his studies at the University of Ghent in Belgium, Daniel Varoujan showed great in-

---

[1] Daniel Varuzhan, *Erkeri liakatar zhoghovatsu* [Complete Collection of Works], 3
vols. (Erevan: Armenian Academy of Sciences, 1986-1987), vol. 3, p. 364.

terest in ancient Roman, Indian, and Greek monuments, which in turn instilled a deeper appreciation toward heathen civilization. He shared similarities in aesthetic conceptions with other contemporaries, such as Levon Esajanian, who believed that intersections of various artistic strands enrich poetic style. Varoujan referred to this as realism, where art represents not only an abstract meaning but also the recognition of true art in its concrete form. Referring to his student days at the university, he wrote to Vardges Aharonian in March 1914: "Flemish art and life caused my proclivity toward realism in art."[2] According to Varoujan, realists were the outstanding representatives of renaissance.

The literary movement urged by Daniel Varoujan stressed adoration of nature and beauty, vivid contrasts between the past and the present, and exposure to pagan freedom. He considered himself a prophet of beauty, as repeatedly demonstrated in his works. He envisaged the parallelism between the charm of the past and his heathen spirit in the present. In one poem, he writes:

Մերկ ըլլաս դուն բանաստեղծի մ'հոգւոյն պէս,
Եւ հեթանոս այդ մերկութեանրդ ներքեւ
Տառապի՛ մարդն ու չկրնայ դպչիլ քեզ.[3]

To be naked like a poet's soul,
And heathen under your nakedness,
To let the man be tortured and not be able to touch you.

The poet can delineate the boundaries and ingredients of the good and harmonious in the mystery of beauty and also develop a pagan aesthetic, philosophical system.[4] The concept of beauty gives rise to his system of imagery. In 1909, in a letter to Levon Esajanian, Varoujan wrote: "Beauty has no schools. It is a multifaceted crystal illuminating through all its aspects."[5] His "multifacted" mystery of beauty is subjective, as found in his "To the Source of Light," which promises multiple pleasures and points of contact with beauty.

---

[2] Ibid., p. 463.
[3] Daniel Varuzhan, *Banasteghtsakan erker* [Poetic Works] (Antelias: Catholicosate of Cilicia, 1986), p. 249.
[4] Varuzhan, *Erkeri liakatar zhoghovatsu*, vol. 3, p. 143.
[5] Ibid., p. 413.

Varoujan's formulation of a "great artist" corresponds to his understanding of perfection. The artist reformulates the heathen beauty through his character's own strength. The creative truth in his "Hero," harkening back to Arthur Schopenhauer, leads the reader "to the kingdom of the ideal." For Schopenhauer, the king of the ideal is the "Superman" for whom the "Hero" represents the third place after the categories of "Saint" and "Genius." Daniel Varoujan believes that in this brutal world every Superman is a victim.[6] This is an expression of his sympathy toward his Hero. Sadly, modern Armenian literature lacks heroes who could realize the dreams of the powerful and courageous nation.

The analysis of the relationships between the Hero and the Superman combines the philosophical understanding and conceptions of freedom with the priority of strength as a political and aesthetical force, thereby determining what is useful in Armenian culture. In the autumn of 1908, Varoujan wrote to Chobanian concerning his heathenist mood: "I have the nostalgia for the mythical age—not only of our culture but the whole world. When will the times of heathen victories return, for which not diplomacy but heroes are needed!"[7] The hero had been ousted not only from life but also from poetry.

The relationship between beauty and liberty is revealed in literary heathenism in the early twentieth century, when Chobanian, Varoujan, Siamanto, and others turned to the pagan gods Anahit and Vahagn for inspiration and cultural regeneration. While the German romantic poet Heinrich Heine in his "Gods of Greece" is willing to be recruited by the defeated gods, Daniel Varoujan in his "To the Dead Gods" presents their defeat as his own:

Ես՝ պարտրուած Արուեստիս դառն սրտէն
Կ'ողբամ ձեր մահն, ո'վ Հեթանոս Աստուածներ.[8]

I, from the embittered heart of my defeated art,
Lament your death, O', pagan Gods.

He considers his mission to be a creator bound in chains with beauty and liberty. His philosophy of liberty is the hope to revive the "glorious lyre," which is a poetic representation of the

---

[6] Ibid., p. 117.
[7] Ibid., p. 386.
[8] Ibid., vol. 2, p. 53.

liberation of the homeland.

The Character of Armenian Literature

In a letter to Garegin Levonian, founder and editor of the *Gegharvest* (Fine Arts) journal, Daniel Varoujan, commenting on the state of Armenian literature, observes that the genre of patriotic literature has often been composed without much regard for fine artistic considerations. Varoujan writes that "in my own poetry, I try to interweave the useful and the beautiful, and to encapsulate within them all forms of objective beauty . . . for it is only thus that one can create solid literature and avoid producing the kind of shallow work . . . which, I regret to say, are sold and continue to be sold like hay on the literary scene."[9] For him, with the exception of a few talented Eastern and Western Armenian writers, most were odd bibliophiles.

Varoujan insisted that the material for national scenes must possess sufficient literary breadth, although such works had always appeared under ideological influences. This was true in the Middle Ages, for example, when historiography and literature could not be clearly distinguished. This was also true in the nineteenth century, as seen in the works of Khachatur Abovian (1809-1848), Raffi (Hakob Melik-Hakobian, 1837-1888), and Muratsan (Grigor Ter-Hovhannesian, 1854-1908), whose literature served as a tribute to national political development. While this proved useful in the nineteenth century, as literature enabled the Armenian people to regain their national consciousness, by the twentieth century that could no longer be valid. This was certainly true in the early twentieth century prior to the Genocide, when literary heathenism had reached its peak, although the character and impact of the movement was subject to debate. The literary critic, Hakob Oshakan (Hagop Oshagan, 1883-1948) in June 1923 wrote to Gegham Gavafian (Kegham Kavafian), the principal of Constantinople's Kedronakan (Central) School, what at first sight seem to be shocking words: "the nation martyred for literature, as it was the books and writers that caused this devastation."[10] The writer reveals an extremely

---

[9] Varuzhan, *Erkeri liakatar zhoghovatsu*, vol. 3, pp. 359-60.

[10] "Lusatuner: Kedronakani sanere ke hishen" [Enlighteners: The Alumni of Central School Remember] (Paris, 1996), p. 29.

subtle and tragic perception of reality. Further, in the absence of an Armenian state, literature, intellectuals, and national identification were closely interrelated, as was the case since the early phases of the cultural reawakening as a national movement.

In the autumn of 1913, the first and the only issue of *Navasard*—long anticipated and carefully prepared by Siruni and Varoujan—was published. With high expectations, Varoujan sought to continue the themes of his *Hetanosakan erger* (Heathen Songs) and considered the periodical an opportunity further to develop the heathen line in literature. The periodical was to join the movement in due course. In fact, Daniel Varoujan was drafting the Credo with Kostan Zarian (1885-1969), Hakob Oshakan, Gegham Barseghian (1883-1915), and Aharon Taturian (Dadurian, 1886-1965). Siruni probably would also have signed the Credo if several lawsuits connected with the newspaper *Azatamart* had not preoccupied his time.

In early 1914, the literary group "Mehyan" (Pagan Temple) attempted to develop the movement, but it soon lost momentum. Disagreements appeared in the May issue of the journal *Mehyan* in the dialogue between Kostan Zarian and Daniel Varoujan. In an article titled "Heathenism?" Zarian tried to distance the journal from heathenism and developed his favored philosophy of futurism, when in fact it was heathenism that had drawn attention to the journal. Siruni comments: "After a heated quarrel," Daniel Varoujan "no longer wanted to work with them for *Mehyan*. He was depressed by K. Zarian's article, where . . . Varoujan seemed to have noticed biting remarks addressed to him."[11] Zarian allegedly believed that in this way he could expropriate the Mehyan movement from Varoujan, Siruni, and Aharon. Zarian ambitiously wished to impose his futurism against the worship of the heathen past. The "neo-futurist" rejected the significance of the Renaissance: "Who said that the Renaissance has been fruitful and progressive for the arts? It was an imitation of Hellenist masterpiece forms with no Hellenist spirit and worldview in them."[12]

---

[11] Hakob Siruni, *Daniel Varuzhan* (Bucharest: Araz, 1940), p. 137.
[12] Ibid.

Eastern Armenian Intellectuals
Confront Daniel Varoujan

The intelligentsia in Eastern Armenia were either ignorant about or contemptuous of the Western Armenian writers. Hovhannes Tumanian (1869-1923) maintained a strange silence about them, although "he had read their works." Yet, in 1917, referring to Western Armenian cultural trends, Tumanian confessed: "I have a huge pain in my heart about how little I know about today's living Armenia."[13] Other critics held no better opinion of Western Armenian literature in general. Vahan Terian (1885-1920) was categorically pessimistic about its future. In his "The Future Days of the Armenian Literature," which appeared in April 1914, Terian declared that he did not believe in the rebirth of Western Armenia and its literature: "I don't think that the literature of Polis [Constantinople] or western literature and language have any charm at all."[14] Rejecting heathenist intellectual ambitions, Terian in fact rejected all Western Armenian literature. His negative attitude was in reaction to the heathenist movement that *Mehyan* represented. He considered the movement false and vain, and the philosophy of liberty as too nationalistic. He commented that he would never compare Tumanian's "Parvana" with "the production of the newly heathenized poets."[15]

This particular conflict dated back to 1911, when Daniel Varoujan expressed an unfavorable opinion in the *Azatamart* newspaper regarding the Eastern Armenian language, while praising Western Armenian literary achievements. He wrote that Eastern Armenian "is more rhetorical than powerful, more propagandistic than idealistic, and notwithstanding the exceptions such as Hovhannes Tumanian and Avetik Isahakian (1875-1957) whose writings share certain characteristics with works of minstrels, and which despite their poetic language are, admittedly, populist."[16] This must have irritated intellectuals in Eastern Armenia, including Vahan Terian, although Varoujan's article did not men-

---

[13] Hovhannes Tumanyan, *Erkeri liakatar zhoghovatsu* [Complete Collection of Works], 10 vols. (Erevan: Armenian Academy of Sciences, 1988-1999), vol. 7, p. 323.
[14] Vahan Teryan, *Erkeri zhoghovatsu* [Collected Works], 4 vols. (Erevan: Sovetakan Grogh, 1972-1979), vol. 3, p. 92.
[15] Ibid., p. 94.
[16] Varuzhan, *Erkeri liakatar zhoghovatsu*, vol. 3, p. 127.

tion Terian. His comments, however, certainly attracted the attention of both Western and Eastern Armenian intellectuals—for example, Chobanian, Shirvanzade, Oshakan, Vrtanes Papazian, Ghazaros Aghayan, and Stepan Lisitsian. *Azatamart* had even formed a board, consisting of Ruben Zardarian, Levon Shant, and Hrand (Melkon Giurjian/Kiurchian), for further discussions on the Armenian language. At the time, Vahan Terian was among the recognized Russian Armenian poets, his first book of poetry having been published in Moscow in 1908. Yet, Daniel Varoujan had dared to criticize the leading intellectuals without a single reference to Terian.[17]

* * *

The tragic events of 1915 did not allow Daniel Varoujan and his cohorts to continue the discussion. Nevertheless, by then he had managed to apply literary heathenism as a conceptual framework in Armenian literature, and through the power of his poetry he had established a movement and integrated Western philosophies into his works.

---

[17] Ibid., p. 128.

Daniel Varoujan

THE VOICE OF KOSTAN ZARIAN:
BEFORE AND AFTER THE CATASTROPHE

Vartan Matiossian

Armenian Constantinople played a central role in Kostan Zarian's life and work in the early twentieth century, and he in turn influenced the community. Born in Shemakh (Shamakhy, in present-day Azerbaijan) in 1885, Zarian had an unstable childhood, as turmoil in the family uprooted him from an early age. When he was four, his father died and the family moved to Baku. He then was separated from his mother and placed with a Russian family, who enrolled him in a Russian school. His brothers subsequently sent him to Paris to study in a French lyceum, and French gradually replaced Russian as his primary language. He earned his Ph.D. in literature and philosophy in 1910 from the Université Nouvelle in Brussels. Zarian became involved in the Russian Social Democratic Party and was personally acquainted with Lenin. After 1909, he was a political exile in Europe, as the tsarist government had reportedly banned his return to the Caucasus because of his revolutionary activities (he spent a year and half in jail in Germany around 1907-08. He published a few poems in Russian in the revolutionary magazine *Raduga* (Rainbow—Geneva) and contributed to Belgian publications with prose, poems, and critical essays in French.[1]

While in Europe, Zarian suffered an identity crisis, which he revealed through the struggles of a character named Iberian, the protagonist in *Bankoope ev mamuti voskornere* (The Bancoop and

---

[1] See Vartan Matiossian, "The Traveler and His Many Roads," *Ararat* (Spring 1994): 26-33, and *Kostan Zariani shurj* [Regarding Kostan Zarian] (Antelias: Catholicosate of Cilicia, 1998); Lawrence Durrell, "Constant Zarian—Triple Exile," *Ararat* (Spring 1994): 34, reprinted from *The Poetry Review* (Jan.-Feb., 1952). Zarian also performed minor roles in Armenian plays in the Caucasus in 1904-05.

the Bones of the Mammoth):

> A moment of great enthusiasm, emotions, beautiful love ad-
> ventures, and flights of thought. Also the nightmare of doubt,
> personal analysis, and the damned philosophical and religious
> questions that fill nights of insomnia and rainy days. Europe and
> its geometrical culture built like a Roman temple was the form:
> cold, beautiful, and indifferent. It lacked the Spirit, the depth,
> which Iberian heartily was looking for. "For our faith—a noted
> Catholic poet had said to him—the personality of the Pope has no
> importance: he can be a Borgia, the most immoral man one can
> imagine, a criminal, a robber, a bandit; we just worship the form,
> the slogan, the symbol."² And Jesus. . . ? Terrified, Iberian had
> gone far from this friend and stopped in the face of new doubts.
>   There, the few words of the once-learnt "Our Father" in Arme-
> nian left in the back of his head; the acute tone of the bell from
> the nearby church ringing on the feast mornings during his child-
> hood; the attraction of the small, insignificant family customs; the
> emotions aroused by the songs he had heard, undulating in him
> until today—all of them amplified in this period of his life, took
> on an extraordinary importance, and, like motherly arms, took him
> into their lap.³

His identity crisis was catalyzed in a conversation with the
famous Belgian poet Emile Verhaeren (1855-1916), with whom
Zarian had a close relationship.⁴ They regularly discussed literary

---

² The identity of this writer is unknown; he might be the Belgian poet George
Ramaekers, about whom Zarian wrote in his 1929 memoir, *West.* See Kostan Zarian,
Erker [Works] (Antelias: Catholicosate of Cilicia, 1975), p. 416.

³ Kostan Zarian, *Bankoope ev mamuti voskornere* (Antelias: Catholicosate of
Cilicia, 1987), p. 168.

⁴ According to Toros Toranian, Zarian's first article in the Belgian press was the
prose poem "Le douleur des larmes" [The Pain of the Tears], and after reading it,
Verhaeren "expressed his satisfaction to the author in a letter and, in reference to his
Armenian origin, despite the fact that this was a French expression, added, 'When
someone prays to his God, he must pray in his mother tongue'." Toros Toranian,
"'Kostan Zarian': Kianke ev gortse" [Kostan Zarian: Life and Work], *Nayiri* (March
1, 1970): 4. Cf. Constant Zarian, "Proses. Nuit de mort/Les flammes de nos larmes
(Fragment)," *Le Thyrse* (Oct. 1909). "Les flammes de nos larmes" bears a dedication:
"A Mlle R. Simchovitch." A footnote (on p. 36) says both pieces were translated from
the Russian by the author. The clipping of "Mer artsunknerun botsere" [The Flames of
Our Tears] tells a slightly different story. See *Azatamarti grakan havelvats* [*Azatamart*'s
Literary Supplement] (Oct. 24/Nov. 6): 6. The French title "Les flammes de nos larmes"

trends, the future of humankind, and the Armenian tragedy.[5] In 1923, Zarian recalled that one day he had gone to see Verhaeren together with two writers, Fernand Cromeleng and Horace Van Offel, to speak about their plans for a new literary journal. A Chauvinist critic in the French paper *Gaulois* had strongly attacked foreigners, especially Belgians of French expression, like Verhaeren, because they "[polluted] our clear and harmonious national genius, and especially [transformed] our language." The three Belgian writers were upset:

> He [Verhaeren] turned to me:
> "If you were a believer and prayed, what language would you use to pray?"
> "Armenian," I answered.
> "Here we are. So, what's poetry, if not an eternal prayer to phenomena and ideas? . . . We, the Flemish, dance with lead feet, we are deprived of that 'doigtée' which is natural to Frenchmen. Throughout the centuries we have created a perfect instrument, tallied to our character and spirit. And then we go into a stranger's home with our untamed nature, our wild German character, and change the places of their lyre's chord in order to express ourselves."
> After talking a lot like this, he confessed that he had never felt satisfied with the French language, and, if he were a newcomer to literature, he would have surely written in Flemish. That night a great desire to learn my mother tongue arose in me.[6]

Zarian, drawn back toward his native culture, began to question

---

has been added at the top of the Armenian one and below we read: "Réponse à M. de Simhovitch [sic] qui lui demande Qui est-tu?" Below the text, another scribble: "Le poète Verharen [sic], après avoir lu ce poème, exclama: 'Ce jeune poète nous apporte une note nouvelle.' 1910 à Bruxelles." The additions belong to Zarian's first wife, Takuhi.

[5] Stepan Kurtikian, *Artasahmani hay groghneri het* [With Armenian Writers Abroad] (Erevan: Loys, 1984), p. 61.

[6] Kostan Zarian, "Emil Verharen" [Emile Verhaeren], *Paykar* (Erevan), March 15, 1923, p. 65; reprinted in Kostan Zarian, *Navatomar* [Ship Log] (Erevan: Sargis Khachents, 1999), pp. 147-49. Zarian later recounted the story with some modifications and contradictions. See, for instance his interview of 1955 in Karo Polatian, *Zroyts* [Conversation], vol. 2 (Cairo: Husaber, 1961), pp. 88-89; Kostan Zarian, "Teghi, zhamanaki ev groghi masin" [About Place, Time, and Writer], *Sovetakan grakanutyun* 6 (1970): 105; cf. Zarian, *Navatomar*, pp. 586-87. For an analysis of the Verhaeren episode, see Matiossian, *Kostan Zariani shurj*, pp. 42-47.

his place in Europe as reports of Armenian suffering again reached the West during the Adana massacre in 1909. Later in his life, Zarian reflected on his reaction to the news of these horrors through the autobiographical eyes of Iberian:

> From those faraway provinces of the homeland that he had never seen, dark voices and deathly cries were heard as floated across the earth like a black flag tainted with blood. That call of his race was cutting into his heart like a terrible dagger. He was used to walking with his head up high, proud and independent, supremely elevated, by the depth of his thought and soul, above his intellectual entourage; he could not take those pious regards, commiserations, and commonplaces which the Europeans uttered to express their sympathy for his people. He would have preferred to be there with his people, in the places of blood and tragedy, rather than here, in this hell of bourgeois Christianity and educated philanthropy which had no fire but still burned his heart.[7]

In 1910, after graduating from the university, Zarian left Brussels, never to return, and went to Constantinople, where he spent nine months. Researchers have overlooked this period, but it is vital to understanding the relationship between Zarian and the Ottoman capital. For instance, in his preface to the 1963 edition of *Nave leran vra* (The Ship on the Mountain), the Soviet Armenian critic Hrachia Grigoryan wrote that "from 1910 to 1913 he lived in Venice, where, for the first time, he started to learn Armenian with the Mekhitarist fathers."[8] Curiously enough, some of Zarian's own autobiographical references—like his statement that, "I liked Verhaeren a lot and his words sounded in my ears like a message. A few days later I was in Venice"[9]—have led many researchers to the inaccurate conclusion that he went directly from Brussels to Venice. In fact, Zarian arrived in Constantinople during the last months (most likely in October) of 1910 and remained there until the summer of 1911. Determined to resolve his identity crisis, he returned to his people to satiate his gnawing hunger for Armenian culture.

---

[7] Zarian, *Bankoope*, p. 168.
[8] Kostan Zarian, *Nave leran vra* (Erevan: Haypethrat, 1963), p. iv.
[9] Polatian, *Zroyts*, p. 89; Zarian, "Teghi," p. 105.

Nine Months in Constantinople (1910-11)

It is not clear why Zarian skipped over his first stay in Constantinople in his autobiographical references to the city. It could have been a mere case of forgetfulness. Nevertheless, in 1929 he mentioned Constantinople as the "missing link" between his time in Brussels and his stay in Venice. In his memoir *West,* he depicts the moments at the Galata Quay as he prepared to board the ship bound for Venice:

> A few months before, I had come here thirsty and tired. I was thirsty for my language, to fit my soul into the traditional niche that the centuries have made for it; thirsty to drink, with my humble two hands, from the source of my race, where it passed from the divine world into the earth and took human form.
>
> I was also tired. I was tired of all those 'truths' from other peoples, enough to pave the streets with; of those common thoughts that everybody has; of those easy concepts that take no thought to grasp; of that surface where it is so easy to float that only the mediocre will swim.[10]

The description of the Constantinople-Athens-Venice journey of 1911 in *West* shows that Zarian departed from the Ottoman capital in late spring or early summer; the next episode is dated in the fall of 1911. A French manuscript with his signature has been kept in his personal archive, titled *copie d'une lettre* by his first wife.[11] We are able to make the logical leap because of a letter dated May 13, 1913, written in Constantinople by Hrand Nazariants, one of Zarian's Armenian colleagues, to the Mekhitarist priest Simeon Eremian, in Venice: "You know how good I was to him during nine long months in Constantinople? And then?"[12]

In December 1910, shortly after his arrival in Constantinople, Zarian published "L'art de la danse" in the periodical *Le Jeune*

---

[10] Zarian, *Erker,* p. 422.

[11] Kostan Zarian, personal archives, Erevan. It has been copied on the clipping of "Venetik" (italics in original). See Vartan Matiossian, "Kostan Zarian Polso mej 'Mehyanen' araj" [Kostan Zarian in Constantinople before "Mehyan"], *Haraj mitk ev arvest* (Dec. 1998): 2. For an Armenian translation, see Zarian, *Navatomar*, p. 598.

[12] Grigor Peltian [Krikor Beledian], "'Haykakan apagayapashtutiun' ev Hrand Nazariants" ["Armenian Futurism" and Hrand Nazariants], *Bazmavep*, no. 3-4 (1990): 386.

Turc.[13] Its Armenian translation appeared a few days later in the literary supplement of *Azatamart* under the title "Letter to the Female Dancer," carrying the following footnote: "Mr. Kostan Zarian, a Caucasian Armenian, has arrived in Constantinople from Belgium, where he was well-known in youthful literary circles for his writings."[14] The piece, a sort of impressionistic essay, was written after a performance by the aspiring dancer Armen Ohanian (Sophia Pirbudaghian), who, like Zarian, was born in Shemakh. This article was the first of many Zarian contributed to *Azatamart*. He had been introduced to the *Azatamart* circle by two writers of his generation, Gegham Barseghian (Kegham Parseghian) and Hrand Nazariants, both of whom were among the driving forces of the brief Western Armenian renaissance between 1909 and 1915. During 1911, Zarian published six other pieces in the literary supplement of *Azatamart*, which can be loosely defined as "prose poems."[15] It is not yet clear who translated them into Armenian,[16] with some sources crediting Barseghian[17] and others, Nazariants.[18]

Nazariants had become interested in futurism Almost immediately after the Italian poet Filippo Tomasso Marinetti published *Manifesto del futurismo* in late 1910, Nazariants published a slim volume in Armenian titled *F.T. Marinetti and Futurism*.[19] His

---

[13] *Le Jeune Turc*, Dec. 21, 1910.

[14] Kostan Zarian, "Namak ar paruhin," *Azatamarti grakan havelvats*, Dec. 13/26, 1910, p. 368. Cf. Zarian, *Navatomar*, pp. 33-35. Zarian was already known to the readers of the supplement, which had reprinted some of his opinions about modern theater, originally published in April 1910 in the Belgian journal *Societé nouvelle*. "Arti tatrone ev ir dere" [The Modern Theater and Its Role], *Azatamarti grakan havelvats* (Aug. 9/26, 1910): 16; cf. Zarian, *Navatomar*, pp. 31-32.

[15] These are: "Antarin mej" [In the Forest], May 1/14, 1911; "Banasteghtse" [The Poet], Oct. 17/30, 1911; "Mer artsunknerun botsere," Oct. 24/Nov. 6, 1911; "Mahvan gishere" [The Night of Death], Nov. 7/20, 1911; see the French originals of the latter two in Zarian, "Proses," pp. 36-38; "Venetik" [Venice], Nov. 14/27, 1911; "Pazilike: Sb. Markosi ekeghetsin" [The Basilic: The Church of St. Mark], Dec. 22, 1911. All of them are reprinted in Zarian, *Navatomar*, pp. 50-61.

[16] Editorial footnotes to "Venetik" (p. 6) and "Pazilike" (p. 9) state that "this and the previous writings have been translated from the French manuscript." For the French originals, see Constant Zarian, "Proses. Venise/Basilikos," *Le Thyrse* (Aug. 1913): 451-52.

[17] This is Hakob Siruni's opinion. See Kurtikian, *Artasahmani*, p. 63.

[18] Beledian, "'Haykakan apagayapashtutiun'," p. 386.

[19] Hrand Nazariants, *F. T. Marinetti ev apagayapashtutiune* (Constantinople: Der Nersessian, 1910).

interest in that movement and later acquaintance with several of its followers has been cause for the widespread belief among literary critics that Nazariants was a futurist.

Nazariants and Zarian made a joint attempt at creating an international literary movement, which Nichanian has rightfully identified as "the only known manifestation of futurism."[20] Until recently, this attempt had been a fleeting reference in Enrico Cardile's translation of Nazariants' first Italian volume of poetry, *I Sogni Crocefissi* (1916). In all likelihood his source was Nazariants; Cardile remarked that he had "tried to form, together with K. Zarian and G. Barseghian, a real cenacle to revive and repair international art, 'Les Volontés Folles,' by the end of 1910."[21] However, one extant copy of the letter-manifest (see Appendix 1) only bears the signatures of Nazariants and Zarian. Apparently, they had planned to create an international literary movement by publishing works by like-minded writers. But this did not materialize.

Shortly thereafter, Nazariants and Zarian signed an open letter on February 13, 1911, "on behalf of the Armenian poets," which called for the release of F.T. Marinetti from prison in Italy. The Italian poet and pioneer of the futurist movement had been sentenced to two months incarceration for his novel *Mafarka le futuriste* (Mafarka the Futurist). In the letter, they state:

> We who love beautiful Italy, the cradle of the arts, deeply regret such acts which weaken our respect for that country which usually glorifies artists and especially its native artists.
> Will an artistic Italy consciously allow such a debilitating and humiliating blow to be struck against poetry itself? Will it allow the walls of the prison to smother the voice of the poet? It is time to choose between the binding chains of human laws and the unbound fire that springs from the poet's imagination.[22]

Neither Nazariants' nor Zarian's literature show any particular inklings toward the futurist movement. Zarian also befriended and worked along with some Armenian and non-Armenian futurists,

---

[20] Marc Nichanian, *Entre l'art et le témoignage: Littératures arméniennes au XXᵉ siècle*, vol. 2: Le deuil de la philologie (Geneva: Metis Presses, 2007), p. 321.

[21] Cf. the Italian quotation in ibid., p. 386.

[22] Ibid., p. 411.

but his interest remained strictly academic.[23] Further, as a follow-er of symbolism, he wrote a powerful article in the *Azatamart* daily about symbolism and classicism, extolling "integral individuality" and making the case for the French symbolist poet Paul Claudel, "a genial poet of elegiac panegyrics, who alas, or fortunately, is only known by a few lovers of literature."[24] Zarian argued in the article that personal intuition should become the foundation of all literary creation and that the poet should commit himself to life rather than to a literary school. He concluded the article with these words:

> Our prose, abandoning the naive simplicity of past times, must take as its foundation the rhythmic and musical elements that are the best medium for evocation, even if it is necessary to sacrifice thought-fulness. Dynamic art must be, above all, the direct expression of the movement of the real; it must evoke the mysteries of the soul and of the cosmic concert, and, sensitizing everything, must pene-trate through intuition into the sublime mirages of the illusions of the future.[25]

A few months later, he published another piece, this time about an exhibition by Armenian, Turkish, and European painters at the Societa Operà Italiana hall in Pera, one of the upscale neigh-borhoods of Constantinople. His scathing critique lambasted the mediocre level of the exhibition, singling out the work of Panos Terlemezian, the painter who later gained considerable fame in Armenian art.[26]

---

[23] In the last years of his life, Zarian wrote about *Mehyan* that "even Marinetti was sending letters to us and giving words of encouragement." "Teghi," p. 106. Other than that, the only evidence of their relationship is a circular sent by Marinetti, which was published by *Mehyan* "for the sake of information." "Nisher" [Notes], *Mehyan* (Feb. 1914): 31.

[24] Zarian praised Claudel again in 1914, this time about his theater. See Kostan Zarian, "Arvesti hamar: Tatron" [For Art: Theater], *Mehyan* (April 1914): 53; Zarian, *Navatomar*, p. 100. Cf. Marc Nichanian [Mark Nshanian], "Kostan Zarian: Ankareli tatrone" [Kostan Zarian: The Impossible Theater], *Bazmavep*, special issue (1994): 181-82.

[25] Kostan Zarian, "Noragoyn dzgtumnere grakanutian mej. senbolizm ev klasisizm" [The Latest Trends in Literature: Symbolism and Classicism], *Azatamart*, Jan. 2/15, 1911, p. 3; Zarian, *Navatomar*, pp. 41-42.

[26] Kostan Zarian, "Gegharvesti ashkharhen: Nkarchakan tsutsahandes me K. Polso mej" [From the World of Art: A Painting Exhibition in Constantinople], *Azatamart*, April 17/30, April 24/May 7, 1911; Zarian, *Navatomar*, pp. 43-49.

Zarian had gone to Constantinople to get in touch with the Armenian world in one of the largest centers of that culture, but nine months later he left the city for Venice, hoping to return when his native culture seemed less alien. His own recollections of his reasons for leaving are enlightening, if slightly jocular: "I had departed, and after the half-hungry days spent in Constantinople, [now] Chianti, cotelette alla milanese and Ionian Sea."[27] He had not been able to find a place in the intellectual environment of Constantinople; he later recalled "the disillusion and the disgust after the initial interest. That terrible and displeasing masquerade."[28] In 1910, the effects of Sultan Abdul Hamid's tyranny still hung like a dark shadow over the city. The few embryonic attempts at cultural renaissance were too weak to counter thirty years of stagnation. Zarian's discomfort was further compounded by the fact that he could not write and speak Armenian properly and had little knowledge of Armenian life. He would later lament the time spent in Constantinople:

> That was such an upsetting year! Like a camel beaten by the winds of the desert, injured, and separated from its owner, I yielded to instinct. My soul had lost all direction. My life seemed to be reflected in ten distorted mirrors. My ideals were crumbling like old plaster from the walls of a hut. My face was yellow; my big head felt heavy on my shoulders and my sadness was palpable. . . . Bitter thoughts were circulating through my head and my heart was filled with hate.
>
> The beer of Bomonti, the *mastika,* the fried *midia,* the Young Turks, the literature of barbers who had seen Paris, the whores of Pera, the easy patriotism of Scutari, the twilights of Istanbul, and the smells of bedbugs and fried oil coming from the wooden houses under a sky burning like the exposed breasts of a mother, were fading. . . .
>
> Foreign among foreigners, foreign among my compatriots.
>
> The Armenian who is not Armenian is, at best, an educated monkey.
>
> And now I was leaving Constantinople. With an emptied soul

---

[27] Zarian, *Erker,* p. 542. In a letter written to Father Eremian on January 21, 1914, Nazariants remarked about Zarian: "And say that that despicable adventurer owes me his existence for nine months; and the one who is being insulted today saved him of dying like a dog in the street." Beledian, "Haykakan apagayapashtutiune," p. 395.

[28] Zarian, *Bankoope,* p. 169.

and lowered eyes. My luggage was filled with ashes, and my heart
with flames.

A cycle was ending, or, who knows, maybe one was starting![29]

It was the end of the beginning, a brief prelude to the long and
tortuous relationship between Zarian and the ancient Byzantine
capital.[30]

Departure and Return

Zarian did not sever his ties with Constantinople. Despite feelings
of despair, during his one and half year stay in Venice, where he
learned Armenian with the Mekhitarist fathers at San Lazzaro and
participated in local cultural life,[31] he continued to correspond with
Nazariants, who sent him a copy of his volume of poetry, *Crucified
Dreams* (1912).[32] Referring to the book in an article on the theory
of poetry and the poet, Zarian wrote:

> And I thought: will people be able to taste these pages, where so
> many tortured reflections and so much grace are found, so many
> signs of more perfect, more personal works to come?
>
> I am making all these comments after reading Nazariants'
> book, where, besides personal and well-said things, there are
> works that are directly influenced by poets of many nationalities,
> who come easily to mind when reading these poems. And this is
> not a fault: he has followed the path of his elders. Let us try to get
> the full picture. A newly beginning youngster will necessarily be
> influenced by this or that genius, the way William Morris was

---

[29] Zarian, *Erker*, pp. 422-23.

[30] Zarian's ambivalent, often negative views regarding Constantinople and the
Armenian community are best summarized in *The Traveler and His Road*. See *Erker*,
pp. 13-45. For an in-depth interpretation, see Marc Nichanian [Mark Nshanian],
"Egherni lrutiune K. Zariani ardzakin mej" [The Silence of the Genocide in K.
Zarian's Prose], *Bazmavep* 1-4 (1995): 370-74.

[31] Besides his article in *Azatamart*, he also published some literary pieces: "Tone"
[The Feast-Day], *Shant*, Nov. 14, 1912; "Char andr-siro" [Discourse beyond Love],
Amenun taretsoytse (Constantinople), 1913; "Erazhshtutiunner" [Music], *Biutania*,
Jan. 1/14, 1913; Zarian, *Navatomar*, pp. 68-73. *Biutania* was actually one of the
names that *Azatamart* adopted each time it encountered problems with Ottoman
censorship.

[32] Hrand Nazariants, *Khachvatz yerazner* [Crucified Dreams] (Constantinople:
Ter Nersessian, 1912). This collection also contains a poem dedicated to Zarian.

influenced by Chaucer; he needs only to become aware of his influences. . . .

Among the poets appearing in the Armenian literary sunrise, Nazariants takes his well-deserved place. His effort gives life to everything that a powerful and definitive work must show. Let us commend this new poet.[33]

Other poets of considerable influence had appeared in the Armenian literary scene of Constantinople by then and sought to energize cultural life. In the summer of 1912, Daniel Varoujan, one of the luminaries of Western Armenian literature, and the young poet Aharon (Dadurian/Taturian), joined budding poet and editor Hakob Siruni to form a group called *Asteghatun* (Constellation), which aimed at publishing a periodical of the same name and organizing literary discussions. Siruni printed a short report in Meruzhan Parsamian's (Meroujan Barsamian) literary bi-weekly, *Shant*, in December 1912. He recalled in 1940:

> We decided not to increase our number. We would be just about ten people in *Asteghatun*. Zapel Yesayan, Komitas Vardapet, Vahan Tekeyan, Ruben Zardarian, Hrand Nazariants, painters [Panos] Terlemezian and [Levon] Kurkjian were readily available. We planned to write to Kostan Zarian, Hakob Oshakan, and Gegham Barseghian, who were out of Constantinople at the time. . . .[34]

Although the group actually dissolved without having produced any issue of the journal, it is worth noting Zarian's name among those mentioned, perhaps included at the suggestion of Nazariants. Zarian had acquired some notoriety among his contemporaries, despite his marginal standing among Constantinople's literati and despite the fact that he did not yet write in Armenian.

Leaving Constantinople on the *S.S. Montenegro* to Venice,

---

[33] Kostan Zarian, "Shrjagitser: Banasteghtsakan hatori me artiv" [Circumferences: On the Occasion of a Volume of Poetry], *Azatamart* (Daily), May 31/June 13, 1912, p. 4; Zarian, *Navatomar*, pp. 63, 66-67.

[34] Albert Sharurian, comp., *Misak Metsarentse ev Daniel Varuzhane zhamanaka-kitsneri husherum* [Misak Medzarents and Daniel Varoujan in the Memoirs of Contemporaries] (Erevan: Sovetakan Grogh, 1986), pp. 213-14. Danielyan has included Siamanto in the group and left out Oshakan, Barseghian, and Zarian. Souren Danielyan, *Hetanosakan grakan sharzhman patmutyunits* [From the History of the Pagan Literary Movement] (Erevan: Loys, 1988), p. 76.

Zarian met his future wife, Takuhi (Rachel) Shahnazarian while on the ship.[35] They were married in Venice on December 4, 1912, and two months later they returned to Constantinople.[36] Soon after Zarian's return, Nazariants married an Italian woman and moved with her to Bari in southern Italy. Under circumstances that remain unclear, the two writers permanently severed their ties, and there are only sparse remarks by Nazariants to help point to the reasons behind the break. In a letter to S. Eremian, dated May 13, 1913, a clearly indignant Nazariants exclaimed: "Did you hear what Kostan did to me? Suddenly he got angry at me; how right you were!"[37]

By 1913, Zarian was again in Constantinople. He was better equipped than his first visit, and the time seemed ripe to start the long hoped for literary movement, which would take the form of a new journal, *Mehyan*.[38]

Mehyan

The year 1913 proved exceptional for Armenian culture. The defeat of Turkey in the Balkan wars and its virtual expulsion from Europe had prompted a reopening of the Armenian Question by the major world powers. This year also marked the 1500th anniversary of the creation of the Armenian alphabet and the 400th anniversary of the first Armenian printed book.[39] Both anniversaries were extraordinarily important to the effort to reaffirm national identity through cultural awareness. Zarian was not one to miss such celebrations. On October 26, 1913, during a tribute to both anniversaries at the Petit Champs Theater, he recited excerpts from Siamanto's recent poem, *Surb Mesrop* (*Saint Mesrop*).[40] The poem is known for its extraordinary sonority and dynamism, especially "when it comes to us from a more or less sensitive soul or a mouth with some skill to recite," Hakob Oshakan (Hagop Oshagan) wrote

---

[35] Zarian, *Erker,* p. 542.

[36] "Mtki haverzhakan chamborde" [The Eternal Traveler of the Mind], interview with Armen Zarian, *Grakan tert,* Feb. 8, 1991, p. 1.

[37] Beledian, "Haykakan apagayapashtutiun," p. 387.

[38] On *Mehyan,* see Matiossian, *Kostan Zariani shurj,* pp. 65-82.

[39] By that time, scholarly research had established that Mesrop Mashtots had created the Armenian alphabet in A.D. 413 and that Hakop Meghapart had printed the first Armenian book in 1513. These dates were later modified.

[40] Sharurian, *Misak Metsarentse,* p. 216.

years later. Zarian had both the soul and the skill:

> I remember the day, in the celebration of the 1913 jubilee, how the crowd which flooded the church of Holy Trinity in Pera, whom all remarks and reproaches from the authorities and the clergy had been unable to silence, suddenly came to its senses when Kostan Zarian recited "Saint Mesrop." And both those who understood and those who did not paid attention.[41]

In the spring of 1913, Varoujan and Siruni decided to revive the project of the journal *Asteghatun* by publishing a yearbook, *Navasard* (name of the first month and New Year's Day according to the Armenian pre-Christian), "which we wanted to become the core of a new literary movement."[42] The first and only issue of the well-crafted yearbook appeared in November. Both Oshakan and Zarian contributed to it, but the yearbook was not enough to bring about the intended literary rejuvenation. A monthly journal was needed to become the focal point of such a movement. Zarian recalled in the mid-1950s:

> 1910 to 1914 were years of great enthusiasm. There was a thing that does not exist today: a fire of faith and self-confidence, a will to reach the future, a desire to forge and be forged through creation, that are the preconditions which allow for the existence of any true literary movement. . . . To make literature is one thing; a literary movement, that irresistible explosion of collective sub-consciousness, is another.[43]

According to Oshakan, one day Zarian summoned him, Daniel Varoujan, Barseghian, and Aharon, and introduced them to his idea for a literary monthly.[44] The exact date is unclear, but it must

---

[41] Hakob Oshakan, *Hamapatker arevmtahay grakanutian* [Panorama of Western Armenian Literature], vol. 8 (Antelias: Catholicosate of Cilicia, 1980), p. 220. See also *Vkayutiun me* [A Testimony] (Aleppo: Nayiri, 1946), pp. 19-21.

[42] Sharurian, *Misak Metsarentse*, p. 217.

[43] Polatian, *Zroyts*, pp. 236-37.

[44] Retold by P[oghos] S[napian], "Irents karotnerun karotov" [With the Longing of Their Longings], *Mehyan* (Aleppo, 1996, facsimile repr.), p. iii. Oshakan states that the meeting was held at a café, but Zarian mentions "a German beerhouse on the bridge of Pera . . . , which became our meeting point." Zarian, "Teghi," p. 106; Zarian, *Navatomar*, p. 587.

have been some time in late 1913. *Mehyan* (Pagan Temple) was born, and with it the group known as the "Mehenakanner" (Mehyanists). No explanation regarding the name was given at the time, but "paganism," a sort of revival of supposedly "pure" Armenian values with ancient roots, attracted much attention among the intellectuals. *Mehyan* seems an echo of *Bagin* (Pagan Altar), the name of the *Azatamart* literary supplement.[45]

The journal would be the place where the greatest Armenian literary minds, such as Varoujan, Oshakan, and Zarian, could come together. The significance of this enterprise for Armenian literature and culture cannot be overemphasized, especially with the advantage of hindsight, nine decades after the genocide. As Nichanian has remarked, "both *Mehyan* and *Navasard* form the core of the encounter and draw the contour of a constellation. This encounter and this constellation mark one of the most important moments in the brief history of Western Armenian literature."[46] Yet, although Western Armenian literature had first-rate writers (Varoujan, Siamanto, Zardarian, Yesayan, Tekeyan, Grigor Zohrap), there was also a sense of fatigue. Oshakan explained this problem quite plainly in the 1930s: "Six years of freedom of the press had developed our lexical senses. The writers, long deprived of youth and creative sap, were busy with words and politics, and had no time for renew themselves. A palpable boredom was the consequence: writers were against themselves and readers, against everyone. To combat that boredom, *Mehyan* had encouraged the transposition of some new trends and ideas, "a drop of madness," and many Western modes into Armenian literature. Its editors were not newcomers and had a significant advantage over their predecessors in the creative arts. When making demands, they were aware that so far the older generation had failed to meet new standards. Rejection, demolition, the emergence of new writers, resistance to the current aesthetics, a few big words (necessary to all credos)—these were the few elements that gave the movement momentum."[47]

---

[45] Beledian writes that "this journal essentially springs out from the groups around *Azatamart*." Krikor Beledian, *Krake shrjanake Daniel Varuzhani shurj* [The Circle of Fire around Daniel Varoujan] (Antelias: Catholicosate of Cilicia, 1988), p. 19.

[46] Nichanian, *Entre l'art et le témoignage*, p. 31. For a thorough analysis of the journal, see pp. 29-56, 309-36, See also Beledian, *Krake shrjanake*, pp. 21-28.

[47] Hakob Oshakan, *Mayrineru shukin tak* [Under the Shadows of the Cedars]

In his more convoluted style, Zarian's own explanation of the movement is equally enlightening:

> The thinking Armenian went back and forth, stopped at a thousand questions, and reconciled himself to a thousand different realities.
>
> The Armenian mind was exiled.
>
> People, the so-called well-educated public, required national ideals in their poetry. Khorenatsi's lament, in new guise, let's say, in new clothes, wandered in front of the editorial offices and received applause from Galata's merchants. Political parties approached literature with unease. Poetry became another form of advertisement and poster, and poets became sandwich men, those people who, like asses, carry signs advertising shops in the big cities.
>
> A select few were oscillating between false realities and cheap idealism. Anarchy reigned. They were jumping barefoot over pieces of coal burned by emotion and inspiration. . . .
>
> . . . . [I]n that dishonorable period, *Mehyan* was preaching heroism, pride, and solitude. *Mehyan* was also preaching madness and freedom. "Madness, freedom?" The Armenian bulls became enraged and the bourgeois screamed.[48]

Polemical overtones and rejection of the past, so common to new literary movements, sufficed to inspire both critical backlash and sympathetic support. Though slightly exaggerated, Zarian's opening remarks for his article in the last issue of *Mehyan* carried a ring of truth when he responded to his critics: "I do not think that any literary gazette has encountered so much enmity, so much misunderstanding, or such a superficial and ignorant environment in the history of Armenian literature, as our small *Mehyan*."[49] Later, Siruni in his comments to Stepan Kurtikian reflected on the early days of *Mehyan*, recalling that "nonconformism with current literary life and a struggle for recognition caused the writers around *Mehyan* and *Navasard* to create their own schools of thought, regardless of previous creative positions and accepted guide-

---

(Beirut: Altapress, 1983), pp. 94-95.

[48] Zarian, *Erker,* pp. 134-35.

[49] Kostan Zarian, "Asbarez!" [Arena], *Mehyan*, July 1914, p. 97; Zarian, *Navatomar*, p. 109.

lines."[50]

Zarian was clearly the driving force behind the Mehyan movement. During the founding meeting, in response to a question from
Oshakan about funding for the publication, Zarian reportedly
pulled a purse from his pocket and laid the Ottoman liras on the
table.[51] In a diary entry dated May 1954, Zarian remarked bitterly that "the Armenians ... rejected *Mehyan*, which I had created on
my own (with my ideas and my money), and which was the last
true movement in Turkish Armenian literature."[52] Yuri Khachatryan has commented that "only the son of the oil-field owner, a
wealthy Russian, had financial resources among the people of
the editorial board."[53] This view is untenable, however, for Zarian
no longer had ties with his family and was not likely to count on
any income from them.[54] Zarian, Barseghian, and Oshakan, who
used his family name, Kufedjian, until 1920 or 1921, were together
responsible for the publication. Zarian appears on the title page
as "director and editor-in-chief," and Barseghian and Kufedjian,
as "editors." The *Mehyan* letterhead reads: "Director-Editor, Kostan Zarian; General Secretary, Gegham Barseghian."[55] Barseghian
carried out editorial tasks and wrote the unsigned sections "Notes"
and "Our Forum." Zarian recalled: "He made all the corrections in
Mehyan and with such love! He argued about the articles, ran to
the print shop, created new sources of enthusiasm."[56] "Follies'
History," also unsigned, bears Oshakan's unequivocal seal. As the
editor-in-chief, the ultimate responsibility for published materials

---

[50] Quoted by Danielyan, *Hetanosakan grakan sharzhman patmutyunits*, p. 140.

[51] Snapian, "Irents karotnerun," p. iv.

[52] Zarian, "Navatomar," p. 22.

[53] Yuri Khachatryan, "Menavor navordi erku 'Navatomare'" [The Two "Log-
books of the Lonely Seafarer], *Nork* 2 (1994): 8.

[54] On January 21, 1914, Nazariants wrote to Eremian: "A Mrs. Shahnazar recently
got a letter from Evgine who informed her that her and Mr. and Mrs. Kostan Zarian's
ties were severed; they have fallen apart; Rachel and Kostan live with a newly-born
baby in a separate house in Arnavoud-koy, Kostan only gets 2 (two...!) pounds from
the Hintlian School, and Rachel has resumed teaching. *Mehyan* is published with the
money earned by Rachel." See Beledian, "Haykakan apagayapashtutiun," p. 395. The
last statement is a second-hand reference which needs further confirmation. Mrs.
Shahnazar and Evgine were probably Zarian's mother-in-law and sister-in-law.

[55] See Barseghian to Zarian, letter, Jan. 1, 1914, in Vartan Matiossian, "Gegham
Barseghiani namaknere Kostan Zarianin" [Gegham Barseghian's Letters to Kostan
Zarian], *Horizon grakan havelvats* (June 1997): 10.

[56] Zarian, *Erker*, p. 35.

must have been reserved for Zarian.

Mehyan launched its inaugural issue in January 1914 with a manifesto titled "Our Credo" and signed by the five founders (see excerpts in Appendix II). The text of the manifesto had been published previously in the December 1/14, 1913 issue of the daily *Azatamart*. It is not clear how this credo came into being, nor is the author confirmed. Zarian claimed in 1955 that he "wrote it mostly . . . in French. Varoujan completed it before translating it into Armenian."[57] In a short recollection written in the 1960s, however, he offered a slightly different version: "My Armenian was not strong enough for me to be able to write the program of *Mehyan* in the mother tongue, so I wrote it in French and Varoujan translated it into Western Armenian."[58] According to Oshakan, "after designing the program of the journal, it was proposed that in the next session everybody would briefly express his ideas, and so it was done, and the composite 'Credo' was written."[59] Krikor Beledian has noticed hints of stylistic futurism in the composition, "which is common of Zarian." Underscoring the "collective" nature of the manifesto, Beledian considers it the product of an Oshakan-Zarian-Varoujan trinity.[60] In 1991, Armen Zarian, stated that "Kostan Zarian himself founded and directed the journal *Mehyan*. He wrote the Credo of the journal, and the others signed it."[61] This is second-hand information, but if accurate, it would exclude the contributions Zarian's companions appear to have made to the theoretical issues underscored by the credo. Nevertheless, the real story concerning the formulation of the credo seems to be a synthesis of both accounts by Zarian and Oshakan: the five writers integrated their thoughts, Zarian gave them their final form in French, and Varoujan rendered them into Armenian. The translation was not mechanical, however; it developed and, as Zarian put it, was "completed" in the translator's creative mind. The

---

[57] Polatian, *Zroyts,* p. 89.

[58] Zarian, "Teghi," p. 106; Kurtikian, *Artasahmani,* p. 62. In his reprint, Yuri Khachatryan has used the typed original of the text, where Zarian had previously written: "and the poet Varoujan and others translated it into Constantinopolitan Armenian." Zarian, *Navatomar,* p. 589.

[59] "Verstin havelvats" [Again an Addenda], *Bagin* 2 (1996): 96.

[60] Krikor Beledian, *Mart* [Battle] (Antelias: Catholicosate of Cilicia, 1997), p. 422.

[61] "Mtki haverzhakan chamborde," p. 2.

language, especially the rhetorical phraseology, has many features distinctive to Varoujan's discourse, but the style, the ideological texture, the apocalyptic imagery, and the analogies—all have traits later displayed in Zarian's *The Traveler and His Road.*

The four points in the manifesto and their respective explanations display certain elements that can be linked with each of the founding members of *Mehyan*. They are: Barseghian, "worship and expression of the Armenian Soul"; Zarian, "originality and individuality of form"; Varoujan, "development of the Armenian language by a revitalizing graft"; and Oshakan, "keeping literature far from politics and journalism."[62] This did not mean that each had exclusive authorship over his section, but the initial formulation was likely to have been his work. Notwithstanding this, if it is accepted that Zarian was the main driving force, he could have likely found some inspiration in European literature for the manifesto, a fact that has not been explored by literary critics. The most natural candidate would be Belgian literature. The groundbreaking manifesto of the journal *La Jeune Belgique* (1881) had announced the intention of creating a literature that was not owing to foreign literatures and turned into a place far from any political influence. The devise of the movement was "Soyons nous" (To Be Ourselves). For the next sixteen years, until its demise in 1897, *La Jeune Belgique* became one of the leading literary journals in the country. As a scholar has observed, "their doctrine is art for the sake of art, art outside history, further away from any utilitarian aim."[63] Of course, the journal had disappeared long before Zarian's arrival to Belgium, but its inspiration as an intellectual source

---

[62] See Gegham Barseghian, "Bazhakachar" [Toast], *Mehyan* (March 1914): 33-34; Kostan Zarian, "Noragoyn dzktumnere," p. 3; Daniel Varuzhan, "Hay lezvi khndire" [The Issue of the Armenian Language], *Azatamart grakan havelvats* (May 24/June 4): 705-10, reprinted in *Erkeri liakatar zhoghovatsu* [Complete Collected Works], vol. 3 (Erevan: Armenian Academy of Sciences, 1987), pp. 121-30, and partially translated into French in Marc Nichanian, *Ages et usages de la langue arménienne* (Paris: Entente, 1988), pp. 407-10. Oshakan's disdain for journalism is well known; he would admonish his students: "Don't be *ghazetajis* [journalists]; journalism killed the literature of Ruben Zardarian, Gegham Barseghian, and other talented men." Mushegh Ishkhan, *Im usutsichners* [My Teachers] (Beirut: Hamazkayin Press, 1984), p. 32.

[63] Albert Heumann, *Le Mouvement litteraire Belge d'expression francaise depuis 1880* (Paris: Mercure de France, 1913), p. 69; Jeanine Paque, *Le symbolisme belge* (Brussels: Editions Labor, 1989), p. 15.

cannot be fully dismissed, especially if we bear in mind that Verhaeren had been one of its old contributors.

It is not by chance that the manifesto had Varoujan and Zarian as its first signers, in that order, for both had a predominant role in its composition. Further, Varoujan's name gave additional weight to the movement, although some time later the great poet left *Mehyan*.[64] The cause of his withdrawal from the project was never fully explained. In the May issue of *Mehyan*, Zarian wrote a polemical essay, titled "Paganism?" perhaps directed against Varoujan, who took it as such. Later, Oshakan wrote of Varoujan:

> His departure was not the result of artistic conflict, but of a superfluous oversensitivity towards K. Zarian's somewhat inflated pretensions, which Gegham Barseghian and I were able to bear because they gave vivacity and freshness to the journal. The interest of our literature was the most important things for us. We were ready to tolerate even laughable pretensions for the sake of that interest; to be talented was enough, and K. Zarian had talent.[65]

Oshakan attributed the problems to personal conflicts but did not delve into the details of the situation.

The tension between Zarian and Varoujan must be placed in the context of the discussions regarding *gavari grakanutiun* (provincial literature), which was considered the paradigm of authentic Armenian literature. In 1893, novelist Arpiar Arpiarian observed:

> The provincial writer does not know the art of bringing those

---

[64] Varoujan did not contribute to the March issue. The journal published the main excerpts of a call for contributors to the second volume of *Navasard*. See "Nisher" [Notes], *Mehyan* (March 1914): 47. Merujan Parsamian (pseudonym Tiran Astvatsatur) wrote in a pamphlet attacking *Mehyan* and feigning to report comments from the group: "Down with Varoujan, who rejected *Mehyan*." Tiran Astvatsatur, "Grakan katakerkutiune: Aytselutiun me *Mehyanin*" [The Literary Comedy: A Visit to *Mehyan*], *Shant*, April 1/14, p. 117. Half a century later, Zarian mentioned a visit paid to Varoujan's home in May 1914, which seems to show they maintained cordial relations even after the split. See Levon Hakhverdyan, "Mi ereko Kostan Zariani het" [An Evening with Kostan Zarian], *Hayreniki dzayn*, Feb. 19, 1967, p. 5.

[65] Hakob Oshakan, *Hamapatker arevmdahay grakanutian* [Panorama of Western Armenian Literature] vol. 6 (Beirut: Hamazkayin, 1968), p. 187. According to Siruni, "after a serious quarrel he had with his companions, he no longer wanted to stay in *Mehyan*. It had been tough for him to accept lessons about writing." Quoted in Danielyan, *Hetanosakan grakan sharzhman patmutyunits*, p. 140.

materials together and erecting a large and beautiful literary edifice. In order to learn that art, it is necessary to read, study the philosophical, poetic, novelistic, historical, and scholarly writings of the Europeans. The mind must become nourished through them, and from them one must learn the secrets of investigating what one sees in his environment and examine their life. Those who carry out that investigation can write great works.[66]

In his 1911 article on the development of the Armenian language in the context of Western Armenian literature, Varoujan wondered:

But where was the *gavar* [province], where the truth lives in the soul of the people? Where was the *gavar* with its plethora of powerful, colorful, realistic troubadours? The language, which was growing up far from its lap, obviously could not express those overarching ideals, those epic sublime images, which belong to the people and to the land. That language did not actually have the universal palpitation that comes from the heart of a people.[67]

The debate was between the "authentic" (*tohmik*) in literature and "foreign" (*otar*) influences. Zarian recalled:

I often discussed European literary currents with Varoujan, along with the main trends of Armenian literature and the problems of its form and content. . . . He was against the direct transfer of European literary influences into the Armenian *tohmik* literature. I was concerned with the level of our art and literature. Both of us were concerned with questions of art.[68]

The cause of the split actually lies in such artistic differences. How does one reconcile one's own with the foreign? Although Oshakan and Barseghian, both aesthetically closer to Varoujan than Zarian, tolerated the latter's "somewhat grandiose pretensions,"

---

[66] Quoted by Krikor Beledian, "From Image to Loss: The Writers of Kharpert and Provincial Literature," in *Armenian Tsopk/Kharpert*, ed. Richard G. Hovannisian (Costa Mesa, CA: Mazda Publishers, 2002), p. 259. I have substituted the word "novelistic" for "romantic" in the translation.

[67] Varuzhan, *Erkeri liakatar zhoghovatsu*, p. 122.

[68] Kurtikian, *Artasahmani hay groghneri het*, pp. 62-63.

Oshakan scorned art and its laws.[69]

Zarian expressed his views on art in a series of essays published in *Mehyan* under the general title of "For the Sake of Art" along with articles[70] and poetry.[71] He asserted that he wrote his articles with the help of dictionaries,[72] but Oshakan claimed, "Gegham Barseghian, a silent martyr to literature, ground his teeth because of this and continued to translate Zarian's French pages into Armenian."[73]

The final issue of *Mehyan* appeared in July 1914, on the eve of World War I. Of course, nothing in the contents reveals that it was meant to be the final issue. There is even an announcement on the last page about a forthcoming *Mehyan* yearbook alongside the journal.[74] The reasons for its demise are unknown. It may have been the result of infighting over questions of artistic integrity and foreign influence. Souren Danielyan writes the following about Aharon, the fifth member of the group:

> He contributed to the seven issues of the journal, but he chose to side with D. Varoujan in the sharp conflict between the "pagan" aesthetics and Mehyanism, leaving *Mehyan* immediately after Varoujan. The conflict between Siruni, Varoujan, and Aharon, and K. Zarian and the other editors took place in April-May 1914. . . . It was losing the interest of its readers after the loss of its

---

[69] On this subject, see Beledian, *Mart*, p. 409-502.

[70] See "Steghtsagortsutiun, khentutiun, diutsaznutiun" [Creativity, Madness, Heroism], *Mehyan* (Jan. 1914); "Hayun Hisuse" [The Jesus of the Armenian], *Mehyan* (Feb. 1914); "Tatrone (hamadrutiun)" [The Theater (Synthesis)], *Mehyan* (April 1914); "Hetanosutiun" [Paganism], *Mehyan* (May 1914); "Hayrenikin sirte" [The Heart of the Fatherland], *Mehyan* (March 1914); "Asparez" [Arena], *Mehyan* (July 1914), all reprinted in Zarian, *Navatomar*, pp. 79-113. For a French translation of these articles, except for the last one, see Nichanian, *Entre l'art et le témoignage*, pp. 383-94, 400-11.

[71] Kostan Zarian, "Meknumner, tsurt gishere" [Departures, the Cold Night], *Mehyan* (Feb. 1914); "Astgheru kertvatse (hatvats)" [The Poem of the Stars (Fragment)], *Mehyan* (June 1914).

[72] Zarian, "Teghi," p. 106; Zarian, *Navatomar*, p. 589.

[73] Hakob Oshakan, *Hamapatker arevmtahay grakanutian*, vol. 10 (Antelias: Catholicosate of Cilicia, 1982), p. 418. According to a recent claim, "it is known that they were translated from French by Gegham Barseghian and Hakob Kufedjian." See Ruzan Aristakesian, "Kostan Zariani *Mehyan* handese," *Garun* 7 (1999): 24. No source, however, including Oshakan, substantiates this statement.

[74] *Mehyan* (July 1914): 112.

well-known authors.[75]

Varoujan was then the only "well-known author." Siruni was an outsider to the journal, and Aharon did not appear in the third and sixth issues. The full frontal clash between Siruni, Varoujan, and Aharon, on one side, and Zarian, Barseghian, and Oshakan, on the other, perhaps did occur. However, Aharon, who supposedly left *Mehyan* immediately after Varoujan, nevertheless continued to contribute up to the final issue.

The demise of *Mehyan* was also a direct result of the general situation in Constantinople. Cultural activities came almost to a complete halt. Between July and November 1914, as Turkey prepared to enter the world war, the state machinery tightened the noose around the Armenian population through various forms of persecution that eventually would take on genocidal proportions.

Before Bardzravank

Zarian fled Constantinople with his family shortly before Turkey entered the war and escaped the grim fate that befell the Armenian intelligentsia in the city. After spending a year in Bulgaria, the family moved to Rome and then to Florence. After the world war, during the fall of 1919, Zarian traveled to the Caucasus as a special correspondent for several Italian newspapers, including *Il Nuovo Giornale* and *Il Secolo* of Florence and *Il Messagero* of Rome. He briefly passed through Constantinople in August and in November, where he wrote his article, "A Menacing Bairam," presenting his first impressions of the postwar city and the situation in Turkey:

> In Constantinople, city of exaggeration, today is the feast of Bairam. Since dawn, cannons have sounded to announce the news of such a major event to the Muslim world. The flag of the Prophet is displayed. The Selamlik has made room for the presence of the few faithful and, in the meantime, for the curiosity of the Allied officers. Groups broken off from the crowd, accompanied by flutes, march through the streets to inspire celebration. While in Pera, the crowd of jobless, cynical and indifferent Levantines feign luxury with fake diamonds waved before the amazed eyes of

---

[75] Danielyan, *Hetanosakan grakan sharzhman patmutyunits*, p. 124.

the winners of yesteryear, the monotonous and sad Istanbul, empty
as a gigantic skull, does not sound as happy as usual and does not
glorify Allah with barbarous music, but instead with pain and
silence, perhaps filled with a fear of tomorrow. Hundreds of thousands were sacrificed with an almighty gesture, and the voice that
sings the chapters of the Quran is now weak and suspicious.[76]

In 1920, after he returned to Italy, Zarian began to contribute to
the literary journal *Vostan*, which had been revived by its founder
and former editor, Mikayel Shamdanjian, himself a survivor.
Zarian's reputation as a poet had grown after publishing *Three
Songs* in Italian translation in 1916. The poem had been widely
praised by the Italian press and had gone through several editions.[77]
Now, in 1920, he attempted to publish the Armenian original in
Constantinople.[78] He and Oshakan also renewed their ties during
this period. No letter written by Oshakan between 1918 and 1922
seems to have survived with the exception of two addressed to
Zarian. They hint at the nature of their relationship. In the first,
dated April 1, 1920, Oshakan wrote:

> I received both your letters. I did not reply because I wanted to
> wait until I could provide the information you had requested re-
> garding your book. I could not have good news for you and was
> forced to write.
>
> The man has stopped the presses, claiming that there is no
> *paper*. Despite Sargisian's statement, work remains at a standstill,
> with just two sections typed. I cannot guarantee that he will re-
> main faithful to his promise.[79]

---

[76] K. Zarian, "Un 'Bairam' minaccioso," *Il Nuovo Giornale*, Sept. 21, 1919.

[77] For the history of this book, see Matiossian, *Kostan Zariani shurj*, pp. 132-72,
and "Kostan Zarian ev Ottorino Respigui" [Kostan Zarian and Ottorino Respighi],
Haraj mitk ev arvest (April 1998): 2-3. See also Yuri Khachatryan, "Ottorino
Respiguin ev Kostan Zariane" [Ottorino Respighi and Kostan Zarian], *Nork* 4 (1997):
102-12.

[78] An editorial note in *Vostan* stated: "As we have previously stated, the manuscripts of this work have already been handed to the Sanjakjian print shop, and we
expect that the volume published will be of the same quality as the Italian edition."
Vostan, March 16, 1920, p. 401.

[79] Vartan Matiossian, "Hakob Oshakanen erku namak Kostan Zarianin" [Two
Letters from Hakob Oshakan to Kostan Zarian], *Hask hayagitakan taregirk* 7-8
(1995-96): 273 (italics in original).

In his second letter, probably written in late May, Oshakan stated that the printing of *Three Songs* had ended in a failure, stopped "for the only reason that you had gone down into the well on the rope of an embezzler."[80] The Armenian text was not published until 1931, and then only in Vienna. Notwithstanding this setback, Zarian continued to publish poetry in *Vostan* in addition to three installments (March, May, and June, 1920) of an unfinished travelogue titled "Towards Ararat," which was intended to depict his trip to the Caucasus.

Despite the apparent cultural revival in Constantinople, the effects of the violent genocidal blow against the Armenian intellectuals in the Ottoman Empire were all too obvious. There was now stagnation, rather similar to the pre-*Mehyan* period, but with one critical difference: in the postwar period, there was no hope for improvement, no possibility of a radical change. Oshakan's letters reflected this despair. In April 1920, he wrote: "There is an eternal grayness here. Letter and literature are more abandoned than ever. People go after politics and one slowly drifts away from literature for want of literati." He was even more somber in May: "If you study Constantinople," he stated, "you will observe the death of the field of literature."[81]

With such grim prospects, it is not clear why Zarian returned to the Turkish capital with his family in November 1921; perhaps his long-standing desire to launch a new Armenian literary movement compelled him to go back. They settled in Scutari, and Zarian worked as a teacher of French literature at the Berberian (Perperian) School in Scutari and at the Kedronakan (Getronagan/Central) School in Constantinople.

Siruni expressed hope that the Armenian intelligentsia in Constantinople could develop a stronger sense of community and that the arrival, in the fall of 1921, of Hovhannes Tumanian, the famous Eastern Armenian poet, in the Turkish capital would miraculously improve the cultural environment. Tumanian visited Constantinople in his official capacity as president of the Committee to Aid Armenia (Hayastani Ognutian Komite, HOK), and on November 26, 1921, he organized a reception in honor of the Armenian literati. During the gathering, the famed poet proposed establishing

---

[80] Ibid., p. 274.
[81] Ibid., pp. 274-75.

a cultural organization, the House of Armenian Arts (Hay Arvesti Tun). Tumanian was president of a similar organization founded earlier that year in Tiflis.[82] Zarian became one of the founding members of the House, and the organization seemed to have a positive influence on the Armenian community in Constantinople. The actor Mkrtich Djanan wrote in 1923: "It is indisputable that the House of Armenian Arts brought many of the people interested in Armenian art together to exchange ideas and get acquainted."[83] The group established a committee of twelve, including Zarian as deputy chairman, to draft the by-laws of the House, which were approved by December 11, 1921. After a subsequent meeting on December 18, they officially proclaimed the existence of the House. It had fifty active members in Constantinople and forty corresponding members from abroad.[84] The "miracle" expected by Siruni had come to pass. A quarter of a century later, Leon Sur-melian, himself a student at the time, wrote: "I must say that in spite of the differences in their political or social views the Armenian writers of Constantinople were able to meet on a com-mon literary ground, with mutual respect and even affection. I observed that what counted was their respective stature as men of letters. . . . And looking back over that wonderful period of my own intellectual growth, I must say we were civilized."[85]

Zarian remained active in the House, although in the end he appeared dissatisfied with the quality of its activities. He served as the chairman of the Literary Committee, the general manager of the Artistic Studio Committee, and a member of the Editorial Com-mittee.[86] The poet Vahan Tekeyan served as chairman of the

---

[82] *Tumanyane zhamanakakitsneri husherum* [Tumanian in the Memoirs of the Contemporaries] (Erevan: Armenian Academy of Sciences, 1969), pp. 816-18. Zarian has a caustic passage about that reception. Tumanian, he wrote, "came and gathered the so-called intelligentsia, gave speeches, made promises, 'It will be this, it will be that.' Then a few people among us went to his room; he insulted this and that person, telling colorful jokes until dawn. . . . We realized that he was the hero; he had understood and figured out everything long before this meeting, yet no one listened." Zarian, *Erker*, p. 37.

[83] *Tumanyane zhamanakakitsneri husherum*, p. 821.

[84] "Hay Arvesti Tun" [House of Armenian Arts], *Amenun taretsoytse* [Everyone's Almanac] (Constantinople), 1923, p. 266.

[85] Leon Zaven Surmelian, "With Vahan Tekeyan in Constantinople," *Armenian Mirror-Spectator*, Feb. 9, 1946, p. 3.

[86] "Hay Arvesti Tune hay zhoghovurdin" [The House of Armenian Arts for the

Central Council. The Artistic Studio, perhaps the most important activity of the House, involved a comprehensive program of studies with five sections: History of Literature, History of Armenian Literature, History of Music, History of Painting, and History of Theater. Zarian and Oshakan headed the History of Theater group; Zarian and the actor Arshavir (Asho) Shahkhatuni were in charge of dramatic recitation and performance. The classes ran from March 27 through May 30, 1922.[87] Zarian also spoke at some of the public activities organized by the House, including the 300th anniversary of Molière's birth[88] and a reception honoring Charles Diehl, the famed specialist of Byzantine Art.[89]

All this notwithstanding, a disappointed Zarian pointed out that "here, too, everything is panoramic, everything is a performance and an illusion. We are deprived of substance. There have been useless attempts at finding a point of unity. We content ourselves with tea receptions, meetings, and theatrical performances."[90] It is understandable that such activities could not sufficiently address the effects of the disruptive violence of the genocide. A sense of cultural crisis had prompted the Western Armenian intellectuals to launch a literary movement in 1914, and after the destruction and the dispersion, another literary movement seemed to be a logical starting point for the rebuilding process. "Constantinople is more of a desert than ever," Oshakan wrote to Zarian in 1920;[91] they had the unenviable responsibility to revive Armenian culture in that "desert."

The time may have seemed ripe for a new literary journal. According to Djanan, during the reception hosted by Tumanian in November 1921, the philosopher and educator Shahan Perperian (Berberian) announced that this group would publish a literary journal, *Bardzravank*, to "elevate Armenian art and artists," and

---

Armenian People], *Chakatamart [Jagadamard]*, Feb. 10, 1922, p. 2.

[87] See the details in Vaché Ghazarian, "Polso Hay Arvesti Tune" [The House of Armenian Arts of Constantinople], *Shirak* 11 (1982): 49.

[88] "Hay Arvesti Tan handese Molieri masin" [The Program of the House of Armenian Arts about Molière], *Chakatamart*, Jan. 31, 1922, p. 2.

[89] "Hay arveste ev Prof. Sharl Dil" [Armenian Arts and Prof. Charles Diehl], *Chakatamart*, April 27, 1922, pp. 1, 4.

[90] Zarian, *Erker,* p. 37.

[91] Matiossian, "Hakob Oshakanen," p. 275.

give further support to the idea of the House of Armenian Art.[92] Perperian, Gegham Gavafian (Kegham Kavafian), a scientist, Zarian, Oshakan, and Tekeyan launched *Bardzravank* in January 1922. The shortlived monthly journal collapsed in June after publishing five issues. Its birth and history have not been satisfactorily explored, but the House of the Armenian Art appears to have been the binding force. Zarian did not dominate *Bardzravank* as he had dominated *Mehyan*, and the five founders served on the editorial board as equals. *Bardzravank* was not *Mehyan*, however, and 1922 was not 1914. Time and age had played a role, together with the gigantic break in the cultural fabric. It was a new attempt, but it lacked the fresh "madness" of the prewar days. The journal did not carry a "credo," but it did include a one-page prefatory note titled "Propositions," with obvious influences from *Mehyan* but far more measured (see Appendix III).

In *The Traveler and His Road*, written from a diary kept between 1922 and 1924, Zarian states:

Today we are trying once again. We collect the still-smoldering coals of the Armenian spirit from beneath the ashes. Like poor village women, we are searching for squalid ears of corn in an already harvested field.

Bardzravank is an essay on self-centeredness. It is an observation post in a burning forest. We watch.

The contents of the journal show that it was intended primarily as a watch post, a reference for high culture. Zarian and Oshakan, the most prolific in the editorial quintet, showed a style more restrained, although they kept their high literary standards and critical stance. The program was more a declaration of aesthetical principles than a call for decisive change. Zarian published some poetry, later included in his 1922 volume *The Crown of Days*,[93] as well as various jottings from his notebooks,[94] a review on paint-

---

[92] *Tumanyane*, p. 823.

[93] Kostan Zarian, "Asatsvats kakhakan bardzratsoghi hamar" [Saying for the One Climbing the Gallows]; "Ays aravot" [This Morning]; "Zhameri kayle [The Passing of the Hours], *Bardzravank* (Jan. 1922): 2-4; Kostan Zarian, *Oreri psake* [The Crown of Days] (Beirut: Bem Editions, 1971), pp. 19, 22, 152-54.

[94] Kostan Zarian, "Zhameri imaste" [The Meaning of the Hours], *Bardzravank* (March 1922): 45-46; "Mtatsumner" [Musings], *Bardzravank* (May 1922): 115, re-

ing,[95] and especially articles on theater, his old interest from his days in Belgium and with *Mehyan*.[96] Nevertheless, as Zarian wrote to Arshak Chopanian (Arshag Chobanian) in April 1922, *Bardzravank* "only [triggered] animal enmity from the generally stupid."[97] A few months after his arrival, Zarian felt completely disillusioned, as the same letter shows:

> In the present condition, when most of the best among us are dead and the rest are far from Constantinople, we are forced to live in an unbearable, terrible environment. To come from abroad and land in this place where the most elementary things have to be explained at length, where customs accepted elsewhere 20 or 30 years ago seem to be strange things fallen from the moon, where the so-called literati and artists are as ignorant as cucumbers, what would you expect? I write all this to you, because I remember you advised me to stay in Paris or abroad and start building the literary movement from there. You were right.[98]

Unlike 1914, when Armenians held hopes for a literary rebirth and a brighter future, in 1922 that faith had dissipated and mediocrity had taken hold. Zarian says as much in *The Traveler and His Road*:

> Pools of water have appeared under the rubble from the extinguished fire and frogs have come forth. After the deaths of the best writers, petty scribblers are unashamedly howling from Istanbul to Pera. The smell of corpses is still coming out. From cheap cafés, drunkards are vomiting up a world with no future. . . . Everything is dying.[99]

---

printed in *Navatomar*, pp. 126-28, 132.

[95] Kostan Zarian, "Nkarchutiun" [Painting], *Bardzravank* (Jan. 1922): 38-39, on an exhibition by painters from Armenia, and *Navatomar*, pp. 123-25.

[96] Kostan Zarian, "Tatron" [Theater], *Bardzravank* (Jan. 1922): 36-37, on Constantinopolitan Armenian theater; "Hay tatron" [Armenian Theater], *Bardzravank* (Feb. 1922): 66-67, on Oshakan's "Nor psak" [New Wedding]; and "Hay tatron," *Bardzravank* (May 1922): 135-36, on a performance of Oscar Wilde's "Salomé." See Zarian, *Navatomar*, pp. 120-22, 129-31, 133-36.

[97] Unpublished letter, April 20, 1922. Museum of Literature and Art, Erevan, Arshak Chopanian file, section I, no. 2131.

[98] Ibid. See also Matiossian, "A Traveler," p. 29.

[99] Zarian, *Erker*, p. 36.

The destruction of Armenian communities and culture had left an irreparable void; little was left to change. In fact, if any attempt had to be made at reconstruction, it would be through the field of literature and the arts. Zarian wrote: "A terrible question has been posed to the modern intellectual generation: should we create, revealing a personality suffused with nationalistic values, or die, adding spiritual annihilation to the physical annihilation of our nation?"[100] This effort, if made, could best be carried out, Zarian believed, in the highly visible field of drama.

It is worth noting that the repertory of Armenian theatrical groups was mostly composed of second-rate European plays. Included among them were a few works by Levon Shant and Shirvanzade, but these plays were not highly regarded by some. Oshakan published a lengthy and damning study of Shirvanzade in *Bardzravank*.[101] Both Oshakan and Zarian had shown a special interest in drama in the pages of *Mehyan* but only as theoreticians and critics. Both also worked on the subject through the House of Armenian Art and experimented as playwrights.

In February 1922, Oshakan's play, *Nor psak* (New Wedding), was performed twice by the Armenian Dramatic Society. The first performance met with public approval, but the critics, with the exceptions of Tekeyan and Gurgen Mekhitarian, brutally attacked the play. Perhaps as a result of such criticism, during the second performance a week later, the hall was nearly empty.[102] Oshakan later attempted to reconcile the novelty of this play with the general atmosphere of the Armenian theater at that time[103] and published an excerpt in the second issue of *Bardzravank*.[104] In an open letter, Zarian indicated that he had clearly perceived the unusual characteristics of the play:

> I will make no attempt at analysis. There are some technical faults in your play, lack of psychological definition in certain characters, and, if we look for them, some other defects, but these are nothing

---

[100] Zarian, "Hay tatron," p. 66.

[101] See Oshakan, *Hamapatker arevmtahay grakanutian*, vol. 10, pp. 258-59, "Shirvanzade, tateragir" [Shirvanzade, Playwright], *Bardzravank* (Jan. 1922): 26-32, (March 1922): 95-100.

[102] See Gevorg Chagerian, "Hakob Oshakan," *Husaber* 4 (1947): 24.

[103] Oshakan, *Hamapatker arevmtahay grakanutian*, vol. 10, pp. 259-62.

[104] Oshakan, "Nor psak," *Bardzravank* (Feb. 1922): 56-58.

in the face of the bold sketching, the beautiful dialogues and the simple, flexible dramatic structure you brought to the starved Armenian scene.

It is beyond question—as the packed audience in the hall felt—that with your *New Wedding* you created the Constantinopolitan Armenian theater, which had not existed until today.[105]

The emphasis on theater is certainly a remarkable feature of the journal. Tekeyan, the poet *par excellence*, published his play "Mayrere" (The Mothers) in *Bardzravank*.[106] Zarian published his three critical essays and the first two installments of the first of the *Three Songs*. The poem clearly has a defined theatrical structure, though readers usually viewed it as no more than poetry.[107] Both Zarian and Oshakan regarded theater as a cultural space for the recreation of a unified community rather than as a mere literary production.[108] According to Zarian, the theater represented "the synthesis of all arts," and as such, "the closest to the people."[109]

While putting into paper his juvenile recollections of those months, Surmelian—who was Zarian's student in his French class in Kedronakan School—remarked that the atmosphere at the school was "one of intense literary and intellectual excitement. Every issue of *Bardzravank,* a new play or criticism by Oshagan, Hovannes Toumanian's visit, the founding of Hai Arvesti Doun—all these were memorable events in our lives."[110]

In addition to his editorial and teaching workload, Zarian also published his first book in Armenian, *Oreri psake* (The Crown of Days), a collection of verses that had been partly published in various periodicals from 1918 to 1922. The book appeared in early April 1922 and received favorable reviews from many authors,

---

[105] Zarian, "Hay tatron," p. 66.

[106] Vahan Tekeyan, "Mayrere," *Bardzravank* (Jan. 1922): 6-11.

[107] Kostan Zarian, "Erek erger aselu hamar vishte erkri u vishte erkinkneri" [Three Songs to Tell the Sadness of the Earth and the Sadness of the Heavens], *Bardzravank* (March 1922): 73-81; (May 1922): 140-49. These excerpts were reprinted as s *Erek erger aselu hamar vishte erkri u vishte erkinkneri: Sirvard, erkri aghchike* [Three Songs to Tell the Sadness of the Earth and the Sadness of the Heavens: Sirvard, the Girl of the Earth] (Constantinople: Arzuman, 1922).

[108] On this subject, see Beledian, *Mart*, pp. 380-96; Nichanian, "Kostan Zarian," pp. 181-88.

[109] Zarian, "Tatron," p. 36.

[110] Surmelian, "With Vahan Tekeyan," p. 3.

including Tekeyan, Perperian, and Oshakan.[111] Perperian wrote that "'The Crown of Days' inspires in me the beautiful hope of a simple pantheistic mystery and of a wide and symphonic new poetry."[112] The book has been considered one of the few lasting Armenian works of the 1920's, although it was not immune to criticism.[113] Surmelian observed that "Zarian, for instance, was not fully recognized yet, and was accused by some of playing with words when he was creating new rhythmic patterns in our language. . . ."[114]

These developments coincided with the rise of Kemalism and the threat of renewed disaster for the Armenians who had returned to Constantinople. Mounting insecurity, as shown by the burning of Smyrna in September 1922, called for an immediate response from the intelligentsia. Those who had survived the genocide were now forced to leave the Ottoman capital for good. As the hysteria began to drive the intellectuals from Constantinople, the Soviet Armenian regime invited many prominent members of the Armenian intelligentsia to the new motherland. Both Oshakan and Zarian received offers to move to Erevan as teachers of Western Armenian Literature and History of European Comparative Literature at the university. Zarian accepted the offer and in October 1922 went with his family to Erevan, where he remained there until June 1924. Constantinople closed its doors behind him.

---

[111] See Vahan Tekeyan, "Oreri psake" [The Crown of Days], *Zhoghovurdi dzayne*, April 30 and May 1, 1922, p. 1 in both; Shahan Perperian, *"Oreri psake* Kostan Zariani" [Kostan Zarian's *The Crown of Days*], *Bardzravank* (May 1922): 132-33.

[112] Perperian, "Oreri psake," p. 133.

[113] See, for instance, Vardan Gevorgian, "Oreri psake," *Shavigh*, May 1 and 8, 1922. *Shavigh* also published several attacks on the book. See the satirical piece by Ervand Otian, "Ignat Agha grakan knnadat (Inch oreru hasank?)" [Ignat Agha, Literary Critic (What Days Have Come upon Us?)], *Shavigh*, April 10, 1922, p. 4; one unsigned piece presents a comparison of a few verses with some Turkish lines: "Tarorinak girk me" [A Strange Book], *Shavigh*, April 3, 1922, p. 3; another unsigned writing announces the preparation, by Oshakan and Tekeyan, of a "key" to the book: "Banali *Oreri psaki*" [Key to the Crown of Days], *Shavigh*, April 10, 1922, p. 2.

[114] Surmelian, "With Vahan Tekeyan," p. 3.

Appendix I

"Les Volontés Folles"
Recueils d'Art
Constantinople, le 191[3][115]
M.

Parmi la Jeunesse Arménienne un mouvement littéraire se dessine en Orient. Voulant combattre la paresse traditionnelle des volontés mourantes, elle s'est groupée a fin par un effort commun et audacieux: imposer l'Art aux esprits refractaires à la Beauté.

Tels les fiers combats qui sont restés gravés éternellement sur les pages resplendissantes de l'Histoire littéraire de vos pays, nous aussi enfin nous voulons créer par nos volontés fortes et folles, des pyramides dont les pierres resteront comme des témoins de nos chiméres diamantisés.

Etoilés d'éspoirs nous jettons un défi rouge aux cadavres effeminés qui empestent les champs dorés de notre Orient. Nous voulons que le Soleil se lève chez nous ardent et jeune et qu'il lance des rayons furieux de sa Force B expression directe de nos volontés.

Sachant d'avance que vos sympathies sont avec nous puisqu'il s'agit de l'Art, nous vous prions de nous honorer de votre collaboration en nous envoyant une de vos oeuvres inédites.

En vous remerciant d'avance, veuillez reçevoir, M.
l'assurance de nos sentiments les plus confraternels.

HRAND NAZARIANTZ   CONSTANT ZARIAN

N.B.CLes œuvres seront imprimées dans leurs langues originales.
Prière d'adresser toutes envois et lettres à

Constant Zarian   Hrand Nazariantz
No. 7, Rue Itir, Tarlapachi   Boite No. 21, Poste Italienne

PÉRA,   GALATA,
CONSTANTINOPLE   CONSTANTINOPLE[116]

---

[115] Initially printed "191," but the "3" inserted with an ink pen.
[116] Kostan Zarian, personal archives, Erevan. First published in Matiossian, "Kostan Zarian Polso mej," p. 2.

Appendix II

MER HANGANAKE
(OUR CREDO)

[Excerpts of the Main Text of *Mehyan*'s Manifesto]

. . . We declare *the need for worshipping and expression of the Armenian Soul*. In fact, the Armenian Soul exists but barely reveals itself. We have to break the seal that has doomed it to silence.

We state: there is no Armenian literature and Armenian art without the Armenian Soul. Every true artist simply expresses the soul of his race. The Armenian Soul, forged from a past filled with somber and glorious images, enlightened by a sadly darkened sun, burned by a life that was ploughed over by the paths of Golgotha, resembles in our day a miracle whose mysteries remain to be revealed. The Armenian Soul is an element of the intellectual universe whose revelation will amaze the thinking humankind. It is the essential duty of every Armenian artist to bring to the light that soul.

We state: external factors—borrowed customs, alien influences, perversion and deformation of feelings—have ruled but have never assimilated it. We perceive the Armenian Soul, we perceive its reflections on the chords of ancient and medieval lutes, and the depth of its sense in our popular legends, brilliant scraps of our national genius. We feel it is hidden in each of us, and always alive through atavistic breath. It will immediately speak after recovering its freedom. We have to free the Armenian Soul from all the strictures and violence of foreign influences, by struggling even against ourselves.

We believe: the Armenian Soul is Light, Force, and Life embodied in the statuesque splendor of the *Aryan* race to whom we belong.

We declare *the need for originality and individuality of form*. Is it even necessary to repeat so basic a truth? Every artist must be original and personal in the form and contents of his writings. Is it yet necessary to say this? Art is the realization of inner self through intuitive creation; therefore, no predetermined influence can be allowed.

We state: our soul, which will be the Armenian Soul itself, will go through all the forms suggested by the sensitivity and inner rhythm within each of us. We reject any enforced submission to a priori determined forms. We prefer as tool of expression all the authentic forms which have carried the Armenian Soul in our ancestral art and literature up to the present day, However, we express, we demand the independence of all media of expression because we believe we will have no particularity, no renewed creative richness until we have achieved originality and individuality of form.

We declare *the need to development of the Armenian language by a revitalizing graft,* because we believe that the ideal of perfection of our language considers insufficient those elements presently used by the Armenian language. No single dialect can fully satisfy it, even a *vostanik* [royal] dialect, as the Armenian dialect of Constantinople is called today.

Declaring the cleansing of the Armenian language from many alien-sounding words [as imperative], we decide to go to the many sources of the Armenian language, Classical Armenian and native dialects, to adopt the authentic and purely Armenian words, explanations, and phrases, and graft them on to our literary language, without sinning against its laws of harmony. We want to found an aesthetics of the language, with the addition of new lines, new colors, new tones.

We declare *the need of keeping pure literature separated from politics and journalism* because nowadays both politics and journalism are the two greatest potential threats to Armenian art. We are not against either of them, neither journalism nor politics, as far as they remain in their role. But we will revolt every time they try to appear on behalf of art and literature or turn them into weapons to pursue their interests. *We call for the complete independence of art. . . .*[117]

---

[117] "Mer hanganake" [Our Credo], *Mehyan* (Jan. 1914): 1-3 (italics in original). See also Zarian, *Navatomar,* pp. 74-76. For a full translation into French, see Nichanian, *Entre l'art et le témoignage,* p. 380-382, who translates it as "Notre Manifeste."

Appendix III

ARAJADRUTIUNNER
(PROPOSITIONS)

[*Bardzravank*'s Prefatory Note]

We elevate Armenian life with mystery and art; we strengthen and give foundation to Armenian mystery and art with life.

We will create a common ground, where the spiritual forces of the Armenian people can find each other and join together for the fatherland, though the world has scattered them.

When will there be, finally, a real Armenian mystery that is not simply a copy or recycling of foreign thinking, a mystery born from the unsleeping depths of the Armenian reality?

The job of the coming generation is to rediscover the Armenian style in the Armenian depths.

Souls reveal themselves in art as in religion.

To be original means to be a deep believer.

Not all people in this enterprise are writers, and the ones who are gladly relinquish that title when they think of those who have usurped that once noble and exalted name.

[We are] workers of the mind who find pleasure, and at the same time satisfaction of conscience, in our work; the one and the other are considered two different, familiar, and solemn ways of saying the same thing.

Withered souls and twisted minds are parasites that kill life; to stigmatize them is a sacred mission.[118]

---

[118] "Arajadrutiunner" [Propositions], *Bardzravank* (Jan. 1922): 1.

352

Hakob Oshakan (Hagop Oshagan)

Kostan Zarian

❋ 15 ❋

THE OTTOMAN EMPIRE AND THE ARMENIAN INTELLIGENTSIA IN CONSTANTINOPLE, 1908-1915

Robert O. Krikorian

On the night of April 23/24, 1915, scores of Armenian intellectuals in the Ottoman capital were rousted out of their beds and arrested. Most of them were deported and then murdered in this mass operation. While there has been much discussion about the meaning of April 24, 1915, there has been less attention devoted to the significance of the Ottoman Armenian intellectual elite and the reasons that the Young Turk Committee of Union and Progress (CUP) targeted them for destruction. This essay presents several hypotheses regarding the Armenian intellectual elite of Constantinople in the period preceding the genocide within the context of Armenian, Russian, and Ottoman history.[1] It examines the role of this elite with special focus on the following: 1) the relationship between the Constantinople Armenian intelligentsia and the wider Ottoman Armenian community during the years between the Young Turk revolution of 1908 and the destruction of the Armenian intelligentsia in 1915; 2) the relationship between these Armenian intellectuals and the Ottoman state; 3) the key political developments in Western Armenia during this period; and 4) general intellectual trends among the Armenians of the Russian Empire and their connections to the Armenians of the Ottoman Empire.

It is frequently argued that the differences between Eastern and Western Armenians were profound and distinct and that the connections between them were minimal; however, each group had an

---

[1] Kevork Sarafian, *The History of Education in Armenia* (LaVerne, CA: LaVerne Leader, 1930), p. 186.

strong interest in the other. In an attempt to explore these connections, this discussion concentrates on the intellectuals of Constantinople, their attitudes toward the situation in Western Armenia, and their connections with their Eastern Armenian and European counterparts.

This subject is important not only because of the light it can shed on the Armenian community in Constantinople and in the Ottoman Empire as a whole but also because of its relevance to the wider scholarly debates regarding the role of the intellectual in the modern state. Throughout Ottoman history, Armenians, Greeks, Jews, Assyrians, Kurds, Arabs, and others had a considerable impact on the development of the empire. Unfortunately, those researching the activities of the Armenians and other non-Turkish nationalities in the Ottoman Empire are faced with certain obstacles. Mainstream Ottoman and Turkish historiography has failed to incorporate the histories of these peoples and their interactions both with the Ottoman state and with each other. In fact, in many instances, it is as if the non-Turkish peoples never existed. There are, of course, political reasons for this, but until such time that the diverse experiences of the peoples who inhabited the Ottoman territories are adequately represented in the historiography of the empire, a distorted version of history will continue to prevail and adversely influence future generations of scholars.

Intellectuals and the State

For the purposes of this chapter, the terms "intellectual" and "intelligentsia" are defined simply as "those who create, distribute and apply culture."[2] These were the educated elite of Ottoman Armenian society, who resided mainly in Constantinople and who held a cosmopolitan worldview. Many of them had been educated in Europe and played an important role in Armenian community life. They also functioned as interpreters and bearers of foreign cultures and influences. Examples include Krikor Zohrab (Grigor Zohrap), Rupen Sevag (Ruben Sevak), and Siamanto (Atom Yarjanian), among others. In the eyes of many Ottoman Muslims, however, these Armenian intellectuals played an uncertain dual

---

[2] Ronald Grigor Suny and Michael D. Kennedy, *Intellectuals and the Articulation of the Nation* (Ann Arbor: University of Michigan Press, 1999), p. 2.

role as bearers of a unique Armenian Christian culture, on the one hand, and as instruments of foreign influence and interference in Ottoman affairs.

It must be noted, however, that the Armenian intellectual and cultural elites of Constantinople were a very heterogeneous group. It would be inappropriate to speak of them as if they were an un-differentiated whole. The terms "intellectual" and "intelligentsia" in the Armenian case refers to a wide range of people from writers and entertainers to politically committed activists concerned about the fate of their compatriots in both the Ottoman and Russian em-pires.

The entries in *Haykakan Harts: Hanragitaran* (Armenian Ques-tion: Encyclopedia) are indicative of the diversity of these intel-lectuals.[3] Some members of the elite wrote in Armenian; others, such as Krikor Zohrab, in Ottoman Turkish as well.[4] Among them were conservatives and liberals, the religious—for example, Gomidas (Komitas)—and agnostics and atheists. Despite their differences, the intellectuals were unified in their sense of belonging to a particular people whose culture they were determined to preserve, develop, and modernize. They were also linked by their growing distrust of the Young Turk rulers.

The important role that intellectuals play in any state must be understood in theoretical terms before one can adequately under-stand the impact of the Armenian intellectuals in the Ottoman Empire. Although there are competing notions of the importance of intellectuals in society, intellectuals need to be "seen, not mere-ly as reflective of what exists, but as constitutive of the nation itself, active agents providing new visions and languages that project a new set of social, cultural, and political possibilities. In-tellectuals here are the creators, not only of nationalisms, but of the more universal discourse of the nation, of the very language and

---

[3] *Haykakan Harts: Hanragitaran,* ed. Konstantin Khudaverdyan (Erevan: Hayka-kan Hanragitaran, 1996).

[4] Avetis Papazyan, "1915 t. Mets Egherni nakhashemin K. Polso Hay Patriar-karani koghmits Bardzragoyn Drane hghvats pashtonakan grutyan masin" [About the Official Correspondence of the Armenian Patriarchate of Constantinople to the Sub-lime Porte on the Threshold of the Great Crime of 1915], in *Merdzavor ev Mijin Arevelki erkrner ev zhoghovurdner* [The Countries and Peoples of the Near and Middle East], vol. 17 (Erevan: Gitutyun, 1998), pp. 201-08.

universe of meaning in which nations become possible."[5]

The Armenian intellectual in the Ottoman Empire was viewed by both Armenians and non-Armenians as an articulator of a qualitatively different Armenian nation than had hitherto existed, making him a potential threat to the Ottoman state.

Armenian Intellectuals and Their Many Worlds

Armenian intellectuals typically operated within three worlds simultaneously—namely, the Armenian community of Constantinople, the wider Ottoman Armenian community, and the world of Ottoman intellectuals. This cosmopolitanism was both an asset and a liability for them. The Young Turk revolution in 1908 deeply affected the peoples of the Ottoman Empire. The overthrow of Sultan Abdul Hamid II (1876-1908/09), who had been responsible for the massacres in the 1890s and had earned the sobriquet "Red Sultan," was forced to allow the reinstitution of the suspended constitution of 1876 and many seemingly progressive developments, including the election of a parliament with Armenian representation.[6]

The heterogeneous makeup of those who had cooperated to overthrow the sultan was indicative of the widespread support that the various liberal elements mobilized for the common Ottoman fatherland (*vatan*). Indeed, many of those involved in the struggle to bring an end to despotism were not thinking along national lines but were striving toward reforms whereby all citizens would be equal before the law.[7] For example, during the first sessions of the Ottoman Parliament in 1908, the Armenian representatives Krikor Zohrab, Vartkes Serengulian (Vardges Serenkulian), and Garegin/Karekin Pasdermajian (Armen Garo) spoke at length of the necessity of defending the Ottoman fatherland and the importance of the concept of Ottomanism. This first Ottoman Parliament had ten Armenian representatives, as follows: [8]

---

[5] Suny and Kennedy, *Intellectuals*, p. 3.

[6] Erik Jan Zürcher, *Turkey: A Modern History* (London: I.B. Tauris, 1994), pp. 97-118; Feroz Ahmad, *The Young Turks: The Committee of Union and Progress in Turkish Politics, 1908-1914* (Oxford: Clarendon Press, 1969).

[7] Mete Tunçay and Erik Jan Zürcher, eds., *Socialism and Nationalism in the Ottoman Empire, 1876-1923* (London and New York: British Academic Press, 1994).

[8] Anahide Ter Minassian, "The Role of the Armenian Community in the Founda-

Deputies	Representing
Krikor Zohrab	Constantinople
Bedros Hallajian	Constantinople
Hagop Babikian	Smyrna (Izmir)
Stepan Spartalian	Smurna
Hampardzum Murad Boyajian	Sis (Kozan)
Karekin Pasdermajian	Erzerum
Vartkes Serengulian	Erzerum
Kegham Der Garabedian	Mush
Nazaret Daghavarian	Sebastia (Sivas)
Vahan Papazian	Van

In the beginning, all the subject nationalities welcomed the Young Turk revolution; its slogans, borrowed from the French Revolution, promised equality and fraternity among all peoples of the empire. For the Armenians, however, disillusionment set in after the attempted countercoup by supporters of the sultan in 1909. Amid the disorder, thousands of Armenians were massacred in the city and province of Adana. The killings alarmed Armenian intellectuals despite Young Turk assurances that they were not involved in the bloodshed. Yet, the regular armed forces sent to halt the massacres participated in a further slaughter of Armenians, and the Young Turk government appointed one of the main instigators to head a relief committee.[9] Krikor Zohrab wearily noted that "Adana is the great sorrow of our nation and, so I believe, also of the entire Ottoman Empire."[10] Armenian suspicions increased as the extreme nationalist wing of the Committee of Union and Progress seized the leadership of the party in 1913. The earlier liberal pronouncements of the Young Turks gave way to the more frightening rhetoric of intellectuals such as the ideologue Zia Gökalp who advocated the cultural homogenization of the empire and the unification of all the Turkic peoples under the Chauvinistic creed of Turanism.[11] Thus, it is within this imperial framework that the

---

tion and Development of the Socialist Movement in the Ottoman Empire and Turkey, 1876-1923," in Tunçay and Zürcher, *Socialism and Nationalism*, p. 140.

[9] Stephan H. Astourian, *The Armenian Genocide: An Interpretation* (The Armenian Genocide Resource Center of Northern California, 2000), pp. 23-24.

[10] Ter Minassian, "Role of the Armenian Community," p. 142.

[11] Zarevand, *United and Independent Turania: Aims and Designs of the Turks*

Armenian intelligentsia needs to be analyzed and studied.

The Armenian Intellectuals in Constantinople

The Armenian community of Constantinople at the turn of the twentieth century was complex, and its constituent parts were in disharmony just as often as they were in accord. Although often portrayed as a homogeneous community led by its patriarch in accordance with the ethno-confessional *millet* system, the reality of the Constantinople Armenian community was far more dynamic. In this modernizing period, contradictions and conflicts deepened between the liberal intellectual elite and the conservative *amira* class of great merchants, financiers, and men of power. There were numerous debates about the seemingly inordinate control of the influential amiras over almost every aspect of Armenian life in the capital. Many Western-educated intellectuals had been exposed to liberal ideologies and were no longer satisfied with the status quo.[12] The party affiliations of the Armenian parliamentarians further reflected the diversity of views within the Armenian intellectual community. According to Anahide Ter Minassian: "Halajian and Babikian were Unionists, Vartkes Serengulian, Garo Pastermadjian, Kegham Der Garabedian and Vahan Papazian were Dashnaks. Murad Boyajian was a Hnchak and Spartal was neutral. Krikor Zohrab was 'liberal' and, at first, voted for the Ahrar [Liberal] party, but . . . drew nearer to the Dashnaks without ever identifying himself with them."[13]

This diversity of views was not new. Since the middle of the nineteenth century, Armenians in increasing numbers traveled to Europe and the Americas to study or work. As aptly summed up by James Etmekjian, they were influenced by Western cultural values in their "struggle for cultural supremacy over the land of Armenia from the period of its earliest inhabitants to the present. There was a battle, not only of armies around and over this historic land, but also of ideas, customs, art, literature, political and social organiza-

---

(Leiden: Brill, 1971).

[12] Christopher Walker, *Armenia: The Survival of a Nation* (New York: St. Martin's Press, 1990), pp. 94-100.

[13] Ter Minassian, "The Role of the Armenian Community," p. 140.

tion, and every other aspect of human life.[14]

The Armenian intellectual elites were in the forefront of the struggle to define and develop the concept of what constituted the nation. By the 1908-15 period, a network of newspapers, schools, orphanages, and charitable foundations established in the capital and led by notable intellectuals participated in the great project of general enlightenment, which focused on the lower classes. For example, Daniel Varoujan taught in the Aramian College of Sebastia from 1909 to 1911, in the National Academy of Tokat from 1911 to 1912, and as director of the Lusavorchian College in Constantinople from 1912 to 1915.[15]

The Intellectuals and Western Armenia

The political and economic situation of the provincial Armenians weighed heavily on the intellectuals in Constantinople. Armenian newspapers of the period routinely discussed the deplorable situation. For example, the Constantinople newspaper *Azadamard* (*Azatamart*) reported on June 17, 1913:

> A savage murder of a young Armenian was perpetrated at Mallu-Khan (Enguri), the victim being a nineteen-year-old farm-hand named Eghia Suluyian, who, when taking his sheep to their grazing ground in the early morning, was suddenly attacked by a Turkish soldier called Ismail, who smashed his skull with a stone and threw his lifeless body in the Alastag River. Only owing to strong protestations of his master, Mr. K. Manukian, did the authorities investigate the matter, arrested Ismail, and recovered the body from the water. When charged, Ismail answered: "It is not a crime to kill a giavur [infidel]." The Armenian population is very agitated.[16]

The condition of the Western Armenian peasantry worsened after the settlement of large numbers of Balkan and Caucasian Muslim refugees on Armenian lands beginning in the 1860s and

---

[14] James Etmekjian, *The French Influence on the Western Armenian Renaissance, 1843-1915* (New York: Twayne Publishers, 1964), p. 25.

[15] *Haykakan Harts*, s.v. "Varuzhan, Daniel," p. 433.

[16] *Azatamart*, June 17, 1913, cited in *Ararat: A Searchlight on Armenia* 1:1 (July 1913): 26.

1870s, culminating in the Hamidian massacres of the 1890s.[17] Thousands of Armenians flocked to the capital in search of security and work, underscoring the urgency of the tragic reality in Western Armenia. Despite differences in dialect, dress, food, and custom among the Armenians, a bond nonetheless existed between natives of Constantinople and those arriving from the eastern *vilayets* (provinces). In fact, since the mid-nineteenth century, the Armenian community of Constantinople had sponsored, financed, and provided expertise to a large network of schools, hospitals, orphanages, and newspapers in Western Armenia.[18] Frequent exchanges between the elites of Constantinople and those in the provinces also brought the gravity of the situation to the attention of the Western powers with which there were extensive contacts. In fact, Krikor Zohrab, among others, frequently interacted with the Western powers in the 1912-14 period regarding the final Armenian reform plan.[19]

Constantinople Armenian Intellectuals and the Ottoman State

The rapidly deteriorating situation in Western Armenia, especially after the Hamidian massacres, forced the Armenian intellectual elite to take a more active political role as advocates for change and reform. While many intellectuals remained unaffiliated with Armenian political parties, some joined the ranks of the Hnchakian Social Democratic Party, Armenian Revolutionary Federation (ARF; Dashnaktsutiun), or other societies. The Young Turk leaders, whose formative experiences had been shaped in the underground opposition to the sultan, soon perceived the growing political awareness and activities by the Armenian intellectuals as a threat to their power.

The position of the Armenian intellectuals in the Ottoman state required that they maintain a precarious balance. As loyal and fairly well integrated subjects of the empire, they easily mixed with their Muslim counterparts. The Armenian and Muslim intellectual

---

[17] Vahakn Dadrian, *A History of the Armenian Genocide: Ethnic Conflict from the Balkans to Anatolia to the Caucasus* (Providence, RI: Berghahn Books, 1995).

[18] Sarafian, *History of Education*, pp. 185-226.

[19] *Haykakan Harts*, s.v. "Zohrap, Grigor," pp. 131-32.

elites shared professional ties and interests, and they often developed personal friendships. Armenians were entrusted with responsible positions in government and industry. The editor of *Erkri dzayn* (Voice of the Homeland), Tigran Zaven, a Marxist and a supporter of Ottomanism, echoed the sentiments of many Armenian intellectuals when he wrote that the Armenian Question, along with the Macedonian and Arab questions, could be solved only through a united front of all the oppressed peoples of the empire; he warned against the dangers of an isolated Armenian national movement.[20]

There were political and legal impediments to equality before the law, and institutional obstacles and cultural prejudices that Armenians had to overcome. Despite the secularizing trends, the Ottoman Empire was an essentially Islamic state, and as such it relegated Christians to an inferior status. As long as Armenians and other Christians, especially the elite and the urban-dwellers, kept their activities within the permitted bounds, they could manage their affairs fairly well. This understanding, however, did not prevail in the eastern vilayets, where the majority of the Armenians lived; rules were made, remade, and enforced by capricious and arbitrary Ottoman officials and Kurdish overlords.[21]

With the rise in national consciousness among both the dominant Turks and the subordinate nationalities in the nineteenth century, the dynamics of relations began to change. Turks and Kurds viewed Armenians with suspicion, both as Christians with ties to their co-religionists in Europe and Russia and as a dominant economic element, competing with the Muslims for a sizable share of the market. The birth of a self-defense movement among the desperate peasantry in the Armenian-populated provinces only exacerbated Turkish and Kurdish animosity.[22] The Armenian intellectuals were particularly disturbed by events in Western Armenia and did not shy away from attempts to alleviate the sufferings of their compatriots. Many intellectuals viewed the rise of pan-Turkist expressions as a direct threat to themselves and their

---

[20] Ter Minasian, "Role of the Armenian Community," p. 135.

[21] Dadrian, *History of the Armenian Genocide*, pp. 3-6.

[22] On this subject, see Louise Nalbandian, *The Armenian Revolutionary Movement: The Development of Armenian Political Parties through the Nineteenth Century* (Berkeley and Los Angeles: University of California Press, 1963).

community and to the very idea of the Ottoman Empire as a multi-national homeland.

A seven-page document written in early 1915 by Krikor Zohrab in Ottoman Turkish and addressed to the Patriarch of Constantinople illustrates the unease felt by the Ottoman Armenian intelligentsia concerning the situation in Western Armenia.[23] He noted that although the Armenians had loyally performed their duties and obligations to the state, they were still subjected to terror and harassment. He detailed the condition in many of the provinces and lamented the pressures to which the rural population was subjected by local officials.[24] This last attempt to bring to light the full extent of the danger facing the Ottoman Armenians is an example of the concern felt by many intellectuals in Constantinople for the fate of their compatriots.

Armenian Intellectuals and the International Arena

Despite their position in the Ottoman Parliament, Armenian leaders like Krikor Zohrab were powerless to influence the direction of politics in the empire because of both internal and external factors. The state of international relations between 1908 and 1915 had an enormous impact on the environment within which the Armenian intellectuals had to operate. Indeed, it could be argued that the international context was a determining factor in the decision to eliminate the Armenian population of the Ottoman Empire. Armenian intellectuals were well aware of developments in other parts of the world and maintained wide-ranging contacts with their compatriots in the Russian Empire, Persia, and Europe. In a sense, the existence of the Armenian intelligentsia may be viewed as a trans-national phenomenon, and it was these cross-border and international connections that allowed them to be both well-informed and instruments of reform. Yet, these connections also caused them to be viewed by the suspicious Young Turks as the bearers of subversive ideas and as potential threats to the territorial integrity of the empire.

Events in Russia, the Balkans, North Africa, and Persia seemed to reinforce the feeling of the Young Turks that they were under

---

[23] Papazyan, "1915," pp. 201-08.
[24] Ibid.

siege. In the period between 1908 and 1914, they had to confront a number of external challenges, including the Austro-Hungarian annexation of Bosnia-Herzegovina; the Bulgarian declaration of independence; union of Crete with Greece; and a war with Italy in North Africa, costing the Turks the important region of Tripolitania (Libya). Further, from 1909 to 1912, the Young Turks also had to deal with revolts in Albania against their "Ottomanization" policies and in 1912 had to grant autonomy to Albania. The most severe blow to the Young Turks was the First Balkan War of 1912-13, during which a coalition of Balkan states soundly defeated the Ottoman military and reduced its area of control in Europe to Constantinople and its environs.[25] The shock of this defeat seriously influenced the attitude of the Young Turks toward the Christians remaining under their rule.

From the perspective of the Young Turk leaders, perhaps the greatest national security threat emanated from the Russian Empire, seen as a strong ally and instigator of the Balkan states. Indeed, there was reason to view Russia as a threat, both in Europe and in the East. Since the eighteenth century, Russia and the Ottoman Empire had been at war at least eight times, and most ended with the defeat or capitulation of the Ottoman Empire and the expansion of the Russian Empire.[26] As for Russia, although the autocracy survived the revolution of 1905, it nevertheless suffered a humiliating defeat by Japan. This fiasco was all the more horrifying for Russia as resulted not from the actions of a European power but from an Asiatic one, something unprecedented in modern times.[27] The government was in no mood to look kindly on revolutionaries. The Young Turk leaders, for their part, noted that during the Russian revolution of 1905 national minorities had attempted to take advantage of the weakening of central authority to push their agendas for reform.

For the Ottoman Empire, the issue of reform in the six Turkish

---

[25] Feroz Ahmad, *The Making of Modern Turkey* (London and New York: Routledge, 1993), pp. 31-51; Charles and Barbara Jelavich, *The Establishment of Balkan National States, 1804-1920* (Seattle: University of Washington Press, 1977), pp. 207-21.

[26] Hugh Seton-Watson, *The Russian Empire, 1801-1917* (Oxford: Clarendon Press, 1977).

[27] Sydney Harcave, *First Blood: The Russian Revolution of 1905* (New York: Macmillan, 1964).

Armenian provinces was viewed with extreme unease. The Young Turks believed that the European powers had frequently exploited the Armenian Question to destabilize the empire and meddle in its internal affairs. Especially worrisome was the fact that Armenians across the border in the Russian Empire had acted and could again act as a vanguard for Russian expansionism into Ottoman territories. Thus, when Armenian intellectuals embraced the idea of reforms for the Armenian provinces, the Young Turks viewed them as a potential subversive element serving the interests of foreign powers rather than the interest of the empire. Many Armenian intellectuals pressed for reforms to modernize the empire and enable the Ottoman Armenians to develop in a more stable and secure environment; independence was not on their agenda at this time.

Interaction between the intellectuals of Eastern and Western Armenia by the turn of the century had become frequent, especially during the period of revolutionary turmoil which gripped Russia, Persia, and Turkey. The confiscation of Armenian Church property in the Caucasus (1903-05) by the tsarist regime united Armenians against the autocracy and the subsequent Armeno-Tatar war[28] (1905-07) in the Caucasus caused concern among Armenian intellectual circles of Constantinople. The constitutional revolution in Persia also saw heavy Armenian participation, with figures such as Eprem Khan actively engaged in the struggle against the Iranian monarchy. Throughout the period after the Young Turk revolution, many Caucasian Armenian intellectuals, such as Paramaz and Vahan Papazian, found refuge in Constantinople.[29] Further, many Eastern and Western Armenian intellectuals became acquainted with each other during their stays in Europe. Thus, they became well acquainted with each other's conditions and problems and interacted continuously during the period leading up to the outbreak of World War I and the Armenian Genocide.

Armenian Reforms, the Intelligentsia, and April 24, 1915

The Armenian reform program of 1914 only exacerbated the distrust of the Young Turk dictators. Stephan Astourian has explained:

---

[28] Armeno-Azerbaijani war.

[29] See the relevant entries of *Haykakan Harts* for details.

By 1914, the Unionist leaders were faced with both a diplomatic and military threat. The reawakening of Russia's interest in the Armenian Question from 1912 on, and the Dashnaktsutiun's request for intercession in 1913 as a result of the worsening situation of the Armenians, led to lengthy negotiations among the powers of the Triple Alliance and Triple Entente. On February 8, 1914, the six European states—France, Great Britain, Russia, Germany, Italy, and Austria-Hungary, assented to a compromise reform act to the effect that the "Armenian" provinces would be divided into two administrative districts, each supervised by a European inspector-general. In addition, mixed Christian-Muslim gendarmeries would be established, the irregular Kurdish units disbanded, and cultural freedom guaranteed. After further negotiations, Major Hoff of Norway and Mr. Westenenk of the Netherlands received approval as inspectors-general. By the summer of 1914, the long and arduous efforts to secure reforms seemed close to fruition. . . . Then, the war broke out, which provided optimal conditions for the genocide.[30]

The Armenian intellectual elites were actively engaged in the debate over the importance and merits of the reform plan. Their active support and encouragement for the project, which was seen as a major step toward improving the security of the Armenians in the Ottoman Empire, made them a target of even greater Young Turk suspicion and anger. The work of the Armenian representatives in the Ottoman Parliament is particularly noteworthy in this respect. Gradually, the Young Turk leaders shifted their suspicion from the relatively few isolated Armenian revolutionary groups to the entire Armenian people, especially its educated elite. The reform agreement of 1914 was regarded as a prelude to the dismemberment of the empire, and all measures that could meet this threat were considered legitimate. For these xenophobic Turkish nationalists, World War I provided the opportunity to dispose of the Armenian problem by disposing of the Armenians.

The Armenian intellectuals viewed the outbreak of the war with great apprehension as they recognized that, in the charged atmosphere of the time, nothing good for the Armenians could be expected from the war. They even tried to warn their colleagues in

---

[30] Astourian, *Armenian Genocide*, p. 31.

Russian Armenia to act judiciously in their pronouncements on the war, especially in their support for the creation of Armenian volunteer units to fight in the Russian army for the liberation of Western Armenia.[31] Caught between warring empires, the Armenians were extremely vulnerable, and the intellectuals of Constantinople recognized this quite clearly. The Young Turks, also aware of this, sought first to silence those in positions of authority, despite the fact that the Armenian religious, political, and cultural leaders had called upon their people to fulfill all obligations as loyal Ottoman subjects. In fact, a great number Armenian men had been called up for service in the ranks of the Ottoman military.

Thus, in the atmosphere created by the successive crises facing the Young Turk regime, a decision was made to destroy the Armenians of the empire. In a well-prepared and lightning-quick operation, the targeted political, cultural, civic, and religious leaders were rounded up on the night of April 23-24, 1915, and sent to their deaths.

Conclusions

The destruction of the Armenian intellectual elite in the Ottoman Empire has had far-reaching effects that are felt even in the present time. The short-term implications are hard to exaggerate. The removal of the leaders of the Armenian community, both in Constantinople and in the provinces, allowed the CUP to carry out the systematic annihilation of the Armenian population without encountering significant organized resistance. The confusion into which the Armenian community was thrown as a result of the operation of April 24, combined with the removal of able-bodied men for military service, eliminated the possibility that the CUP and its Special Organization death-squads would meet opposition from the deported population. The unorganized Armenian masses appeared to have no choice but to acquiesce in their own destruction, exactly as the CUP had envisioned. The isolated and usually unsuccessful attempts at armed resistance at Van, Urfa, Shabin-Karahisar, Musa Dagh, and a few other places attest to the efficiency with which the operation was carried out. Further, the

---

[31] Richard G. Hovannisian, *Armenia on the Road to Independence, 1918* (Los Angeles and Berkeley: University of California Press, 1967), pp. 40-58.

elimination of Constantinople's Armenian elite silenced voices arguing moderation and restraint. As is well known, however, the CUP, led by Mehmed Talaat, Ismail Enver, and Ahmed Jemal, was not interested in moderation or restraint in its handling of the Armenian Question. The continued presence of Armenian intellectuals in the Ottoman capital was not desirable for those committed to the eradication of the Armenian people.

Although the short-term consequences of the destruction of the Armenian elite were devastating in their own right, this calamity had grave implications for the future as well. In the aftermath of the Russian revolutions in 1917, the remnants of the Armenian people were presented with the opportunity to create an independent state, the first since the fall of the Cilician kingdom in 1375. But the nascent Armenian republic that was created in May 1918 was denied the possibility of utilizing the talents and experience of the Constantinople Armenian intellectuals. Although there were numerous political and strategic variables involved in the ultimate demise and Sovietization of that state in December 1920, it may be argued that the loss of the tremendous potential of the Constantinople Armenian intellectual elite robbed the Armenian people of some of its finest minds, which could have played a critical role in affecting the fate of the Republic. One can only speculate about how differently Armenia may have developed had it been able to draw upon the resources of Constantinople's Armenian elite. The lack of intellectual cadres was also to affect Soviet Armenia and the Armenian Diaspora in the succeeding decades.

The activities of the Constantinople Armenian intelligentsia in the pre-1915 era stand out as a high point in cultural achievement and productivity. The loss of their talents for the Armenian nation had wide-ranging consequences that are still felt today. Even now, the Armenian intelligentsia is undergoing one of its most serious trials, as post-Soviet economic collapse and massive emigration deplete their ranks. But when put in historical perspective, the present difficulties cannot be compared with the tribulations of the intellectual elite in Constantinople and across historic Armenia in 1915. Yet, each time Armenian intellectuals have been dealt a merciless blow, they have picked up the pieces of their shattered lives and strived to create anew. The spirit of the Armenian intellectuals was perhaps best portrayed by Krikor

Zohrab:

> One should confront the misfortunes of life not with despair and
> dejection but in the same way that one confronts the sudden
> arrival of an unwelcome guest—with a smiling face. We Arme-
> nians should sing and laugh more often in order to develop that
> degree of emotional health and intellectual balance without which
> we can achieve very little in this world. A nation that is given to
> lamentations will never amount to anything.[32]

---

[32] Ara Baliozian, *Zohrab: An Introduction* (Kitchener, Ontario: Impressions, and
Cambridge, MA: National Association for Armenian Studies and Research, 1985),
pp. 71-72.

✽ 16 ✽

THE ARMENIAN REVOLUTIONARY FEDERATION IN CONSTANTINOPLE, 1908-1914

Dikran M. Kaligian

In 1900, the Armenian Revolutionary Federation (ARF) and the Hnchakian Social Democratic Party entered into a dialogue in Paris with Turkish groups opposed to the autocratic rule of Sultan Abdul Hamid II (1876-1908/09). Both Armenian parties participated in the First Congress of Ottoman Opposition in 1902, along with Turkish, Arab, Greek, Kurdish, Albanian, Circassian, and Jewish representatives. The resolutions adopted by the congress called for local self-administration and the restoration of the Ottoman Constitution of 1876, which Abdul Hamid had suspended in 1878. In late 1907, the Second Congress of Ottoman Opposition convened in Paris on the initiative of the ARF and resolved to overthrow Abdul Hamid II and to restore the Constitution by all possible means, including refusal to pay taxes, propaganda, and even armed rebellion.[1] When in the following summer a mutinous Turkish army led the revolution against the sultan, most Ottoman subjects greeted it with jubilation. According to one ARF leader, Mikayel Varandian, Constantinople "rippled with unusual enthusiasm." E. Aknuni described the celebrations:

---

[1] Hratch Tasnapetian, *History of the Armenian Revolutionary Federation Dashnaktsutiun, 1890-1924* (Milan: Oemme Edizioni, 1990), p. 87. The Armenian Revolutionary Federation (Hay Heghapokhakan Dashnaktsutiun) was founded in 1890 in Tiflis and became the leading Armenian political party in both the Ottoman and Russian empires after 1900. The Hnchakian Revolutionary Party (or Hnchak Party) was founded in 1887 in Geneva and was the leading Armenian party in the Ottoman Empire until internal divisions weakened it after 1896. The Ittihad ve Terakki (Committee of Union and Progress; CUP) was the driving force behind the 1908 revolution. Its central committee directed the government behind the scenes from 1908 to 1912 and openly after it seized power in a coup d'état in January 1913.

> You cannot imagine how happy I am that I write you from this
> city, without fear of the ubiquitous spies. A city where mouths
> that had been silenced for 32 years together cry "freedom." . . .
> The crowd is intoxicated. Let it be that way. After 30 years of
> silence, it is possible to scream and get drunk.[2]

The ARF distributed a proclamation that praised the revolution
and expressed hope for greater freedom, equality, and justice
under the new constitutional regime. The party subsequently published a program that reaffirmed its support for the territorial
integrity of the Ottoman Empire and called for a federal system
with the widest possible degree of local autonomy. The party then
prepared a list of demands for consideration by the Ottoman Parliament, including guarantees for the freedom of speech, assembly,
and religion, freedom of the press, and the legal right to strike. The
proclamation advocated the elimination of class privileges and
equality of all ethnic and religious communities. For that purpose,
the party declared: "All parliamentary, judiciary, and local administrative bodies will be elected on the principle of universal,
equal, secret, and proportional voting. This principle will be implemented for all peoples and religions equally."[3] In fact, whereas
for years the ARF (among other parties) was forced to print its
newspapers in Europe and to smuggle copies to Constantinople and
the provinces, the reinstitution of the Constitution allowed the
party to publish its official organ, *Azadamard* (*Azatamart*), in
Constantinople beginning in 1909.

In order to influence government policy and improve conditions for the Armenians, the ARF needed to work closely with the
CUP. Communications between the two parties were initially
hindered, however, by the fact that neither was headquartered in
the capital. The CUP Central Committee headquarters were in
Salonika, while the ARF Western Bureau was based in Geneva and

---

[2] Mikayel Varandian, *H.H. Dashnaktsutian patmutiun* [History of the A(rmenian)
R(evolutionary) Federation], vol. 2 (Paris: Imp. de Navarre, 1932), p. 8. Varandian
was the main theoretician of the ARF, an active political commentator, and a member
of the Western Bureau. Aknuni (Khachatur Malumian) was a member of the Western
Bureau and one of the organizers of the Congress of Ottoman Opposition. He moved
to Constantinople after the 1908 revolution where he was a prolific political commentator, writer, and public speaker.

[3] Ibid., pp. 10-12; Aykut Kansu, *The Revolution of 1908 in Turkey* (Leiden: Brill,
1997), pp. 167-68.

the Eastern Bureau in Tiflis. To address this problem, the ARF established a Responsible Body for Constantinople, and in September 1909 the party's Fifth World Congress elected a Western Bureau that included a "Turkish Section" to be based in the Ottoman capital. In 1913, the entire Western Bureau moved its headquarters to the city.[4] The CUP headquarters, however, remained in Salonika. As a result, while the ARF met regularly with CUP ministers in Constantinople, it had to rely on delegations to Salonika for direct communications with the CUP Central Committee.

The restoration of the Constitution permitted the Armenian parties to participate in the elections. In late 1908, elections were held throughout the empire and a multiethnic parliament was seated. Although a majority of its 283 members could be classified as ethnically Turkish, the body also included 53 Arabs, 27 Albanians, 22 Greeks, 11 Armenians, 7 Slavs, 6 Kurds, and 4 Jews. Of the 11 Armenian deputies, 4 were ARF members representing the eastern provinces, and 2, Krikor Zohrab and Bedros Hallajian, represented the Armenian community of Constantinople.[5]

In an atmosphere of reduced governmental control, an armed insurrection broke out in Constantinople in April 1909 and drove the CUP out of the capital. Liberal opponents of the CUP as well as reactionaries favoring Sultan Abdul Hamid supported the coup, but within two weeks troops under Mahmud Shevket Pasha suppressed the revolt. Amid the unrest, anti-Armenian massacres broke out in the city of Adana and other parts of the Adana *vilayet* (province). The *vali* (provincial governor) Jevad (Cevat) Bey and the commandant of the gendarmes took no action to protect the Armenians, and the massacres continued for three days. Nine days

---

[4] Hrach Tasnapetian, *H.H. Dashnaktsutian kazmakerpakan karoytsi holovoyte* [The Evolution of the Organizational Structure of the ARF] (Beirut: Hamazkayin Press, 1974). Subordinate to each Bureau was a number of central committees, each overseeing local ARF committees (*komite* or *gomide*) and responsible for party activities in its respective region. The party operated under the principle of decentralization in which each elected body governed the organizational activities within the guidelines set by the higher bodies. The Eastern Bureau oversaw the central committees of Van, Taron/Mush, Erzerum-Erzinjan, and Trebizond as well as the Baghesh/Bitlis gomide. The Western Bureau oversaw the central committees of Tigranakert/Diarbekir, Kharpert-Malatia, Sebastia/Sivas, Kesaria/Gesaria, and Samsun, as well as bodies in Cilicia, Smyrna, and Constantinople.

[5] Kansu, *Revolution*, pp. 238-301.

later, the arrival of troops dispatched by the CUP to restore order set off another round of massacres and led to the burning of thousands of Armenian houses in the city. In all, some 25,000 Armenians perished in the two rounds of massacres.[6]

In the aftermath of the crisis, the ARF had to decide, in the face of mounting Armenian opinion, whether to continue its cooperation with the CUP. It was essential, therefore, to determine if the massacres were the result of loss of control by a new regime, or if the CUP held intolerant tendencies heretofore hidden beneath the rhetoric of liberal democracy. The ARF and the Armenian population at large, drawing on past experiences, realized that the events in Adana could be a harbinger of violence elsewhere. To a degree, the fears of the Armenians were borne out by the increased restiveness of Turks and Kurds in the eastern provinces, although the tensions did not escalate into violence. It is not clear if the perpetrators were encouraged by the attempted coup in the capital and the massacres in Adana.[7] Nevertheless, some in the Armenian community demanded an end to further cooperation with the CUP, and popular anger towards the ARF and the Armenian parliamentary deputies grew. Krikor Zohrab responded to the criticism:

> We Armenian deputies are reproached for having sympathetic relations and providing assistance to the Ittihad. You should know, compatriots, that the famed revolution of the Ottoman Constitution is still far from accomplishing its entire work. Indeed, the fact that circumstance where the Muslim element, full of hatred, resumes their criminal oppression, is a sign that the Turk has not matured enough for constitutional order. We have not been idle and uncaring, but rather we have been cautious and slow, taking steady steps. We cannot salve our wounds with speeches from the rostrum of the Parliament.[8]

---

[6] Erik Jan Zürcher, *Turkey: A Modern History* (London: I.B. Tauris, 1993), pp. 101-02; Vahakn N. Dadrian, *The History of the Armenian Genocide: Ethnic Conflict from the Balkans to Anatolia to the Caucasus* (Providence, RI: Berghahn Books, 1995), pp. 181-83; Christopher Walker, *Armenia: The Survival of a Nation* (London: Croom Helm, 1980), pp. 183-86.

[7] Vahan Papazian, *Im hushere* [My Memoirs], vol. 2 (Beirut: Hamazkayin Press, 1952), pp. 123-24. Papazian (also known as Goms or Koms) was elected to Parliament in 1908, representing Van vilayet. From 1904 to 1908, he served as a leading figure in the ARF in Van and organized the arms and ammunition route from the Caucasus.

[8] Papazian, *Im hushere*, p. 126. Krikor Zohrab (Grigor Zohrap), a renowned

Weighing the Options

The ARF found itself in a serious dilemma, torn between its solidarity with the progressive elements of the CUP and its revulsion at the murderous acts of its more chauvinistic elements. Should the progressives lose power, or should their profession of faith in constitutionalism be mere empty gestures, the consequences for the Armenians could prove deadly. As the self-defense units had been disbanded after the Young Turk revolution, the Armenian population in the eastern provinces and Cilicia were at the mercy of Kurdish and Turkish mobs. Vahan Papazian commented regarding the dilemma as seen by the ARF leadership:

> At that moment, it would perhaps have been the right decision to all make the break and end our relations once and for with the CUP. But with that, we would have added fuel to the flames for the watchful treacherous opposition elements. We had no doubt that they would undertake further rash actions and perhaps even jeopardize those few liberties that remained. We were faced with a heavy dilemma; we had never before faced such a psychological crisis. Our trust and hope were deeply shaken.[9]

After some deliberation, the Western Bureau decided to make a final attempt at continued cooperation with the CUP, but that relationship depended on government action on a number of critical issues that the massacres had brought into sharp relief. In this vein, the Bureau sent the following directive to its executive body in Constantinople:

> The ARF, believing in its principles and modus operandi, will continue, with the same effort but a broader scope, to work with the Young Turk party and the intelligentsia *in defense of the constitution*. And it will gather around that cooperation all supportive elements, Armenian and non-Armenian alike, that have an appreciation for, and a goal of defending, the new order and the interests of the oppressed peoples.
> The ARF will continue, along with its defense of the constitu-

---

lawyer, law professor, and author of short stories, was one of the foremost figures of the Ottoman Parliament. He was elected as a representative of Constantinople. Although not a member of the ARF, he worked closely with the party's deputies.

[9] Ibid.

tional order, to struggle against the government in those cases where it betrays its responsibility by allowing deviations from constitutional norms which harm not only the national interests, but also create inequalities among the peoples . . . and thus jeopardize their national bond. . . .

Based on this, and the events of the Adana massacres, the ARF demands the following:

1. The legal punishment of officials who failed in their duties and of the leaders of the carnage, and corporal punishment for the masses responsible;

2. The return of property or compensation to Armenians for their financial losses;

3. The securing of an annuity for widows or relatives of the dead;

4. The relief of the population from the usual taxes for a few years;

5. The recognition of ownerless land and properties as the possessions of the church or the school;

6. The reorganization of the gendarmerie and the establishment of security forces composed of all nationalities; organization of government-armed Armenian guards in Armenian villages.

On this basis, the ARF does not end its cooperation with the CUP.[10]

The CUP took great pains to reassure the ARF of its sincerity and support for the reforms to ensure the security of the Armenian community. The two parties met in Salonika to draw up an accord so that they could "work hand-in-hand to save Turkey from new disasters," as the Western Bureau reported:

The August 20 accord was important. . . . We dare to think that for Turkey's political prestige, with the Adana calamity coming at such a critical time, the signing of the accord by the main political party of the suffering Armenians was a significant extension of the olive branch. However, the position taken by those who signed the accord on behalf of the ARF was inspired by the belief that advances could be made on the federal level.[11]

---

[10] Ibid., pp. 124-26.

[11] ARF Archives, Hairenik Building, Watertown Massachusetts, C/78a-2, Western Bureau-Turkish Section memorandum on the relations between the ARF and CUP.

The terms of the accord committed both parties to the preservation of the empire, to a broader devolution of power to the provinces, and to the defense of the constitution against reactionary movements. The two parties thus agreed on the following points:

> In order to strengthen permanently the implementation of the constitution and public improvements in the country, they will work and struggle with combined forces, sparing no sacrifice:
>
> 1. They will cooperate with total mutual support and unified direction, using all options as permitted by law, to counter the likely reactionary movements;
>
> 2. As preserving the sacred Ottoman fatherland from partition and division is a reason for the joint cooperation of the two organizations, they will work practically to dispel the false impression in public opinion inherited from the despotic regime that the Armenians strive for independence;
>
> 3. The two parties also wish to announce that they are in agreement on the subject of "expanding provincial rights," which will guarantee further development and progress for the Ottoman fatherland as a whole; and
>
> 4. The CUP and the ARF, accepting the events of March 31 and the grievous Adana massacres as a warning of possible atrocities to come, have decided to work hand-in-hand to realize the goals listed above.
>
> CUP General Headquarters
> ARF Constantinople Responsible Body[12]

Agreeing to continue cooperation was a serious political gamble for the ARF. The credibility that the ARF had gained through years of defending the Armenian people and conducting political education and organizing activities, all would be lost if the CUP failed to deliver on its promises. But such was the faith of the ARF leadership in the benefits of constitutionalism that they pursued cooperation at great risk.

At the same time, however, one cannot rule out some degree of self-interest on the part of the ARF. Faced with criticism, its leadership may not have been willing to admit that the policy of cooperation had been a failure. Given that the party had invested

---

[12] Varandian, *Dashnaktsutian patmutiun*, pp. 18-19.

years in the relationship with the Young Turks, the leaders had to overcome a certain degree of institutional inertia to change that policy. There may also have been internal factors. The party leadership had made cooperation a centerpiece of its policy and therefore could have felt vulnerable to the minority within the organization that had opposed such cooperation. Yet there is little evidence that the opposing faction had either the numbers or the credibility needed to mount a serious challenge.

Nevertheless, the ARF viewed the Adana massacres as an example of the dangers that the Armenians faced should the Turkish nationalists gain power over the liberal faction of the CUP. If the CUP, which had limited room to maneuver because of its own internal tensions, failed to fulfill its promises, the ARF would be forced to sever relations. While the Armenians began to recover from the shock of the Adana massacres, the CUP had to come to terms with its own political vulnerability and was still reeling from the counterrevolution.

ARF-CUP Relations

For the first eighteen months after the revolution, the Western Bureau's relations with the CUP were irregular due to the CUP's internal difficulties.[13] Also, it was not until August 1910, two years after the revolution, that the government legalized the ARF—a fact that had added to the frustrations in relations between the two parties, especially considering that other non-Turkish parties had been legalized sooner.[14] Nevertheless, communications between the two parties became more regular beginning in 1910 with the formation of a "Joint Body," in which each side was represented by three members, of whom two were deputies in the Parliament. The ARF appointed Armen Garo, Vartkes Serengulian, and Arshag Vramian, and the CUP appointed Midhat Bey, Hachim Bey, and Haji Nazim.[15] According to the Western Bureau, al-

---

[13] ARF Archives, C/106-31, Western Bureau-Turkish Section to Mush Central Committee, Dec. 10, 1909.

[14] ARF Archives, C/106-22, Western Bureau-Turkish Section to *Droshak* Editorial Board, Geneva, Nov. 29, 1909; C/107-107, Western Bureau-Turkish Section to Eastern Bureau-Turkish Section, Aug. 11, 1910.

[15] ARF Archives, C/78a-1, Western Bureau-Turkish Section, report on relations with the Ittihad ve Terakki, Nov. 1909-Aug. 1911. The report was presented to the ARF

though progress was slow, the parties were continuing their negotiations in the Joint Body. The ARF delegation had hoped to obtain positive results, particularly as the CUP appeared to favor a rapprochement. The delegates agreed to establish joint committees to oversee the administrative affairs of three eastern provinces, and the CUP pledged to dispatch special inspectors for that purpose. The Western Bureau took this promise with a grain of salt but urged the Eastern Bureau to maintain friendly relations with CUP representatives in their region.[16]

Meanwhile, conditions in the provinces deteriorated, and the numerous ARF protests and demands remained unanswered. On March 20, 1910, Vramian and Harutiun Shahrigian, representing the Western Bureau, met with the members of the CUP Central Committee in Salonika to discuss the pressing issues of the physical security of the Armenians in the eastern provinces, educational and land policies, and the continued harassment of ARF members in certain areas.[17] The CUP leaders received them cordially and assured the Armenian representatives that their party had not changed its policy toward the ARF. The CUP was aware of Armenian loyalty with respect to the Ottoman Constitution and did not have a policy of assimilation. In fact, the CUP was using the Armenians as an example to demonstrate how an ethnic group could maintain its rights as a distinct community while being part

---

Sixth World Congress. The role of the congress was to review and analyze the operations of the Western and Eastern Bureaus and determine the political and organizational policy guidelines for the following years by the two bureaus.

Armen Garo (Garegin Pasdermajian) was born in Erzerum and played a leading role in the seizure of the Ottoman Bank in 1896 and the defense of Tiflis during the Armeno-Tatar (Armeno-Azerbaijani) conflict of 1905-07. He was twice elected to the Ottoman Parliament and in 1913 became a member of the Western Bureau. Vartkes Serengulian (Vardges Serenkulian) was born in Erzerum and was engaged in ARF activities in Constantinople from 1891 to 1896. He was imprisoned from 1903 to 1908 and was then elected to Parliament in 1908 and 1912. Arshag (Arshak) Vramian was born in Constantinople and was a central figure in the city until the Ottoman Bank occupation in 1896 made him a wanted man. He spent several years in the United States as an editor and ARF field-worker but returned to Constantinople as a member of the Western Bureau after the Young Turk revolution.

[16] ARF Archives, C/107-17, Western Bureau-Turkish Section to Eastern Bureau-Turkish Section (Erzerum), Jan. 26, 1910.

[17] Harutiun Shahrigian (Shahrikian) was born in Shabin-Karahisar but educated in Constantinople. He was a prominent figure in the party in the city and a member of the Armenian National Assembly.

of the Ottoman nation. The ARF representatives were pleasantly surprised to see the large number of social science books that the CUP was to distribute to the field workers in the provinces to study and apply. The Western Bureau deemed the results of the Salonika meeting satisfactory. The accord was submitted to the Joint Body to be implemented, and that body in turn agreed on the following working points: land issues to be addressed administratively; security matters; the judiciary; political issues; and change in government employees. On April 6, 1910, the Turkish translation of these points was given to Talaat Bey.[18]

At a joint meeting soon thereafter, the CUP members announced that they had received orders from Salonika regarding the accord to instruct the executive bodies to put in motion the decisions that had been agreed upon. An ARF parliamentary deputy would accompany the CUP representative to meet with the various ministries to that effect.[19] By July, the Western Bureau reported that relations with the CUP had become closer. Despite this progress, a report from the Western Bureau on the two years of relations with the CUP stated that the Joint Body did not meet regularly. Although ARF members met informally with individual ministers and CUP leaders, the Joint Body held only sixteen formal meetings from the time of its formation to the middle of 1911. Among the reasons cited were the frequent crises within the CUP and the ministries, their inexperience and inefficiency, and their reluctance to admit failure regarding the implementation of objectives agreed upon with the ARF.[20]

The Land Issue

Peasants comprised the overwhelming majority of the Armenian

---

[18] ARF Archives, C/78a-1, Western Bureau-Turkish Section report on relations with the Ittihad ve Terakki, Nov. 1909-Aug. 1911. Mehmed Talaat was the most important civilian member of the CUP, a member of its central committee, and a parliamentary deputy. He served in the cabinet as minister of the interior in 1909 and from 1913 to 1917.

[19] Ibid.

[20] ARF Archives, C/107-102, Mgrdich Sahagian (Mkrtich Sahakian) on behalf of the Western Bureau to Taron Central Committee, July 17, 1910; C/78a-1, Western Bureau-Turkish Section, report on relations with the Ittihad ve Terakki, Nov. 1909-Aug. 1911.

population in the provinces. The restoration of the constitution had raised hopes among the dispossessed Armenians for the restitution of lands, which, together with the promised equal status as Ottoman citizens before the law, would secure their economic survival in historically Armenian regions. Land dispossession, economic deprivation, abuses by Kurdish tribes, and official indifference to such issues, over decades had resulted in large-scale Armenian migration from rural areas to cities, such as Constantinople and Smyrna, and emigration abroad. This westward movement, hastened by economic deprivation and massacres as experienced under Sultan Abdul Hamid, made the government's goal of reducing the number of Armenians in the eastern vilayets and Cilicia a reality. The sultan had realized that Armenian appeals for European intervention and demands for autonomy would be weakened if Armenians made up a smaller percentage of the population. The ARF was acutely aware of the political impact of such demographic changes. Anahide Ter Minassian has noted: "For several years they had witnessed with concern the decline of the Armenian population, particularly in the eastern vilayets where wars, massacres, famines, a rural exodus, and the installation of the *muhajirs* (Muslim refugees) favored regional Islamization."[21] The ARF believed that recovery of the lost lands would arrest the migratory trend.

The hopeless position of the dispossessed under the *ancien regime* was one reason for the jubilant reaction to the Young Turk revolution. The promised equal status as Ottoman citizens would remedy past injustices and restore the usurped lands to their rightful owners. The prospect of equal status was so appealing that many of those from the countryside who had fled to the cities or abroad now returned home, which in turn sparked further land disputes.[22] Initially, the CUP appeared determined to redistribute land and to improve conditions for peasants. From their early days

---

[21] Anahide Ter Minassian, "The Role of the Armenian Community in the Foundation and Development of the Socialist Movement in the Ottoman Empire and Turkey, 1876-1923," in *Socialism and Nationalism in the Ottoman Empire 1876-1923*, ed. Mete Tuncay and Erik Jan Zürcher (London and New York: British Academic Press, 1994), p. 137. *Muhajirs* were Muslim refugees from other parts of the Ottoman Empire and the Caucasus.

[22] Roderic H. Davison, *Essays in Ottoman and Turkish History, 1774-1923: The Impact of the West* (Austin: University of Texas Press, 1990), p. 181.

in the political underground, they were well aware of the significant role rural conditions had played in fostering discontent and hence the convenient pretext they provided for European intervention in Ottoman affairs.[23]

The CUP and the ARF agreed to establish a joint Armenian-Turkish commission to address the land issue. Local ARF representatives were familiar with conditions and the history of dispossessions, and CUP leaders carried the authority of the government and could reassure Muslims in the provinces of impartial treatment. The CUP, however, soon retreated from the idea of joint commission, perhaps because of the party's unwillingness to expend political capital on an issue favoring exclusively Armenians. The Turkish and Kurdish deputies from the eastern vilayets, and the large landowners whose interests they represented, were the most significant obstacles to the implementation of land policies. The ARF was not wholly unrealistic in its estimates of the speed at which reforms could be instituted. While the party leadership continued to pursue the matter, it also cautioned the central committees not to press for too many demands in view of the increasing discontent with the government and a renewal of "threatening sentiments in the provinces."[24]

The government repeatedly postponed resolution of the land question. Mehmed Talaat, as Minister of Interior, did not take steps to resolve the issue either because he chose not to or because he could not. The Kurdish deputies continued to pressure the government for land policies favorable to them; in order to counter such lobbying, the ARF presented statements from municipal officials in the provinces supportive of the Armenian position.[25] By late 1910, it had become clear that no substantial progress would

---

[23] Tarik Zafer Tunaya, *Türkiye'de siyasi partiler, 1859-1952* (Istanbul, 1952), pp. 206-10, as cited by Feroz Ahmad, "Agrarian Policy of the Young Turks, 1908-1918," in *Économie et sociétés dans l'Empire ottoman (fin du XVIIIᵉ-début du XXᵉ siècle)*, ed. Jean-Louis Bacqué-Grammont and Paul Dumont (Paris: Editions du Centre national de la recherche scientifique, 1983), p. 278.

[24] ARF Archives, C/107-10, Western Bureau-Turkish Section to Taron Central Committee, Jan. 22, 1910.

[25] ARF Archives, C/99-26, Rostom, April 16, 1910. Rostom (Stepan Zoryan) was one of the three founders of the ARF and perhaps the most influential figure in the party for the rest of his life. He engineered ARF-Macedonian cooperation and fought in the Iranian Constitutional Revolution. He had a leading role in the Armeno-Tatar war in 1905-07 and in the Eastern Bureau's Turkish Section from 1909 to 1914.

be made in the near future in settling land disputes.[26] Despite the ARF's commitment to cooperation, even after the Adana massacres, the CUP appeared to have been unwilling in the end to implement land restitution and reform. Given the ARF's investment in the issue and the fundamental role it played in any determination of the extent of justice and equal status for Armenians under the constitution, this problem would prove crucial in the party's decision in 1912 to sever ties with the CUP and to go into political opposition. Delays in the implementation of land restitution could be countenanced, but the abandonment of the issue could not.

Gerald Henry Fitzmaurice, First Secretary at the British Embassy, perhaps best summed up in 1913 the centrality of the land issue in Armeno-Turkish relations:

> After the revival of the Constitution in 1908, large numbers of Armenians returned, especially from the Caucasus, and, though the Committee of Union and Progress repeatedly promised to deal with the matter, especially in the case of Armenians who are in possession of the title-deeds of their lands, nothing has been done. . . . This failure to settle the usurped lands question had been interpreted by the Armenians as evidence of bad faith on the part of the Committee, and of their secret intention to persist in the old methods of breaking up the peasantry.[27]

The Deterioration of Relations with the CUP

Talaat resigned from the government in 1911, but the ARF believed that his election as head of the CUP parliamentary delegation actually strengthened his position. Thus a bolder intervention with him might become possible. This seemed to be the case when the Western Bureau requested the resumption of meetings by the Joint Body for consultation regarding internal and external issues.

---

[26] ARF Archives, C/78a-2, Western Bureau-Turkish Section memorandum on the relations between the ARF and CUP.

[27] British Foreign Office [FO] Archives, FO 40170/19208/13/44, encl. Mr. Fitzmaurice (Constantinople), Aug. 10, 1913, annexed to a report by Mr. Marling to Sir Edward Grey, in *British Documents on the Origins of the War 1898-1914*, ed. G.P. Gooch and Harold Temperley, 11 vols. (London: H.M.S.O., 1926-1938), vol. 10, pt. 1, pp. 513-14.

Talaat agreed and insisted that he, Midhat, and Haji Nazim represent the CUP at the Joint Body. He also agreed to hold meetings regularly every two weeks.[28] This modified Joint Body met for the first time in February 1911. In heated discussions on the conditions in the provinces, the CUP representatives admitted their party's weak position in the interior and agreed to communicate to the governors of Erzerum and Bitlis their protest concerning the killings and the prosecution of a number of ARF leaders in their respective vilayets. The ARF representatives for their part agreed to send one of their field workers, Nigol Tuman (Nikol Duman), to the affected area to investigate the killings in hopes of averting further bloodshed.[29]

In March 1911, a meeting between the Western Bureau and the Armenian parliamentary deputies concluded that, in spite of growing protests in the provinces, local government employees were still biased against Armenians and that the central government had not shown good will and had failed to ameliorate the situation. The ARF decided to send Vramian and Shahrigian to Salonika to discuss with the CUP leaders such matters as land, security, and education in the Armenian provinces. The response from Salonika would determine the Western Bureau's position towards the CUP.[30]

Vramian and Shahrigian met with the CUP Central Committee for five days in Salonika. They reported that they had received satisfactory responses to their demands and that they had taken new approaches toward resolving some of the outstanding issues. Regarding the land issue, a top priority for the ARF, the CUP had agreed that it would be addressed administratively rather than through the Parliament. On the issue of security, the party promised to make an effort to send trouble-making *beys* out of the country to prevent the nomads from doing further damage. Both parties would direct their branches in Constantinople to continue negotiations with respect to the implementation of the agreements

---

[28] ARF Archives, C/108-18, Western Bureau-Turkish Section to Eastern Bureau-Turkish Section, Feb. 12, 1911.

[29] Ibid.

[30] ARF Archives, C/108-42, Western Bureau-Turkish Section to Eastern Bureau-Turkish Section, April 2/15, 1911; C/115-14, Minutes of the Western Bureau-Turkish Section, March 4, 1911. The Bureau also decided to inform the Armenian Patriarchate of Constantinople to that effect.

secured in Salonika.[31]

The CUP and the Western Bureau held a meeting of the Joint Body in Constantinople on April 1, 1911. Present were Vramian, Mar (Mikayel Der Mardirosian), Kalfa (Hmayag Yeridanian), Vartkes, and Armen Garo from the ARF, and Talaat, Haji Nazim, and Midhat from the CUP. The Bureau postponed discussion on other matters and concentrated on the land and security issues. The CUP representatives, concurring that the Armenian population was truly in need of assistance, promised to do all that was possible to satisfy the ARF demands.[32] The CUP also agreed to take measures to prevent the persecution of Armenians but cautioned that such steps be taken gradually. Accordingly, the parties concurred that the government arm all villages, Armenian and Kurdish alike, to enable the inhabitants to defend themselves against the nomadic Kurds who had previously received arms from the government for service as irregular troops. They also agreed to find the means to settle the nomads.[33]

Rostom expressed satisfaction to the Western Bureau concerning the CUP's acceptance of the Armenian demands, but he cautioned that Armenians would again be disappointed, as the CUP had promised more than it could feasibly accomplish. It would have been preferable, he added, if the CUP agreed to fewer items and secured their implementation. In any event, the Bureau needed to persist in its demands so that promises would be kept.[34] The Western Bureau took Rostom's advice and on April 24, 1911, met with Talaat, Haji Adil, and Midhat. The CUP representatives explained that they had been weakened politically and would be unable at this time to press for reforms. They proposed instead to urge their deputies to introduce the issues in the Parliament and claimed that they had already distributed copies of the accord to

---

[31] ARF Archives, C/115-14, Minutes of the Western Bureau-Turkish Section. March 29, 1911; C/108-42, Western Bureau-Turkish Section to Eastern Bureau-Turkish Section, April 2/15, 1911.

[32] ARF Archives, C/115-14, Minutes of the Western Bureau-Turkish Section, March 30 and April 1, 1911.

[33] ARF Archives, C/108-42, Western Bureau-Turkish Section to Eastern Bureau-Turkish Section, April 2/15, 1911.

[34] ARF Archives, C/100-25, Rostom to Western Bureau-Turkish Section, April 17, 1911.

them.[35]

The Armenian deputies would soon submit their specific demands to the Ministry of Interior, and the Western Bureau would present the same to the CUP prior to the ARF World Congress, but the lack of progress had brought the ARF to a state of near despair.[36] ARF deputy Vahan Papazian described the atmosphere:

> In face of this hopeless situation that gradually developed a complicated and dangerous quality and having lost all trust in the CUP's abilities or benevolent attitude, the Armenian deputies presented a new list of demands to both the government and the CUP headquarters. We openly stated the pan-Armenian nature of the demands, in this case the complete agreement of the National Assembly, the Armenian deputies, and the ARF on the terms. Separately the ARF announced that if the intolerable and worrisome condition of the country and for the Armenians was not ended soon, the ARF would renounce its friendship accord and probably recall the ARF deputies in the Ottoman Parliament.[37]

The Sixth World Congress of the ARF convened under these conditions in Constantinople in the summer of 1911. The main item on the agenda was the question of cooperation with the CUP. The meeting ratified the list of demands presented by the Western Bureau to the CUP.[38] The endorsement of past ARF-CUP cooperation notwithstanding, the Sixth Congress was critical of the CUP's duplicity and failure to live up to its promises. A related resolution stated:

> We note with sorrow that, despite a series of hopeful initiatives, in the three years of constitutional rule the government's policies not only have failed to create an improved life for, and reconciliation between, peoples of all religions and races, but they have generally given way to a fostering of distrust between peoples and a denial of national rights. The CUP, rather than progressively eliminating the land privileges of the feudal classes inherited from

---

[35] ARF Archives, C/115-14, Minutes of the Western Bureau-Turkish Section, April 24, 1911.

[36] ARF Archives, C/108-70b, Western Bureau-Turkish Section to *Droshak* Editorial Board, June 1/14, 1911.

[37] Papazian, *Im hushere*, pp. 157-58.

[38] Ibid., p. 158.

the Middle Ages, has encouraged those elements through policies aimed at winning them over.

The CUP has gradually withdrawn from constitutional and democratic principles. The CUP has failed to take steps to combat and cleanse itself of rightwing elements which, increasing their numbers over time, have developed a preponderant influence. . . .

And also, despots, ravishers, and corrupt elements have been left unpunished and have even been encouraged to continue the looting, the massacres, and the marauding.

Therefore the Congress resolves:

That the ARF send the CUP a declaration based on the above observations, verifying the two parties' relations and the explicit conditions for the present cooperation; To attach to it a memorandum about the reigning anarchy in the Armenian-populated provinces. . . . To propose decisive and fundamental means to remedy the Armenian people's extraordinary situation and to implement a number of reforms in a broad egalitarian spirit.

If, after the party's appeal, the CUP and the cabinets drawn from it fail to demonstrate by action that the realization of their repeated promises are imminent, the Western Bureau is authorized to cease its relations with the CUP.[39]

The Government's Precarious Position and Divisions within the CUP

The Western Bureau observed that the government's position was very shaky.[40] All the cabinet ministers had not been appointed yet, and the political situation could easily change. The lack of confidence in the authorities and internal instability compelled the government to depend on the military to maintain power, but this in fact limited the utility of that power in matters of policy, for it would be difficult to rely on the military to enforce the constitution.[41] As the Western Bureau viewed it, the crisis stemmed from the chronic clashes between two competing CUP factions in the Parliament. The ARF sympathized with the progressive and

---

[39] Ibid., pp. 159-60.

[40] For a discussion of the difficulties faced by the government, see Feroz Ahmad, *The Young Turks: The Committee of Union and Progress in Turkish Politics, 1908-1914* (London: Oxford University Press, 1969), p. 86.

[41] ARF Archives, C/108-19, Western Bureau-Turkish Section to *Droshak* Editorial Board, Feb. 16, 1911.

European-oriented group and realized that reforms for national rights and increased autonomy could not be achieved should the conservative faction consolidate power.[42] The abdication of the throne by Sultan Abdul Hamid, the Bureau believed, had shocked some CUP members, who had decided to remain in the party so as to hide their true inclinations but, given the opportunity, would attempt to overthrow the new regime. Some of the dissident leaders, motivated by sheer self-interest, were clearly envious of the lucrative government posts others had obtained. There were also rumors of the army's discontent with CUP rule. The dissidents therefore hoped to seize the reins of power either by relying on the Parliament to vote the current cabinet out of office or by gaining the support of the army.[43] The army command, however, immediately and forcefully denied the existence of any disagreements with the CUP and insisted that the armed forces would defend the constitution and the laws enacted under it. This announcement undermined the dissident faction and hopefully would lead to the end of the crisis.

The Western Bureau announced in *Azadamard* that it supported, without reservation, the constitutional regime against any regressive action. At the same time, the Bureau also informed its bodies that it would publicly criticize the government once the crisis passed and calm was restored. The Bureau then directed its central committees and local bodies to stand ready to defend the constitutional regime and to support the CUP. It also ordered its members, and warned the Armenian population, to avoid providing the conservatives with any pretext that could be used to fan the flames of nationalistic and religious fanaticism among the Muslim population. The Bureau even urged its Daron (Taron) Central Committee to help strengthen the CUP in its region.[44] Although the crisis ended, the Bureau believed that the mere memory of such conflicts would negatively affect Ottoman political life in general and ARF-CUP relations in particular.

---

[42] ARF Archives, C/115-14, Minutes of the Western Bureau-Turkish Section, April 11, 1911.

[43] ARF Archives, C/108-47, Western Bureau-Turkish Section circular number 14 to ARF bodies, April 16, 1911.

[44] Ibid.; C/100-26, Eastern Bureau-Turkish Section to Taron Central Committee, April 29, 1911.

The 1912 Elections and
the End of Cooperation with the CUP

The lack of progress in land reform or in improving conditions for Armenians and the ascendancy of reactionary elements within and without the CUP strained ARF-CUP relations to the breaking point. The parliamentary elections of 1912 would tax the interparty cooperation even further. The two parties had formed an electoral accord for the 1908 elections that had resulted in significant Armenian representation in the Parliament, which included a number of ARF members. The CUP, however, was politically in a weak position in 1912 due to its failure to deliver on many of its promises since 1908 and setbacks in the Libyan war. As a result, the CUP had little freedom to maneuver and resisted bold action concerning the ARF demands for reforms for fear of backlash from the reactionaries. The CUP leadership focused on controlling the reins of power and directed its resources toward that end.

An imperial decree dissolved the Ottoman Parliament on January 17, 1912, with new elections to be held within a month. The CUP leadership believed that it needed to strengthen the cabinet and its own position in it. By the middle of February, three new CUP members were added to the cabinet: Haji Adil as Minister of Interior, Talaat as Minister of Posts and Telegraphs, and Javid as Minister of Public Works.[45]

Negotiations between the Western Bureau and the CUP Central Committee over an electoral alliance dragged out and, in the meantime, the Bureau instructed the central committees to avoid making any promises to the local CUP officials until the completion of negotiations.[46] In planning for an Armenian bloc in the Parliament, the ARF expected to secure seats for its representatives as guaranteed by the CUP as well as support of Armenian candidates. The Bureau opposed allocating three seats to the Azadagan/ Azatakan (Liberal) Party, as its only strength was in Constantinople and Krikor Zohrab already represented its views. The Bureau would cede one or two seats to the Hnchakian Party and one seat

---

[45] Aykut Kansu, *Politics in Post-Revolutionary Turkey, 1908-1913* (Leiden: Brill, 2000), pp. 319-21; Ahmad, *Young Turks*, p. 102.

[46] ARF Archives, C/109-13, Western Bureau-Turkish Section to Izmir ARF Committee, Feb. 4, 1912.

each to the Armenian Catholics and the Armenian Protestants.[47]

The CUP and the Western Bureau agreed that Armenian candidates would be put forward in all locations where Armenians constituted a significant percentage of the population; however, the definition of that percentage immediately became an issue. Further, the CUP attempted to renege on its promises regarding Armenian representation in a number of locations, including Erzinjan, Diarbekir, Kharpert, and Marash. It appeared that the CUP Central Committee had not instructed its branches in the provinces to implement its accord with the ARF. This became obvious in a number of regions. Encountering opposition to having an Armenian deputy from the Trebizond vilayet, the Bureau instructed the Trebizond Central Committee to convince the governor and local CUP officials, who refused to cede even one seat out of seven, of the need for Armenian representation. They should be informed, the Bureau's directive read, that the CUP Central Committee was in complete agreement on the issue of Armenian representation from Trebizond. If this effort failed, the Bureau would consider supporting the leftist candidate. A similar problem developed in Van vilayet, where the ARF had wished to secure at least two seats out of six. In Erzerum, the CUP repeatedly postponed meetings that had been arranged to coordinate and consult with the Eastern Bureau on the elections and reluctantly ceded two seats to the ARF. The ARF in Bitlis and Diarbekir failed to set up consultative meetings with the CUP, much less claim their promised parliamentary seats.[48]

The Western Bureau's relations with the CUP deteriorated as the electoral machinations continued, but the CUP eventually guaranteed thirteen Armenian deputies and promised to assist in the election of another two in Marash and Marsovan, explaining that the lack of a census, the weakness of local CUP chapters, and the existence of the new opposition party, the Itilaf, made inclusion of additional Armenian deputies politically impossible.[49] The West-

---

[47] ARF Archives, C/101-5, Eastern Bureau-Turkish Section to Western Bureau-Turkish Section, Feb. 5, 1912.

[48] ARF Archives, C/109-30, Western Bureau-Turkish Section to Trebizond Central Committee, Feb. 25, 1912; C/101-15, Eastern Bureau-Turkish Section to Western Bureau-Turkish Section, March 4, 1912; C/109-45, Western Bureau-Turkish Section to Trebizond Central Committee, March 17, 1912.

[49] ARF Archives, C/109-58, Western Bureau-Turkish Section to *Droshak* Editorial Board, April 23, 1912.

ern Bureau was also concerned that the CUP would enter into separate alliances with the other Armenian parties and thereby disrupt plans for a unified Armenian bloc led by the ARF. It reached an agreement with Talaat that electoral negotiations with other Armenian parties would be conducted through the ARF. The Bureau instructed its local committees to inform their CUP counterparts of this agreement and to expect further instructions from Constantinople.[50] Yet, while the ARF struggled to sort out its relations with the CUP, its local and regional bodies were deteriorating. The organization had been in poor shape in many regions, and the Western Bureau had refused many requests for fieldwork because it could not spare its own members from Constantinople while the crisis with the CUP continued.[51]

The CUP failed to comply with nearly all of the points contained in the accord regarding the elections, and its behavior caused discontent among the Armenian public and the ARF rank and file. The CUP appeared dishonest in its negotiations as it had lowered the number of Armenian deputies.[52] The Western Bureau reported that the duplicity shown by the CUP was "beyond belief." Rostom also expressed his disappointment about Talaat's role in the affair. In April, the Bureau presented an ultimatum to the CUP to implement the accord and stressed the following points, among others:

> 1. Creation of a committee to oversee the implementation of the accord;
> 2. Formation of Armenian and Kurdish village guards in the Van and Bitlis vilayets in the ratio of one guard for every ten houses;
> 3. Guarantee of the right of return with a government subsidy for Armenian refugees as determined by prelacy lists;
> 4. Recruitment of 200 gendarmes for each of the Armenian vilayets drawn from the ranks of Armenian soldiers; and
> 5. Appropriation to the Armenian Patriarchate of the 12,000 pounds promised to Armenian schools for 1912.

---

[50] ARF Archives, C/109-31, Western Bureau-Turkish Section to Izmir ARF Committee, Feb. 28, 1912.

[51] ARF Archives, C/109-69, Western Bureau to Izmir ARF Committee, May 12, 1912.

[52] ARF Archives, C/60-31, Western Bureau to U.S. Central Committee, April 30, 1912.

If the CUP failed to implement the administrative changes within fifteen days, the ARF would end its relationship, as authorized by the Sixth World Congress.[53] The party would also publish the contents of the ARF-CUP accord and other correspondence in *Droshak* and *Pro-Armenia*.[54]

While waiting for a response to the ultimatum, the Western Bureau effectively halted all contacts with the CUP. In fact, the ARF parliamentary deputies not only avoided contact with their CUP colleagues but also opposed the CUP in the Parliament.[55] The Bureau believed that, faced with many political difficulties, the CUP would eventually yield to the ARF demands. A week after the ultimatum had been issued, the Bureau reported that the CUP was "acting insulted and wounded" and therefore refused to reply, although some CUP military officers attempted to meet with the Bureau. The latter responded to these overtures by stressing the need for "positive work" and fulfillment of its demands rather than pursuing what it referred to as "empty promises." The Western Bureau then asked for advice from their central committees and the Eastern Bureau.[56]

The Eastern Bureau disagreed with this condemnation of the CUP and maintained that the Turkish leaders had not been as deceptive as portrayed. The CUP could not immediately execute all the points that had been agreed upon.[57] The Eastern Bureau maintained that, although the World Congress had authorized the Western Bureau to break relations, the latter acted prematurely. There had been changes in the political climate, and the World Congress had not anticipated the political complications surrounding the elections and other matters. The Eastern Bureau suggested that an appeal be made to the CUP in Erzerum to press the CUP Central

---

[53] Ibid.; C/109-60, Western Bureau-Turkish Section to Van Central Committee, April 28, 1912; C/101-30, Rostom to Western Bureau-Turkish Section, April 29, 1912; C/109-106, Western Bureau-Turkish Section to U.S. Central Committee, Aug. 6, 1912.

[54] ARF Archives, C/109-61, Western Bureau-Turkish Section to *Droshak* Editorial Board, April 30, 1912.

[55] ARF Archives, C/109-69, Western Bureau to Izmir ARF Committee, May 12, 1912.

[56] ARF Archives, C/109-73, Western Bureau-Turkish Section to Trebizond Central Committee, May 19, 1912.

[57] ARF Archives, C/101-34, Eastern Bureau-Turkish Section to Western Bureau-Turkish Section, May 6, 1912.

Committee to execute the interparty accord. The Eastern Bureau further believed that the ARF should wait a little longer for the CUP to regroup to assure that it had the necessary political strength to implement the ARF demands. If the CUP failed, the ARF could then officially sever relations and side with the opposition. Should the party break off relations prematurely, the Eastern Bureau cautioned, it would make the implementation of the accord all the more difficult. The ARF had to conduct itself in a diplomatic manner, the Eastern Bureau advised.[58]

On July 15, 1912, Grand Vizier Said Halim Pasha's cabinet won a vote of confidence by a vote of 194 to 4, one of the largest majorities any cabinet had ever received.[59] The ARF deputies abstained, stating that they would wait for positive action from the cabinet before declaring their support. The large majority of votes secured by the government seemed to indicate that the country supported the cabinet led by Said, Talaat, and Javid, but two days later the cabinet fell. Nazim Pasha (soon to be Minister of War) organized a praetorian guard, the League of Savior Officers, to manipulate the political system and the CUP gave in without a fight.[60]

The Western Bureau found itself in a no win situation. Despite the CUP's deceptions, manipulations, false promises, and delays in reforms, it remained the only party with which the ARF could negotiate. Viewing the CUP as a lesser evil than the opposition, the ARF briefly stopped criticizing it in the press.[61] But in the second week of August, the ARF organs in Constantinople (*Azadamard*) and Erzerum (*Harach*) announced that the party had severed relations with the CUP. Further, the declaration stated that the ARF would remain neutral in any conflicts between the Turkish parties in the Parliament. In an editorial titled "Bitter Confession," the ARF argued that Javid Bey's recent comment that the CUP's greatest error had been its failure to punish Sultan Abdul Hamid and his cronies was too little, too late. The editorial further maintained that the sultan and those surrounding him should have

---

[58] ARF Archives, C/101-35, Eastern Bureau-Turkish Section to Western Bureau-Turkish Section, May 9, 1912.

[59] Ahmad, *Young Turks*, p. 107.

[60] ARF Archives, C/109-106, Western Bureau-Turkish Section to U.S. Central Committee, Aug. 6, 1912.

[61] Ibid.

been put to death, and there were a number of other failings that the CUP needed to confess before it could return to power.[62]

In late September 1912, the Balkan states and the Ottoman Empire began mobilization and, on October 8, Montenegro was the first member of the Balkan League to declare war on the Ottoman Empire.[63] The ensuing war, coupled with the ARF's break with the CUP, placed the Armenian population in serious danger of a violent nationalistic backlash. In hopes of averting bloodshed, Rostom, Murad, and Simon Zavarian met in Constantinople to discuss ways to arm and protect the Armenian communities. The reorganization of self-defense units, they agreed, would require time, leadership, and resources, particularly weapons.[64]

By October, as the Ottoman army was losing considerable ground, an intense debate occurred within the ARF. There would soon be a peace conference to conclude the Balkan War, and the Europeans would divide the spoils. The postwar conference, party leaders believed, would provide an opportunity to present the Armenian case for reforms and to obtain guarantees for the security and livelihood of their compatriots in the Armenian vilayets. The war had created political pressure for the Ottoman government to address the issue. Two conflicting views appeared in the party regarding the best approach to secure the desired reforms. The first of these believed that nothing would be given to beggars and that, in the absence of a national liberation movement, the Armenians would remain powerless in international forums, as experienced since the Congress of Berlin in 1878. Such movements by the Balkan peoples had won them their independence. The Armenian people, this view held, had to organize an armed liberation struggle in order to convince the government of the seriousness of their

---

[62] FO 424/232/237, Mr. Marling to Sir Edward Grey (Constantinople), Sep. 11, 1912, encl. 1, Consul Monahan to Sir G. Lowther (Erzerum), Aug. 22, 1912.

[63] M. Naim Turfan, *Rise of the Young Turks: Politics, the Military and Ottoman Collapse* (London: I.B. Tauris, 2000), pp. 194-95.

[64] ARF Archives, C/109-129, Simon Zavarian to Mikayel Varandian (Constantinople), Sep. 22, 1912; C/60-64, Mikayel Varandian to Simon Zavarian (Geneva), Sep. 17, 1912. Simon Zavarian was one of the founders of the ARF and was considered the "conscience of the party." He moved to Constantinople in 1908 and was a key figure in the Western Bureau-Turkish Section until his death in October of 1913. Murad of Sebastia was one of the foremost partisan (*fedayi*) commanders and a leader of the 1904 Sasun uprising. After the 1908 revolution, he became a fieldworker and organizer in Sivas (Sebastia) province.

demands for reform. The second approach, on the other hand, warned that an armed movement would only harm the Armenian people under the existing circumstances. Moreover, the party lacked an organized military force. This second view represented the concerns expressed by most ARF members, and the party adopted a wait-and-see attitude. Armenians had no choice but to pursue their cause in diplomatic circles.[65]

In the meantime, rumors spread that Armenians serving in the Bulgarian army had massacred Turkish soldiers near Kavala. These rumors, the ARF feared, were intended to incite massacres of Armenians in Anatolia. The party pointed out that telegrams received from the Balkans mentioned no Armenian names among those accused of murdering Turks and that survivors from the Turkish army units had stated that Armenian troops were not responsible for the killings. The party prominently published in *Azadamard* Nazim Pasha's statement commending the conduct and bravery of the Armenians serving in the Turkish army in the Balkans.[66]

Peace Negotiations and the Armenian Reforms

In 1913, the Armenian community was largely preoccupied with the ongoing negotiations between the European and the Ottoman governments. While the primary objectives of the negotiations were to end the Balkan War and to determine the new borders, they eventually included issues of reform in the Ottoman Empire. On January 23, 1913, the nationalists in the CUP seized power in a coup d'état, assisted by army officers who opposed ending the war. Following the coup, the Balkan League resumed hostilities, and the Ottoman army suffered a series of defeats in March and April.[67]

Meanwhile, the Russian government sought to assume the leading role in the resolution of the Armenian Question and presented the Ottomans with three demands: no massacres in the Armenian provinces, no muhajirs settling in the same provinces, and imple-

---

[65] ARF Archives, C/117-1, ARF Self-Defense Body to *Droshak* Editorial Board, Oct. 27, 1912.
    [66] ARF Archives, C/117-8, ARF Self-Defense Body to Samsun Central Committee, Nov. 26, 1912.
    [67] Ernst Christian Helmreich, *The Diplomacy of the Balkan Wars, 1912-1913* (Cambridge, MA: Harvard University Press, 1938), pp. 302, 313.

mentation of reforms.[68] Concerned with potential Russian influence in the Armenian provinces, the British took a greater interest in the proposed reforms. The British consul in Van reported:
"The Armenian race as a whole, though preferring to remain a
nationality under Ottoman rule, . . . would accept Russian rule as
the lesser of two evils." Unless fundamental reforms approaching
autonomy were instituted and guaranteed by the European powers,
the Armenians would press to be removed from Ottoman rule,
"though they recognise that Russian rule would mean absorption,
an absorption which would destroy their existence as a national
entity, [but] they would accept this, the lesser evil, confident of the
individual prosperity which would accrue to them."[69]

The ARF, however, sought autonomy within the Ottoman
Empire and used the specter of Russian rule as an implied threat to
force Ottoman and European action on reforms.[70] The party real-
ized that it had to maintain political pressure on the Western powers
lest they allow the Ottomans merely to implement token reforms.
Accordingly, the ARF Self-Defense Body in Constantinople, for
example, wrote to criticize the ARF Central Committee in the
United States for failing to publicize the Armenian Question in the
United States. The directive stressed the urgent need to lobby the
U.S. government.[71]

A joint committee formed in Constantinople by the ARF and
the Patriarchate prepared a list of demands on behalf of the Armenians in the eastern provinces. The Patriarchate, which had initially
supported the ARF demands, later asked for explanations for every
point prior to final approval. While the original proposal called for
equal numbers of deputies for Christians and non-Christians, the
ARF Eastern Bureau soon offered a modified proposal calling for

---

[68] Russian Foreign Policy Archives, Fond Politarchiv, File 1605, Russian Vice-
Consul at Van to Giers, Jan. 1, 1913, as quoted in Manoog J. Somakian, *Empires in
Conflict: Armenia and the Great Powers 1895-1920* (London: I.B. Tauris, 1995), p.
58; ARF Archives, C/118-11, ARF Self-Defense Body to U.S. Central Committee,
Jan. 9, 1913.

[69] FO 424/237/12, Sir Gerard Lowther to Sir Edward Grey (Constantinople), Dec.
31, 1912, encl. 1, Vice-Consul Molyneux-Seel to Sir G. Lowther (Van), Dec. 6, 1912.

[70] ARF Archives, C/110-1, Aknuni to *Droshak* Editorial Board (Constantinople),
Jan. 9, 1913.

[71] ARF Archives, C/118-10, ARF Self-Defense Body to U.S. Central Committee,
Jan. 7, 1913.

each nationality to elect deputies proportional to its population. It also proposed that the six Great Powers of Europe (Great Britain, France, Russia, Germany, Austria-Hungary, and Italy) guarantee the reforms without naming any one power to act unilaterally on behalf of the Armenian people. Patriarch Zaven Der Yeghiayan raised objections but eventually agreed to study the changes; however, claiming that the hour for such negotiations had long passed, he showed no interest in further discussions with the party concerning these changes. Instead, he introduced his own plan without explanation.[72] The ARF demands were eventually combined with those of the Armenian National Assembly without removing any of the major points, and rather than call for a governor-general of the Armenian provinces to be appointed by only the European states, it requested that the appointment be made jointly by the Europeans and the sultan.[73]

Since the Treaty of Berlin in 1878, the Armenians had been leery of reform plans that required a consensus of the powers to take action rather than a single guarantor. Then, as in this case, Russia was prepared to step in and be the guarantor of reforms in the Armenian provinces. In 1878, the tsarist government had done so under the terms of the Treaty of San Stefano, which was rejected by the other major powers. The Armenian reforms in the superseding Treaty of Berlin had been guaranteed by all the powers collectively, but its terms remained largely a dead letter.

Although the CUP had headed off many of the other Russian proposals, it found itself in an extremely difficult position and attempted to improve its situation by inviting several other political parties to cooperate, including those in the opposition. They invited Prince Sabaheddin to join the cabinet and approached the ARF, but these calls for cooperation were rebuffed.[74] Near the end of September 1913, Russia and Germany, with the support of other European powers, finally agreed to divide the Armenian provinces into two sectors, each governed by an inspector-general. Most

---

[72] ARF Archives, C/118-10, ARF Self-Defense Body to U.S. Central Committee, Jan. 7, 1913; C/110-5A, Simon Zavarian to *Droshak* Editorial Board (Constantinople), Feb. 6, 1913.

[73] ARF Archives, C/118-44, ARF Self-Defense Body to U.S. Central Committee, April 25, 1913.

[74] ARF Archives, C/118-29, ARF Self-Defense Body to U.S. Central Committee, March 4, 1913.

provincial officials would be replaced and elective councils, with equal numbers of Muslims and Christians, would be established and supervised by the European powers through the two inspectors-general.[75]

In the meantime, conditions worsened in Constantinople and many Armenian leaders, including ARF members and Patriarch Zaven, received death threats. Turkish newspapers, especially those of the CUP, began a "poisonous and inflammatory" propaganda campaign against the Armenians. The Western Bureau believed that these signaled preparations for a massacre. At night, groups made black marks on stores owned by Armenians, Greeks, and other non-Turks. Graffiti containing extremist slogans became common. One night, all the Armenian and Greek churches in the Derekoy neighborhood were defaced. The Western Bureau considered these acts of intimidation as an attempt to force the Armenians to declare their rejection of foreign "control." Some ARF members had heard similar sentiments expressed in official circles.[76] After months of stalling and obstruction, the government finally yielded at the end of 1913 and allowed for the appointment of two European inspectors-general, a provision included in the final compromise reform package in February 1914.

ARF Preparations for Self-Defense

The deteriorating situation in the provinces and the dim prospects for resumption of cooperation with the CUP created an urgent need for the Armenians to purchase arms for self-defense to prevent massacres. Armenians, however, lacked the organizational framework and resources for self-defense. In February 1913, Varandian reported that the ARF was turning all its attention toward self-defense and raising funds for armaments.[77] Vramian was sent to the Caucasus to collect funds. There students and workers donated about 3,000 rubles, but members of the bourgeoisie class refused to contribute.

---

[75] Joseph Heller, *British Policy towards the Ottoman Empire, 1908-1914* (London: Frank Cass, 1983), p. 90.

[76] ARF Archives, C/61-77, Western Bureau-Turkish Section to U.S. Central Committee, Nov. 18, 1913.

[77] ARF Archives, C/61-5, Mikayel Varandian (Geneva) to Iran Central Committee, Feb. 3, 1913.

The Armenian community in Egypt was fearful of a revolutionary movement and invoked Boghos Nubar Pasha's name to dispute the need for such action and to reject appeals for funds.[78] Varandian was instructed to approach Nubar to solicit his assistance in the matter. Nubar warned that pressuring wealthy Armenians for funds and importing weapons would attract negative attention from the government. He was particularly apprehensive that involvement in such affairs would harm his official diplomatic negotiations. In case the negotiations failed, Nubar said, he would not hesitate to help the ARF, promising Varandian: "I will put all my skills into the revolutionary effort." He expressed his anger that his name was being used as an excuse by members of the bourgeoisie who did not want to contribute. Nubar indicated that he would write to Egypt and Bulgaria to explain that he was not opposed to arming the people for their own defense but feared that distribution of arms would lead to a premature uprising. He did, however, privately state his belief that the ARF would use every available means to preserve the peace and would take up arms only if it served the best interest of the Armenian people.[79]

The ARF Eighth World Congress and the Approach of War

The ARF held its World Congress in Erzerum in July 1914 but had to adjourn early because of the outbreak of war in Europe. A committee comprised of nine members was formed to stay behind to complete certain tasks that the congress had been unable to get to. While the committee was meeting, Dr. Behaeddin Shakir and Naji (Naci) Bey arrived as envoys of the CUP and the government. They met with Rostom, Aknuni, and Vramian for three days. They asked how the ARF would react to two possible developments that they were predicting. The first was a Russian invasion of Ottoman territory, and the second involved either a Turkish advance into

---

[78] ARF Archives, C/61-33, Western Bureau to U.S. Central Committee, June 14, 1913. Boghos Nubar Pasha was the son of the former prime minister of Egypt. He cofounded the Armenian General Benevolent Union in 1906 and in 1912 was appointed to head an Armenian delegation to Europe to publicize the Armenian case.

[79] ARF Archives, C/61-32, Mikayel Varandian to *Pour les peoples d'Orient* directors (Paris), June 12, 1913; C/61-33, Western Bureau to U.S. Central Committee, June 14, 1913.

Russia or Turkish support for a Caucasian rebellion against Russia. The ARF representatives responded that in the first case the party would obviously defend the sovereignty of the Ottoman Empire, including its lands and its constitutional laws. This response reportedly pleased the CUP representatives. Concerning the second case, however, the ARF representatives stated that they could not answer without additional information, particularly as it was only by chance that the two parties were discussing the issue.[80]

After lengthy discussions, the CUP representatives disclosed that the government intended to take advantage of the anticipated German defeat of France and Russia and to complete their own unfinished business, including the separation of Turkish-inhabited lands from Serbian rule, recovery of the Dodecanese islands, and cancellation of the Capitulations. Further, should the Russians be completely defeated, the Ottoman army would advance to the Caucasus either to conquer or to incite revolution. According to Shakir and Naji, the Georgians and the Muslims in the Caucasus were preparing to rebel against Russian rule, and Armenian support was essential for Turkish success. The CUP believed that the ARF had the power and the ability to persuade the Russian Armenians to act as a subversive element, remaining loyal to the Russian government until a critical juncture, at which time they would ally with the Turks. They gave assurances that the Ottoman government had no interest in occupying the Caucasus; it merely wished to remove the region from the Russian orbit and then grant it autonomy. The degree of such autonomy, the CUP representatives stressed, would depend on the extent of "dedication and service" which the peoples of the Caucasus demonstrated to the Ottoman Empire. Finally, they noted that Germany was committed to the execution of the entire plan.[81]

The ARF representatives responded that they did not possess the authority to enter into such a commitment and that such authority rested with the two Bureaus. In any event, they added, the Russian Armenians no longer exhibited the enthusiasm for Ottoman constitutional rule that they had from 1908 to 1910. The errors made by the government and the CUP in their treatment of the Ottoman Armenians inspired no confidence among the Russian

---

[80] ARF Archives, C/103-30, Arshak Vramian to Western Bureau, Aug. 17, 1914.
[81] Ibid.

Armenians so as to support the Ottoman government. Before promising autonomy to the Armenians in the Caucasus, the government needed to implement policies to assist and gain the support of the Ottoman Armenians.[82]

In Constantinople, Talaat expressed to Armen Garo his disappointment in the position adopted by the ARF. The Bureau convened a consultative meeting with leading party members as well as Krikor Zohrab, where two views emerged. One group expected a speedy Russian victory over the Ottoman armies, and the other feared that a lengthy campaign would be fought in Armenian-inhabited lands. In either case, volunteer units were needed to defend the Armenians but without appearing to act as a threat to the Ottoman government in order not to provide a pretext for massacres. All agreed that the Turkish-Armenians had to fulfill their responsibilities as citizens, including enlisting in the Ottoman army or paying special war taxes.[83] This was the tightrope the ARF had to walk as the guns of war approached.

---

[82] Ibid.

[83] Papazian, *Im hushere*, pp. 278-80.

Krikor Zohrab (Grigor Zohrap)

Armen Garo and Arshag Vramian

❦ 17 ❦

La Renaissance and the Aftermath of World War I

Hervé Georgelin

The Armenian Patriarchate of Constantinople established and funded *La Renaissance*, a daily newspaper in French published from December 9, 1918 to February 10, 1920, for the purpose of defending Armenian interests.[1] Its editorial team included the editor-in-chief Tigrane Tchaïan (Tigran Chayan), and two staff members, Garabed Nurian and Dr. Topjian.[2] Tigrane Tchaïan, the person primarily responsible for the content of the paper, was born in Constantinople in 1882 into a relatively wealthy family of civil servants. His father, Ilia Bey Tchaïan, held the office of *Evrak müdürü* or head of documents at the Sublime Porte. Tigrane Tchaïan was educated in a French school, probably the Collège Saint-Benoît in Galata. He may have also studied at the Armenian lycée, the Kedronakan (Getronagan/Central) School. A well-rounded intellectual and fluent in French, Tchaïan was recruited by the Sublime Porte to serve in the Ministry of Foreign Affairs. After the Young Turks revolution of 1908 had restored the Ottoman Constitution, he established close ties with the Armenian Revolutionary Federation (Dashnaktsutiun), one of the principal political parties in which his brother, Hovhannes Tchaïan, was a prominent member. Tigrane

---

[1] The author gratefully acknowledges the assistance of Raymond H. Kévorkian, director of the Nubarian Library in Paris.

[2] The full title and address of the newspaper reads "*La Renaissance*, Journal Quotidien, politique, littéraire et financier, Direction et Administration: 343, Grande Rue de Péra, 343, Téléphone: Péra, no. 203, Adresse telegraphique: 'Renaissance' Constantinople." Some issues in 1919 appeared in four pages. The newspaper dedicated scant space to financial matters and contained only a short table of quotations from the Galata Stock Exchange. The rare literary short sections pertained exclusively to the past.

Tchaïan was appointed editor of *La Renaissance* after the Mudros Armistice between the Allied Powers and the Ottoman Empire on October 30, 1918.[3] According to him, his articles attracted the attention of the Allied representatives who used the newspaper as a valuable source of information.[4] In most issues of *La Renaissance*, Tchaïan inserted French translations of excerpts from articles that appeared in Turkish, Greek, and Armenian newspapers in Constantinople. The newspaper ceased publication with its final issue on February 10, 1920, after which Tchaïan departed for Europe with the Armenian Patriarch of Constantinople, Zaven Der Yeghiayan (Ter-Eghiayan).[5]

The publication of an Armenian newspaper in the French language was not surprising, as Constantinople and the entire Near East then used French as the lingua franca.[6] *La Renaissance* therefore could provide its foreign readership with news about Armenians that otherwise would not have been accessible. This initiative was especially important in the immediate aftermath of World War I when Constantinople witnessed an influx of Westerners, in addition to the Allied troops and diplomatic staff who occupied the Ottoman capital and the Straits while the peace treaty was being prepared. Tchaïan sought to

---

[3] *Haratch* (daily), Nov. 18, 1952, p. 1.

[4] Handwritten note by Tigrane Tchaïan on the cover of the first of the two volumes of *La Renaissance*, Nubarian Library, Paris.

[5] They traveled through Salonika to Athens, then Marseilles and Paris, and arrived in London on February 23, 1920. Tchaïan accompanied the Patriarch on all his official appointments and meetings with the political leaders of the British Empire. He was appointed technical counselor to the Armenian Delegation in Paris and briefly served as Minister of the Republic of Armenia at the Legation of Athens September-October 1920. See Richard G. Hovannisian, *The Republic of Armenia*, vol. 3: *From London to Sèvres, February-August 1920* (Berkeley, Los Angeles, London: University of California Press, 1996), p. 405. After the fall of the Armenian republic in December 1920, Tchaïan remained in Athens until 1924. He later returned to Paris and embarked on a couple of unsuccessful business ventures. He remained faithful to the Delegation of the former Republic and lent his assistance whenever he could. He died at Sainte-Anne's Hospital in Paris on November 14, 1952 and was buried at the cemetery of Thiais. See *Haratch*, Nov. 18, 1952, p. 1; *Aysor Abaka,* Nov. 18, 1952, p. 1, "Obituary."

[6] See Max Roche, "L'éducation et la culture françaises à Constantinople et à Smyrna dans la première moitié du XIXe siècle"; Klaus Kreiser, "Le rôle de la langue française en Turquie et la politique culturelle allemande au début du XXe siècle," in *L'Empire Ottoman, la République de Turquie et la France*, ed. Hâmit Batu and Jean-Louis Bacqué-Grammont (Istanbul: Isis, 1986), pp. 233-46, 403-17.

inform the Allied Powers about the situation and the aspirations of the Armenians, hoping to secure the fulfillment of the many pledges they had made to the Armenians, particularly in light of the genocidal policies pursued by the Young Turk (Committee of Union and Progress; CUP) regime since 1915.[7]

Further, examination of *La Renaissance* offers an insight into the way Armenians in Constantinople perceived themselves and into the kind of information disseminated to Western representatives posted in the city. The paper is a rich source of information about the ongoing persecutions and the crises facing the Armenians in the empire after the armistice. *La Renaissance* sought to project an image of a unified community, but in doing so it also avoided serious discussion of internal affairs, disputes among the Armenian political parties, and personal disagreements. An assessment is in order to determine the extent to which *La Renaissance* served its purpose and whether the Armenians in Constantinople experienced the renaissance Tigrane Tchaïan so optimistically promoted in its pages.

Constantinople at the End of 1918: The Occupied Capital of a Defeated Empire

In 1918, the Armenian community in Constantinople, which numbered more than 100,000 individuals, was the only one in the Ottoman Empire, aside from Smyrna, to have lived through the war without having been deported and annihilated. On the night of April 23-24, 1915, more than 200 Armenian intellectuals had been arrested, deported, and murdered.[8] The government abolished the Armenian Patriarchate in the summer of

---

[7] British officials frequently met with Armenian representatives. See Levon Marashlian, "Finishing the Genocide: Cleansing Turkey of Armenian Survivors, 1920-1923, in *Remembrance and Denial: The Case of the Armenian Genocide*, ed. Richard G. Hovannisian (Detroit: Wayne State University Press, 1998), p. 117nn10-11. They undoubtedly followed closely the news and views published in *La Renaissance*.

[8] Arthur Beylérian, ed. and comp., *Les Grandes Puissances, l'Empire ottoman et les Arméniens dans les archives françaises (1914-1918)* (Paris: Publications de la Sorbonne, 1983), pp. 16-17, no. 21, Telegram of M. Ledoulx, Drogman at the Embassy of France in Constantinople, to M. Delcassé, Minister of Foreign Affairs, May 1, 1915.

1916 and sent Patriarch Zaven into exile to Mosul, his birth-place.[9] The Ottoman authorities kept a detailed record of the residents of Constantinople, which made it easier for them to apprehend and deport individuals summarily.[10] Even Armenians in Thrace and Bithynia in the vicinity of the imperial capital were victimized,[11] while Armenian males born in the provinces but residing in Constantinople were also deported and most were killed.[12] Rumors of imminent deportations spread throughout the terrorized community.[13] To exacerbate matters further, the CUP regime used the Armenians of Constantinople as hostages in an effort to prevent Armenians living abroad from participating actively in war operations against the Ottoman Empire.[14] The armistice signed with the Allies on October 30, 1918, brought some relief and the prospect of safety for the survivors.

Allied forces began to land in Constantinople on November 13, 1918.[15] Apart from being a military presence, the Allies did not interfere in the internal affairs of the city. In fact, they lacked

---

[9] Yervant P'erdahdjian, "Évènements et faits observés à Constantinople par le vicaire [patriarcal] (1914-1916)," trans. R.-H. Kévorkian, *Revue d'histoire armé-nienne contemporaine* (1995): 249-82; Beylérian, *Les Grandes Puissances,* pp. 328-40, no. 335, Letter of M. Beau, French Ambassador to Bern, to M. Aristide Briand, Prime Minister, Minister of Foreign Affairs, Feb. 24, 1917, encl. Communiqué of the Milli News Agency, Aug. 11, 1916: "The Status of the Armenian Patriarchate"; *Tanine,* "The Armenian Patriarchate," editorial, Aug. 11, 1916.

[10] Johannes Lepsius, ed., *Deutschland und Armenien, 1914-1918: Sammlung diplomatischer Aktenstücke,* 2d ed. (Bremen: Donat & Temmen Verlag, 1986), p. 200, no. 206, Letter of Dr. Johannes Lepsius, Chairman of the German-Armenian Society, from Potsdam to the Imperial Chancellor, Dr. Von Bethmann Hollweg, Berlin, Nov. 29, 1915.

[11] James Bryce and Arnold Toynbee, *The Treatment of Armenians in the Otto-man Empire, 1915-1916* (Princeton, NJ: Gomidas Institute, 2001), pp. 407-22.

[12] Beylérian, *Les Grandes Puissances,* pp. 285-90, no. 298, Letter of Colonel de La Panousse, Military Attaché of France in London, to General Joffre, Command-er in Chief of the French Armies, Dec. 1, 1916, encl. French trans. of "Report by an Inhabitant of Athlit, Region of Mount Carmel (Syria) about the Massacres of Armenians, Nov. 27, 1916"; Lepsius, *Deutschland und Armenien,* p. 206, no. 214, Letter from the Imperial German Ambassador, Mordtmann to His Excellency, the Imperial Chancellor, Herr von Bethmann Hollweg, Dec. 16, 1915.

[13] Beylérian, *Les Grandes Puissances,* p. 134, no. 132, Report from the British Intelligence Service to the Ministry of War, no. 363, Secret, Athens, Oct. 29, 1915.

[14] Ibid., p. 345, no. 343, translation of letter of Gabriel Simbad (American Citizen) to Cheraz, opinion sent to Boghos Nubar Pasha.

[15] Paul Dumont and François Georgeon, "La mort d'un empire (1908-1923)," in *Histoire de l'Empire ottoman,* ed. Robert Mantran (Paris: Fayard, 1989), pp. 577-647.

the means of controlling the Ottoman administration or events transpiring in Ottoman politics.[16] The Turkish press remained highly critical of the Allied presence and of the imminent peace treaty with the defeated empire. Mass protests against the Allied presence occurred frequently in front of the Sultan Ahmed Mosque, especially after the Greek landing at Smyrna on May 15, 1919. Local Muslim officers and civil servants were hostile toward the Allied Powers, and public violence against Christians was not a rare occurrence. Often, the windows of Armenian orphanages were broken at night; the Allied presence in the city failed to prevent such attacks. The Allied supervision in Constantinople, though humiliating for the Muslims, remained largely ineffectual and symbolic.[17]

Documenting the Genocide

La Renaissance informed its readers who had little access to the Armenian language sources about the genocide perpetrated by the Young Turk regime against the Armenian subjects. Almost daily, under the heading "Faits et documents," the paper published eyewitness accounts of the deportations and the mass murders that had taken place throughout the empire. It is not clear whether the Ottoman authorities censored the texts, as they were not yet unanimous in their denial of the crimes perpetrated against the Armenians. In fact, some officials admitted that the government had been engaged in such excesses. Liberal Turkish newspapers expressed their worries about the absence of punishment for those responsible for the Armenian sufferings. As a private person, Grand Vizier Damad Ferid Pasha donated some money to an Armenian orphanage.[18] Fearing possible re-

---

[16] *La Renaissance*, Jan. 20, 1920. On different views concerning the severity of the Allied occupation of Constantinople, see Dumont, "L'Empire," p. 638; Sina Aksin, "Le dernier des Ottomans," in *Istanbul 1914-1923, Capitale d'un monde illusoire ou l'agonie des vieux empires*, ed. Stéphane Yerasimos (Paris: Editions Autrement, 1992). pp. 121-32; Erik J. Zürcher, *Turkey: A Modern History* (London and New York: I.B. Tauris, 1997), pp. 145-47.

[17] *La Renaissance*, Feb. 25, April 2, 1919.

[18] Ibid., July 22, 1919, editorial, "Turkey Facing the Peace Conference." The paper reported on April 12, 1919: "The *Alemdar* [Standard-Bearer] writes that a death sentence alone is very little for so many victims whose blood demands vengeance."

taliation, however, most reports published in *La Renaissance* regarding the atrocities remained anonymous and were neither signed nor dated, making it difficult for the historian to determine the authors or the dates of the events described.

One of the many striking and elaborate articles about the genocidal process deals with the deportations of Armenians in Erzerum. The text in question is long and relatively well researched and was published in two parts.[19] The author, who uses the pseudonym Alexis, identifies himself in the text as a survivor from the second deportation caravan that left Erzerum in June 1915. According to his account, only a few of the deportees reached Suruj, a town near Urfa, three months later. Even fewer made it to Rakka, where they stayed an additional three years. Alexis does not account directly for his survival, but his text does provide some explanation: the caravan was not butchered at once and deportees were even permitted to drive carts or use pack animals until they reached Erzinjan. Alexis at least twice escaped death during the deportation, when other men were massacred. He seems to have been a relatively wealthy man and may have been carrying some money with him at least until August 15, 1915, when the caravan reached the neighborhood of Malatia, where it was searched and robbed. The two-part article presents facts about the Armenians of Erzerum and the surrounding areas, with detailed descriptions of their deportation and their eventual annihilation.

The author mentions the names of numerous perpetrators of atrocities on the deportation routes. He notes that the governor (*vali*) of Erzerum, Tahsin Bey, received orders from Constantinople and ignored complaints by the Ottoman Armenians in his province. Ottoman officials in the region, such as Manduh Bey, the *mutesarif* (county governor) of Erzinjan, were informed of the annihilation taking place. Manduh Bey mocked the complaints of some deportees, reportedly telling them: "We are taking advantage of the opportunity. If the opportunity were given to you, you would do the same." The article also mentions specific Muslim civilians (for example, Jambas Mehmed, Ivan Oglu Mehmed, Kuchek Shukri) who collaborated with the authorities and accused Armenians of conspiring against the

---

[19] Ibid., April 17-18, 1919, "Faits et documents."

government. They benefited from stealing properties Armenians left behind and from the exploitation of women and children. Ottoman officials and the police organized as executioners brigand *chete* bands, including hardened criminals. Mulazim Nusret, who was in charge of the deportees, is described as a "calm and serene" sadist, able to slaughter hundreds of people in cold blood. The Kurd Zeinar Bey, his brother Bedir Agha, and Kurdish tribes like the Reschvan located in the mountains of Keakhta functioned as auxiliaries of the Ottoman state. When a deportation caravan from Erzerum reached Malatia, these Kurdish tribes robbed, raped, and murdered the survivors. The Ottoman official who authorized the attack is identified as "Behaeddin Shakir, special envoy of Talaat, who came to deliver orders and give instructions." The text describes the various methods of physical, sexual, and psychological violence the perpetrators employed against the defenseless and emaciated deportees.

Most readers of *La Renaissance* in Constantinople probably had only indirect contact with Armenians in the provinces. Extensive reports, such as the one about Erzerum, were intended to compensate for this lack of information. The details as to dates, place names, and the names of perpetrators would have left no doubt regarding the massacres. These reports may have also served to remind its Armenian readers in Constantinople of their good fortune in having escaped the suffering experienced by their compatriots in other parts of the empire since 1915 and to strengthen the community's sense of solidarity with and duty toward the ragged, needy Armenian orphans and refugees arriving in the capital. Indeed, according to Patriarch Zaven, the Bolsetsi Armenians did contribute financially to the relief work organized by various institutions for the needy orphans and survivors.[20]

In the newspaper, the testimonies of Armenian survivors are interspersed with those of non-Armenians as a way to confirm Armenian accounts. Such reports by non-Armenians were deemed particularly valuable if the witness quoted was a Jew, since re-

---

[20] Zaven Arkepiskopos [Ter-Eghiayan], *Patriarkakan hushers: Vaveragirner ev vkayutiunner* [My Patriarchal Memoirs: Documents and Testimonies] (Cairo: Nor Astgh, 1947), pp. 280-81; trans. Ared Misirliyan as Zaven Der Yeghiayan, *My Patriarchal Memoirs* (Barrington, RI: Mayreni Publishing, 2002).

lations between Christians and Jews at the end of the Ottoman
Empire were tense.[21] Further, articles published in the column
"Faits et documents" illustrate how absorbed the Armenians were
with the calamity, as the paper presented detail upon detail to
document the deportations and the massacres. What remained
problematic was the official stance of the defeated empire,
which not long after the Mudros Armistice launched a propaganda campaign to trivialize the events and to undermine any
document that validated the accusations against the Ottoman
authorities.[22] This campaign of denial was driven purely for
political reasons, and no amount of documentary evidence
presented by Tchaïan could alter the official stance.

La Renaissance reported regularly about public ceremonies
of mourning, especially in the issues published in the first six
months. The Armenians of Constantinople frequently attended
religious services to honor the memory of those who had
perished.[23] Such memorials served to bring together the Armenians of the capital and the refugees from the provinces, on the
one hand, and Catholic, Protestant, and Apostolic (Gregorian)
Armenians, on the other hand, as they collectively mourned the
victims. There are also accounts of a rapprochement between
the often antagonistic Armenian and Greek communities. Armenians mourned in public for the Armenian and Greek victims of
the deportations and massacres. *La Renaissance* also printed
calls for information about missing people, although such announcements were not as frequent as they were in the Armenian-
language press.[24]

Reorganization of the Remnants
of the Armenian Nation

La Renaissance reported in detail on the reorganization of the
Armenian *millet*. Patriarch Zaven resumed his leadership on

---

[21] *La Renaissance*, Jan. 22, 1919, "Faits et documents," and May 7-8, 1919.

[22] See the issue of July 22, 1919, for Damad Ferid Pasha's quotation while
advocating the Ottoman cause in Paris.

[23] Ibid., Jan. 12, 1919: "A requiem mass: A solemn requiem mass will be
celebrated today in the Armenian Holy Trinity Church in Pera (Ballouk Bazar) for
the repose of the souls of Armenian and Greek martyrs."

[24] Ibid., Dec. 21, 1918, July 22, 1919, p. 3.

returning to Constantinople on February 19, 1919, after nearly three years in exile.[25] During the war, the Young Turk government had also abolished the Armenian National Assembly and suspended the Armenian National Constitution of 1863.[26] Tchaïan reported on the arrival of the Patriarch in Constantinople, where a large crowd of Armenians and non-Armenians welcomed him.[27] Soon after his return, he reinstituted the Armenian Constitution and convened the National Armenian Assembly in March 1919. The revived Assembly, however, did not include all its previous members, as many of them had perished during the genocide.[28] The Armenian Apostolic Church cooperated closely at this time with the Armenian Catholic and Protestant churches. Quite often, the Patriarch was joined by the heads of the sister communities during visits and consultations with Western dignitaries.[29]

Patriarch Zaven, with the National Assembly and its Civil Council, organized relief efforts for the refugees and orphans in the provinces. Despite the fact that Armenian political organizations cooperated with the Ottoman authorities, they did not receive any funds from the government for their relief work. They repeatedly requested that the government repeal the iniquitous laws instituted by the Young Turk regime, that public order be restored in the provinces, and that officials assist the Armenians in retrieving their orphans from Muslim households.[30] The postwar government, however, not only failed to

---

[25] Zaven Arkeps., *Patriarkakan hushers*, p. 277; *La Renaissance*, Dec. 18, 1918, p. 2.

[26] The National Constitution provided for radical changes in the management of the Armenian millet. It introduced, for the first time in the Ottoman Empire, significant democratic representation of the male population and secularization of the decision-making process at the local and national levels.

[27] Zaven Arkeps., *Patriarkakan hushers*, p. 276.

[28] *La Renaissance*, March 13 and March 18, 1919, p. 2, "La nation arménienne, L'Assemblée nationale": "In his speech at the beginning of the session, His Beatitude expressed his joy at yet again addressing the representatives of the nation. The Patriarch pointed out that, despite the unprecedented catastrophe that had just befallen the Armenian nation, it was necessary to put the tragic events of the past behind and to focus on fulfilling the needs of the present. Prayers were said in memory of the Assembly members who had fallen victim to the Unionist tyranny."

[29] Ibid., March 7, Aug. 2, 1919.

[30] Ibid., Feb. 7, 1920, p. 2. On the inauguration of an orphanage by Patriarch

assist Armenians to recover their children but also attempted to
prevent institutions and families from releasing the orphans. In
some cases, Armenian agents responsible for searching for
orphans were arrested, although they possessed the required
identification documents or *vesikas*.[31]

The Armenians formally withdrew from Ottoman politics by
refusing to participate in the parliamentary elections in late
1919. *La Renaissance* published a translation of an interview
with Patriarch Zaven, as the *millet bashi* (head of the nation),
informing his community of the reasons behind the boycott.[32]
He was not the first leader to act this way. The Greek Orthodox
Patriarch had adopted a similar position in March 1919. In
addition, the Ottoman political party, Entente Libérale, also
refused to participate. These election boycotts were intended to
deprive the new government of political legitimacy.

Orphans and Refugees

The fate of Armenian orphans and refugees, the opening of
orphanages, the fundraising initiatives, and the impact of these
on the Armenian community in Constantinople are recurring
themes in *La Renaissance*. The influx of survivors created practical problems for the weakened Armenian institutions, although
Armenian and non-Armenian organizations alike attempted to
collect funds and run hospitals and orphanages in order to
ameliorate the human catastrophe. These activities dominated
much of Armenian life in the capital. The editorial on December 11, 1918 addresses the stark reality:

> Massive numbers of orphans are coming from all over the country. It
> is hard to estimate their precise numbers. They are only a small

---

Zaven, see the issue of April 2, 1919; on the financial problems facing the Civil
Council regarding the relief work for the orphans, Aug. 31, 1919, p. 2. An overall
assessment of the relief work for Armenian orphans appears in Anna Welles
Brown, "Orphanages in Constantinople," in *Constantinople To-Day or the Path-
finder Survey of Constantinople*, ed. Clarence Richard Johnson (New York: Macmillan, 1922), pp. 228-57. Armenians in Constantinople operated 25 orphanages
in 1922; Turks, 8; Greeks, 4; Jews, 2; and Russians, 2.

[31] On Ottoman politics and official protestation by Patriarch Zaven, see *La Renaissance*, May 18, 1919, p. 2.

[32] Ibid., Oct. 11, 1919.

part of those countless others held captive by their abductors. We have made great efforts to gather these victims who arrive at the main railway stations deprived of everything, waiting for some happy coincidence that enables them to continue their trip to Constantinople. Eventually they reach the promised land! One would assume that the process of relieving these orphans would start immediately, but it does not. Relief committees, in fact, do step in but none of them receives any support from the government. The work of gathering and providing for the orphans rests squarely on the shoulders of the victimized nations themselves. Given the circumstances, sometimes it is amazing that these committees are able to function at all.[33]

Constantinople served as a magnet. Orphans and refugees converged on the city where the Armenian institutions could offer some help to the destitute. To cope with the influx of needy people, the Armenian National Assembly levied a tax to finance the many organizations in charge of the orphans. Armenians had the largest number of orphanages in the city and its environs in the early 1920s. *La Renaissance* published news from Urfa, Marsovan (Merzifon), Erzinjan, and Van.

In city after city, the same fate befell the survivors: isolation, destitution, unemployment, epidemics, and lack of resources to care for the orphans. Relief work was slow to be organized and to reach the provinces. Thanks largely to a network of correspondents in large cities, such as Adana and Trebizond, with a remaining or returning Armenian population, the paper was able to shed light on the fate of Armenian orphans in the provinces. The post and telegraph systems continued to function and provided the newspaper with information. To these reports were added accounts of travelers or newcomers from different parts of the country. Also, due tribute was regularly paid to efforts made by American missionaries, the Orthodox authorities, Hellenic officials in Smyrna, and the Armenians themselves.[34]

---

[33] Ibid., Dec. 11, 1918, editorial.

[34] Ibid., Aug. 1, 2, 31, 1919, p. 2 in all. For a testimony by Vahan Loussiguian, a survivor who had wandered in Anatolia for five years in order to escape the massacres, see the issue of Jan. 18, 1920. On the difficulties encountered in the Armenian orphanage in Smyrna, see the issue of June 21, 1919, and on American orphanages in other cities such as Kharpert, Sivas, and Erzinjan, the issues of June

Rescuing the orphans and saving their national identity also served the political purpose of lending legitimacy to the territorial claims made by the two Armenian delegations in Paris led by Boghos Nubar Pasha and Avetis Aharonian (who often collaborated as the Delegation for Integral Armenia). Demographic considerations became a key issue in the debates concerning the future of the Ottoman Empire. The Turkish press and Ottoman officials did everything in their power to undermine Armenian territorial claims. The eastern Ottoman provinces, they asserted, had nothing but a few traces of an Armenian population left within an overwhelming majority of Muslim inhabitants. As a counter-argument, Armenian spokesmen stressed that the voice of every Armenian victim, survivor, and orphan be counted in determining the future boundaries of Armenia.

La Renaissance described the difficulties involved in reclaiming Armenian orphans from the so-called "Neutral House" in Constantinople, where orphans gathered from Muslim households were assembled to determine their ethnic identity before transferring them to an appropriate Armenian or Turkish orphanage. The task became especially difficult when children or teenagers realized that they had little to gain by returning to their Armenian community. For many such orphans who had lost their families in the deportations and massacres, life with their Turkish foster parents and their subsequent acceptance into Turkish society offered a better alternative than life in an orphanage.[35]

There are apparently no articles in *La Renaissance* dealing specifically with the refugee population in Constantinople, although there were at least 3,000 and probably more of them in the city.[36] Various reasons could account for this omission. One is that despite the overall economic hardships prevailing in the Ottoman capital, most Armenian refugees succeeded in becoming self-sufficient soon after their arrival in Constantinople and

---

22 and Aug. 2, 1919.

[35] Ibid., Sept. 2, 1919. See also Donald Miller and Lorne Tourian Miller, *Survivors: An Oral History of the Armenian Genocide* (Berkeley, Los Angeles, London: University of California Press, 1993), pp. 94-136.

[36] C. Calflin Davis, "The Refugee Situation in Constantinople," in Johnson, *Constantinople*, pp. 203-26.

did not remain a burden on the community for long. There may have also been political reasons for circumventing the real numbers. It was not in the interest of the Armenians to emphasize the fact that the surviving population was converging on Constantinople, thus emptying the territories of Western Armenia, the very land claimed by the Delegation of Integral Armenia at the Paris Peace Conference. In fact, even if the survivors tried, it was extremely difficult for them to resettle in the provinces from which they had been forcefully removed only a few years earlier.

Tigrane Tchaïan and his colleagues regularly covered the anarchic conditions and insecurity in the provinces. Patriarch Zaven apprised the Ottoman authorities of the troubling situation and personally visited the Sublime Porte to protest the lack of law and order in these regions.[37] The authorities responded with the usual promises and issued occasional *pro forma* orders to the local authorities. Tchaïan realized that the CUP regime and its crimes had caused major transformations in the social structure of the provinces which the Mudros Armistice could not reverse. A new Muslim bourgeoisie had emerged in the provinces, and the perpetrators of the genocide and those who had socially and financially benefited from it tried to block the return of refugees to their native cities, towns, and villages. The new Turkish society was ready to employ any means at its disposal to maintain the status quo. In his editorials, Tchaïan urged the government to address the problems and to remove corrupt local functionaries, but he was relatively mild in his criticism of the government of Damad Ferid Pasha.[38]

Cultural and Social life in Constantinople

Cultural and social life in Constantinople, with its inescapable superficiality, bloomed anew after the war. An Armenian bourgeoisie had survived there and reestablished its way of life. As

---

[37] *La Renaissance*, Dec. 11, 1918, p. 2, "Presse arménienne, Nor Giank": "The massacres came to an end, but small-scale lootings and isolated murders go on. Every day, new aggressions, new thefts, new murders take place even in the capital! What is the situation in the provinces?"; March 18, 1919, p. 2.

[38] Ibid., April 3, 1919, editorial.

a result, the same pages that contained alarming news and commentary on political developments in the country also presented the life of a privileged world as if there had been no war.

La Renaissance was not a literary paper, and it focused mainly on the restoration of Armenian culture in Constantinople. It did not provide an ideal forum for debates on the cultural issues and conflicts within the Armenian community. From time to time, it published brief pieces about established Armenian writers, while emphasizing connections to the West, probably to convince readers of the Western cultural standards achieved by Armenians. *La Renaissance* reported about Armenian and non-Armenian public cultural events. Theatrical performances received regular coverage. The newspaper carried advertisements for plays, operas, and concerts. In January 1919, an Armenian theatrical company was established, and its first performances were Avetis Aharonian's play, *The Valley of Tears,* and Krikor Zohrab's *Postal*, both of which were staged in the Theater of Piccolo Campo. The folk opera, *Anush*, was performed at the same theater in February 1919. Some of the performers were professional artists who had survived or escaped the deportations. Since Armenian theater and stage production had a long history in Constantinople, a series of related public lectures was organized; Patriarch Zaven often attended these and similar cultural events.[39] These programs, most of which were organized by volunteers, school children, and residents of orphanages, served to rally Armenians around the Armenian artistic heritage as a unifying force. They also demonstrated to the non-Armenian and at least a partly hostile public the vitality and the indomitable spirit of the Armenian people.

La Renaissance's readers might have wondered whether Western Armenians were capable of any cultural renewal after the genocide and whether the deportations and destruction had not condemned the survivors, in their desperate attempt to compensate for the cultural loss, to sterile imitations of what had been erased. It was becoming increasingly clear that by "Armenian culture" people understood not something that belonged to the present, but something in their past, a heritage that needed to be saved and preserved. Classical Armenian choral music as

---

[39] Ibid., Jan. 29, Feb. 13, July 11, Nov. 2, 1919.

standardized by Gomidas (Komitas) Vartabed became a key cultural emblem for Armenians.[40] In its issue of January 16, 1920, *La Renaissance* reported:

> Students of Gomidas Vartabed, Ganachian, Sarkisian, and Toumadjian are organizing a series of concerts, hoping to use the proceeds to complete their Master's degrees in France. The choirs that had taken Gomidas Vartabed so long to organize here [in Constantinople] and in the provinces have been scattered during the storm which has swept down upon the Armenian nation. But the work had to be resumed and the fervor that had almost been extinguished had to be rekindled. The students set to work and published an announcement in the paper. In a few weeks, they received quite a few applications and more than 250 people came to sign up. Twenty days ago, those auditioning for the choir were invited to a general rehearsal of the first concert which will be held tomorrow.
>
> Although the choir is still young and has not yet established itself and although the program is flawed, one has to congratulate the organizers for their efforts. The voices are still too young and do not have enough self-control. In the program, far too much space has been devoted to modern music, which lacks originality. However, one cannot but admire the will of these four young artists to reconstruct the ruined edifice, and the fervor of these young men and women to perform the music of their Fatherland.[41]

Social Life in Constantinople and Remedying Social Inequities

Cultural and social revival was not a phenomenon peculiar to Armenian life. For example, the Philharmonic Society although largely but not exclusively Armenian, was reestablished after the war, and *La Renaissance* placed a call for volunteers to revive its activities. Other announcements referred to entertainment offered in French with no obvious connection to the Armenian world but served the wider Constantinopolitan society. For instance, a French theater troupe, Georges Delatour's Company, performed at the Théâtre Municipal des Petits-Champs in Jan-

---

[40] Ibid., Jan. 25, 1920.
[41] Ibid., Jan. 16, 1920.

uary 1920, and placed advertisements in *La Renaissance*. It would be safe to assume that these announcements indicate the existence of a privileged class whose fortunes remained largely untouched by the recent upheavals and which could resume its luxurious life-style after the war.[42]

La Renaissance also carried advertisements on its last page for goods and services available in the capital. Constantinople and Smyrna were the only cities in the Ottoman Empire where some form of economic activity was taking place, as trade resumed with the Allied Powers and Bulgaria by March 1919, some five months after the armistice. Most of the items and services could be found at business addresses located in Pera and Galata, as on the Grand'rue de Péra, near the Central Post office of Stambul, a renovated area of the old city, and in Kadi-koy, a well-to-do quarter on the Asiatic shore. Furthermore, despite the shortage of housing for the thousands of refugees of various nationalities in Constantinople, furnished and unfurl-nished villas were available for rent during the summer months at Therapia, an idyllic spot on the European side of the Bos-phorus, where foreign representatives had their official summer residences.[43] It appears that only the bourgeois Armenians and non-Armenian Christians of Constantinople placed advertise-ments in *La Renaissance*.

The upper classes in Constantinople, perhaps in hopes of legitimizing their privileged social position, shared some of their wealth with those less fortunate through charitable and philanthropic activities. The economy of the city had worsened during the war as the Ottoman Empire had severed its com-mercial ties with the Allied Powers and the Caucasus and the economic infrastructure in Anatolia was destroyed. High un-employment rates and shortages in housing and food char-acterized the everyday life of the many refugees streaming into Constantinople. Yet, despite the uncertainty of the postwar era, life in Constantinople tended toward normalcy, as the more fortunate groups in society organized various events to raise funds for institutions that cared for the displaced and orphaned. For instance, the Alumni Association of the Tbrotsaser School

---

[42] Ibid., Feb. 14, July 30, Aug. 12, 1919, Jan. 13, 1920.
[43] Ibid., March 4, May 1, 1919.

regularly organized charity concerts in various places, as in the Cinéma Pathé in Pangalti. Often, money collected from ticket sales was totally or in part allocated to a specific charity cause, including orphanages, schools, and refugee shelters. Ironically, the needs and the misery of the destitute seemed to have justified the most outlandish soirées held in upscale social clubs in post-war Turkey.[44]

Other advertisers in *La Renaissance* included photographers. There were also Western style restaurants, bars, hotels, and cafes, such as the famous Armenian-owned hotel Tokatli (Tokatlian), which referred to itself as the meeting point of Allied officers, in hopes of attracting them and their Constantinopolitan sympathizers. Then, as trade with the outside world resumed, export companies began to advertise their services. Dentists, ophthalmologists, and physicians who could treat syphilis appear to have been in high demand in Constantinople.[45] High quality medical care was, however, still limited in the city and remained the preserve of an elite group.

Despite supply shortages in postwar Constantinople and the continuation of a rationing system for staples such as bread, trade relations with the rest of the world began to normalize after the war. *La Renaissance* published advertisements for tea (more accurately "special teas" sold at Thés Yavrouyan). Garments and textiles from Europe were available at the department store Samaritaine, or at the Bazar du Levant. Beauty and health items for women were available at the Droguerie Centrale d'Orient. The last page of *La Renaissance* reveals a European-styled, radically-Christian Constantinopolitan society, busy and rich, far removed from political issues, or the repercussions of genocide still experienced by a majority of Armenians. With its seemingly innocent advertisements, this page projected an image of a Westernized Turkey devoid of social and ethnic divisions.[46]

Constantinople was also one of the few places in the empire, along with Smyrna, with educational facilities for non-Muslims that resumed their function immediately after the war, with

---

[44] Ibid., Dec. 11, 1918, Aug. 12, 1919, Jan. 13, 1920.

[45] Ibid., Jan. 22, March 30, 1919.

[46] Ibid., Jan. 22, March 30, May 1, 1919.

Western curricula and personnel. The traditional system was already established in institutions such as the French Catholic Collège Saint-Benoît of Galata, which placed advertisements to recruit new students. Summer course offerings may explain the attempt of many of these institutions to bring future students to the level required for regular coursework. Similar announcements for Armenian schools did not appear in the newspaper, probably because they did not need to advertise in a French-language newspaper to fill their classrooms. Besides, the elite readership of *La Renaissance* may not have been particularly interested in sending their children to Armenian schools. Education and professional training were a good investment for the future, regardless of the ultimate terms of the peace treaty between the Ottoman Empire and the Allies. *La Renaissance* also published advertisements for lessons in French and English and courses in bookkeeping, and business correspondence.[47]

The Matter of Crime and Punishment

The historical value of *La Renaissance* is particularly high as a measure of the political expectations of the Ottoman Armenians in the postwar period. Tigrane Tchaïan's editorials clearly reflect the political climate among the Armenian elite of Constantinople. He served on the Mixed Consultative Council of the Armenian Patriarchate, and, as one of the counselors of Patriarch Zaven, he was well informed about the inner workings of the Patriarchate and the Armenian National Assembly.[48] An enlightened Armenian nationalist of the post-genocide period, he commented on the political developments in Turkey, the court-martial of the former Young Turk leaders, events in the Caucasus, and the negotiations at the Paris Peace Conference. He emphasized the need for justice in Ottoman society after

---

[47] Ibid., April 18, July 12, 1919.

[48] Ibid., March 7, 1919, "La Nation Arménienne, Le conseil consultatif mixte." Elected members of the Mixed Consultative Council of the Patriarchate included Dr. Krikor Tavitian (Grigor Davitian), Maître Hmayiag Khosrovian, Haig Khojasarian, and Tigrane Tchaïan. The word "mixed" may be misleading because it refers both to a mix of secular and religious members of an assembly or council and to an inter-confessional body of Armenian Apostolic, Catholic, and Protestant representatives.

five years of CUP rule.

From the Ottoman constitutionalist perspective, Tchaïan asserted that justice was the very foundation of human society. Indeed, the defeat of the Ottoman Empire had made possible a resumption of constitutional rule, including court-martial proceedings to try those responsible for atrocities committed against the Armenians. He criticized the leadership of the Grand Vizier Ahmed Izzet Pasha (October 14-November 8, 1918), which had permitted the flight of the CUP leaders who had organized the annihilation of the Armenian population. The government of the Grand Vizier Ahmed Tevfik Pasha (November 11, 1918-March 10, 1919), however, gave no reason to hope for greater justice. On the first day of the court-martial proceedings, Sami Bey, the imperial attorney (procureur impérial), attempted to distort the facts and to reverse the responsibilities. Tchaïan expressed his despair in his editorial. Tevfik Pasha's condemnation of the CUP regime amounted to mere lip service in order to satisfy the Allies. Those responsible for the atrocities continued to live undisturbed. The situation seemed to improve slightly under Grand Vizier Damad Ferid Pasha (March-October, 1919). His government promised some reparations and apparently supported the normal process of justice within the legal Ottoman framework as prominent members of the CUP were arrested and a few placed on trial. Tchaïan expressed his satisfaction in *La Renaissance*.[49]

The newspaper's editorials reflect Tchaïan's cautious attitude in the face of seemingly positive developments. Revealing a subtle distrust toward the postwar authorities, he reminded his readership of the disillusionment that followed the enthusiasm of 1908. A few arrests and kind words clearly could not satisfy the Armenians in Constantinople. *La Renaissance* bore testimony to some gestures of goodwill by the Ottoman authorities. Damad Ferid Pasha contributed privately to the funding of an Armenian orphanage, as if he felt some responsibility for the fate of the destitute children. The first words of repentance from the interior minister of Damad Ferid Pasha's cabinet immediately triggered a strong reaction among Turkish nationalist circles. Vocal criticism in the Turkish press

---

[49] Ibid., Dec. 11, 18, 1918, and Jan. 19, Feb. 8, March 14, 1919, editorials.

prompted the minister to retract his statement on the following day. Liberal Ottoman officials were not granted the freedom to reconcile with Armenians. As reported by *La Renaissance*, these events served to illustrate that while as yet there was no consensus among Turkish officials to deny the crime, denial and distortions of the truth were nevertheless being promoted by the Turkish state itself, by the press, and by acts of violence.[50]

La Renaissance offered thorough coverage of the sessions of the postwar trials, providing the historian considerable insights into the court proceedings. The paper reported many incidents, declarations, accusations, and condemnations, as well as the extent to which the French-reading public and the Western diplomatic chancelleries were familiar with these proceedings.[51] The trials became a major disappointment for the Armenians. Although the composition of the court was exclusively Ottoman, Turkish nationalists rejected the legitimacy of its judgments and treated those convicted as national heroes. Tchaïan, disturbed by the Turkish attitude, pointed out the chasm between Armenians and Turks and between Christians and Muslims, even in Constantinople. He observed that Turkey lacked a justice system independent of one's ethnic or religious background.[52]

After the Greek landing in Smyrna, Tchaïan on May 25, 1919 contrasted the laxity of the Ottoman administration of justice with the stringent punishments meted out by the Greek military courts. Greek offenders in Smyrna were rightfully punished at the very time that most Ottoman genocidal criminals were permitted to live a normal life in Constantinople.[53] From Tchaïan's perspective, this demonstrated the superiority of the Christian state over the Ottoman state, and he stressed this point to convince the reader that an Armenian state would be more just and reliable than the Ottoman Empire.

---

[50] Ibid., March 20, 1919, editorial, April 12, 1919.

[51] *La Renaissance* was apparently the only newspaper to document these proceedings. Taner Akçam asserts that the "trial of the Bosphorus" is documented only by reports in *La Renaissance*. On this subject, see his *Armenien und der Völkermord: Die Istanbuler Prozesse und die türkische Nationalbewegung* (Hamburg: Hamburger Edition, 1996), pp. 163-364 *passim*.

[52] *La Renaissance*, March 20, April 15, May 8, 1919, editorials.

[53] Ibid., July 30, 1919, p. 2.

Tchaïan's constitutionalist stance was difficult to maintain while *La Renaissance* continued to champion the future of the Armenian people in an Integral Armenia separated from the Turkish territories. Some readers may have doubted the credibility of Tchaïan's concern for Ottoman affairs, but he countered such attacks by quoting the liberal Turkish press (for example, *Alemdar* and *Sabah*), which contained many assessments similar to his own but which were also unpopular and subject to strong criticism by Turkish nationalists.[54] There was some ambiguity in Tchaïan's despair. One might have wondered whether he was speaking as an Ottoman citizen desperately awaiting the renewal of the state, or whether he supported a nationalist Armenian narrative that would encourage Turkey to compensate for the damages it had caused.

Material Compensations

Material damages suffered by Ottoman Armenians during the genocide were one of the main subjects of the early editorials in *La Renaissance*. The Patriarchate requested information from all communities to establish a balance sheet of losses, as well as lists of those who benefited from expropriating Armenian goods and properties. *La Renaissance* commented that "new terms are needed for each new situation. They call the properties of the Greeks and the Armenians, who were taken violently from their homes, scattered here and there, decimated, massacred in the most dreadful crime that history has ever witnessed, 'Abandoned Properties.' These are not Abandoned Properties, but rather Despoiled Properties. The euphemism does not veil the crime."[55] Tchaïan's newspaper continued to expose the criminal nature of the understatements in official Ottoman discourse. In March 1919, the newspaper printed a thorough evaluation of the damages in a detailed report published in five parts.

The assessment was based on an informed evaluation of the prewar Armenian demographics in the empire. There had been a

---

[54] Ibid., May 1, 1919, "Revue de la presse, Presse turque, *Justice*, Du Sabah," stating: "Yes, we are plagued! The world hesitates to approach us." See also Aug. 21, 1919, editorial.

[55] Ibid., Dec. 29, 1918, March 8, 1919.

broad social and economic survey of Armenian activities before 1914 in order to account for Armenian properties in the
empire. The final figure of the various damages suffered by
Armenians was valued at approximately 10 billion francs, or
some 474,270,000 Turkish pounds at the postwar rate. The key
issue for the Ottoman Armenian elite after the war was how to
indemnify the Armenian people as a whole rather than according to losses suffered by each Armenian family or individual. *La
Renaissance* demanded, along with the Ottoman Armenian authorities, a complete revision of the Law on Abandoned Properties
to secure reparations at the community level when no individual
heirs of a particular victim survived. The creation of an Armenian state would make it possible to obtain reparations from the
Ottoman Empire for losses suffered by the Ottoman Armenian
population as a whole: "[The share of Armenia] will be the
cornerstone of the economically reconstituted [state]. It will
serve to rebuild the destroyed homes of the resurrected state."[56]

The final law on this issue, adopted by the government of
the Grand Vizier Ali Riza Pasha (October 1919-March 1920),
offered no reparation. The Armenian Patriarchate refused to
recognize this law and terminated all official relations with the
Ottoman authorities. Tchaïan also refused to publish the articles
and expressed the utter dismay of the surviving Ottoman Armenians. Rather than making provisions for reparation, the new
law legalized usurpations and thefts when the former owner was
dead without leaving any heirs. With the backing of the three
heads of the Armenian religious communities, Patriarch Zaven
drafted a memorandum to be presented to the Allied Powers in
Constantinople, but this had no greater effect than the protests
and complaints that were sent to successive Ottoman governments by the Armenian leaders.[57]

International Perspectives

The general tone of *La Renaissance* echoed the pronouncements
of the Allied Powers, which pretended to have won a war of

---

[56] See the series, "L'indemnisation des Arméniens," in the issues of March 13-
19, 1919.

[57] *La Renaissance*, Jan. 23, 29, 30, Feb. 7, 1920.

principles. The Allies promised justice and reparation to the Armenian people, whose condition in the Ottoman Empire had been an international issue at least since the treaties of San Stefano and Berlin in 1878. The Armenians of Constantinople expected the fulfillment of these promises. Tchaïan and the circles to which he belonged looked forward to the creation of a much larger Armenian state than the one formed in the Caucasus and the inclusion in the new Armenia of the provinces of Diarbekir, Mamuret-ul-Aziz (Kharpert), Van, Bitlis, Erzerum, Sivas, Trebizond, and Adana.[58] This Armenian state would represent the new reign of justice in that part of the world, and it would be a civilized one in relations with the non-Armenian populations on its territory. Armenia would advance the principle of equality and thereby benefit all nations in the region. Tchaïan argued that, if the division of the Austro-Hungarian and the Russian empires could be justified, such partitions were all the more justifiable in the former Ottoman lands, where the defeated empire had perpetrated recurrent massacres that were unheard of in the other two empires. He believed that the rightful demands of the subject peoples would eventually prevail.[59]

Tchaïan placed much emphasis on demographic issues and refused to accept the contention that the newly formed Muslim majority in the Armenian provinces had the right to decide the fate of the remnants of the Armenian nation. The Muslim majority appeared so overwhelming, he argued, only because of the CUP's criminal policies of "denationalization" in Western Armenia. Ottoman officials should not be allowed to misuse the Wilsonian principle of self-determination to deprive the Armenian nation of its homeland. Tchaïan maintained that two and a half million Armenians worldwide—the survivors in Syria, Constantinople, and Smyrna, in the Diaspora, in the Russian Empire, and elsewhere—were ready to repatriate to Armenia, which would nullify Turkish claims of territorial integrity based on a Muslim majority. Moreover, the Muslims themselves had experienced demographic losses and did not surpass one million

---

[58] Richard G. Hovannisian, *Armenia on the Road to Independence, 1918* (Berkeley and Los Angeles: University of California Press, 1967), pp. 24-39; *La Renaissance*, March 8, 1919, editorial.

[59] *La Renaissance*, Feb. 15, July 20, 1919, editorials.

in the Armenian provinces, he argued, and they were divided
into several different, often mutually-hostile, groups. If public
safety as well as free access to the territories were secured, he
believed, the predominant element would soon be Armenian, despite the annihilation of half of the Ottoman Armenian population.[60]

La Renaissance published numerous appeals from the various Armenian communities around the world expressing their
wish to immigrate to the new Armenian state when it was given
definitive boundaries. The paper sought to convince readers that
Armenia could easily be repopulated by those returning from
the Diaspora. The Armenian nation "possesses today in non-
Turkish Armenia [that is, outside the eastern Ottoman provinces
to be included in Armenia], in Russia, in Arabia, in Persia, in
Romania, in Bulgaria and in America, colonies strongly organized, conscious of their nationality, who are waiting for Independence Day to return to their homeland."[61]

In his moralizing editorials, Tchaïan zealously supported
the Allied Powers, whose victory he presented as the triumph
of good over evil. One of his editorials greeted with delirious
enthusiasm the solemn entry of French General Franchet
d'Espérey into Constantinople.[62] Yet, despite his firm belief in
the ability of the Allies to impose their peace terms on the defeated empire, Tchaïan oscillated between hope and despair, as
the Allied discourse contrasted sharply with their actual
practices regarding Ottoman territories. The terms of the Mudros
Armistice already showed leniency toward the Ottoman Empire
as far as Western Armenia was concerned: there was to be no
evacuation of the Turkish army and no disarmament of the
Muslim population in the region. Furthermore, the Allies lacked
any immediate plans to occupy the Armenian provinces. In fact,
Ottoman Yemen received better treatment than Ottoman Ar-

---

[60] Tchaïan quoted the *Journal des Débats* (Paris) as his source for this political
concept. *La Renaissance*, March 12, 1919, editorial, "Dénationalisation," and March
8, 1919.

[61] Ibid., April 4, July 4, 1919.

[62] Ibid., Feb. 8, 1919. On the dismay of the Constantinopolitan Muslim population on this occasion, see Robert Mantran, *Histoire d'Istanbul* (Paris: Fayard, 1996),
p. 315.

menia.[63] Western policy toward the Ottoman Armenians was at best passive. Nevertheless, Tchaïan repeated his statements favoring the Allies in order to remind his readers of the numerous promises that had been made to the Armenian people. His constant repetition of such promises, however, appears to have been a desperate cry to escape the postwar realities in Turkey. In contrast, Tchaïan used harsh terms to characterize Turkish society, so much so that his lack of political caution was to preclude any possibility of future residence in Constantinople after the victory of the Turkish Nationalists. This sharp difference in his political approach may be explained only if he truly expected that the Paris Peace Conference would ultimately take firm action against the Turkish perpetrator side and in favor of the Armenian victim side.

Ottoman Armenians and Diplomacy

The Allies negotiating at the Peace Conference, more concerned about pursuing their own interests in the Near East, appeared in no hurry to satisfy Armenian claims. Colonial competition, despite the moralizing rhetoric of the time, left little room for reparations for the Ottoman Armenians.[64] In addition, the Ottoman delegation in Paris did not give in to sentiments of remorse or political pressures. Tchaïan devoted many editorials to the two memoranda presented by the Sublime Porte to the peace conference. The first, issued under Tevfik Pasha, not only misrepresented the Wilsonian principles to the benefit of the Ottoman Empire but even blamed the Armenians for massacring a million Muslims, thereby reversing the accusation of annihilation. The memorandum proclaimed that since Muslims

---

[63] Beylérian, *Les Grandes Puissances*, pp. 707-08, no. 730, Letter of M. Camille Barrère, Ambassador of France in Rome, to M. Stéphen Pichon, Minister of Foreign Affairs, T. no. 2594, Secret, Nov. 3, 1918, with a copy of the Telegram of Sir Mark Sykes to Lord Robert Cecil, Parliamentary Under-Secretary of State for Foreign Affairs. Boghos Nubar Pasha expressed consternation about the armistice clauses to Sir Mark Sykes in Paris. See also p. 709, no. 733, Letter of Mikaël Varandian, ARF Delegate in Europe (Lausanne), to M. Stéphen Pichon, Minister of Foreign Affairs, Nov. 3, 1918.

[64] Beylérian, *Les Grandes Puissances,* p. lxiii: "The Allies never seriously envisioned creating an independent Armenia in Asia Minor."

constituted a majority everywhere in Anatolia, the empire should not surrender any part of its territory. Reacting strongly to this document, Tchaïan contended that the Muslim population did not consist exclusively of Turks and that the logic of the Ottoman position was rooted in the annihilation of the Ottoman Armenians as well as the persecution of the Greeks and other Christians in the empire.[65]

The second memorandum presented Ottoman territorial claims that were inconsistent with the creation of an independent Armenia or Kurdistan. Moreover, the usual anti-Armenian propaganda of the Ottomans continued. Tchaïan believed the Ottoman position lacked realism. Yet, even prior to the signing of the Treaty of Sèvres in August 1920, the Allied Powers began to withdraw their military forces, clearly indicating that none of them planned any large-scale intervention in Ottoman affairs, which clearly favored Mustafa Kemal and his Nationalist movement. The Ottoman cabinet protested against the perpetuation of the unstable status quo, while Kemal proceeded to create a counter-government.[66]

The postwar disillusionment felt by the Armenian elite in Constantinople was not so much about their own personal situation as with their hope and belief that the Allied victory would bring justice and satisfy the Armenian collective demands. Tchaïan's articles reveal an incredible faith in the Western world, European and American alike. He and Constantinopolitan Armenians in general expected the major powers to be morally superior and just. In his memoirs, Patriarch Zaven criticized this naive belief. Armenians, he observed, were waiting with outstretched hands while the Turks were using every means, including the honor of their women, to influence the Allied representatives.[67]

The Republic of Armenia

Armenians in Constantinople had mixed feelings about the

---

[65] *La Renaissance*, March 7, 13, 1919, editorials.

[66] Ibid., April 2, July 25, 1919, Feb. 10, 1920, editorials.

[67] Zaven Arkeps., *Patriarkakan hushers*, p. 302: "Our people were sitting with folded hands, waiting for the Powers to make every sacrifice for the sake of their dark eyes."

Republic of Armenia in the Caucasus. Much like Boghos Nubar Pasha, who led the Armenian National Delegation and represented the Ottoman Armenians at the Paris Peace Conference, they wished for another kind of state for themselves and for the remnants of the Ottoman Armenians. The Allies recognized the existing republic in early 1920, a decision that caused the Armenian political parties to organize public feasts and the churches throughout the capital to hold services in honor of the newly recognized Republic of Armenia. The Patriarch, however, distanced himself from these public celebrations.[68] According to *La Renaissance*, on the eve of the de facto recognition of the Republic by the Allied Powers, the leaders of the Armenian Catholic church and the Armenian Protestant community paid a visit to Ferdinand Tahtadjian, the representative of the Armenian republic in Constantinople. Patriarch Zaven, however, did not join the two other religious leaders.

Although Tchaïan expressed some pride when the Republic was recognized by the Allies, he referred to it as "the Caucasian Republic" or "the Republic of Erevan," which, he complained, did not yet include Western Armenia within its boundaries. He viewed the Allied recognition as a preliminary step toward the justice promised to Armenians, although he was highly skeptical of the Allied assurance that this initial recognition would have no effect on the final definitive boundaries of the Armenian state.[69] Tchaïan was in full agreement with Boghos Nubar, who, along with many Western Armenians, opposed any attempt by the Caucasian republic to speak in their name and insisted that an all-inclusive united Armenian state be created immediately. *La Renaissance* regularly reported news about the hardships and achievements in the republic (for example, the establishment of the first university).[70] Even in his cautious editorial about Allied recognition of the republic, Tchaïan did pay tribute to that state: "The Armenian republic, despite its imperfections, is fully deserving of humanity. Let us greet its blossoming

---

[68] *La Renaissance*, Feb. 1, 1920.

[69] Richard G. Hovannisian, *The Republic of Armenia,* vol. 2: *From Versailles to London, 1919-1920* (Berkeley, Los Angeles, London: University of California Press, 1982), pp. 482-530; *La Renaissance*, Jan. 28, 1920, editorial.

[70] *La Renaissance*, Aug. 17, 21, 1919, Feb. 7, 1920.

under the great sun of the future, awaiting the fulfillment of all its destinies."[71]

The Triumphant Metamorphosis of Unionism

By the time the Allied Powers recognized the Armenian republic at the beginning of 1920, the Ottoman government in Constantinople had lost control over the political-military situation in the country, as Mustafa Kemal's open rebellion against the sultan's government had gained considerable momentum. Kemal and his movement received increasing coverage in the columns of *La Renaissance*, although the subject was suppressed for a long time by government censors. While the majority of the Turkish press supported the Nationalist insurgents against the legitimate Constantinopolitan government, they portrayed the rebellion as a mere misunderstanding between the central authorities and Kemal.[72]

As early as August 1919, Tchaïan was certain that the Nationalist movement of Mustafa Kemal would control Anatolia and resist any peace treaty imposed by the Allies.[73] He understood that individuals such as Kemal rose to power in periods of moral depletion in the aftermath of cataclysms, but he nonetheless condemned the actions of those officers "rebelling against the destiny of Turkey," as if they wanted "to erase the Turkish defeat." He appealed to the Allied Powers to intervene militarily. He appears to have been aware of the fact that with the rise of Mustafa Kemal the situation in Anatolia would change dramatically, dealing a crushing blow to Armenian aspirations to a united nation state. As feared, the rise of the Nationalist movement in the provinces posed yet another threat to the Armenian survivors who, heartened by the armistice, had returned home but were being either exiled again or massacred by the local Muslims.[74]

---

[71] Ibid., Jan. 28, 1920, editorial.

[72] Ibid., June 26, Aug. 7, p. 2, Aug. 19, 1919, editorial.

[73] Ibid., Aug. 1, 1919, editorial.

[74] Ibid., Aug. 19, Oct. 11, 1919, Feb. 10, 1920, editorials, and Feb. 8, 1920, p. 2; Antranig Dakessian, "The Armenians in Post-WWI Turkey (1919-1938)," *Haigazian Armenological Review*, pt. 1, vol. 15 (1990): 401-31, and pt. 2, vol. 17 (1997): 127-57.

Conclusion

The last editorial of *La Renaissance* was intensely bitter. The long period since the armistice had done little to improve the situation in Turkey. Even worse, the Ottoman government in Constantinople now appeared to agree with the Nationalists led by Mustafa Kemal, whose rebellion had gained even more legitimacy by the election of the "new Unionist" Parliament. The Allies had lost every opportunity for Western Armenia—that is, for justice, according to Tchaïan—and instead had preferred to "save the Turks in spite of themselves." The only form of justice for which there was still hope, at least in the columns of *La Renaissance*, was an Allied intervention to bring the empire and the Nationalist forces to account for their treatment of the Ottoman Armenians.[75] Tchaïan continued to assume that the Allies would eventually defeat Kemal's Nationalist movement. Perhaps he could not imagine a different scenario. Perhaps he found it necessary to express these beliefs in French in hopes of convincing the Allied military authorities and the diplomatic corps in Constantinople of the necessity of helping the Armenian survivors. His editorials, however, evince a total divorce between the realities on the ground under the postwar Turkish regime and the Armenian expectations. In fact, Patriarch Zaven's memoirs emphasize the inability of the Armenians to influence Allied policies.[76]

La Renaissance was published for only fifteen months, but in that short period the paper and its editor, Tigrane Tchaïan, sought to inform and influence the French-language readership of Constantinople, especially Western diplomats, about the miserable plight of Ottoman Armenians and the Armenian aspirations for statehood. Further research will be able to assess the role and content of *La Renaissance* in light of the news and commentaries then appearing in other contemporary Armenian and non-Armenian periodic press in Constantinople.

---

[75] *La Renaissance*, Jan. 22, Feb. 1, 8, 10, 1920, editorials.

[76] Zaven Arkeps., *Patriarkakan hushers*, p. 302.

La Renaissance Masthead

✣ 18 ✣

REDEFINING ARMENIAN LITERARY IDENTITY IN ISTANBUL

S. Peter Cowe

Over the last thirty years, scholars have paid increasing attention to the phenomenon of nationalism within the context of modernity and globalization.[1] The creation and sustenance of nationalism has been associated with a process of differentiation from perceived "others" and the establishment of a sense of unity by means of appeal to common bonds of homeland, language, and shared historical experience. This acculturation then becomes one of the central aims and products of educational institutions and cultural media.[2] Significant parallels exist, though in a more fragmentary perspective, in the situation of transnational ethnic minorities within a host state, whose members maintain their community ties within the broader spectrum of relations and articulations of individual identity.[3]

---

[1] For the impact of globalization on ethnic identity, see Richard H. Robbins, *Global Problems and the Culture of Capitalism* (Needham Heights, MA: Allyn and Bacon, 1999), pp. 270-302. Within this burgeoning field one might cite the following seminal works, each approaching the issue from a fundamentally different perspective: Miroslav Hroch, *Social Preconditions of National Revival in Europe: A Comparative Analysis of the Social Composition of Patriotic Groups among the Smaller European Nations*, trans. Ben Fowkes (New York: Columbia University Press, 2000); Anthony D. Smith, *Theories of Nationalism*, 2d ed. (New York: Holmes and Meier, 1983); Eric Hobsbawm, *Nations and Nationalism since 1780: Programme, Myth, Reality*, 2d ed. (Cambridge: Cambridge University Press, 1992); Ernest Gellner, *Nations and Nationalism* (Ithaca, NY: Cornell University Press, 1983); Benedict Anderson, *Imagined Communities* (London: Verso, 1991).

[2] Gellner, *Nations and Nationalism*, pp. 54-55, 59-60.

[3] For an application of these theoretical perspectives to the transformation of Armenian ethnic identity in the United States, see Anny Bakalian, *Armenian-Americans: From Being to Feeling Armenian* (New Brunswick, NJ: Transaction Publishers, 1993).

As Benedict Anderson and others have demonstrated, the role of the intelligentsia and of print capitalism was of seminal importance in promoting nationalist yearnings.[4] Literature proved a potent vehicle for the articulation and promotion of Armenian nationalist aspirations during the nineteenth century when the historical homeland was partitioned between the Russian and Ottoman empires.[5] Although these found fleeting expression in the first Republic of Armenia (1918-20), they were stifled immediately with the region's incorporation into the Soviet Union. Meanwhile, in the Ottoman territories to the west, Armenians suffered the destruction of genocide and deportation, precipitating the creation of the current worldwide dispersion.[6] In the absence of a national state, certain writers in Soviet Armenia and in the diasporan communities provided the intellectual leadership as spokesmen for the silent majority and in doing so held in common the different sides of what came to be the Cold War divide.[7]

This essay concentrates on Zahrad (Zahrat—Zareh Yaldizian, 1924-2007) and Zareh Khrakhuni (Artin Jiumbiushian, 1926-), the two most seasoned Armenian poets in Istanbul since World War II.[8] They represent an emerging diversity of literary approaches to culture and identity, and their prolific output over several decades has been referred to as the Istanbul school with a sense of an

---

[4] Anderson, *Imagined Communities*, pp. 67-82.

[5] See Ronald G. Suny, *Looking Toward Ararat* (Bloomington: Indiana University Press, 1993), pp. 52-62.

[6] For an overview of the phenomenon, see Robin Cohen, *Global Diasporas: An Introduction* (Seattle: University of Washington Press, 1997), pp. 31-55.

[7] In this regard one might single out poets like Hovhannes Shiraz (1915-1984) and Paruyr Sevak (1924-1971). For a critical assessment of the former, see Kevork B. Bardakjian, *A Reference Guide to Modern Armenian Literature, 1500-1920* (Detroit: Wayne State Press, 2000), pp. 226-28, 506-09, and for the latter, Seyran Grigoryan, *Paruyr Sevak: Ardzagankogh antare* [Echoing Forest] (Erevan: Van Aryan, 1998).

[8] For a fairly comprehensive bibliography of Khrakhuni's publications up to 1998, see Suren Danielian, *Zareh Khrakhuni: Banasteghtsutian azatagrume* [Zareh Khrakhuni: The Liberation of Poetry] (Echmiadzin: Catholicosate of the Mother See, 1999), pp. 273-75. Since then his major collections are *Hobelenakan* [Jubilee] (Istanbul: Murad Ofset, 2002) and *Andradardzumner: Antskali veradardz, husheru otabar* [Reflections: Desirable Return, Balloon of Memories] (Istanbul: Murad Ofset, 2002). It is significant that in more recent years Khrakhuni has branched out into drama. His two main contributions to that genre are *Potorik* [Storm] (Istanbul: Murad Ofset, 1999) and *Dimaki etev* [Behind the Mask] (Istanbul: Murad Ofset, 2000).

unparalleled tradition in most diasporan centers.[9] Moreover, their continuity in diversity reveals some of the tensions involved in negotiating Armenian identity in the old Ottoman capital.

Once the bustling hub of the Armenian ethno-religious *millet* or community in the vast empire, the now-diminished community has had to come to terms with its current status as a small ethnic minority in the Turkish nation state. The Armenians of Istanbul have faced important changes and challenges, although, unlike their deported compatriots, their experiences did not involve the physical dislocation and international dispersion, which demanded that the immigrants grapple with a totally unfamiliar environment, social practices, and cultural expectations.[10] In Ottoman times, as a confessional minority, Armenians enjoyed a certain degree of autonomy in the conduct of their internal affairs.[11] The corporate association was with the millet, which mediated their participation in the affairs of state, whereas now as Turkish citizens, it is their community affiliation which is problematized. Previously, the imposition of various taxes and dress codes highlighted their distinctiveness, while now there is pressure to conform.[12] Moreover, periodically arbitrary restrictions have been placed on the Armenian Patriarchate, which remains as one of the few loci for ethnic identity.[13] As the two poets were honing their craft in the

---

[9] For the contrasting sense of alienation from the past and the disruption of tradition that characterized Armenian writing in the significant early diasporan literary center of Paris, see Talar Chahinian, "Paris Attempt: Rearticulation of (National) Belonging and the Inscription of Aftermath Experience in French Armenian Literature between the Wars," Ph.D. diss., University of California, Los Angeles, 2008.

[10] For a survey of these changes, see Richard H. Dekmejian, "The Armenian Diaspora," in *The Armenian People from Ancient to Modern Times*, vol. 2: *Foreign Dominion to Statehood: The Fifteenth Century to the Twentieth Century*, ed. Richard G. Hovannisian (New York: St. Martin's Press, 1997), pp. 422-23.

[11] Hagop Barsoumian, "The Eastern Question and the Tanzimat Era," in Hovannisian, *Armenian People*, pp. 182-201; Mesrob Ashjian, "The Millet System," in *Armenian Church Patristic and Other Essays* (New York: Armenian Prelacy, 1994), pp. 227-51.

[12] For the imposition of a wealth tax on non-Muslim citizens in Turkey during World War II, see Dekmejian, "The Armenian Diaspora," p. 422; Faik Ökte, *The Tragedy of the Turkish Capital Tax*, trans. Geoffrey Cox (London: Croom Helm, 1987). I am indebted to Mr. Kurken Alyanakian for drawing my attention to this latter source. Another aspect of the issue is the alteration of their surnames to render them less ostensibly Armenian. Thus, Balian becomes Bal and Nalbandian becomes Nalbandoğlu.

[13] The patriarchate has published an official organ *Shoghakat* from time to time. It

middle of the 1950s, tensions over the Cyprus issue erupted in Istanbul, resulting in the desecration of Armenian and Greek churches and cemeteries.[14] Further, Turkish authorities repeatedly attempted to interfere in the election of a successor at the death of patriarchs Karekin I Khachadourian (Garegin I Khachaturian, 1951-61), Shnork I Kalustian (Galustian, 1963-90), and Karekin II Kazanjian (Garegin II Gazanjian, 1990-98).[15]

The poets also had to contend with significant demographic and social changes within the Armenian community. Armenian emigration from Turkey gained momentum and reduced the Armenian population of the city to less than 40,000, taking a certain toll on the community's morale.[16] Heir to the illustrious traditions of the renaissance of West Armenian letters in the second half of the nineteenth century, the community's cultural impact was eclipsed by other diasporan centers beginning in the 1920s.[17]

Beyond the specifics of the Armenian situation, one must also consider the more general atmosphere of conformism in the Turkish polity and the debates concerning Kurdish nationalism and Muslim fundamentalism.[18] In the absence of multicultural media, the articulation of ethnic or other differentiated identity within the state perforce maintains a lower profile. These are some of the factors delineating the parameters that have defined the oeuvre of Zahrad and Khrakhuni over their literary career spanning the last half-century.

Born in Istanbul, Zahrad and Khrakhuni attended the Mekhi-

---

also oversees the Surp Prgich (Surb Prkich) Hospital in Istanbul, which maintains a periodical of its own.

[14] Dekmejian, "Armenian Diaspora," pp. 422-23.

[15] Ibid., p. 423.

[16] In the absence of reliable statistics, the above figure has been conservatively drawn. Other sources state the current population as thirty to thirty-five thousand.

[17] For a treatment of the literary impact of these developments, see Bardakjian, *Reference*, pp. 230-36. For the same trend in Jerusalem, see Victor Azarya, *The Armenian Quarter of Jerusalem: Urban Life behind Monastery Walls* (Berkeley, Los Angeles, London: University of California Press, 1984), and my review of this work in *Journal of the Society for Armenian Studies* 2 (1986): 208-14.

[18] See inter alia Michelle Penner Angrist, "Party Systems and Regime Formation: Turkish Exceptionalism in Comparative Perspective," in *Authoritarianism in the Middle East: Regimes and Resistance*, ed. Marsha Pripstein Posusney and Michelle Penner Angrist (Boulder, CO: Lynne Rienner Publications, 2005), pp. 165-202.

tarist Academy, one of the finest schools for boys in the city.[19] In the absence of political organizations promoting Armenian identity, the Sanuts Miutiun or school alumni group is one of the main forms of secular association for the Armenian community. The alumni newsletter, which Zahrad edited for a while, became one of the first for presenting their literary works.[20]

The poetic movement Zahrad and Khrakhuni helped shape, the latter being the main theoretician, sought to introduce a break with the earlier generations of the city's literary past (for example, Varoujan, Tekeyan, and Zarifian), the mourning of its passing, and attempts at its slavish imitation.[21] The movement stressed the themes of simplicity of language and form and focused on contemporary realities, as uninspiring as they might be.[22] Poetry was to be harnessed to the known, through what was termed Objective Symbolism. As Khrakhuni put it, "poetry should not be an inaccessible ivory tower, but rather a beautifully constructed house, which anyone could comprehend, and where they would feel at home."[23] Its manifesto may be broadly paralleled by that of the trio of poets forming the Garip coterie of Turkish writers Orhan Veli Kamik (1914-1950), Oktay Rifat (1914-1988), and Melih Cevdet Anday (1915-2002), who similarly strove to distance themselves from the outmoded and restrictive conventions of Ottoman court poetry with its complex meters and abstruse vocabulary. They made literature more accessible to the public in a more modern idiom closer to that of colloquial speech.[24]

---

[19] Hilta Galfaian-Panosian, *Polsahay nor banasteghtsutiune* [Modern Armenian Poetry of Istanbul] (Antelias: Catholicosate of Cilicia, 1998), pp. 103, 168.

[20] Karo Abrahamian, *Zhamanakakits istanpulahay groghner* [Contemporary Armenian Writers of Istanbul] (Antelias: Catholicosate of Cilicia, 2004), vol. 1, p. 109.

[21] These principles were enunciated by Khrakhuni in an article "Mayr Gitse" [The Main Line] published in the Istanbul literary journal *T O*, whose first issue appeared in May 1959.

[22] See Aleksandr Topchian's introduction in Zareh Khrakhuni, *Es ev urishner* [I and Others] (Erevan: Sovetakan Grogh, 1982), p. 4.

[23] Ibid., p. 6.

[24] Talat S. Halman, *Living Poets of Turkey: An Anthology of Modern Poems* (Istanbul: Dost Publications, 1989), pp. 18-19. Zahrad also alludes to certain parallels in an interview with Edward H. Foster, "An Interview with Zahrad: An Armenian Poet in Istanbul," *Ararat* 28/1 (1987): 41-42; see also Nermin Menemencioglu and Fahir Iz, eds., *The Penguin Book of Turkish Verse* (Harmondsworth: Penguin Books, 1978), pp. 254-82.

Zahrad

This direct and informal approach, employing blank unrhymed, basically unpunctuated verse, is well illustrated by Zahrad's "Ayspes amen aravot" (Every Morning Like This) from his collection *Bari erkink* (Good Sky, 1971).[25] Here the poet parallels the daily movement from home to work with the existential distancing, which accompanies this process as we put on our public face to interact with those of others, while our inner selves stand anxiously at the window and stare at our departure. Although this observation has general significance, it speaks with particular poignancy to the ethnic minority, since the public sphere is associated with the majority, dominant culture. Zahrad's uncanny ability of the image to illustrate the dull daily soul-destroying routine of the megalopolis is also exemplified in a poem titled "Vosp stkogh kine" (The Woman Cleaning Lentils) in his first collection *Mets kaghake* (The Big City, 1960).[26] As J. Alfred Prufrock measured out his life with coffee spoons, so the poet's staccato rhythmic presentation of this monotonous, relentless ritual of going through the lentils to extract the stones powerfully embodies the quotidian of the small man in the urban conglomerate.[27] The poem highlights Zahrad's focus on the individual and its intimations of the universal. The very fact that the work is written in Armenian, however, implies a particular bond of solidarity with his community and readership. In this lack of spatial closeness or ghetto mentality, the reader potentially "buys into" and shares the values the work encodes.

Zahrad's concern for alienation and loneliness in part may reflect the Istanbul Armenian's social setting. Similarly, the reference to nuclear war in his poem "Grahashiv" (Algebra) gains greater moment considering Turkey's strategic position on the Cold War divide. On occasion Zahrad's presentation of the human

---

[25] For the original, see *Zahrat* (Paris: Erebuni Publications, 1971), p. 42, trans. Ralph Setian, *Zahrad: Selected Poems* (Hull, Canada: Manna Publishing, 1974), p. 22. In addition to English, a number of Zahrad's poems have been translated into French, Greek, Arabic, Russian, Lithuanian, Latvian, and Estonian.

[26] *Zahrat*, pp. 25-26; Setian, *Zahrad*, p. 13.

[27] T.S. Eliot, "The Love Song of J. Alfred Prufrock," in *The Complete Poems and Plays 1909-1950* (New York: Harcourt, Brace and World, 1971), p. 5.

condition is extremely bleak, as in "Kurch" (Rags).[28] When the poet describes the snow-white body revealed when the ragged clothing is removed, the reader may foresee a more positive contrast between inner and outer being set up. However, precisely at that point the impression is unexpectedly dashed by the fact that "disillusioned egos" within the body "crumpled like rags." The poetic circle has been drawn and congruence has been established between outer and inner realism: both are torn and fragmented.

In "Krkes" (Circus), not unlike some of the works in Khra-khuni's cycle *Hrashkneru srahen* (From the Hall of Miracles, 1968), such as "Odzapar" (Snake Dance), Zahrad comments on the similarities of man and beast.[29] For a time the trainer not only controls the animals but holds the audience in his thrall as well. Human mortality and insignificance is starkly handled in the epigram titled "Antsav" (It Passed), encapsulating a life within the brief moment of a funeral cortege:

They were sitting,
They stood up,
They sat down again,
A coffin passed by.[30]

True to his modernist creed, Zahrad allows no room for religious sentimentality. In "Latsi gisher" (Night of Weeping), alluding to Christ's crucifixion, humanity commiserates with his suffering but remonstrates that he, being divine, simply cannot comprehend the profound tedium of human existence.[31] Yet, in the poet's estimation, man's lot is not ultimately tragic, but tragicomic, a state he describes with much ironic humor. Focusing on the determination of the small man to survive, in "Erknavar" (Celestial Flame), Zahrad contrasts the obfuscation of the stars by autumn

---

[28] Zahrat, *Mets kaghake* [The Big City] (Erevan: Sovetakan Grogh, 1978), pp. 59, 68; Setian, *Zahrad*, pp. 9, 11.

[29] Zahrat, *Mets kaghake*, pp. 80-81; Setian, *Zahrad*, p. 14. For Khrakhuni's poem "Odzapar" [Snake Dance], see Khrakhuni, *Es ev urishner*, p. 199, and trans. Agop J. Hacikyan and Arsène Mamourian, *Selected Poems of Zareh Khrakhouni* (Lewiston, NY: Edwin Mellen Press, 1990), p. 47.

[30] Zahrat, *Mets kaghake*, p. 142; Setian, *Zahrad*, p. 40.

[31] Zahrat, *Mets kaghake*, p. 76; Setian, *Zahrad*, p. 12.

winds with the power of the tiny, feeble lamp to endure.[32] Suspicious of great undertakings, in "Herosamart" (Heroic Struggle) he employs a mock-heroic spirit to fit the images of martial conflict to the inner problems of the individual.[33] Similarly, in "Atenk 1969" (Athens 1969), Zahrad indulges in an irreverent juxtaposition of classical antiquity with modern reality. Discussing a temple at Vouliagmeni, he quips: "I used to think Venus was born somewhere around here—I saw one—when I asked her, she said she was born in Sweden."[34] His most popular embodiment of man's tragicomic predicament is undoubtedly Gigo (Kiko) and his continuing saga. The latest installment "Kikoyi verjin arkatsakhndrutiune" (Kiko's Final Adventure) from the collection *Tsayre tsayrin* (Barely Enough) pokes fun at the achievements of the space age by suggesting that, in fact, nothing is new under the sun. Once Kiko rises rocket-like into the atmosphere, he makes the amazing discovery that he is actually revolving round the sun, just like the age-old planets, and as he used to do sunbathing at the seashore back on Mother Earth.[35]

Although reticent about concretizing the ethnic element, Zahrad indicates his attachment to neighbors and neighborhood, as a poet in society, articulating their colorful dreams and assuring them of their fulfillment. At the same time, in his cycle *Gunavor sahmanner* (Colorful Borders), he relativizes various types of spatial perspective. One of these, "Sahmanaglukh" (Frontier), once again underlines his broad view of humanity. With pithy conciseness, he states that people are just as mad on that side of the border as on this. Both sides are deceived in imagining they are different from the rest.[36]

Zahrad vents his irreverence not only against tradition but also against his readers, who are constantly teased and cajoled. In the foreword to his first collection he humorously contrasts the public record of the written word with the privacy of the spoken in terms

---

[32] *Zahrat*, p. 50; Setian, *Zahrad*, p. 34.

[33] *Zahrat*, p. 48; Setian, *Zahrad*, p. 29.

[34] Zahrat, *Mets kaghake*, pp. 127-28; Setian, *Zahrad*, pp. 27-28.

[35] Zahrat, *Tsayre tsayrin* [End to End] (Istanbul: Murad Ofset, 2001), pp. 54-55.

[36] Zahrat, *Zahrat, Banasteghtsutiunner* [Zahrat Poems], vol. 1 (Istanbul: Sena Ofset, 2006), p. 172; Setian, *Zahrad*, p. 18. See also the development of the theme of boundaries, borders, limitations, and the possibility of exploring beyond them in Zahrat, *Magh me jur* [A Sieve of Water] (Istanbul: Murad Ofset, 1995), pp. 91-98.

of lovers' intimate secrets. This relationship with his readers is only amplified in his book *Magh me jur* (A Sieve of Water), whose quizzical title reveals the poet in the role of *homo ludens*. While in one poem he portrays himself as an itinerant peddler parceling out wisdom to customers,[37] in another he celebrates the licit magic of poetry in spreading illusion from his sieve as he darts from shore to shore.[38] In a rare personal glimpse under the title "Hartsazruyts banasteghtsin het" (Interview with the Poet), when posed the question whether he has any complaints, with wry humor he responds that he is perplexed when a theme for a new poem comes to mind. He confesses that he may often lack the right mood or frame of mind to write, but on days when he does not put pen to paper he feels empty and frustrated that he has nothing to give.[39]

Khrakhuni

Khrakhuni was the theoretician of the Istanbul group of poets. He continued his education at Istanbul University, where he studied law, philosophy, and psychology, and pursued advanced studies in literature in Paris.[40] Although most of Khrakhuni's poems are relatively short, he tends to employ longer periods than Zahrad and is even more prone to sustain themes over several poems, as in his cycles on the natural elements of water and birds in his collection *Tsaghikneru pes* (Like Flowers, 2000).[41] It is striking that the poet dates most of his compositions, holding some in reserve for several years until a suitable collection emerges for their publication.

As wordplay is important for Zahrad, it is arguably more so for Khrakhuni. A good example of his verbal artifice is provided by "Mayramut" (Sunset, 1971), which reflects on various relations between beauty and death:

The sunset dies like all beautiful things,
The sunset is beautiful like all dying things,

---

[37] Zahrat, *Magh me jur*, p. 136.
[38] Ibid., p. 5.
[39] Zahrat, *Tsayre tsayrin*, p. 87.
[40] Galfaian-Panosian, *Polsahay nor banasteghtsutiune*, p. 168.
[41] Zareh Khrakhuni, *Tsaghikneru pes* [Like Flowers] (Istanbul: Murad Ofset, 2000).

The sunset is very beautiful because it dies.[42]

Similarly, "Tsatktuk" (Hopping About) of 1987 exhibits something of Zahrad's irony in arguing that by engaging in the activity of hopping you may on the one hand break a record, but on the other break a leg.[43] Unlike Zahrad, however, he concludes that even if you are lame "you can still hop from one heart to another," Khrakhuni provides powerful examples of what he termed Objective Symbolism, such as "Karayr" (Cave, 1964), which parallels physical and psychic space. Describing a cave of prehistoric man where "only yesterday, it appears, they roasted a deer," he also suggests how close modern man is to his ancestors in his unconscious, dreams, and imagination.[44] Likewise, he discusses the limits of human freedom in the poem "Vkayutiun" (Witnessing) in conjunction with an orangutan in a zoo cage.[45]

One of Khrakhuni's recurring images is the path or road of life. In "Kar" (Stone, 1963) he employs it with regard to the meaning and significance of his poetic output. Likening his craft to that of a stonemason, carving at the roadside as people hurry past, he ponders on whether it will be regarded in the present, hailed in the future, seen as a "dedication to ancient heritage" or simply ignored at the curb. Particularly in his early composition he devotes attention to small everyday themes, as in "Npatak" (Goal, 1954), which describes the elation of someone on the ferryboat watching another person left at the quayside or a passenger in a streetcar looking at others stranded at the stop, both of which are ironically referred to as the author's "one supreme goal." Unlike Zahrad, Khrakhuni handles Christian subjects more positively, as in his early self-explanatory works "Surb Tsnund" (Christmas) and "Avetaran" (Gospel), as well as his "Srbankar" (Icon, 1984), which offers an *ekphrasis* of a painting of the Madonna and Child.[46]

---

[42] Zareh Khrakhuni, *zbosaptoyt* [Excursion] (Istanbul: Murad Ofset, 1978), p. 12, trans. Hacikyan and Mamourian, *Selected Poems*, p. 71.

[43] Zareh Khrakhuni, *Ughiner* [Paths] (Istanbul: Murad Ofset, 1987) p. 93, trans. Hacikyan and Mamourian, *Selected Poems*, p. 124.

[44] Khrakhuni, *Es ev urishner*, pp. 16-18, trans. Hacikyan and Mamourian, *Selected Poems*, pp. 19-21.

[45] Khrakhuni, *Es ev urishner*, pp. 157-58, trans. Hacikyan and Mamourian, *Selected Poems*, pp. 37-38.

[46] Khrakhuni, *Es ev urishner*, pp. 9-11, 120-21; Khrakhuni, *Tonakarg* [Order of

More salient for our purpose is his gradual espousal of more explicitly national themes in the 1970s. His "Requiem" (1972), though fundamentally universal in its reaching out to "all those who had no grave," contains certain phrases that may be interpreted as alluding to the Armenian Genocide—for example, "roads with no return that lead nowhere," "those who were sacrificed in vain," "penitence and expiation to all cowards disproportionately stronger, richer than us, yet owing," and "dreams which had no tomorrow."[47]

Khrakhuni visited the former Soviet republic of Armenia in the middle of the 1970s, which is reflected in a number of works in his collection *Zbosaptoyt* (Excursion). Employing a term to refer to Armenia popularized by Charents,[48] Khrakhuni states that he wakes up to "the song of simple Naïrian chimes" and instead of "soft alien carpets" he steps onto a wool rug woven in his fatherland.[49] Similarly, in a series of rhetorical questions the point at issue is the proper relationship that should subsist between the poet and his native land, especially a poet of the Diaspora. Armenia should not be presented as a distant fable, but a mother (that is, Mayr Hayastan).[50] Khrakhuni asks how he should breathe so "that you'd still be free," the territory would become a country, and his poems an anthem. The issue of liberty is revisited in the poem "Botse" (The Flame, 1980), which, although talking in general terms about "that flame which burns with the spirit of freedom for the sake of freedom," also refers to the symbol of Prometheus being freed from his chains.[51] The site of the demigod's confinement was a Caucasian crag. The region generated two Armenian variants to the legend, one associated with King Artavazd, who was removed by the *dev*s, and the other with Pokr Mher of the Sasun epic.[52]

Feasts] (Istanbul: Hagop Abelyan Publishers, 1973), pp. 22-23; Khrakhuni, *Ughiner* [Paths] (Istanbul: Murad Ofset, 1987), p. 89, trans. Hacikyan and Mamourian, *Selected Poems,* pp. 22-24, 39, 51-52, 117-18.

[47] Hacikyan and Mamourian, *Selected Poems,* pp. 55-56.

[48] Eghishe Charents, *Erkir Nairi* [Land of Nairi] (Erevan: Sovetakan Grogh, 1977 [1926]).

[49] Khrakhuni, *Zbosaptoyt*, p. 115, trans. Hacikyan and Mamourian, *Selected Poems*, pp. 63-64.

[50] Hacikyan and Mamourian, *Selected Poems*, pp. 55-56.

[51] Zareh Khrakhuni, *Diutsaznahandes* [Heroic Contest] (Istanbul: Murad Ofset, 1984), p. 7, trans. Hacikyan and Mamourian, *Selected Poems*, pp. 91-92.

[52] Georges Charachidzé, *Prométhée ou le Caucase: essai de mythologie contrastive*

Another indirect allusion to a potent national symbol seems encoded in a poem in the series "Roads" (1977). Querying whether all roads lead to Rome, Khrakhuni states that his only road takes him to a mountain, beyond which the road rises toward the sky, a most likely reference to Mount Ararat. The skyward ascent might then allude to the author's flight to Armenia. Certainly, the poem "Kanch" (Call, 1978), the most explicitly national of this period, locates the author at various tourist sites of the republic—Garni, Geghard, and so forth.[53] The distressing cries from afar are revealed in the concluding line as uttering the name Ani—the Bagratuni (Bagratid) capital of historic Armenia in the tenth to eleventh centuries,[54] which, as in Shnorhali's lament, is portrayed as an orphan of its widowed mother Armenia.[55] Situated on the western banks of the Akhurian River, which marks the current border between Turkey and Armenia, the city has been severed from the latter albeit by only a few hundred feet.[56]

The earthquake of 1988, the declaration of the independent republic in 1991, and the presidential elections in the following year form the background to several of the poems in Khrakhuni's collection *Azatergutiun* (Liberty Song, 1993),[57] and the themes are

---

(Paris: Flammarion, 1986), pp. 95-103.

[53] Khrakhuni, *Zbosaptoyt*, pp. 105, 113, trans. Hacikyan and Mamourian, *Selected Poems*, pp. 65-66, 79.

[54] For a collection of studies on the city's history, economy, and artistic significance, see S. Peter Cowe, ed., *Ani: World Architectural Heritage of a Medieval Armenian Capital* (Leuven: Peeters, 2001).

[55] For Shnorhali's original lament, see Manik Mkrtchian, ed., *Oghb Edesioy* [Lament on Edessa] (Erevan: Armenian Academy of Sciences, 1973), trans. Theo M. van Lint, "Lament on Edessa by Nerses Shnorhali," in *East and West in the Crusader States*, ed. Krijna Ciggaar (Leuven: Peeters, 1999), pp. 29-47, 49-105. For a study of the lament tradition in general, a significant genre of medieval Armenian poetry, see Poghos Khachatrian, *Hay mijnadaryan patmakan oghber (XIV-XVII dd.)* [Medieval Armenian Historical Laments (14th-17th Centuries)] (Erevan: Armenian Academy of Sciences, 1969).

[56] The city has maintained its numinous fascination for more recent generations of Armenian writers, of whom one might especially mention the poems of Daniel Varujan, Eghishe Charents, and Avetik Isahakian, as well as Levon Shant's deeply symbolic drama *Shghtayvatse* [The Enchained]. For Ani's impact on the urban development of Gyumri in the second half of the nineteenth century, see S. Peter Cowe, "A Tale of Two Cities: Ani-Leninakan," *Armenian Review* 43:4 (1990): 133-40.

[57] Zareh Khrakhuni, *Azatergutiun* [Liberty Song] (Los Angeles: Abril, 1993).

continued in *Kar Hayastani* (Stone of Armenia, 1997).[58] He poses one of his customary riddles in the title of the poem "616," dedicated to President Levon Ter-Petrosyan. Gradually, the first part of the composition unfolds details concerning the Armenian kingdom of Cilicia, which collapsed in 1375 with the capture of King Levon V. Khrakhuni reflects widespread popular sentiment of the time in depicting the coming to power of another Levon of lion heart (with wordplay on the name Leo), who shatters the chains in which his people have languished for seventy years. At the same time, Khrakhuni maintains an ironic distance from the events described in posing the question whether the coincidence might be endowed with supernatural or magical significance, or there again is a matter of pure historical happenstance.[59]

* * *

Comparison of Zahrad and Khrakhuni, united in time and space and sharing the same overall aesthetic approach, reveals an interesting diversity in perspective with regard to the articulation of ethnic identity in their works. Zahrad has fundamentally maintained his focus on the meticulous observation of life in his native city, writing about the individual and the universal through the medium of the Armenian language. Khrakhuni, in contrast, has felt impelled to broach explicitly Armenian issues and symbols in his writing, including politics in the Armenian republic, while maintaining his fascination with the imponderables of the human condition as a whole. One wonders how the next generation will respond to the challenge they accepted half a century ago.[60]

---

[58] Zareh Khrakhuni, *Kar Hayastani* [Stone of Armenia] (Beirut: Sipan, 1997).

[59] Khrakhuni, *Azatergutiun*, pp. 53-57.

[60] On the new generation of Armenian poets of Istanbul, see Abrahamian, *Zhamanakakits istanpulahay groghner*, vol. 1, pp. 25-26.

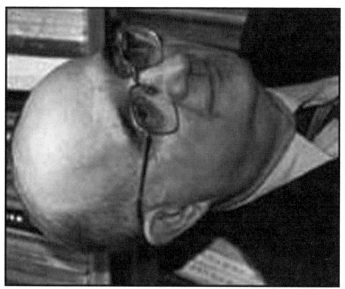

Zareh Khrakhuni

Zahrad

�֍ 19 ✷

FROM CONSTANTINOPLE TO EREVAN:
THE ODYSSEY OF VAHRAM PAPAZIAN

Robert H. Hewsen

Vahram Papazian (1888-1968) was one of the most revered celebrities of the Armenian theatrical profession in Constantinople, his birthplace.[1] He began his career in the Ottoman capital in 1904 and later become one of the few Armenian cultural icons who survived the Armenian Genocide. His circle of friends included Siamanto, Daniel Varoujan, and other writers. Papazian left Constantinople early in his career, but his influence extended well beyond the Ottoman capital. He became the foremost Armenian actor of his day and, after he fled to Russia, was widely regarded as the greatest Shakespearean actor in the Soviet Union.

Vahram Papazian was born to a middle class Armenian Catholic family. His father, Kamer Papazian, owned a factory that manufactured shirts. His mother, Takuhi Tashjian, was the granddaughter of a surgeon who had served with the Ottoman army during the Crimean War (1853-56).[2] Papazian was one of four children. His brother Diran was an engineer and lived in Marseilles along with his sisters Srpuhi and Nvart. Vahram attended the Yesayan School and upon graduation in 1902 entered the secondary school in Kadikoy. He continued his education at the Mekhitarist Moorat-Raphael College in Venice from 1905 to 1907. He journeyed to Paris in 1907, from there to Tiflis, and thence to Baku, where he spent a few months acting with the local Armenian

---

[1] Most of the biographical details in this paper are drawn from Papazian's two-volume memoirs, *Hetadardz hayatsk* [Retrospective View], 2 vols. (Erevan: Haypethrat, 1957), and my interviews with him in August 1961. See also *Haykakan Sovetakan Hanragitaran* [Armenian Soviet Encyclopedia], 12 vols. (Erevan: Armenian Academy of Sciences, 1974-1986), vol. 12, pp. 326-27, s.v. "Papazyan, Vahram Kameri."

[2] My grandmother's first cousin, Henry Hewsen, personal reminiscences, 1948.

theater company.[3]

Papazian's parents had regularly taken him to the theater in Constantinople, where his relatives, on his father's side, performed. It was his father's cousin, Philomene, who nurtured his early interest in acting and arranged for his first public appearance on stage at the age of sixteen. He acted in a Turkish translation of a play by Alexandre Dumas in 1904. In Baku, Papazian performed for a few months and then returned to Constantinople where, in 1908, at the age of twenty, he formed his own theatrical company and dared to perform Shakespeare's *Othello* (in Armenian) in a cosmopolitan city where Armenian audiences had seen Bernhardt and Duse on tour. The French Armenologist, Frédéric Macler, who saw Papazian perform that year, described him as "assez médiocre."[4] When I related this anecdote to Papazian more than fifty years later, he shook his head, smiling, and said: "We were sparrows trying to be eagles."[5] The production, however amateurish it may have seemed to a French visitor at the time, was significant in that it ended a fourteen-year ban on Armenian theater in the Ottoman capital, and the exuberant audience would not leave the auditorium until Papazian stepped forward and recited the poem "The Massacre" by Daniel Varoujan.[6] In his old age, Papazian acknowledged that his first wife, a member of this primitive company and ten years older than he, had been his first teacher. The marriage did not last.[7]

Determined to master his art, Papazian journeyed to Milan, where from 1908 to 1911 he studied acting at the Academy of Fine Arts, training under E. Novelli, E. Zakoni, and Eleonora Duse, herself widely regarded as the greatest actress among her contemporaries. During this period, Papazian prepared his basic repertoire: Othello, Romeo, and Hamlet, though from time to time he also played other roles, such as that of Corrado in Giacometti's *Criminal Family*. In the years immediately following his departure from Milan, 1913 through 1917, he regularly played in the Ar-

---

[3] *Haykakan Sovetakan Hanragitaran,* vol. 12, p. 326.

[4] Frédéric Macler, *Rapport sur une Mission scientifique en Arménie russe et en Arménie turque* (Paris: Imp. Nationale, 1911), p. 114.

[5] Vahram Papazian, personal interview, Aug. 1961.

[6] Nishan Parlakian, "Shakespeare and the Armenian Theater," in *Council on National Literatures Quarterly World* Report 5:4 (Oct. 1982): 9.

[7] V. Papazian, personal interview, Aug. 1961.

menian theaters of Constantinople, Smyrna, and Tiflis, and again in Baku until the Russian Revolution made further performances there impossible.[8] As a result of these travels, Papazian became fluent in French and Italian, although curiously, considering his devotion to Shakespeare, he never learned English.

It was in this period that my father's family saw Papazian most often. My father told me of one occasion when Papazian appeared in Smyrna playing Othello with his cousin, Philomene's daughter Marie, as Desdemona. Although Papazian had probably never even heard of the Stanislavsky Method at this time, he had already mastered the technique of losing himself within the characters he portrayed. In the scene where Othello strangles his wife, the attack was so real that Marie became terrified and, shoving him away from herself, said before the entire audience "Vahro, you can find yourself another Desdemona," whereupon, she stalked off the set. And Papazian? He continued the scene strangling a Desdemona whose presence on the stage he conjured up solely through the genius of his art.[9]

On another occasion, my uncle recalled how Papazian was playing a young poet dying because of the unrequited love of a young girl. Half way through the death scene, a woman in the audience leaped to her feet in tears crying "Akh! Akh! Enough, Papazian! You're breaking my heart!" Whereupon, her husband jumped up, smacked her, shoved her into the aisle, and drove her— still sobbing—out of the theater.[10] Later still, while strangling Desdemona yet again, a man from the audience, who, thinking that he was actually killing the actress, climbed onto the stage and shot at Papazian; he missed his target and was dragged from the set.

World War I and the years following it were horrific for the Armenian people and for Armenian artists of every kind. The cultural world of Armenian Constantinople was destroyed, the situation in Tiflis and Baku was unstable, and almost everywhere else Armenian communities were too impoverished and too preoccupied with sheer survival to support them. Actors performed wherever they could and for whatever audiences could be mustered. In the

---

[8] *Haykakan Sovetakan Hanragitaran,* vol. 12, p. 236.
[9] Henry Hewsen, personal reminiscences, 1948.
[10] Archavir Hewsenian, personal reminiscences, 1985-1990.

years from 1917 to 1920, Papazian performed in Moscow and Yalta, surviving the Russian Revolution and Civil War as best he could.

Returning to Constantinople, Papazian performed for two years, but the Armenian world was never the same after 1915. When the allies left the city in 1922, he departed as well. Returning to Russia with another rising actor, Hrach Nersisyan, he married a Russian girl and remained in the newly formed Soviet Union. The exciting new possibilities in the burgeoning Soviet theater beckoned the young actor of only thirty-four. Like so many others of his generation, he, too, saw the creation of the Soviet Union as the dawn of a new world, bright with promise and filled with wonderful opportunities. It was a mistake that he freely admitted—at least to me—but it had its rewards as well.[11]

Unable to speak Russian, Papazian at first appeared only before Armenian audiences in Erevan, Tbilisi, and Baku. Later, as his reputation grew, he went on to perform with Russian companies, speaking in French while the rest of the cast performed in Russian. In Baku, to the delight and admiration of Azeri audiences, he delivered his lines in Ottoman Turkish, full of the rich Persian and Arabic vocabulary which Kemal Ataturk had banned in the new Turkish republic. Eventually, the Soviets assigned Papazian a tutor who lived in his home for ten years to give him Russian instruction. His first performances in Russian were warmly and graciously received.[12]

In the days of the Stalinist terror, Papazian was in grave danger. A foreigner by birth, a member of the intelligentsia, and a man of bourgeois background and cultivated bearing, he matched the profile of a typical candidate for arrest and deportation to the labor camps in Siberia. Sensing his peril, Papazian arranged to be sent on an extensive tour to the Soviet Far East on the assumption (correct, as it turned out) that the Secret Police could not send him to Siberia if he were already there. When it became safe to do so, he returned to Leningrad unharmed.[13]

In the years 1934-35, Papazian toured to perform throughout

---

[11] V. Papazian, personal interview, Aug., 1961.

[12] Ibid.

[13] Hagop Jack Touryantz, "Vahram Papazian: A Memoir," *Ararat* (New York) (Summer 1985): 38.

Transcaucasia, and from 1936 to 1941 in Russia and Ukraine. In 1941, he performed as Othello at the Gorky Theater in Moscow and the Great Drama Theater in Leningrad.[14] Papazian had made his home in Leningrad, which, though no longer the capital, was still a more polished and cultivated city than Moscow. There, between performances and tours, he lived with his wife and daughter, Zhana, in a villa in the suburb of Olgino, on his own lands, complete with its own lake, enjoying the life of a country gentleman from a nineteenth century Russian novel. "It is incredibly like the old days," he told me in 1961, referring to the years before the Russian Revolution. "I go hunting with my dogs and I even have peasants who live on my land, and when they have a baby they come to me with the newborn in their arms and ask me to be the Godfather!"[15]

Papazian, unfortunately, was in Leningrad when the Nazis attacked the Soviet Union in the summer of 1941, and, along with three million other Soviet citizens, he was trapped in the city as it was surrounded by the German army and besieged for the next three years. During this time Leningrad starved. There was a list, however, especially prepared by the secret police, the dreaded NKVD, on which were recorded the names of the Leningrad elite who were to be assisted in surviving the dark days of the siege at any cost. It is a tribute to the esteem in which Papazian was held that his name was on that list. While a million people perished during the siege—one third of the population—Papazian and his family received everything that they needed. He was very emphatic on that point: "everything!" *"On a eu tous qu'il faut."* Alas, however, he was still not spared the horrors of war. His wife was killed by shrapnel one morning while they were having breakfast in the garden of their country home. Later, his daughter lost her husband at the front. In 1961, she was still living with Papazian and a daughter of her own. At that time, the losses in the siege of Leningrad were still a taboo subject in the Soviet Union and Papazian's account was the first that I had ever heard of them. The famine had been unbelievable in the city during the siege and there were those, he assured me, who had been desperate enough to taste the flesh

---

[14] *Haykakan Sovetakan Hanragitaran,* vol. 12, p. 327.
[15] V. Papazian, personal interview, Aug. 1961.

of the dead.[16]

The fame of Vahram Papazian will always be linked to the role of Othello, a part in which he excelled and of which he was said to have been the master. This was, of course, Papazian's great forte and the role for which he will always be most remembered. Some critics said that he seemed born to play the Moor of Venice; others remarked that the part seemed to have been almost written specifically for his talents. Some reviewers even considered his interpretation of the role to have been the best they had ever seen. Over the years, Papazian appeared in the role on hundreds of occasions, and his interpretation of it slowly evolved as the years went on. In his youth, he saw Othello as a romantic hero tragically brought down by jealousy, the fatal flaw in his own otherwise sterling character. In the days of the Stalinist terror, he played him as a persecuted alien destroyed by racial prejudice. Finally, in his later years, when Soviet censorship had grown more relaxed, he portrayed the Moor as an abstract man, overcome by treachery, spite, and deceit.[17] Whatever his interpretation of Othello, Papazian consistently tried the patience of his co-stars. His most frequent Desdemona, Mataxia Simonian, constantly complained that he almost killed her during the supposedly simulated strangulation.

Othello, however, was by no means the only role that Papazian played; he was not even totally committed to Shakespeare. He had played Arpenini in Lermontov's *The Masked Ball*, and the title roles in Dumas' *Kean*, Moliere's *Don Juan*, and Rostand's *Cyrano de Bergerac*. I had the good fortune of seeing Papazian on the opening night of William Saroyan's *My Heart's in the Highlands*, performed in Armenian translation at the Sundukyan Theater in Erevan in August 1961. When he entered the stage and introduced himself as Jasper McGregor the world's greatest Shakespearean actor, the audience gave him a standing ovation.[18]

A true intellectual, Papazian was interested in everything, and, unlike many people in the theatrical profession, he was able to talk freely and keenly on a variety of subjects. Witty, full of anecdotes and stories, he commanded the conversation in his home and at his table. He was also a gifted writer and took full advantage of

---

[16] Ibid.

[17] Parlakian, "Shakespeare," pp. 3-12.

[18] V. Papazian personal interview, Aug. 1961.

his age and his reputation to write a two-volume memoir, *Hetadardz hayatsk*, that are relatively free of the cant required of Soviet artists writing their autobiographies in those days. Sometimes exaggerated, occasionally far-fetched, always candid, Papazian's memoirs deserve to be recognized as a significant contribution to Western Armenian literature.

Although he lived in Leningrad, Vahram Papazian felt obliged to visit Erevan annually to perform and, as he put it, "to raise the standards of the local people." "Would you believe it," he told me in 1961, "when I first came here they used to hiss the villain; they would hiss Iago when he came upon the stage!" In Erevan, Papazian also taught at the Sundukyan Theater and, in this way, brought the traditions and acting style of the Constantinople theater to Soviet Armenia.

Papazian had an impact on theater well beyond Erevan. He toured constantly, having been to China before World War II and in Aleppo and Beirut as late as 1966, two years before he died. In 1956, he was sent to Tehran to help the Iranian government to establish its own national theater, an enterprise in which many local Armenian theatrical professionals played a leading role.[19] Already designated the People's Artist of Armenia, Georgia, and Azerbaijan in 1933-34, in 1956, after the ten-day festival of Armenian Art in Moscow, he was awarded the title of People's Artist of the USSR, one of the highest cultural honors that the Soviet Union bestowed.[20] At the banquet tendered him on his seventieth birthday, he thanked the Soviets warmly for their recognition but then asked: "All my life, I have wanted to visit England to perform Shakespeare in the land of his birth. I have repeatedly asked for permission to do so but you have always refused. If you really want to honor me, let me go to Stratford-upon-Avon." "Well, they didn't like that," Papazian complained to me, and shortly afterwards, an article appeared in the press comparing him to Hrach Nersisyan, which deemed Nersisyan the greater of the two. "But now," Papazian told me over dinner, "Nersisyan is dying of cancer, so I suppose that I am the greatest again."

As a man, Vahram Papazian was of medium height and rather stocky; not really handsome, he had a twinkling eye and a pixie-

---

[19] V. Papazian, personal interview, Aug. 1961.

[20] *Haykakan Sovetakan Hanragitaran*, vol. 12, p. 327.

like grin that made him instantly likable. He was a keenly intelligent man, however, and I remember well—after forty years—
his piercing glance when he was making a point that he particularly
wished me to remember. Though he was known to be a philander-
er and a heavy drinker, women adored him, and he went through
more than one wife and had numerous affairs.[21] He had charm
and self-confidence in abundance and this served him well both
on and off the stage. One of my Smyrna uncles, visiting the family
in Constantinople about 1912, recalled being taken out by Papazian
to see the town. Before he began the tour, however, Papazian,
unwilling to be hampered by a lack of ready cash, took my uncle
to the mansion of a wealthy Armenian merchant in the middle of
the day and passed a note to the maid who had admitted them into the foyer. The maid went upstairs with the note and in a few
moments the merchant's wife—another lady who was no longer
young—descended with a handful of gold coins. Pressing the coins
into Papazian's hands, she smiled and in a purring voice said
chidingly "And Vahro, do come and see me once in a while."[22] In
his last years, Papazian drew comfort and moral support from the
actress Anahit Dadrian, a French Armenian repatriate, who eventually lived with him as his wife in all but name.[23]

My fondest memory of my meeting with Papazian was walking
with him from the Hotel Armenia to the Ararat Restaurant where
we were to have dinner together. Nattily dressed (which was no
small feat in the Soviet Union in 1961), he strolled along swinging
his cane—strictly a prop—touching it to his Panama hat tipped
rakishly to one side as he smiled and greeted the many people he
knew along the way. He still spoke the Western Armenian language
and when I mentioned this, he confided that it gave him "*un espèce
de charme avec ces gens*—a kind of charm with these people."[24]

More than forty years have passed since Vahram Papazian died,
but fortunately he made a number of films that help to preserve the
memory of his art though, even without these, the force of his
talent and personality remain a permanent part of the foundation
of the theater in the Armenian republic. In Stepanakert, the Kara-

---

[21] Henry Hewsen, personal reminiscences, 1948.

[22] Archavir Hewsenian, personal reminiscences, 1985-90.

[23] Touryantz, "Vahram Papazian," p. 39.

[24] V. Papazian, personal reminiscences, Aug. 1961.

bagh Armenians have immortalized his memory by renaming their national theater in his honor. At home, I take a great satisfaction that through some marvel of human genetics, my son, unlike myself or my father, bears a striking resemblance to Vahram Papazian, a man whose face was seen by tens of thousands for so many years upon the Armenian stage and perhaps by millions on the Soviet screen.

Vahram Papazian

❋ 20 ❋

THE ARMENIAN ORAL TRADITION IN ISTANBUL

Verjiné Svazlian

The oral tradition of the Armenian community in Istanbul has over the centuries adhered to certain principles of Armenian folklore, although in time it developed its own distinctive characteristics reflecting the city's cultural life.[1] Some of the important elements in Armenian oral tradition as developed in Istanbul include religious-moral stories, fables, legends, parables, and animal tales. Since the 1915 genocide, which not only eliminated the Armenian population from its historic homelands in the Ottoman Empire but also destroyed most of its cultural infrastructure, the community has not been able to preserve much traditional folklore. Nevertheless, some of it endured in the memory of those who fled to the Caucasus region and were subsequently recorded in Erevan. Other survivors living in Istanbul were recorded in 1996 and 1997. Clearly, no survey can provide an exhaustive account of such a multifaceted subject. This brief discussion can offer only a small sample of the essential components of the Armenian oral tradition.

Oral Tradition in Prose

Rich in genre and thematic diversity, the Armenian oral tradition consists of stories and fables that are believed to reflect actual events and characters in ancient Armenian and Greek cultures. They are obviously embellished with supernatural qualities and often appear to bring about events of great historical significance. Fables in prose include "King Aram's Son, Ara the Handsome" and "The Capture of Troy." In addition, philosophical and moral

---

[1] This chapter is based on materials in Verjine Svazlian, *Polsahayots banahyusutyune* [The Folklore of the Constantinopolitan Armenians] (Erevan: National Academy of Sciences, 2000).

tales praise diligence and honesty—for example, "Do Good, Toss It into the Sea"; "The Shepherdess"; "The Force of Craftsmanship"; "The Boy Who Had Seen the World"; "Man's Fortune"; and "The Power of Liquor." They portray men as seeking the meaning of happiness while confronting their daily concerns and the mysteries of a transitory life.

In addition, legends consist of tales of Armenians in Turkey and, as indicated by their toponymic titles, narrate their interpretations in the context of local traditions. These include, for instance, "The Monastery of Hope of the Heybeli Island"; "Surb Gevorg Sanctuary of the Large Island"; "Surb Hovhannes Church of Burgas Island"; and "Surb Karapet, the Dream-Giver."

The religious-moral tales reflect the belief that "The Bible should become the root of morality for everyone." This category consists of tales based mainly on themes and stories found in the Bible, including, among others, "God's Message"; "The Fortune God Has Bestowed"; "The Punishment God Has Given"; and "Providence." As an example, "Father Abraham's Grapevine" relates:

> One day, an angel came as a guest to the house of Father Abraham, who had no food to offer the angel. So he went to the stable, took out a calf, slaughtered it, and offered it to the angel. The calf's mother returned from the pasture in the evening and, seeing that the calf had disappeared, began to shed salty tears. The angel became very distressed and said to Father Abraham: "Fetch me the calf's hide and bones." Father Abraham brought the remnants of the calf. The angel blessed the hide and the bones and the calf came back to life. The remnants were buried in the orchard. The following year a grapevine grew in the same place.[2]

These religious-moral tales, however, are not mere reproductions of biblical episodes; instead, each possesses a special style of development, which, upon reaching the climax, imparts particular moral values. Their titles include "If You Give, God Will Give You More"; "Mohammed and the Armenian Hagop"; and "Unity Is Power." One such moral tale states:

One day there was a funeral procession in the street. The people

---

[2] Ibid., p. 96.

were watching it in silence. An old man spoke to himself aloud.

"I wonder if this man is dead or if he will live on." A young man, who heard him, said, "When someone dies, that's the end; how can he be living?"

"Eh, my son," replied the old man, "if the deceased has not done any good works in his life and has not left any good memories, then he is really dead. But if the deceased has left behind him good children, good deeds, and good memories, then he does not die and his memory is immortal."[3]

Another story, "The Young Men and the Wealthy," depicts the choices presented by life itself:

Two young men saw a beautiful building in a garden. One of them said to the other, "Look! What a beautiful building!"

The owner of the building heard this, came out of the building and said to the young men, "I will give you this building, if only you give me your youth."[4]

In addition to philosophical, religious, and moral teachings, humorous tales appear in popular aphorisms. A subset of this section consists specifically of tales pertaining to familiar humorous characters such as the famous Molla Nasraddin or Nasraddin Hoja. Humor, as in satires, is often used to criticize human faults, as in "The Lazy Daughter-in-Law"; "The Shoemaker Who Did Not Pay His Debt"; "The Judge and the Robber"; "The Thief of the Church"; and "The Vindictive Man."

In a similar vein, parables and animal tales, compact in form and allegoric in content, portray the same human shortcomings through animal characters. The villains in these parables are always punished. Samples of such parables include "The Wolves and the Shepherd," on deceitfulness; "The Snake and the Man" and "The Fish and the Man," on greed; "The Mournful Partridge," on imposters; and "The Tortoise and the Scorpion," on ingratitude. Other parables praise admirable traits in kind and innocent animals, as in the case of "The Grateful Bear" and "The Sensitive Seagulls." In one such story, dolphins become the personification of gratitude:

---

[3] Ibid., p. 137.
[4] Ibid., p. 177.

One day, two fishermen were in their boat fishing. When they were pulling their net out of the water, they saw that about forty dolphins had surrounded their boat and, their heads out of the water, were crying plaintively.

"What do they want?" asked one fisherman the other.

"I do not understand their language," replied the other.

When they drew the net out of the sea, they understood the behavior of the dolphins, since a baby dolphin had fallen into the net. The fishermen took it out and dropped it back into the sea. When the fishermen returned to the wharf they were astonished to see about forty dolphins encircling and jumping round the boat and expressing their gratitude to the kind fishermen with squeals of delight.[5]

There are also tales related to cultural differences, which reflect local conditions and depict with vibrant, albeit stereotypical, imagery the distinctive lifestyles and moral standards of Armenians and other ethno-religious groups in the provinces. The residents of Constantinople presumed to represent the height of Ottoman culture and viewed the poor provincials as ignorant and backward "outsiders." When newcomers arrived in the capital, they had little knowledge of the Turkish language and felt confused and embarrassed in their new environment. This culture shock prompted many humorous situations and often served as the basis for local folklore. Such stories include "The Provincial Who Did Not Know Turkish"; "The Provincial in Pera"; and "The Kesaratsi and the Bolsetsi." Further, stereotypical anecdotes are embellished with colorful pictures, as the tale describing the cleverness of those from Caesarea ("The Kesaratsi Father and Son"); the wittiness of those from Tomarza ("The Tomarzatsis and the Airplane"); the frugality of the inhabitants of Tekirdagh ("The Tekirdaghtsi Mother-in-Law"); the patriarchal character of those from Yozghat ("The Betrothed Yozghatsi Couple" and "The Yozghatsi Girl at the Beach"); the taciturn young women of Adana ("The Adanatsi Bride"); and the naïveté of the inhabitants of Agn ("The Provincial and the Agntsi Innkeeper").

Similar stories highlight the peculiar features, conduct, customs, lifestyles, and habits of Armenians from different parts of the Diaspora. A common comic theme is the perplexed Armenian

---

[5] Ibid., p. 210.

provincial in foreign countries, as in "The Provincial Who Did Not Know French"; "The Zeituntsi in France"; and "The Tomarzatsi in America," which make fun of the provincial's naive ignorance of the language, laws, and regulations in the United States:

> Mr. Harutiun from Tomarza and his friend went to America. There they entered a factory to work without knowing a word of English. The boss showed, on a big clock placed on the table, the time until which they would have to work. Then, another worker came in and the chief showed the hours on his wristwatch, saying, "You will have to work from this hour to that one."
>
> "You saw that, didn't you?" said Mr. Harutiun to his friend, "the boss showed us the time on the big clock, therefore he will make us work longer than the other worker."
>
> "This man is deceiving us," agreed his friend.
> And both of them fled from the factory.[6]

Tales told like a novel with surprise endings capture Armenian perceptions of the conduct and customs of other ethnic and religious groups. Such tales include, for example, "The Jew Who Helped the Jew"; "The Advice of the Jewish Father"; "Mournful Mannig and the Greek Neighbor"; "The Traveling Laz"; "The Yugoslav Pastor"; and "Don't Boast Like a Persian." Other tales emphasize Armenian dignity and portray good neighborly relations between Armenians and peoples of other cultures. These include "The Priest of Kesaria and the Foreigners" and "The Charm of the Armenian Alphabet." The following is meant to show Armenian national character in a positive light:

> An Armenian from Bolis was traveling on a ship to the Far East— to China, Japan, and Australia. Naturally, there were on the ship people of various nationalities. They decided, one day, that every one of them would make a speech in his own language so that the others could hear it. The Jew stood up and made a speech in his language. The Indian rose next and spoke in Indian. Then it was the Armenian's turn; he was not well educated, so he decided to recite all the letters of the Armenian alphabet, but he recited with such a strong feeling that all the spectators clapped and congratulated the Armenian, saying, "Your speech was wonderful.

---

[6] Ibid., p. 264.

Your language is so beautiful!"[7]

Historical Tales and Memoirs

Folk tales and memoirs reproduce historically significant events and characters. One story narrates the establishment of the Armenian Patriarchate of Constantinople shortly after the Ottoman conquest of the city. Other stories are about Harutiun Amira Bezjian, the sultan's counselor; the Duzian brothers, directors of the Ottoman mint; the Balians, the famed family of architects; the talented actors Mardiros Mnakian, Hagop Vartovian, and Marie Nvart; the renowned musicians Tateos Effendi, Kemanji Sarkis, and Oudi Hrant; and numerous intellectuals who contributed to the cultural development of Constantinople.

The stories also involve the Armenian Church. The historical tale, "Sultan Hamid and Patriarch Maghakia Ormanian," is of interest:

One day the advisors of Sultan Abdul Hamid told him:

"Do you know, Sultan, that the Armenian Patriarch does not take a meal without saying grace? He crosses himself without fail before the meal."

"Honestly? If so, let us invite him to dinner; we will see if he dares to cross himself before me."

Abdul Hamid gave orders to organize a grand dinner and to invite the Armenian Patriarch.

Maghakia Ormanian appeared augustly before the Sultan and saw the sumptuously laid table. All sat round the table. Before starting to eat, Patriarch Ormanian raised his right hand and, pretending to point to the various delicious dishes on the table, he unnoticeably made the sign of the cross, saying, "At first, we shall taste that delicious dish, then eat this one, then that dainty one, and then this one, and finally that's all!"[8]

And he started eating. When the banquet was over, Patriarch Ormanian expressed his appreciation for the reception and took his leave. The Sultan told his advisors with satisfaction:

"Did you see that the Armenian Patriarch was afraid of me and did not make the sign of the cross?"

The advisors replied, "You are mistaken, Sultan, before the

---

[7] Ibid., p. 281.

[8] The word "all" in Armenian is "amen," which is synonymous with "Amen," as in praying.

dinner, the Armenian Patriarch, pointing to the dishes, already made the sign of the cross on your table, but he made it in such a way that you did not notice."[9]

There are also stories about the Armenian Patriarchate during the tenure of Archbishop Zaven Der-Yeghiayan, including the sheltering of thousands of orphaned children and widows in the Kalfayan and the Karageuzian orphanages and the National Surb Prkich (Surp Prgich) Hospital after the Armenian Genocide.

Oral Traditions in Verse

The poetic oral traditions reflect emotions, joy and love, sorrow and affliction. Traditional songs of Constantinople include lullabies, children's songs, love songs, immigrant songs, and ritual songs. The following is an example of a lullaby:

Sleep, my dear baby,
I'll sing you a lullaby,
The bright moon is gently
Looking at your cradle.
I'll tell you many tales
And sing lovely songs,
While you rest in your bed
In sweet sleep.[10]

Children's songs use simple language, such as *Eghrig-Meghrig* (Butter-Honey), and *Dan-Dan* (Clap-Clap). Some also include religious symbolism, as follows:

My little boy's eye
Looks like the cross of the church,
My little boy's mouth
Looks like the altar of the church,
My little boy's nose
Looks like the beam of the church,
My little boy's back
Looks like the door of the church,
My little boy's hands

---

[9] Svazlian, *Polsahayots banahyusutyune*, p. 301.
[10] Ibid., p. 387.

Look like the books of the church.[11]

Children's songs also include patriotic themes, as "I Am an Armenian," which emphasize national dignity:

> I am an Armenian, a noble Haigazian,[12]
> I speak the language of Haig and Aram,[13]
> I have no crown, throne, gold, or diamond,
> But my heart is rich and especially honest.[14]

Armenians of Istanbul have a number of love songs. Some are composed in the style of medieval musical *hayren*s, which express tender and delicate feelings and echo rustic expressions—for example, "You Come Picking Roses, Sweetheart" and "My Heart Is Turning Like a Millstone." The following is an example of a traditional Armenian love song:

> The sea of Istanbul is curling in waves,
> How sweet is the breeze of love blowing,
> May the Lord give me the fortune to see her,
> To fulfill my dream and then to fall into the sea.[15]

There are also immigrant (*bandught*) and ritual songs. Immigrant songs are about Armenians who migrated from the provinces to Constantinople to earn money and support their families. In the song "Call, Crane, Call," the immigrant longingly awaits news from his native land. Ritual songs contain nuptial, baptismal, and funeral rites. Nuptial songs are ancient songs that praise the bride as she dresses and carries her dowry to the bridegroom's house. Examples include "You Are Fortunate, Girl"; "The Priest Gives Nuptial Blessings"; and "They Are Taking Away the Girl, Weeping, Lamenting," which depicts the sad farewell as a child bride leaves her parents' home:

> They are taking away the girl, weeping, lamenting,

---

[11] Ibid., p. 391.
[12] Descendants of Haik, the progenitor of the Armenian people.
[13] Armenian king.
[14] Svazlian, *Polsahayots banahyusutyune*, p. 393.
[15] Ibid., p. 396.

They are combing her hair with a silver comb,
And wrapping her head with the nightingale-decorated shawl,
Do not cry, pretty girl, your eyes and brows will be stained,
Cursed be he who gave you in marriage so young.[16]

While traditional rituals have been modernized to a great degree, the Armenians of Istanbul have preserved their Christian holidays, together with practices of pagan origin and popular songs performed on such days. These include, for example, "Song of Christmas"; "Song of the New Year"; "Easter Has Come"; and songs and melodies of the Ascension and of the Transfiguration of Christ, which were composed both in the Armenian and in Turkish languages. In the following Ascension song, pagan sun worship is intertwined with biblical characters:

The key descended from the sky,
Our house was filled with sunshine,
Our bread is Father Abraham's bread,
Our water is Virgin Mary's milk,
Bride, pull your good lot!
And may Ascension fulfill your wish![17]

A number of songs regarding *Vartavar* (Transfiguration) have been composed in the Turkish language as well:

Hey! Mentivar, Mentivar,[18]
Mentivar has a definite time,
He who loves Mentivar
Has five divans in Heaven.[19]

Most Armenians of Istanbul know church prayers, which are recited in Armenian and Turkish and are addressed to Jesus, to the Virgin Mary, and to Saint Sarkis and other saints. The following is an example:

May the angels witness my religion and faith,
God is my head,

---

[16] Ibid., pp. 406-07.
[17] Ibid.
[18] Mentivar means Vartavar.
[19] Svazlian, *Polsahayots banahyusutyune*, p. 425.

Jesus is my companion,
He who does evil to anyone
Will have his mouth locked
and his tongue turned to stone.
Amen.[20]

Other prayers implore God to grant peace and grace:

Holy Trinity,
Give healing to the sick
And remission of our sins,
Love and unity to the Armenians
And peace to the world.
Amen.[21]

There are, however, less familiar incantation-like prayers; for example, "The Evil Eye" and "The Evil Nazar," which are taboos. The narrators in these cases believe that, upon reciting the incantations aloud, they would be barred from heaven.

Armenian traditional songs concern not only rites of religion and custom but also nature. Some of the important themes include the Sea of Marmara ("On the Sea"); birds ("The Stork"); and fruits ("What Place is Renowned for What"), which lists the products of various quarters of Istanbul, on Marmara shores, and various regions of Turkey:

The fish of Kumkapu,
The mulberry of Topkapu,
The lettuce of Yedikule,
The plum of Yenikapu,
The apple of Amasia,
The cucumber of Langa,
The fig of Izmir,
The chickpeas of Nigde,
The peach of Bursa,
The pear of Tokat,
The water of Tashdelen,
The chestnut of Konia,
The cotton of Adana,

---

[20] Ibid., p. 514.
[21] Ibid.

The pistachio of Aintab,
The potato of Adabazar,
The basturma[22] of Kesaria,
The coal of Zonguldak,
The honey of Erzerum,
The apricot of Malatia,
The watermelon of Dikranagerd,
The kishmish[23] of Urgup.[24]

Phraseological Oral Tradition

The Armenian oral tradition also consists of proverbs, didactic aphorisms, benedictions, and riddles. Proverbs are concise sayings that reflect the realities of Armenian life in Istanbul, the peculiarities of Armenian character and temperament, their moral faculties, their national customs, and their beliefs and religion. Among the examples are "We went to Tokat and became disabled"; "Worry for a year, work for a day"; and "A man with a trade remains hungry till noon; one without remains hungry till night."[25]

Didactic aphorisms implicitly portray the elderly as possessing broad life experiences and wisdom. They exhort the youth not to fall into the traps of various physical and moral "dangers." These include, for example, such sayings as "Do not rely on your power, money, or beauty, since they are transient," "Before being happy yourself, make your companion happy," and "The only thing which will remain is the monument made up of your virtue and your good deeds."[26]

Benedictions in secular form are concise sayings which in most cases emphasize nature. The sun, soil, water, and flowers symbolize life and appear in blessings and good wishes. Examples include sayings such as "May your sun be bright"; "May the soil become green in your hands"; and "May you live as many years as there are leaves on the olive tree."[27]

The Constantinopolitan Armenian oral tradition is replete with

---

[22] Cured spiced beef.
[23] Raisins.
[24] Svazlian, *Polsahayots banahyusutyune*, p. 432.
[25] Ibid., pp. 438-58.
[26] Ibid., pp. 459-70.
[27] Ibid., pp. 474-79.

meaningful idioms expressed in a colorful language, while riddles allegorically describe an object and its properties. For example, what is the answer to the following riddle?

> What is it?
> That is man's best friend,
> Has no evil and no malice,
> Does not require bread, does not demand water,
> Does not give trouble,
> It is, on the contrary, useful.[28]

The correct answer is "a book."

Although the Armenians are Christian, popular superstitions remain and appear in daily life. Examples include "If your eye is twitching, a guest is expected"; "If salt is spilled, a fight will occur in the house"; "If sugar is spilled, love will prevail in the home."[29]

* * *

The Armenian community of Constantinople/Istanbul has held on to its traditions and transmitted them to new generations. The community has maintained its bonds with the Christian faith and has preserved its mother tongue. It is hoped that the ethnographic fragments of oral tradition, as presented in this brief outline, can be saved from loss amid the general cultural retreat in the Armenian Diaspora.

---

[28] Ibid., pp. 495-501.
[29] Ibid., pp. 506-07.

✳ 21 ✳

THE FRENCH CONNECTION:
PETER SOURIAN AND CONSTANTINOPLE

David Stephen Calonne

The responses of American-Armenian writers to the Armenian Genocide are conditioned by their educational and social backgrounds as well as by their parents' place of origin. In many cases, the principal issue they address is not the genocide but rather the complexity and ambivalence involved in simply being Armenian in America. We cannot separate Peter Balakian and Peter Najarian from ancient Diarbekir, David Kherdian from Adana, Leon Surmelian from Trebizond, Emmanuel Varandyan from Urmia, or William Saroyan from Bitlis. Peter Sourian's family roots in Constantinople (in addition to the influence of French culture) had a significant impact on his Armenian identity; it further shaped his initial perceptions of the genocide and his attempts to find its meaning.

Born in 1933 in Boston, and educated at Philips Academy and Harvard, Peter Sourian authored three novels—*Miri* (1957), *The Best and Worst of Times* (1961), and *The Gate* (1965). He lived in Europe as a young man, studied at the Lycée Hoche in Versailles, and spent two years in the U.S. Army in Germany. His fiction is characterized by variations on recurring themes, including the relationship between a young man and his difficult Constantinopolitan father, the intricate sorrows of triangular love, class relations in America, the "pride and shame" of wealth, and the complexity of Armenian identity. These themes do not resolve their inherent ambiguity in Sourian's works. The dilemmas associated with assimilation into the dominant American culture surface time and again in the works of Armenian-American writers, and Sourian is no exception. His life experience follows the familiar path taken by several other Armenian authors: first, a rejection of his Armenian past, tradition, and heritage, followed by a desire to learn about Armenian history, including self-exploration, and concluding with a newfound awareness of a complex identity.

Sourian's Armenian identity was largely defined by his familial roots in Constantinople and French culture. Historically, there is an unbroken connection between the French and Armenian cultures, beginning with commercial relations in the Middle Ages followed by close interaction during the Crusades, and extending to William Saroyan's stay in Paris at 74 Rue Taitbout in the 1960s and 1970s. Vahe Oshagan has pointed out that in the nineteenth century "31 bright students from the schools [in Constantinople] were sent to European, mainly French, universities between 1843 and 1848. . . . They adulated the French Romantics, in particular Lamartine, Hugo and Chateaubriand. . . . The first to appear in print were articles on Voltaire's *Dictionnaire Philosophique* and Rousseau's *Emile* . . . in 1851 in Constantinople."[1]

Sourian's essays, novels, and short stories also demonstrate that it is neither Armenian nor American traditions which have exercised the strongest influence on his writing, but rather French literature and thought. In the television criticism he published in *The Nation* from 1975 to 1980, Sourian frequently commented incisively on French culture. In his review of the classic film *Les Enfants du Paradis*, Sourian wrote: "It is the air of ideas and aesthetics that the French cast abroad perennially, whether their own or not. Their slender language conveys this; it is serious and silver, not serious meat-and-potatoes, like ours."[2]

Sourian's affinity for France may be seen as part of this long Armenian tradition. James Etmekjian has stressed the centrality of the French language and literature in the curriculum of Constantinople's schools.[3] The Armenian literary elite, including

---

[1] Vahe Oshagan, "From Enlightenment to Renaissance: The Armenian Experience," in *Enlightenment and Diaspora: The Armenian and Jewish Cases*, ed. Richard G. Hovannisian and David Myers (Atlanta: Scholars Press, 1999), p. 159.

[2] Peter Sourian, *At the French Embassy in Sofia* (New York: Ashod Press, 1992), p. 94.

[3] James Etmekjian, *The French Influence on the Western Armenian Renaissance* (New York: Twayne, 1964). See ch. 6: "The French Language in Armenian Schools." See also Vahe Oshagan, *The English Influence on West Armenian Literature in the Nineteenth Century* (Cleveland: Caravan Books, 1982), p. 13. Oshagan writes concerning the influence of English literature: "But English had a hard time because, for

Sourian's family, was deeply tied to French culture in Constantinople. In *The Gate*, where Sourian's treatment of the Armenian theme fully emerges, Paul, the protagonist, finds in Constantinople among his family's cache of "translations of French plays and novels into Armenian—*Les Miserables*." We are told that Paul's father, Sarkis Stepanyan, remembers "everything" in Victor Hugo's novel "from forty years ago—Fantine, Cossette, Jean Valjean, Inspector Javert."[4] The novel traces the history of the Stepanyan family from its beginnings in Constantinople to its flight to America during the genocide. The narrator, Paul Stepanyan, an aspiring writer, states: "I sensed that out of my Armenian background, my family's immigrant past—out of that mere available substance—I could concoct something: mix, through a remarkable alchemy, a number of elements, and pour out a molten fool's gold of narrative. I went over to my parents' house telling myself that tomorrow I would continue to write."[5] *The Gate* is the story of Paul's attempts to write a novel based on his own Armenian experience.

Sourian reveals that Paul's "father refused to teach [them] Armenian as children."[6] Further, Sarkis wants his son to first learn French, and then, if he chooses, to learn Armenian. Thus Sourian, in some sense, has to embark on a solitary quest for his Armenian self, combining his historical research in chapter 3 regarding Ambassador Morgenthau with the narrative of his own life. In this autobiographical-historical search, Sourian depicts a severe father who has a hard time dealing with his past as an Armenian in Constantinople, setting a precedent for later Armenian-American authors including Michael Arlen in *Passage to Ararat* (1975) and Peter Balakian in *Black Dog of Fate* (1997), both of whom portray Armenian fathers frozen in time by anguish, psychological detachment, and denial. Arlen states that his father was born in Bulgaria, but "before that the Kouyoumjians had been in Constantinople."[7] Balakian describes not only his father, who down-

---

complex historical reasons, West Armenians had for centuries accepted the undisputed ascendancy of the Mediterranean culture, particularly French, and to a lesser degree Italian, over any other culture."

[4] Peter Sourian, *The Gate* (New York: Harcourt, Brace, 1965), pp. 126, 277.

[5] Ibid., p. 89.

[6] Ibid., p. 121.

[7] Michael Arlen, *Passage to Ararat* (Harmondsworth: Penguin, 1982), p. 190.

plays his Armenian roots but also devotes a chapter to "The Princess of Byzantium," his aunt Anna Balakian, the doyenne of French Surrealism scholars. Anna Balakian's roots were also in Constantinople; she tries to forget the terror of genocide by locking herself in an ivory tower of high art and aesthetic pleasure.

Paul's father, however, cannot completely forget the past. When he reads sections of the memoirs of his own father, Vahan, retrieved by Paul during a journey to Constantinople, Paul observes that he "began to weep. His shoulders trembled. Once I heard a sort of *aohh*-sound come from him. I saw him bite his lip. Tears were touching it now. Then he set the book blindly down on the black coffee table, began to wipe his eyes with his hands, clumsily. He stopped and pulled the handkerchief from his breast pocket. 'I can't any more. . . . Your grandfather was a wonderful man'."[8] It is a rare and welcome moment: Sarkis at last confronts the horrors of Constantinople, allowing himself to feel intense grief and the catharsis of tears.

Another character in *The Gate*, Boghosian, who is writing a history of Armenia in the novel, asks Paul at one point: "'Why don't you write about the Armenians?' . . . It was no question. He already knew why I did not write about the Armenians. It was because I was definitely, fatally evil. I would triumph, as true Armenians never triumphed."[9] In ignoring his Armenian heritage of "defeat," Paul attempts to leave Constantinople behind and "triumph" in a kind of Faustian bargain with the devil of American "success" as his father had done. Again, one sees parallels with Michael Arlen, whose father Dickran Kouyoumjian also rejected his Armenian heritage in order to blend in with the English literary scene.

A lecture that Sarkis Stepanyan gives to his son-in-law Lew Johnson is perhaps the most significant passage of *The Gate*. Sarkis exclaims:

> You should try reading an Armenian newspaper sometime. They're still talking about what the Turks did to us. Every week on the editorial page. My God! I hate the Turks myself. I can't help it. But those Armenians are *so proud* of what they went

---

[8] Sourian, *The Gate*, p. 131.
[9] Ibid., p.179.

through. Why can't they be proud of themselves today? I'll tell you why. Because they haven't done anything for themselves as individual people. They suffered and so they think it's up to the world to live for them. So they suffered. It was horrible. It was. So what?[10]

It is an argument that comes up today as it did in 1965. There is some fierce need to reject Armenian "victimhood," yet there is also the implicit, hidden self-rejection that may occasion such declarations: "pride as a defense against shame."

So, too, for the son Paul. Despite Paul's efforts to fathom the mystery of his family's past in Constantinople, Armenia remains an abstraction: "Armenia, what was Armenia? How could one grasp it? It was everything, yet it was not in the air, not in a room, like a chair or a table."[11] Paul wants to imagine the Armenians as heroes, not victims. When his brother-in-law Lew states that the Stepanyan family seemed at first to him like "tribal chieftains," Paul laughs but is "a touch pleased at that tribal chieftain idea. As if they were really brute, savage, strong people, like Kurds. I discovered that this was an attractive idea to me."[12] Rather than being submerged in self-pity and the catastrophe of the Genocide, both father and son demand a more heroic character from the Armenians anchored in toughness—a rigorousness defined by a kind of Nietzschean—or Kurdish—strength of will.

Sourian's ambivalent relationship with the Armenian past, with Constantinople, and with his Armenian identity weaves in and out of his work. In his review of the television series *Centennial*, he writes: "I'm not sure how much I like all this ethnicity, even if in the case of *Centennial* it's a sound representation of historical facts concerning our origins . . . in our obsession with 'identity' we seem at times to have regressed to tribalism."[13] One notes here the reversion to the word "tribal" as Lew had described the Stepanyan family in *The Gate*.

In his review of Marjorie Housepian Dobkin's *The Smyrna Affair*, Sourian writes:

---

[10] Ibid., p. 219.
[11] Ibid., p. 204.
[12] Ibid., p. 210.
[13] Sourian, *At the French Embassy*, p. 123.

Nearly every Armenian of the diaspora has had his quota of family horror stories to tell. Some feel that proper attention has never been paid to the causes and results of Turkish behavior toward the Armenians and, subsequently, toward the Greek Christian population of Smyrna. But what is the point of raking over these ashes once again? Is it not simply an instance of self-righteous ethnic groups, perversely proud to have been victims, insatiably seeking morbid satisfaction in the narcissistic, chauvinistic totting-up of old scores?[14]

The language here also sounds familiar: there is an echo of Sarkis Stepanyan's speech concerning masochistic Armenian pleasure in victimhood. Sourian ends his essay by answering his own rhetorical question: "Of all these things, Miss Housepian writes compellingly. Her book rakes over the old ashes to some purpose, rekindling our anger in a potentially useful way—the more so because of her evident scrupulousness in not sacrificing truth for effect."[15] One appreciates the reserve here: anger can be "potentially useful"; Housepian has not become a propagandist "sacrificing truth for effect." Yet Sourian's dispassionateness may be interpreted as both a strength and a weakness, and one speculates on the emotional and psychological reasons for such a stance. What is the relation between this reserve and questions of class? What does it have to do with his family's history in Constantinople? This seems an unexplored theme in Sourian's work, although the scandal is plain to see: to be an upper-class Armenian-American intellectual with roots in French Constantinople is to deny the Genocide, is to deny one's affiliation, connection, fellowship with those "other tragic suffering Armenians back in the homeland."

Sourian is an author of fiction, and due caution must of course be taken to avoid assuming his work is "autobiographical" in any obvious sense. Yet one may still inquire: to what degree has Sourian, the son, carried on the Constantinopolitan father's rejection of the "messy" aspects of being Armenian in favor of a sanitized version of Armenian history, or a rapprochement with what is perceived as American or French/European ways of behavior? Is he also assimilating his identity to what has been considered the "superior" culture—France and its great literary

---

[14] Ibid., p. 177.
[15] Ibid., p. 179.

tradition—and abandoning his Armenian self, as Michael Arlen Senior (Dickran Kouyoumjian—author of *The Green Hat*) had in England when he spent time with D.H. Lawrence and Arnold Bennett?

Was a writer like William Saroyan, whose parents were from Bitlis, driven to take on the badge of his "Armenianness" as just one more way to identify himself as "different" and "unique" in relation to the "privileged" Anglo-Saxon Establishment from which he was excluded by ethnicity and class? As an orphan child from an impoverished background, did Saroyan have any choice but to "identify" with the oppressed and marginalized in America? Saroyan in any case denied that the Establishment had any privileges he coveted. As for snobs and the wealthy, he simply made fun of them as in his riotous sending-up of the "sophisticated" couple who invade and pollute Nick's bar of sensitive memory and dream in *The Time of Your Life*.

Yet later in his career, Sourian moved away from Constantinople and towards a more direct acknowledgment of the trauma that the Armenian people had experienced but which he had earlier sought to avoid confronting directly. In a 1993 essay titled "Arshile Gorky's Drawing of a Remembered Armenian Arquebus," Sourian writes:

> The Turks, of course, had subjugated the Armenians, transforming them from a once proud nation of warriors to a land of captives. The birdlike figure in the upper right, about to rise above the cloud at the left, also resembles a crossbow oddly in flight. The image, however, is still more like a bird, which abounds in Armenian poetry and folksongs to convey the helplessness of the Armenians against their neighbors. Often the earthbound poet addresses a bird because of its power of flight.
>
> Every Armenian knows the song to the crane. Seeing the crane in the sky, the poet asks if the crane has come from its home, from whence it has been exiled, as had been Gorky himself, whose beloved mother had perished at home from starvation. Full of both hope and fear the poet begs for more news that the bird has the power to bring. The Drawing of a Remembered Armenian Arquebus is not an arquebus, nor a crossbow, but a bird. The bird, like the arquebus, is a conquering weapon. It is a small, graceful

sign of the soaring power of art.[16]

It seems that here Sourian has found a way out of the aesthetic distance of Constantinople and towards a way of combining the poet in himself and the man struggling to comprehend the suffering and anguish of Armenian history.

The most significant themes in Sourian's work are the relations between past and present, father and son, privilege and want, Armenian and American, and Constantinople and Boston. He presents the struggle, but eschews easy answers or ideological positions. In this way, he occupies a unique position in Armenian-American literature; he forces the reader to consider just how complicated issues of ethnic identity and class affiliation are. His work is an important source of inspiration for later writers who echo his concerns such as Michael Arlen, Peter Najarian, and Peter Balakian, all of whom have combined historical narrative with autobiographical quests for the Armenian past.

For W.B. Yeats, Constantinople was Byzantium, with its fantastic mosaics arranged with small colored exquisite stones, and it became, for Yeats, a symbol of escape into a pure world of artistic, timeless form. He writes in "Sailing to Byzantium":

Once out of nature I shall never take
My bodily form from any natural thing,
But such a form as Grecian goldsmiths make
Of hammered gold and gold enameling
To keep a drowsy Emperor awake;
Or set upon a golden bough to sing
To lords and ladies of Byzantium
Of what is past, or passing, or to come.[17]

Yeats observes in a note: "I have read somewhere that in the Emperor's palace at Byzantium was a tree made of gold and silver, and artificial birds that sang."[18] Peter Sourian has moved out of Yeats' Byzantium and Mallarme's static world of French fin-de-

---

[16] Peter Sourian, "Arshile Gorky's Drawing of a Remembered Armenian Arquebus," *Drawing Magazine* (Winter 1993-94), p. 108.

[17] W.B. Yeats, "Sailing to Byzantium," in *The Collected Poems* (New York: MacMillan, 1974), p. 192.

[18] Ibid., p. 453.

siècle symbolic timelessness—and in Arshile Gorky's bird found
not an artificial creature made of gold or silver but the realities of
the Armenian Genocide—the real, warm, alive, tragic Armenian
crane. Yeats' "complexities of mire or blood" had been what
Sourian sought to escape, just as his father had done. But he has
begun to see at last in this essay on Arshile Gorky the tragic
complexities of history, the real mire and the real Armenian blood
splattered over the walls of Constantinople.

Peter Sourian

INDEX